MW01071575

KANJI IN MANGALAND

Volume 2

Basic to intermediate kanji course through manga

Marc Bernabe
Veronica Calafell
Alberto Aldarabi

Illustrations:
Javier Bolado

Cover illustration:
Inma R.

Translation:
Olinda Cordukes

Kanji in MangaLand Volume 2
Basic to intermediate kanji course through manga.
By Marc Bernabe, Veronica Calafell and Alberto Aldarabi

Published and distributed: *Japan Publications Trading Co., Ltd.,*
1-2-1 Sarugaku-cho, Chiyoda-ku, Tokyo, 101-0064 Japan.

(First edition)
1st printing: August 2009

Overseas Distributors

UNITED STATES:
Kodansha America, LLC. through Oxford University Press,
198 Madison Avenue, New York, NY 10016.
CANADA:
Fitzhenry & Whiteside Ltd., 195 Allstate Parkway, Markham,
Ontario L3R 4T8.
ASIA AND OTHER COUNTRIES:
Japan Publications Trading Co., Ltd.,
1-2-1 Sarugaku-cho, Chiyoda-ku, Tokyo, 101-0064 Japan.

ISBN: 978-4-88996-261-1

Printed in Spain

The authors 著者について

Marc Bernabe (L'Ametlla del Vallès, Barcelona, 1976) is a Japanese-Spanish/Catalan translator and interpreter, working mainly on manga and anime translations. He also specializes in Japanese language and culture didactics for Spanish speakers. His published works are many: the five-book *Japanese in MangaLand* collection (Japan Publications); *Apuntes de Japón* (*Notes on Japan*, Glenat, 2002); the series *Kanji para recordar* (*Remembering the Kanji*, Herder), together with J. W. Heisig and V. Calafell; and the travel guide *Rumbo a Japón* (*Bound for Japan*, Laertes, 2005), together with V. Calafell and J. Espi. http://www.nipoweb.com

Veronica Calafell (Palau de Plegamans, Barcelona, 1978) is a Japanese translator and interpreter, and specializes in translation of leisure products. She has lived several years in Japan, where she combined her translation work with her specialization in International Relations. She is coauthor of the series *Kanji para recordar* (*Remembering the kanji*, Herder, 2001, 2003, and 2004, together with J. W. Heisig and M. Bernabe); the travel guide *Rumbo a Japón* (*Bound for Japan*, Laertes, 2005) together with M. Bernabe and J. Espi; and *Apuntes de Japón* (*Notes on Japan*, Glenat, 2002) with M. Bernabe.

Alberto Aldarabi (Toledo, 1973) is presently working in manga and anime translation, after graduating in Japanese from the Official Language School, Madrid. Besides being editor of the magazine *Shirase* between 2001 and 2003, he has been linked to the entire *Japanese in Mangaland* series, as well as the book *Kanji to Remember II*, revising the texts for publication. He also has collaborated in various projects related to Japanese language and culture.

Javier Bolado (Valencia, 1980) started out as a manga artist at the age of 17, with the creation of his first comic book *Myth Wars*. Later, he published *Evan SD* and *TwoSides*. He has contributed to comic and videogame magazines, as either feature writer or as editor in chief. His most recent work is the first volume of his fantasy novel *La Canción de la Princesa Oscura* (*The Song of the Dark Princess*) for Timun Mas, as both author and artist.

Table of contents 目次

Introduction はじめに

This is the second book (out of three) in the *Kanji in MangaLand* series, with which we intend to help the Japanese language student effectively master the 1,006 教育漢字 *Kyōiku kanji* (education kanji), which Japanese children learn during their six years in Elementary School. In the first book, we studied the kanji for the first and second years of elementary school; this time, we will introduce those for the third and fourth years. They will add up to 400 new characters (200 for the third grade level and 200 for the fourth grade level), which implies a considerable difference and greater effort to learn than in the previous book (240 kanji, 80 for the first grade level and 160 for the second grade level).

We are not going to repeat here what we have already said in the introduction for the first book of the series about the motivations that led us to create this method, nor about its advantages and possible faults. But it is certainly important that you remember the book is structured in lessons where 8 or 12 kanji are studied at a time, these being complemented with a comic book page, an exercise page, the answers to the exercises, and the translation of the comic book. At the end of each lesson, you will find the "New elements" to be featured in the following lesson, both in their original form and in their pictorial representation, which will help you in the mnemonic process. Finally, at the end of each grade you study, you will find a couple of pages with comprehensive review exercises, with which you will be able to assess your progress before moving on to the next grade.

Kanji in MangaLand is a cumulative study method, where we assume that you have assimilated what you have previously learned. Accordingly, we start with lesson 22, after the 21 lessons you should have studied in *Kanji in MangaLand 1*. This time, there are 17 lessons for grade 3, and 17 lessons for grade 4, which add up to a total of 55 lessons and 640 kanji between both books. Therefore, due to the peculiarity of this study method, which is based on associating an original picture with each "element" that constitutes a kanji, we do not recommend starting directly with book 2 without at least having had a look at book 1. The "elements," which appeared in the first book, have all found their way back into this book; therefore, you will come across many familiar pictures: Kim, the watering alien, the sitting Indian, and so on.

The tables

The essence of *Kanji in MangaLand* is the kanji tables for study. Within them, the pictograms graphically represent all of the elements, which comprise each of the kanji. They are what make this learning method original and fun. This also makes this method suitable for a very wide age bracket. Here we have, in detail, a learning table, where we can see the thirteen parts:

Breakdown of a table

261 ① (2級) ②

ブ

一部 (いちぶ) a part
全部 (ぜんぶ) all
部下 (ぶか) subordinate (bottom part)
本部 (ほんぶ) headquarters ③
学部 (がくぶ) faculty
部長 (ぶちょう) department head.

Especial

部屋 (へや) room

PART, DEPARTMENT ④

部 ⑤

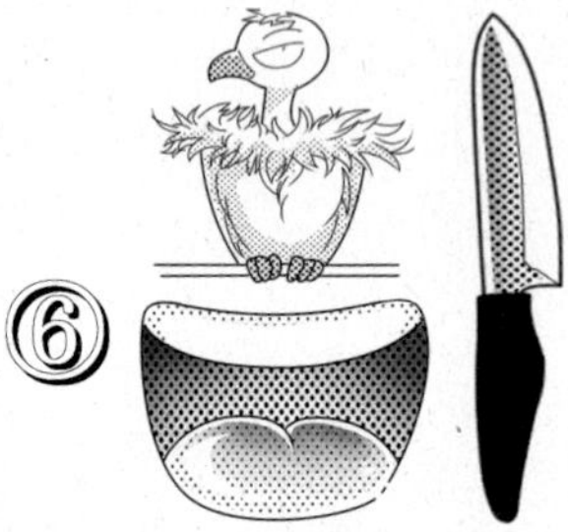

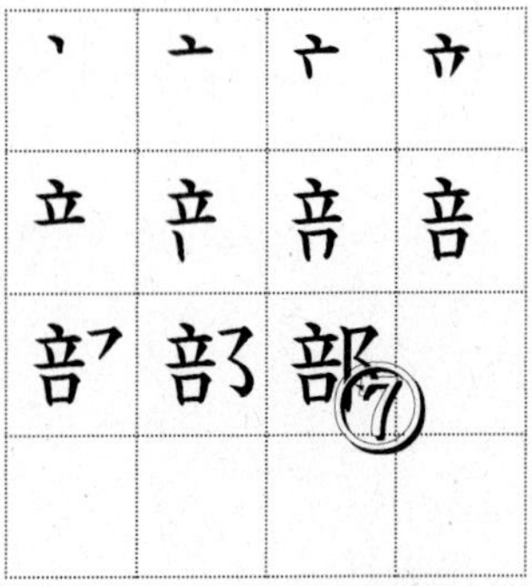

⑥

⑦

(11 strokes) ⑧

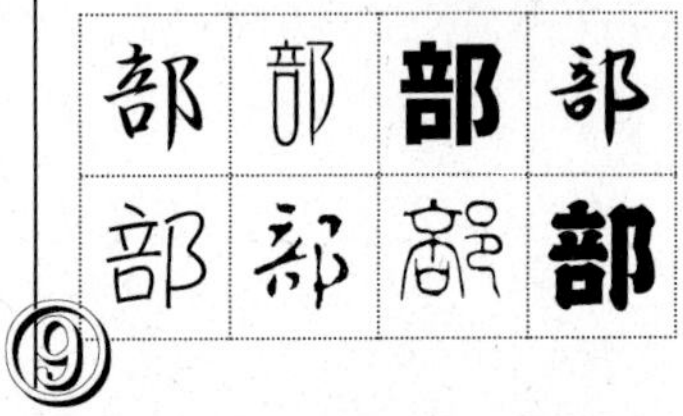

⑨

注 倍 (260) ⑩
都 (263)

学 To put a vulture in your mouth, take a knife and cut it in *parts*. ⑪

特 [咅邑] (alt) ⑫

① **Kanji number:** its number in our method. Kanji will be numbered from 1 to 1,006. This book will cover numbers 241 to 640.

② ***Nōken* level:** level of the kanji in the official test for Japanese as a foreign language, the *Nihongo Nōryoku Shiken (Nōken)*. The *Nōken* standards differ quite a lot from the Ministry of Education. This is why we will surprisingly come across simple kanji, which appear in advanced levels of the test (level 4 being the most basic, and level 1 the most advanced).

③ **Readings and *jukugo*:** the reading or readings of the kanji we are studying (in katakana the *on'yomi* [Chinese reading], and in hiragana the *kun'yomi* [Japanese reading]), as well as several examples of *jukugo* (compound words). Be careful with velarization, occlusion, and sound division phenomes that some readings undergo in combination with other kanji to make their pronunciation easier, a perfectly normal occurrence (see the introduction in *Kanji in MangaLand 1* for more information). Unfortunately, in these cases, the only solution is to learn them by heart.

④ **Meaning:** general meaning of the kanji.

⑤ **Kanji:** the kanji we are studying.

⑥ **Pictogram:** picture representation of the kanji. Each "element," or radical, forming the kanji has been assigned a picture, and the sum of the various pictograms provides us with an effective and original way to remember the kanji. The slogan is this: the more absurd and flamboyant, the better! You will also find the new elements featured in each lesson detailed on the last page of the previous lesson.

⑦ **Stroke order:** a detailed, step by step, order of strokes in which the kanji is written, which is very important in order to write it properly.

⑧ **Stroke number:** the number of strokes the kanji has.

⑨ **Other written styles:** Japanese, like Western languages, has many calligraphic styles of writing. Here we give different ways of writing the same kanji, so that you can understand how important stroke order is, as well as be able to recognize different versions of the same kanji. This will help you to clarify possible doubts when trying to identify handwritten kanji.

⑩ **Easily confused kanji:** different kanji that is easily confused with the kanji we are currently studying; this is usually due to similarity. The number after each kanji indicates its order in books 1 and 2. On the other hand, "5th" or "6th" indicates which of the corresponding levels of *Kyōiku kanji* they belong to; thus, the kanji with these level indications will appear in *Kanji in MangaLand 3*. When we indicate "Jōyō," it means that kanji is one of the 939 "common use kanji" (常用漢字, *Jōyō kanji*) which are not studied in elementary school. "Not Jōyō" indicates the kanji is not in the list of *Jōyō kanji.*

⑪ **Mnemonic caption for the picture:** so that you can remember the picture better, and the kanji by extension, we offer a simple sentence using the "elements" and the general meaning of the kanji.

⑫ **alternative forms:** alternative or archaic forms of the kanji we are studying. We offer them basically for the purpose of reference, and you don't need to study them. Here are the meanings of the different abbreviations: "alt" indicates it is an alternative version; "old" indicates an archaic form, now obsolete; "hom" indicates kanji that are read the same way and have similar meanings, though slightly different nuance usages; and, last of all, "simp" indicates a simplified form of the kanji (generally used with handwritten kanji).

The History of Kanji

Although several traces of the native Japanese culture remain in the Japanese archipelago, which date back to the Paleolithic Era, as far as we know, there was no writing system used to represent the Japanese language.

Kanji emerged in China more than 6,000 years ago, as a set of pictographic symbols representing scenes from nature and life: the sun, the moon, man, and so on. This was similar to the ancient tribal cave paintings of indigenous people or to the hieroglyphics of ancient Egypt. These figurative drawings –together with the addition of simple strokes to express action or movement, or the combination of several drawings to form a more elaborate idea (for example, the Sun, 日, with the Moon, 月, give the idea of "light, clarity", 明)– gave rise to other more complex drawings. By 1500 BC, during the Shang Dynasty, we already have evidence of an authentic and complete writing system based on ideograms. As proof of this, inscriptions on bones and turtle shells had been uncovered and still survive in museums today. Throughout the centuries, these kanji characters continued to develop, and adapted themselves to the varying dialects throughout the huge Chinese Empire.

From the 3rd century AD, the main kingdom of ancient Japan, the Yamato court, began to import the Chinese culture through travelling wise men, who arrived from Korea. Confucianism was introduced together with literature, Chinese etiquette, and... kanji. In the year 405, the imperial court of Japan officially adopted the Chinese writing system to represent their own language. At first, however, characters were only taken in their phonetic form to represent similar sounds in Japanese. Later, they would be used for their meaning, which would be ascribed to equal or similar meanings already existing in the Japanese language. However, considering that every kanji came to Japan with its own Chinese pronunciation, it happened that characters thus acquired two readings: the *on'yomi*, 音読み, derived from its original Chinese pronunciation; and the *kun'yomi*, 訓読み, the already existing word in the Japanese spoken language, which was adscribed to that kanji.

In this first stage, writing was only accessible to the highest classes, and, therefore, resulted in limited spreading. However, in the 6th century, a new cultural wave began with the introduction of Buddhism and its holy scriptures. With the rapid and wide spread of the new faith, together with being promoted by the State, writing reached a greater circle of people. This process spanned the entire Nara Era (710-794), until the beginning of the Heian Era (794-1185). From the 7th century on, we can say that the kanji writing system had become a characteristic of Japan, and had begun developing on its own independently from China.

The arrival of the kanji system in Japan with its various readings was the result of centuries of the mingling of Chinese dialects, emerging mainly from two different sources:

first, from the Wu region (pronounced "Go" by the Japanese) in Southern China and, later, from the ruling Han dynasty (called "Kan" in Japan) in Northern China. This merging explains why many of the current kanji have two Chinese pronunciations: *Go-on*, 呉音, and *Kan-on*, 漢音. That is, as well, where the etymology of the word kanji, 漢字, comes from: word (or ideogram, 字) from China (from the Kan dynasty, 漢).

Generally speaking, the *Go-on* reading, which is older, is found in concepts associated to Buddhism; whereas the *Kan-on* reading with which they read texts on religion, medicine, science, and so on and which was brought by scholars from the Asian continent, constitutes the main body of the learned vocabulary and most of the compound words used nowadays in Japanese.

There is still a third pronunciation, the Tō-on, 唐音, from the Tang Dynasty, which had been brought and introduced by monks and merchants since the Kamakura Era (1185-1333). Although it is rare, we can find its usage in a few words, such as the reading "pekin" of 北京 (north capital, Peking).

As we mentioned before, kanji have been fully implanted and integrated in the Japanese culture since the 8th century. Not only were new kanji created exclusively for the Japanese language, such as 働, 畑, or 峠, but also two writing systems of their own were developed in order to represent words through phonemes or to write down word endings and grammatical particles: the hiragana and katakana syllabaries (about which we have already spoke in the first volume of *Kanji in MangaLand*), which are collectively referred to as Kana. Generally speaking, hiragana are curvilinear characters coming from the simplification of certain kanji from which they borrow their pronunciation; whereas katakana, with squarer and straighter strokes, comes from the writing of just one part of another set of ideograms.

Kana aside, kanji have not yet stopped developing. There exists, as well, several writing styles: some more ornamental, such as *sōsho* (草書, "grass writing"); others more rectilinear, such as *kaisho*, 楷書, the basis of present-day print.

Since the Meiji Era (1868-1912), the new government started reducing the number of Chinese-origin characters, in an attempt to systemize and simplify them. In 1923, a list of 2,500 common use kanji was published, where many complex kanji were changed into others with a simpler form. In 1946, when the Second World War had just finished, a new education reform was enacted, approving the *Tōyō-kanji*, 当用漢字, list, "common-use characters." The 1,850 characters appearing on the list were, according to the experts, the most frequently used kanji in newspapers and magazines. From then on, all publications had to restrict themselves to that list. The idea, promoted by the American administration, was to keep revising the list every certain number of years, in order to remove the less used characters and replace them with their kana equivalents until writing with kanji was completely eliminated, as it later happened in Korea.

However, reality proved to be very different. Shortly after the *Tōyō-kanji* list was announced, an additional list had to be approved with almost 100 extra ideograms to compensate for proper nouns of the people who had "officially" been left unable to write the kanji of their own name. When the main list was finally revised, in 1981, far from reducing it, they had to increase the list up to 1,945 kanji (including the 166 extra kanji for proper nouns, which then increased to 284 characters nine years later, totaling 2,229 altogether). The current list of *Jōyō-kanji* (常用漢字, "common-use characters") is where (once again) those kanji with many strokes or complex structures have been replaced with simpler variants. But the intended eradication of kanji, besides the destruction of an extremely valuable cultural legacy, causes more problems than advantages, given the characteristics of the Japanese language: a great number of words are homophonous, and are only distinguished by the characters with which they are written.

The last reform was the approval of a substantial increase in the kanji list for proper nouns, in September 2004, with 488 extra kanji added, and the recognition of another 205 kanji written in less common variants. Consequently, nowadays almost 3,000 kanji are used officially, and that's without including those kanji that may appear in poetry, specialized books, or history books. As you can see, in spite of what one might think in this age of globalization, the kanji writing system enjoys perfect health. Moreover, the number of people outside Japan who feel fascinated by these millenarian symbols keeps growing, as it is proved by the publication of this very book. We hope our method has helped to break the initial "inaccessibility" barrier, which seems to have shielded kanji from non-expert eyes, and to encourage students to fearlessly immerse themselves in the study of kanji.

New elements 新しい部首

丁 corkscrew 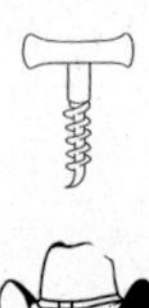

几 cowboy hat

 director´s chair 

Grade 3
小学校三年生

Lesson 22
第二十二課

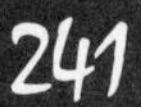

241 (1級)

(STREET) BLOCK, POLITE, EVEN (NUMBER)

チョウ

一丁目（いっちょうめ） the first block, one city block

三丁（さんちょう） three blocks

丁度（ちょうど） just, exact, precisely

丁半（ちょうはん） even and odd numbers

テイ

丁寧（ていねい） polite, courteous

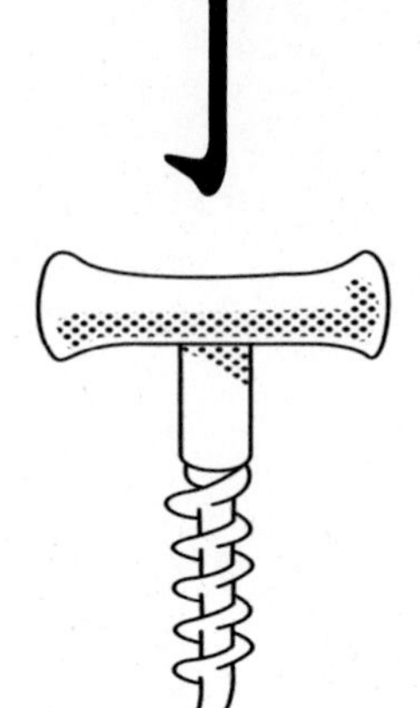

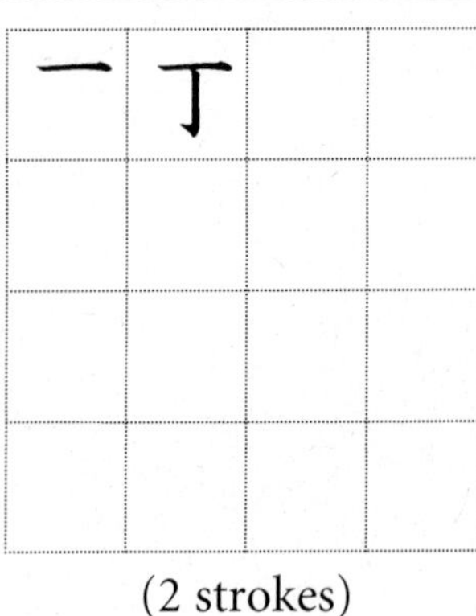

(2 strokes)

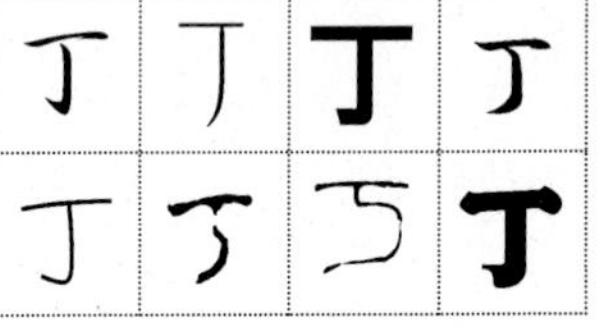

注 テ (katakana)
庁 (6th)

Find the oddly *even* corkscrew a *few blocks* ahead.

242 (2級)

TO HIT, TO STRIKE

ダ

長打（ちょうだ） long hit

安打（あんだ） safe hit

う(つ/ち)

打つ（うつ） to hit, to strike, to impress

心を打つ（こころをうつ） to impress

打ち上げる（うちあげる） to throw

打ち合わせ（うちあわせ） preliminary meeting

値打ち（ねうち） value, price

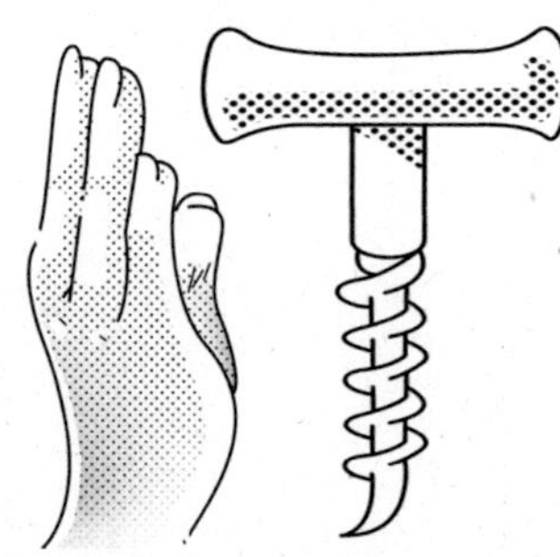

(5 strokes)

行 (136)
町 (73)

A hand *hits* with the corkscrew.

一	十	扌	扌
扒	拎	拎	拾
拾			

(9 strokes)

拾	拾	**拾**	拾
拾	拾	拾	**拾**

TO PICK UP

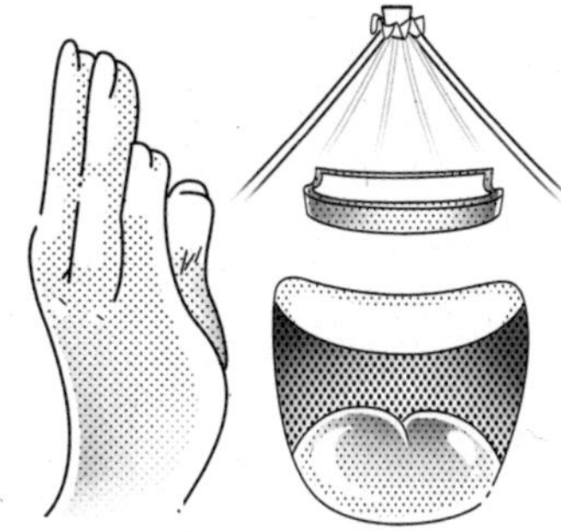

(2級)

243

シュウ

拾得（しゅうとく） to pick up, to find

収拾（しゅうしゅう） to have under control

ひろ(う)

拾（ひろ）う to pick up

拾（ひろ）い物（もの） a thing picked up, a bargain

拾（ひろ）い出（だ）す to select

拾（ひろ）い読（よ）み browsing

特

学 What does *pick up* mean? To join something with our hand.

注 捨 (6th)
塔 (Jōyō)

一	十	扌	扌
扌	扌	指	指
指			

(9 strokes)

指	指	**指**	指
指	指	指	**指**

FINGER, TO POINT TO

(2級)

244

シ

指名（しめい） nomination

指導（しどう） guide, to guide

ゆび

指（ゆび） finger

小指（こゆび） little finger

指輪（ゆびわ） ring

さ(す/し)

指（さ）す to point to

目指（めざ）す to aim at

 The *finger* in the sitting Indian's hand (or "the hand") points to the sun.

 脂 (Jōyō)
拍 (Jōyō)

245 (2級)

TO THROW, TO HURL

投

トウ
投票（とうひょう） to vote
投合（とうごう） agreement

な(げる)
投げる（なげる） to throw, to fling
身投げ（みなげ） to throw oneself (to commit suicide)
投売り（なげうり） to sell at loss (bargain sale)

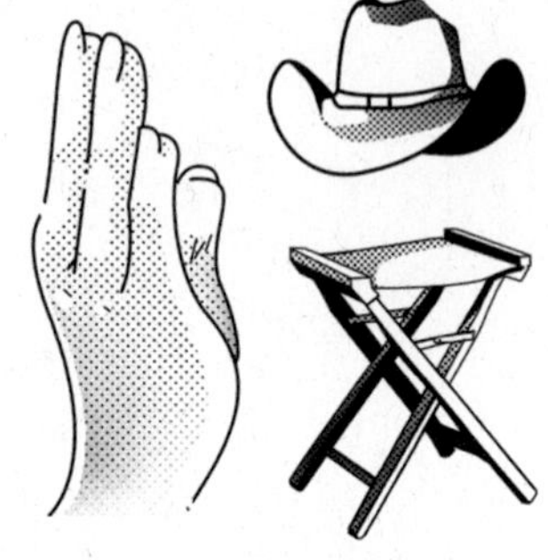

Stroke order: 一 扌 扌 扌 扌 投 投 (7 strokes)

注 役 (245)
技 (5th)

学 With his hands, the upset director *throws* his cowboy hat from the chair...

特

246 (2級)

ROLE (IN THEATRE OR CINEMA), OFFICIAL

役

エキ
労役（ろうえき） work
懲役（ちょうえき） penal servitude

ヤク
役立つ（やくだつ） to be useful
役に立つ（やくにたつ） is of use
役目（やくめ） role, duty, function
下役（したやく） subordinate
役者（やくしゃ） actor

Stroke order: ノ 彡 彳 彳 彳 役 役 (7 strokes)

注 投 (245)
後 (157)

学 ...As he fires the actor, who takes the highway to heaven as he does not have his *role* anymore.

特

一	十	扌	扌
扌	扌	挂	持
持			

(9 strokes)

持	持	持	持
持	持	持	持

TO HOLD, TO HAVE

(3級)

247

ジ

維持(いじ) maintenance

も(つ/ち/てる)

持(も)つ to hold, to endure
長持(ながも)ち lasting, durable
金持(かねも)ち rich person
力持(ちからも)ち strong (to have strength)
持(も)てる to be popular, to be a womanizer

 A hand *holds* the ancient Buddhist temple.

 待 (248)
侍 (Jōyō)
特 (484)

丿	彡	彳	彳
彳	往	待	待
待			

(9 strokes)

待	待	待	待
待	待	待	待

TO WAIT

(3級)

248

タイ

招待(ちょうたい) invitation
待機(たいき) to wait for an opportunity

ま(つ/ち)

待(ま)つ to wait
待(ま)ち合(あ)わせ to meet (someone)
待(ま)ち時間(じかん) waiting time

 The temple *waits* for the faithful to come through the highway.

 侍 (247)
侍 (Jōyō)
特 (484)

249 (1級)

POEM, POETRY

詩

シ

- 詩(し) poem, poetry
- 詩語(しご) poetic language
- 詩人(しじん) poet
- 詩形(しけい) verse, poetic form
- 詩学(しがく) study of poetry
- 近代詩(きんだいし) modern poetry
- 古詩(こし) ancient poetry

(13 strokes)

注 読 (114)
誌 (6th)
討 (6th)

学 Originally, *poetry* was "words that came out of a temple."

250 (3級)

TO GATHER, TO COLLECT

集

シュウ

- 集中(しゅうちゅう) concentration
- 集会(しゅうかい) meeting
- 集金(しゅうきん) to collect money
- 詩集(ししゅう) a collection of poems

あつ(まる/める)

- (人(ひと)が)集(あつ)まる to gather (people)
- (コインを)集(あつ)め to collect (coins)

(12 strokes)

注 東 (199)
業 (300)
乗 (368)

学 Swans *gather* on top of a tree.

251 TONE, INVESTIGATION

(15 strokes)

(2級)

チョウ

- 声調（せいちょう） (voice) tone
- 順調（じゅんちょう）に progress favorably, smoothly
- 体調（たいちょう） (physical) condition
- 調査（ちょうさ） investigation
- 調査団（ちょうさだん） investigation group

しら(べる)

- 調（しら）べる to investigate

 調 (alt)

 To *investigate* smoothly is nothing like speaking nonsense while wearing a mask and a wig.

 詞 (6th)

252 TO CONVERSE

(15 strokes)

(2級)

ダン

- 談合（だんごう） agreement
- 談話（だんわ） conversation
- 相談（そうだん） consult
- 冗談（じょうだん） joke
- 怪談（かいだん） ghost story
- 談（だん）じる to talk, to negotiate

 Two fires *converse* with words only they can hear.

 認 (6th)
評 (5th)
誘 (Jōyō)

ん？拾い物ですか？
まあ…こんなもの、役に立たない。古くて汚い指輪だけね…すてるわ！
わぁあああああ!!
待って！川に投げないでよ！
おそらく…それは「一つの指輪」かもしれない！
信じてください。
丁度、あたしは神話、伝説、怪談などの調査団に入っているわ。
「一つの指輪はすべてを集め…」せめて指輪の詩は知っているでしょ？
…
たしか、それは「力の指輪」の一番強いリング!!
そんな値打ちのある指輪を持つことができれば、なんでもできる!!!
じゃ…どうしてこのものすごい指輪、プラスティック製なの？

Exercises 練習

1. Develop the stroke order of the following kanji.

打
投
集
調

2. Choose the correct reading for each kanji or kanji combination.

a) 待って！冗談じゃないよ。相談にのるから、何でも言ってね。

Wait! I'm not joking. We can consult him if you want to; just say what you want to know.

待って:	1．まて	2．もて	3．まって	4．もって
冗談:	1．じょうだん	2．じょうたん	3．じょうた	4．じょた
相談:	1．そたん	2．そた	3．そうたん	4．そうだん

b) お金持ちの友人に招待されたけど、待ち合わせ時間までは余裕(よゆう)がある。

A rich friend of mine has invited me, but there's plenty of time until the appointment.

金持ち:	1．かねもち	2．かねまち	3．かねじち	4．かねみち
招待:	1．しょうまち	2．しょうま	3．しょうだい	4．しょうたい
待ち合:	1．うちあわせ	2．うちあい	3．まちあい	4．まちあ

c) 詩人が集中しているから、静(しず)かにしてください。

Since the poet is concentrating, please be quiet.

詩人:	1．じじん	2．ししん	3．じしん	4．しじん
集中:	1．ちゅうしゅう	2．しゅちゅ	3．しゅうちゅう	4．しゅちゅう

3. Write the kanji (one or more) and the meaning of the following words.

いっちょうめ	＿＿＿	＿＿＿	やくしゃ	＿＿＿	＿＿＿
うちあわせ	ち　わせ	＿＿＿	こし	＿＿＿	＿＿＿
ひろいだす	い　す	＿＿＿	しらべる	べる	＿＿＿

4. Correct either the reading or the writing mistakes in the following words.

小拾	こゆび	役票	とうひょう	集る	あつまる
目指す	めさす	力持ち	ちからまち	体周	たいちょう
拾得	しゅうとく	指導	じどう	懲役	ちょうやく

Answers to exercises 練習解答

1. (Check them in the corresponding kanji tables: #242, #245, #250, and #251)

2. a) 待って: 3 | 冗談: 1 | 相談: 4 / b) 金持ち: 1 | 招待: 4 | 待ち合(わせ): 4 / c) 詩人: 4 | 集中: 3

3. いっちょうめ: 一丁目, the first block | うちあわせ: 打ち合わせ, previous arrangement | ひろいだす: 拾い出す, to select | やくしゃ: 役者, actor | こし: 古詩, ancient poetry | しらべる: 調べる, to investigate

4. 小指 こゆび | 投票 とうひょう | 集まる あつまる | 目指す めざす | 力持ち ちからもち | 体調 たいちょう | 拾得 しゅうとく | 指導 しどう | 懲役 ちょうえき

Manga translation マンガ翻訳

Friend 2: So? Have you found anything?

Friend 1: Huh! This is useless. It's only a dirty old ring. I'll throw it away!

Friend 2: Aaah! No, wait! Don't throw that into the river!

Friend 2: It could be... the One Ring.

Friend 1: ...

Friend 2: Trust me, just now I belong to an investigation group dealing with myths, legends, and ghost stories.

Friend 2: "One ring to gather them all..." At least the Poem of the Ring will sound familiar to you, won't it?

Friend 2: I'm sure that this is the most powerful of the Rings of Power!

Friend 2: Whoever has this really valuable ring can do anything!

Friend 1: Okay, then, why is this legendary ring made of plastic?

Friend 2: ...

New elements 新しい部首

弋 Robin Hood 

吏 Astaire turtle 

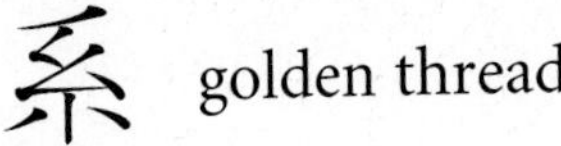

系 golden thread 

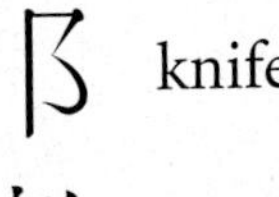

阝 knife 

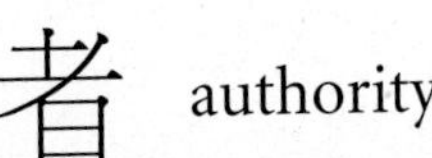

者 authority

Lesson 23
第二十三課

253 (3級)

DEATH, TO DIE

シ

死(し) death

死語(しご) dead language

死肉(しにく) dead flesh

死体(したい) corpse

死地(しち) grave, place of death

し(ぬ/に)

死(し)ぬ to die

死神(しにがみ) god of death

一 丆 歹 歹 歹 死

(6 strokes)

死 死 死 死 死 死 死 死

 花 (70) 夜 (148)

 Under his last slice of bread, at dusk, the sitting Indian is ready to *die*.

254 (2級)

TO CHANGE, TO TRANSFORM

カ

文化(ぶんか) culture

化学(かがく) chemistry

悪化(あっか) to worsen

ケ

化粧(けしょう) makeup

ば(ける/かす)

お化(ば)け ghost

化(ば)け物(もの) monster

化(ば)ける to become, to disguise as

ノ イ イ' 化

(4 strokes)

化 化 化 化 化 化 化 化

注 花 (70) 北 (197) 比 (5th)

 Kim and the sitting Indian: their friendship has *changed* them.

 化 (alt)

255

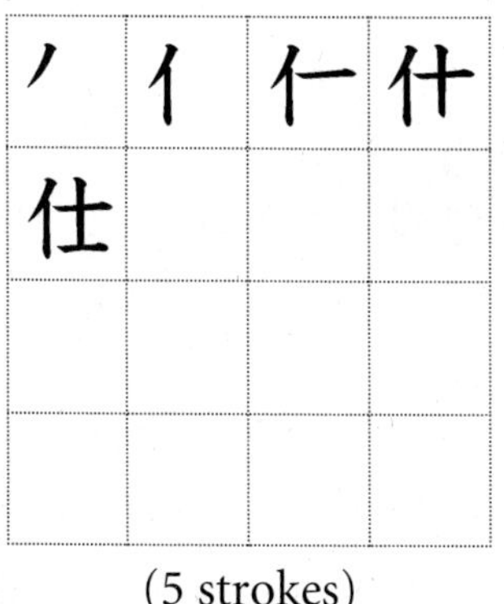

(5 strokes)

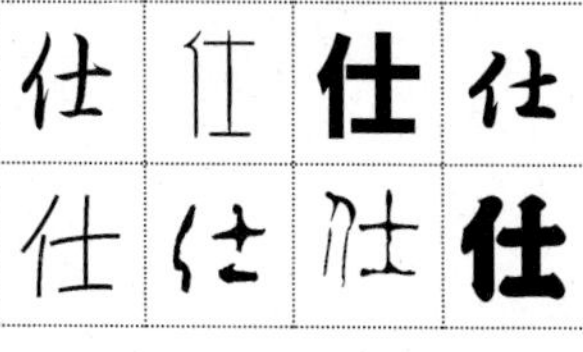

TO SERVE, TO WORK

(3級)

シ

仕事(しごと) work, job
仕方(しかた) way of doing
仕打(しう)ち treat, treatment
仕組(しく)み structure

つか(える)

仕(つか)える to serve (somebody or something)

Kim *works* as a frog caretaker.

社 (255)
任 (5th)
壮 (Jōyō)

256

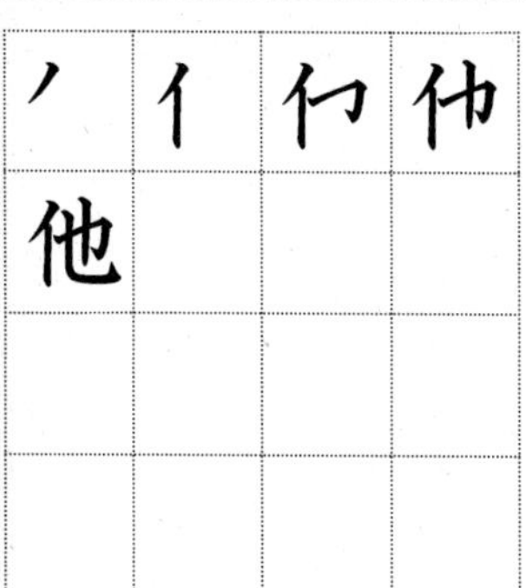

(5 strokes)

OTHER(S)

(2級)

タ

他人(たにん) another person, someone else's
他方(たほう) on the other hand
他言(たごん) to divulge

ほか

他(ほか)の another
～他(ほか) and the like

Kim has short hair: the hair bun must be *someone else's*.

地 (169)

257 (3級)

TO REPLACE

ダイ

時代（じだい） era, period

代金（だいきん） expense, payment

タイ

交代（こうたい） turns, shifts

か(わる/わり/える)

代（か）わる to replace (A with B)

～代（か）わりに instead of

よ

代（よ） era, reign

ノ	イ	仁	代
代			

(5 strokes)

代	代	代	代
代	代	代	代

 式 (427)

 Kim *replaces* Robin Hood, the prince of thieves.

258 (3級)

TO USE

シ

天使（てんし） angel

行使（こうし） use, employ

大使（たいし） ambassador

使命（しめい） misison, task

つか(う/い)

使（つか）う to use

使（つか）い手（て） client

魔法使（まほうつか）い magician, sorcerer

ノ	イ	仁	仁
佰	佰	伊	使

(8 strokes)

使	使	使	使
使	使	使	使

 便 (451)

 Kim learns how *to use* a cane by the teachings of the Astaire turtle.

 使 (alt)

259 PERSON IN CHARGE

(9 strokes)

(2級)

ケイ

関係（かんけい） relationship, bond
係累（けいるい） dependent relatives

かか(る/り/わる)

係（かか）る to involve
係（かかり）の人（ひと） person in charge
係長（かかりちょう） chief clerk
係（かか）わる to be involved, to have to do with

学 Kim is the *person in charge* here: he pulls the golden threads.

 系 (6th)
孫 (547)

260 DOUBLE, TIMES

(10 strokes)

(2級)

バイ

倍（ばい） double
二倍（にばい） twice
五倍（ごばい） five times
数倍（すうばい） several times
倍大（ばいだい） twice as large
倍（ばい）にする to double

 Kim is a vulture with a mouth: he always eats *twice*.

 部 (261)
位 (448)
借 (450)

261 (2級)

PART, DEPARTMENT

部

ブ

一部（いちぶ） a part
全部（ぜんぶ） all
部下（ぶか） subordinate (bottom part)
本部（ほんぶ） headquarters
学部（がくぶ） faculty
部長（ぶちょう） department head

Special

部屋（へや） room

丶	亠	六	立
立	立	音	音
部	部	部	

(11 strokes)

部	部	部	部
部	部	部	部

注 倍 (260)
都 (263)

 To put a vulture in your mouth, take a knife and cut it *in parts.*

 郶 (alt)

262 (3級)

PERSON, SOMEBODY

者

シャ

学者（がくしゃ） investigator
読者（どくしゃ） reader
記者（きしゃ） journalist
芸者（げいしゃ） geisha

ジャ

忍者（にんじゃ） ninja

もの

者（もの） person
若者（わかもの） young person

一	十	土	耂
老	者	者	者

(8 strokes)

者	者	者	者
者	者	者	者

 青 (36)
暑 (264)
老 (575)

 The old wise man on the sun is *somebody* (an "authority") in the world.

 者 (alt)

(11 strokes)

都	都	都	都
都	都	都	都

METROPOLIS

(3級) **263**

ト

都心（としん） the center of the city
都内（とない） within the city
都会（とかい） large city
京都（きょうと） Kyoto

ツ

都合（つごう） one's convenience, circumstances

みやこ

都（みやこ） capital

 都 (alt)

 The *metropolis* is where an authority rules the capital using a knife.

注 者 (262)
部 (261)

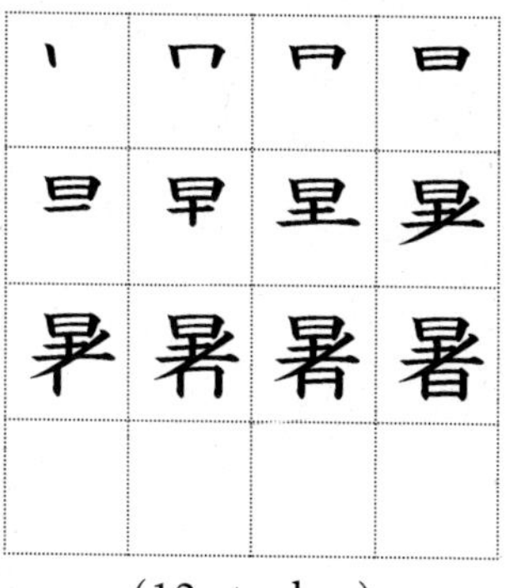

(12 strokes)

暑	暑	暑	暑
暑	暑	暑	暑

HEAT

(3級) **264**

ショ

暑中（しょちゅう） midsummer
暑気（しょき） sensation of heat

あつ(い)

暑い（あつい） hot
暑さ（あつさ） heat
蒸し暑い（むしあつい） humid, sultry
暑苦しい（あつくるしい） sweltering

 An authority under the sun also feels the *heat.*

 景 (555)
曇 (Jōyō)

京都 ー 9:15 AM
イカサマ株式会社本部
社長… あれ？ そんなに暑いですか、社長？

おお、山田くんか！ よくがんばる人だね、きみ！ ね、係長… いや、部長に昇進してあげよう。どう？
わ… 私ですか？ たぶん、他の山田さんと間違っておられるのかもしれません…
いやぁ… きみなら完璧な部長になるよ。すごく能力があるから!! 化け物なみだ！

そして、給料は倍にしよう。どうだ？
O… OK！ どうもありがとうございます、社長！

あの… すみませんが、具体的に、私のやる仕事って何ですか？
そうね… とりあえず、きみの初の使命は…

…僕の代わりにそのヤクザの若者を迎えることじゃ。
がんばれ！
死にたいヤツって、お前か？

Exercises 練習

1. Develop the stroke order of the following kanji.

他											
使											
都											
暑											

2. Choose the correct reading for each kanji or kanji combination.

a) あの死体を見たら、私(わたし)の学部時代の知り合いだった。

When I saw that corpse, he happened to be an acquaintance from my university period.

死体:　1．したい　2．じたい　3．しにたい　4．しぬたい

学部:　1．がくぶん　2．がくふ　3．がくぶ　4．がふん

時代:　1．ときたい　2．ときだい　3．じだい　4．じたい

b) 仕事の都合により、子供を他人に預(あず)かってもらうことがあります。

Due to work circumstances, I sometimes leave someone else looking after the children.

仕事:　1．つかこと　2．つかごと　3．じごと　4．しごと

都合:　1．つうごう　2．つうご　3．つご　4．つごう

他人:　1．ほかにん　2．ほかじん　3．たんいん　4．たにん

c) 全部調べてから、いい記者は記事を書き始める。

A good journalist starts writing an article once he has investigated everything.

全部:　1．きんぶ　2．きんぷ　3．ぜんぶ　4．せんぷ

記者:　1．きもの　2．きじゃ　3．きしゃ　4．きじょの

3. Write the kanji (one or more) and the meaning of the following words.

しにがみ　______　______　げいしゃ　______　______

ぶんか　______　______　みやこ　______　______

てんし　______　______　あつい　______　______

4. Correct either the reading or the writing mistakes in the following words.

都屋	へや	仕かえる	つかえる	若者	わかしゃ
化粧	かしょう	他の	たの	忍都	にんじゃ
お化け	おぼけ	関系	かんけい	暑苦しい	しょくるしい

Answers to exercises 練習解答

1. (Check them in the corresponding kanji table: #256, #258, #263, and #264)

2. a) 死体: 1 | 学部: 3 | 時代: 3
b) 仕事: 4 | 都合: 4 | 他人: 4 / c) 全部: 3 | 記者: 3

3. しにがみ: 死神, god of death | ぶんか: 文化, culture | てんし: 天使, angel
げいしゃ: 芸者, geisha | みやこ: 都, capital | あつい: 暑い, hot

4. 部屋 へや | 仕える つかえる | 若者 わかもの | 化粧 けしょう | 他の ほかの | 忍者 にんじゃ | お化け おばけ | 関係 かんけい | 暑苦しい あつくるしい

Manga translation マンガ翻訳

Text panel: Kyoto. 9:15 AM. Racket Inc. headquarters.

Employee: Director... Oh, are you that hot, Director?

Boss: Ah, it's you, Yamada! A great worker, yes, indeed! Look, I'm going to promote you to chief clerk... No, to department head, what do you think about that?

Employee: M-me? Perhaps you are mistaking me for another Yamada.

Boss: Not at all! You will be a perfect department head. You have tons of potential! Yes, you're like a monster!

Boss: Besides, I'll double your wages. How's that?

Employee: O... OK! Thank you very much, Director!

Employee: And... by the way, what, exactly, will my job involve?

Boss: Oh, yes. Well, for the meantime, your first task...

Boss: ...will be to deal with those young yakuza on my behalf. Good luck!

Yakuza: Are you the guy who's willing to die?

New elements 新しい部首

主 magician king

羊 lamb

氺 roots

反 slope (cliff + chair)

失 drill

Lesson 24
第二十四課

265 (3級)

MAIN

シュ

主人（しゅじん） boss, husband

主力（しゅりょく） main force

ぬし

家主（やぬし） house owner, landlord

飼い主（かいぬし） owner (of an animal)

おも(な)

主な（おもな） main

主に（おもに） mainly

(5 strokes)

注 王 (15)
玉 (16)

The *main* magician king.

主 (alt)

266 (3級)

TO LIVE, TO RESIDE

住

ジュウ

住所（じゅうしょ） postal address

住宅（じゅうたく） house, residence

先住（せんじゅう） previous occupant

す(む)

住む（すむ） to live

住まい（すまい） residence

(7 strokes)

注 柱 (267)
狂 (Jōyō)

Kim (who is not a fool) *lives* in the magician king's residence.

住 (alt)

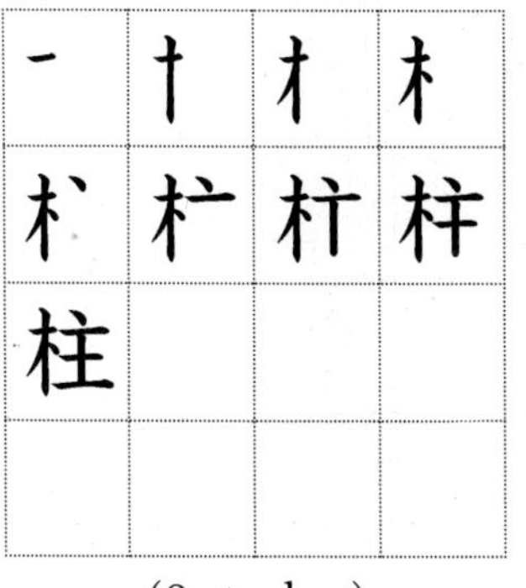

(9 strokes)

柱 柱 柱 柱
柱 柱 柱 柱

PILLAR, COLUMN

（2級）

267

チュウ

電柱（でんちゅう） electric-light pole
柱石（ちゅうせき） pillar (of society)

はしら

柱（はしら） pole, pillar, column
柱時計（はしらどけい） wall clock

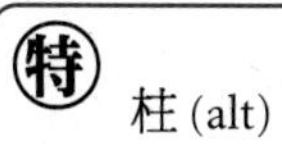

 (alt)

学 As a *pillar* of society, the magician king has the makings of a leader.

住 (266)

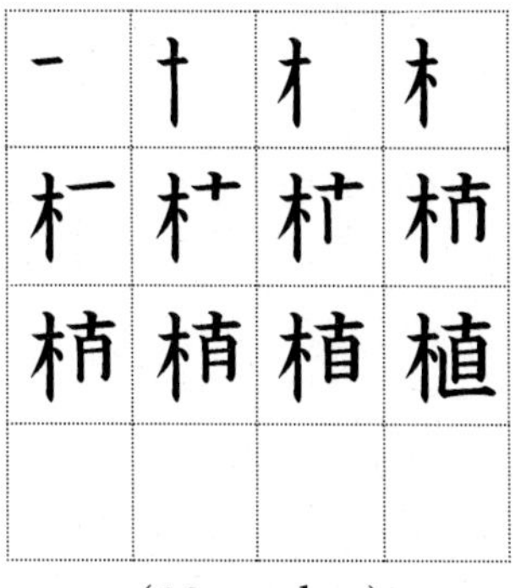

(12 strokes)

植 植 植 植
植 植 植 植

PLANT, VEGETABLE

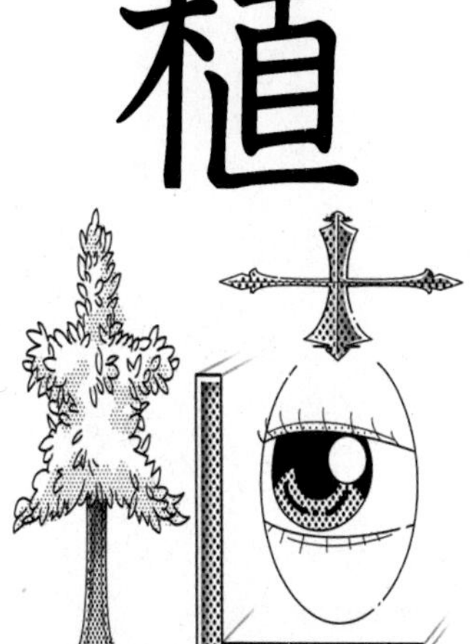

（2級）

268

ショク

植物園（しょくぶつえん） botanical garden
植生（しょくせい） vegetation
植民地（しょくみんち） colony
植林（しょくりん） tree planting

う（える）

植木（うえき） (potted) plant
植える（うえる） to plant

特

学 In the world of *plants*, planting trees is the right thing to do.

注  権 (6th)

 殖 (Jōyō)

269 (2級)

WAY, APPEARENCE

ヨウ

- 同様（どうよう） equal(ly)
- 多様（たよう） various, diverse
- 文様（もんよう） design, pattern

さま

- やの様（さま） Mr. Yano
- 有（あ）り様（さま） status quo
- 様様（さまざま） various

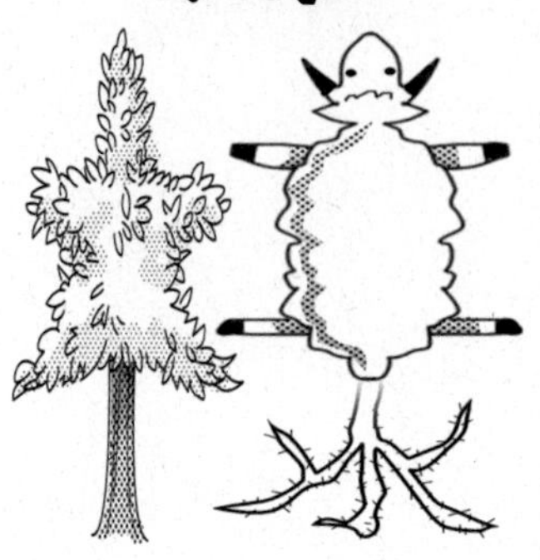

(14 strokes)

注 横 (270)
構 (5th)

学 To achieve the *appearance* of a tree, the lamb takes root.

特  (ant)

270 (2級)

(BE) SIDE, LATERAL

横

オウ

- 横断（おうだん） crossing
- 横死（おうし） violent death
- 横柄（おうへい） impertinent

よこ

- 横（よこ） side, lateral, horizontal
- 横顔（よこがお） profile (of the face)
- 横綱（よこづな） *Yokozuna* (sumo champion)
- 横雨（よこあめ） slating rain (from wind)

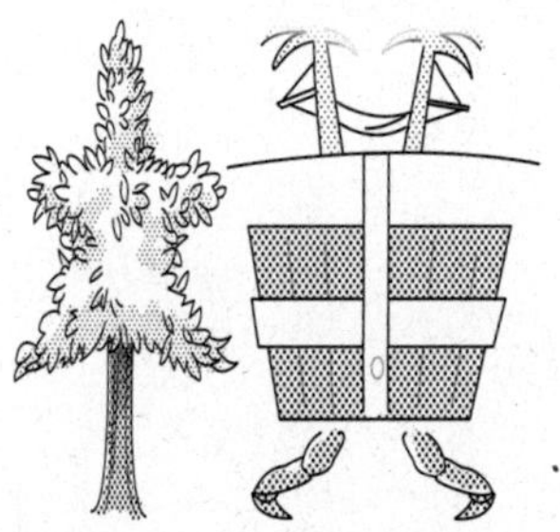

(15 strokes)

注 様 (269)
演 (5th)

学 When a tree is yellow it starts leaning horizontally toward the *side*.

特  (alt)

271 BRIDGE

橋

(16 strokes)

(2級)

キョウ

- 鉄橋（てっきょう） steel bridge
- 歩道橋（ほどうきょう） pedestrian overpass

はし

- 橋（はし） bridge
- 橋渡し（はしわたし） to cross a bridge
- 石橋（いしばし） stone bridge
- 隅田川橋（すみだがわばし） bridge on the river Sumida

特

学 Made of wood is the *bridge* over which Kim rises higher and higher on his way to Paradise.

注 稿 (Jōyō)

272 SLOPE, HILL

(7 strokes)

(2級)

ハン

- 登坂（とうはん） to go uphill
- 急坂（きゅうはん） steep hill

さか

- 坂（さか） hill, slope
- 坂道（さかみち） sloping road
- 下り坂（くだりざか） downhill

特 阪 (alt)

学 A *slope* of fertile land.

注 地 (169)
板 (273)

273 (2級)

SIGN, BOARD

ハン/バン

- 板木（はんぎ） engraving block
- 板書（ばんしょ） writing on the blackboard
- 黒板（こくばん） blackboard
- 掲示板（けいじばん） bulletin board

いた

- 板（いた） plank
- 板前（いたまえ） cook
- 板の間（いたのま） wooden floor
- 板切れ（いたぎれ） piece of wood

(8 strokes)

板	板	板	板
板	板	板	板

注 枚 (6th)
仮 (5th)
析 (Jōyō)

On to the top of a slope with trees, a *sign* tells you when you've arrived home.

274 (2級)

ROOT

コン

- 大根（だいこん） daikon (a Japanese giant radish)
- 根本（こんぽん） basis, fundation
- 根治（こんじ） full recovery (of a root)
- 根性（こんじょう） character, disposition

ね

- 根（ね） root
- 根元（ねもと） root, base
- 根回し（ねまわし） groundwork

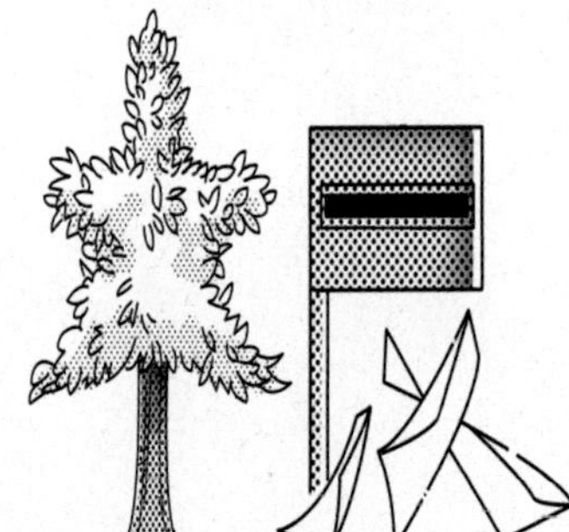

(10 strokes)

根	根	根	根
根	根	根	根

注 銀 (275)
桟 (Jōyō)

学 One has decided to put down *roots* where one plants a tree and a mailbox.

(14 strokes)

銀	銀	銀	銀
銀	銀	銀	銀

SILVER

銀

(3級)

275

ギン

銀（ぎん） silver
銀行（ぎんこう） bank
銀山（ぎんざん） silver mine
銀色（ぎんいろ） silver color
銀座（ぎんざ） Ginza (a suburb in Tokyo)
銀閣寺（ぎんかくじ） Ginkakuji (the Silver Temple of Kyoto)
金銀（きんぎん） gold and silver (money)

特

If you put money in a mailbox, it must be *silver*.

注 録 (604)

(13 strokes)

鉄	鉄	鉄	鉄
鉄	鉄	鉄	鉄

IRON

鉄

(2級)

276

テツ

鉄（てつ） iron
鉄人（てつじん） iron man
鉄板（てっぱん） iron plate (to cook)
鉄道（てつどう） railroad
鉄砲（てっぽう） firearm
鉄板焼き（てっぱんやき） to roast on a a hot plate
近鉄（きんてつ） Kintetsu (railroad company)
地下鉄（ちかてつ） subway (train)

特 鐵 (ant) 銕 (alt) 鐡 (alt)

With money we pay for the drill which cuts through *iron.*

銃 (Jōyō)
釣 (Jōyō)
鋭 (Jōyō)

ご主人様、お風呂の用意ができました。
はあ…
ご主人様は、真に根性のある方でございます…
ふん…
まずしい家庭生まれなのに、貧乏の坂をのぼり、銀行の社長にまでなられまして、立派でございます。
大変だったぞ。電柱を立てたり、木を植えたり、鉄板焼きの前で立ったり… いや… いろいろあったな!
しかし… どうも失礼しますが、質問してもよろしいでしょうか?
なぜ橋の下で住んでおられるのですか
横柄な口をきくな!! ケチだから。以上だ。

Exercises 練習

1. Develop the stroke order of the following kanji.

柱												
様												
坂												
銀												

2. Choose the correct reading for each kanji or kanji combination.

a) この柱時計はこの住宅の家主のものですから、触(さわ)らないでください。

This wall clock belongs to the house owner; so, please, don't touch it.

柱時計: 1．はしどけい　2．はしらどけい　3．ちゅうとけい　4．ちゅうどけい

住宅: 1．しゅたく　2．じゅたく　3．じゅうたく　4．しゅうたく

家主: 1．かぬし　2．やぬし　3．かしゅ　4．やしゅ

b) 昔(むかし)、坂道の多い、石橋という町に住んでいた。

Long ago, I lived in a village called Ishibashi that had many slopes.

坂道: 1．はんどう　2．はんとう　3．さかどう　4．さかみち

石橋: 1．せっきゅう　2．せききゅう　3．いしばし　4．いしはし

住: 1．すむ　2．す　3．じゅん　4．じゅう

c) あの銀行の人は「鉄人」と言われるぐらい根性のある人です。

That banker has character, to the point of being called "iron man."

銀行: 1．きんこう　2．ぎんこう　3．きんこ　4．ぎんこ

鉄人: 1．てっじん　2．てつにん　3．てつじん　4．てんにん

根性: 1．こんせい　2．ねせい　3．ねじょう　4．こんじょう

3. Write the kanji (one or more) and the meaning of the following words.

しゅじん ______ ______　くだりざか ______り______

じゅうしょ ______ ______　こくばん ______ ______

よこ ______ ______　ちかてつ ______ ______

4. Correct either the reading or the writing mistakes in the following words.

横物園　しょくぶつえん　黄断　おうだん　歩道橋　ほどうばし

植回し　ねまわし　金座　ぎんざ　植民地　ちょくみんち

Answers to exercises 練習解答

1. (Check them in the corresponding kanji table: #267, #269, #272, and #275)

2. a) 柱時計: 2 |住宅: 3 | 家主: 2 / b) 坂道: 4 | 石橋: 3 | 住: 2 / c) 銀行: 2 | 鉄人: 3 | 根性: 4

3. しゅじん: 主人, boss, husband | じゅうしょ: 住所, postal address | よこ: 横, side, lateral | くだりざか: 下り坂, downhill | こくばん: 黒板, blackboard | ちかてつ: 地下鉄, subway (train)

4. **植**物園 しょくぶつえん | **横**断 おうだん | 歩道**橋** ほどうきょう | **根**回し ねまわし | **銀**座 ぎんざ | **植**民地 しょくみんち

Manga translation マンガ翻訳

Butler: The bath is ready, sir.

Gentleman: Uh-huh

Butler: Sir, you really are a person of strong character.

Gentleman: Hum.

Butler: It's impressive how, having been born in a humble family, you overcame the hill of poverty, and became a bank manager.

Gentleman: It wasn't easy at all. I did all sorts of things: stood telephone poles, planted trees, work at the hot plate in a restaurant...

Butler: However..., begging your pardon, but may I ask you something?

Butler: Why do you live under a bridge?

Gentleman: Don't be impertinent! Because I'm stingy. And that's it!

New elements 新しい部首

癶	crown of thorns	厶	pantry
旡	hurdles	冂	cane
匚	box	其	easel
区	cemetery	关	divided half

Lesson 25
第二十五課

277 (1級)

BEAN

豆

トウ

豆腐（とうふ） tofu
豆乳（とうにゅう） soy milk
納豆（なっとう） nattō, (fermented soybeans)

ズ

大豆（だいず） soybean

まめ

豆（まめ） bean, pea
黒豆（くろまめ） black soybean
豆鉄砲（まめてっぽう） pea shooter

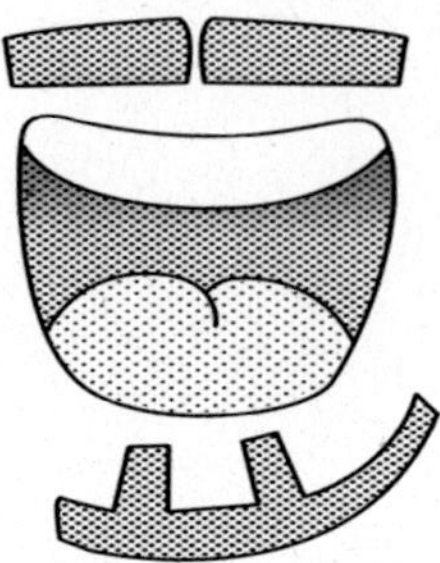

(7 strokes)

豆	豆	豆	豆
豆	豆	豆	豆

注 立 (42)
谷 (95)
登 (279)

学 Did you know facial hair grows from eating *beans?*

特  荳 (alt)

278 (3級)

SHORT

短

タン

短期（たんき） short-term
短気（たんき） short temper
短見（たんけん） narrow-minded

みじか(い)

短い（みじかい） short
手短に（てみじかに） in short, briefly

(12 strokes)

短	短	短	短
短	短	短	短

注 知 (234)

学 With the tip of an arrow, shave your facial hair *short.*

特

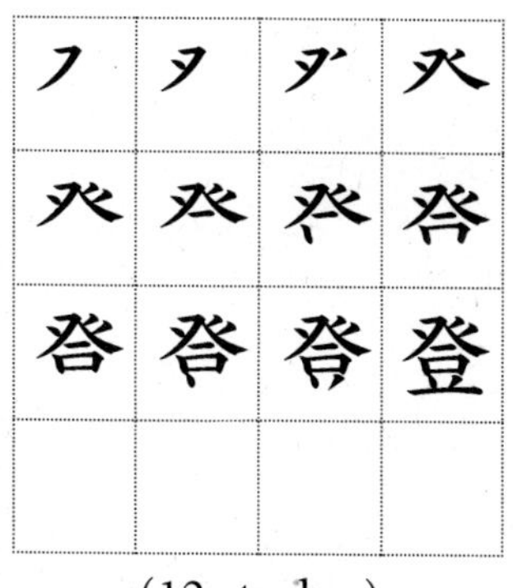

(12 strokes)

TO CLIMB

(2級)

279

トウ

登頂（とうちょう） to reach the summit
登記（とうき） registration, registry
登校（とうこう） to go to school

ト

登山（とざん） to climb a mountain

のぼ(る)

登る（のぼる） to climb
山登り（やまのぼり） to climb mountains

学 With a crown of thorns and several days' growth of facial hair, the martyr *climbs* the hill.

容 (5th)
発 (280)

(9 strokes)

DEPARTURE, START

(3級)

280

ハツ

出発（しゅっぱつ） departure
発射（はっしゃ） shot
発送（はっそう） shipment
発達（はったつ） development, growth
発売（はつばい） on sale
発表（はっぴょう） (oral) presentation
発見（はっけん） discovery, find

發 (ant)

With their crown of thorns, the long-suffering runners wait for the gun to be fired to *start* the hurdle race.

究 (410)
登 (279)

281 (3級)

イ

医者 (いしゃ) doctor
医学 (いがく) medicine
医療 (いりょう) medical treatment
医書 (いしょ) medical book

DOCTOR

(7 strokes)

 区 (282)
図 (183)

 A terrible *doctor*: he who operates only with a box full of arrows.

 醫 (ant)

282 (3級)

ク

区別 (くべつ) to distinguish, to classify
区域 (くいき) territory
二十三区 (にじゅうさんく) 23 wards (of Tokyo)
中央区 (ちゅうおうく) Chūō ward
港区 (みなとく) Minato ward
区役所 (くやくしょ) ward office

WARD, TO DIVIDE

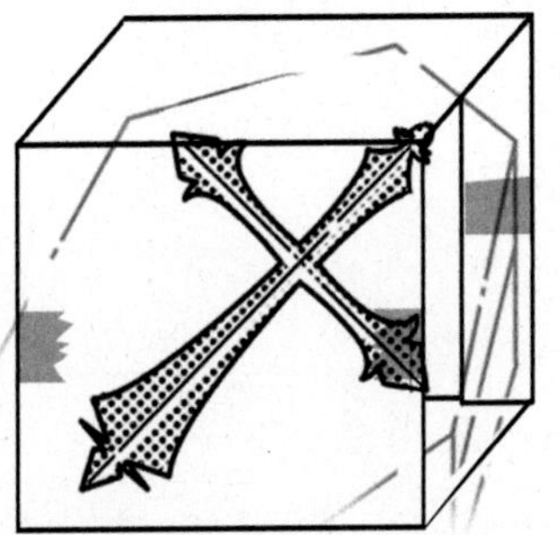

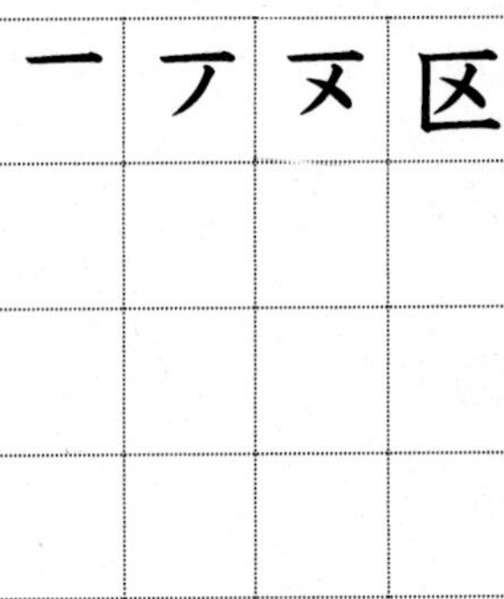

(4 strokes)

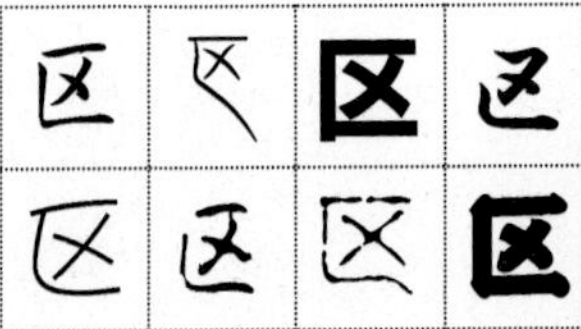

 医 (281)
図 (183)
凶 (Jōyō)

 There is a cemetery in every *ward.*

 區 (ant)

丶 亠 ナ 文
文 対 対

(7 strokes)

OPPOSITE

対

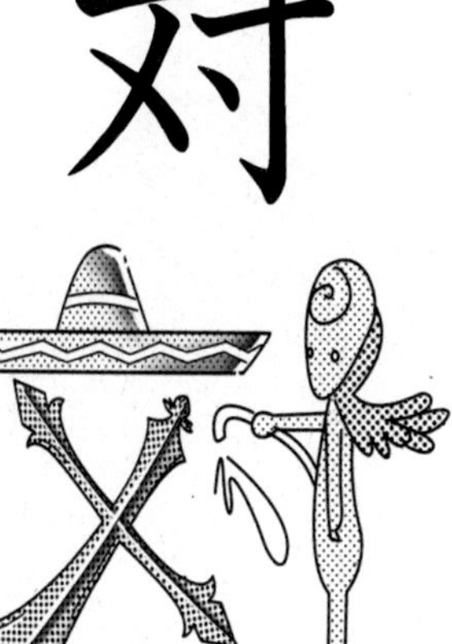

(2級)

283

タイ

対(たい) against, versus
反対(はんたい) opposition
絶対(ぜったい) sure, absolute
対(たい)する to oppose
対立(たいりつ) opposition, rivalry
対戦(たいせん) confrontation (war)

 對 (ant)

 Two *opposites* personified: the religious scribe and the pagan alien.

 村 (64)
効 (5th)

丶 亠 云 云
产 育 育 育

(8 strokes)

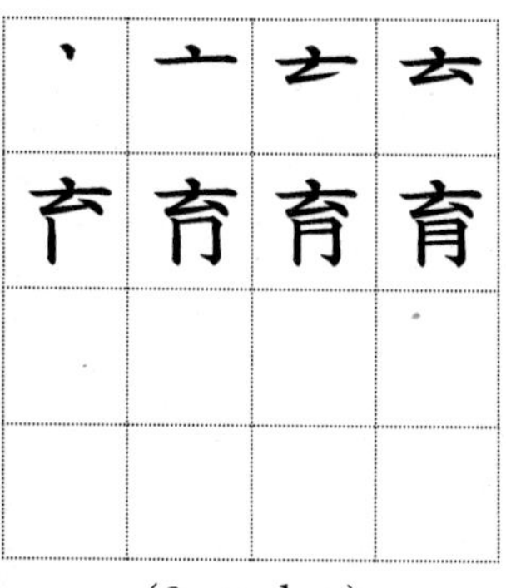

TO RAISE, TO NOURISH

育

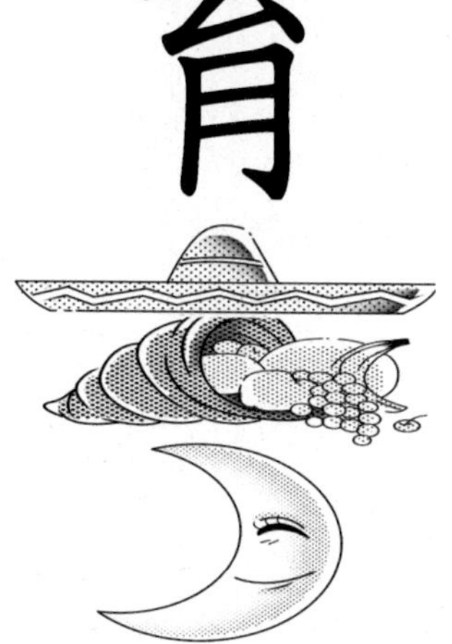

(2級)

284

イク

教育(きょういく) education
体育(たいいく) physical education

そ(だつ/てる)

育(そだ)つ to grow up
生(う)まれ育(そだ)ち born and raised
育(そだ)てる to raise, to educate

 毓 (alt)

 *To raise* your children, if necessary, you would give them everything in the pantry... even the moon.

 有 (285)
青 (36)
玄 (Jōyō)

285 (3級)

TO BE, TO EXIST

ユウ
- 有名（ゆうめい） famous
- 有能（ゆうのう） capable, able
- 有利（ゆうり） advantageous, productive
- 有（ゆう）する to exist

あ(る)
- 有（あ）る to be, there is/are
- 有（あ）り様（さま） status quo
- 有（あ）り難（がと）う thank you

ノ	ナ	冇	有
有	有		

(6 strokes)

有	有	有	有
有	有	有	有

注 育 (284)
右 (29)

The thing that *is there*, always in the sky, is the moon; it looks as if you could catch it with chopsticks.

有 (alt)

286 (3級)

CLOTHES, TO OBEY

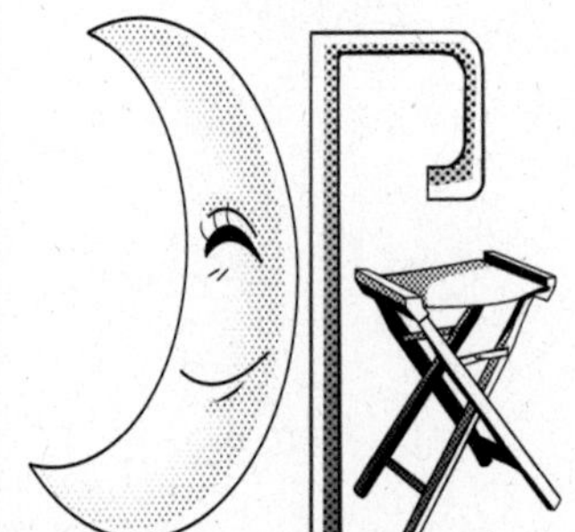

フク
- 服（ふく） clothes
- 衣服（いふく） clothing, apparel
- 和服（わふく） Japanese clothes
- 洋服（ようふく） Western clothes
- 一服（いっぷく） a temporary pause / break, smoke, a dose
- 服（ふく）する to obey
- 服用（ふくよう） to take (medicine)

丿	月	月	月
月⺈	肌	服	服

(8 strokes)

服	服	服	服
服	服	服	服

報 (5th)
被 (Jōyō)

The moon watches as you leave your cane and take off your *clothes*.

服 (alt)

287 (2級)

TIME, PERIOD

期

一	十	廾	廾
甘	甘	其	其
其	期	期	期

(12 strokes)

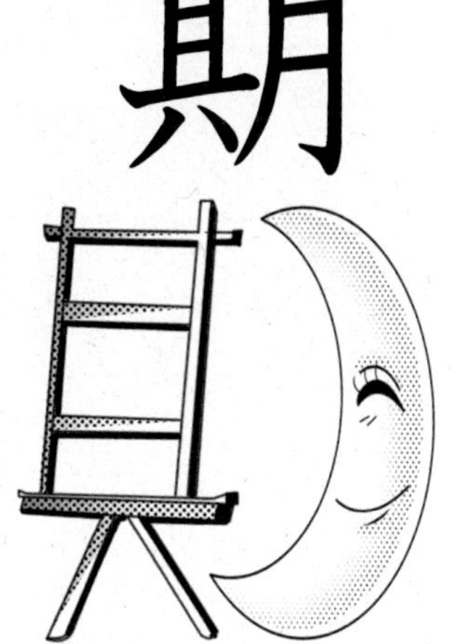

キ

短期（たんき） short-term
期間（きかん） period
学期（がっき） school term
期限（きげん） deadline

ゴ

最期（さいご） one's last moment (death)

期 (alt)

学 To paint the moon takes *time*.

旗 (609)

288 (2級)

TO WIN, VICTORY

勝

ノ	刀	月	月
月	月′	月⺈	月⺈
胖	朕	勝	勝

(12 strokes)

ショウ

勝負（しょうぶ） challenge, match
勝利（しょうり） victory
勝者（しょうしゃ） winner

か(つ)

勝つ（かつ） to win
勝ち組（かちぐみ） winning team
勝手（かって） selfish (not taking others into account)

学 The moon, even when it's a divided half, retains its strength and *wins* the night's challenge.

数 (82)
藤 (no Jōyō)

服を着替えてね。おじいちゃんは話を読むから。
わ〜い！わ〜い！
むかしむかし、ジャックという子がいた。ある日、豆を植えて、小さな苗がでたの…
短期で、苗がすごく発達して、天にいたるまでの大きな木まで育った。魔法の豆だったので！
元気で有能なジャックは、その木を登り、雲の上まで行った。その不思議な区域にきれいな城があった。
でも、その城に恐ろしい鬼も住んでいた!!そして…
ジャック対鬼
それで？ジャックが勝ったんでしょ？
ま…勝ったことは勝ったけど…
家宅侵入罪で、医療費とか、賠償金とか、鬼に払わざるをえなかった。

Exercises 練習

1. Develop the stroke order of the following kanji.

登												
医												
服												
勝												

2. Choose the correct reading for each kanji or kanji combination.

a) 豆腐や納豆を食べるようにお医者さんに言われました。

The doctor has recommended that I eat tofu and nattō.

豆腐:	1．とうふう	2．とふう	3．とうふ	4．とふ
納豆:	1．なとう	2．なと	3．なっとう	4．なっと
医者:	1．いもの	2．いしゃ	3．いじゃ	4．いもん

b) あの有名な洋服のブランド、いよいよ新しいコレクションを発売するよ！

That famous clothing brand has finally put its new collection on sale!

有名:	1．ゆうめい	2．ありめい	3．ゆうな	4．ありな
洋服:	1．ようふ	2．ようふく	3．ようぷ	4．ようぷく
発売:	1．ははい	2．はばい	3．はっぱい	4．はつばい

c) プランに反対するなら、勝負しよう！勝利はこっちのもんだから。

If you are against the plan, I challenge you! The victory will be mine.

反対	1．はたい	2．はんだい	3．はんたい	4．はだい
勝負:	1．かふ	2．かぶ	3．かつぶ	4．しょうぶ
勝利:	1．かつり	2．かっり	3．しょうり	4．しょり

3. Write the kanji (one or more) and the meaning of the following words.

まめ	______	______	いがく	______	______
やまのぼり	____り	______	きょういく	______	______
しゅっぱつ	______	______	ゆうり	______	______

4. Correct either the reading or the writing mistakes in the following words.

短汽	たんき	中央図	ちゅうおうく	生育	うまれそだち
発山	とざん	豆期	たんき	勝手	かて

Answers to exercises 練習解答

1. (Check them in the corresponding kanji table: #279, #281, #286, and #288)

2. a) 豆腐: 3 | 納豆: 3 | 医者: 2 / b) 有名: 1 | 洋服: 2 | 発売: 4 / c) 反対: 3 | 勝負: 4 | 勝利: 3

3. まめ: 豆, bean, pea | やまのぼり: 山登り, to climb a mountain | しゅっぱつ: 出発, departure | いがく: 医学, medicine | きょういく: 教育, education | ゆうり: 有利, advantageous, productive

4. 短気 たんき | 中央区 ちゅうおうく | 生まれ育ち うまれそだち | 登山 とざん | 短期 たんき | 勝手 かって

Manga translation マンガ翻訳

Grandfather: Come on, change your clothes, and grandfather will read you a story.

Grandson: Yippee! Yippee!

Grandfather: A long, long time ago, there was a boy called Jack. One day he planted a bean and a little plant sprouted from it, but...

Grandfather: ...in a short period of time, it grew and grew until it became a big tree which reached the sky. It was a magic bean!

Grandfather: Jack, who was a strong and able boy, climbed the tree up to the clouds. There, in a fantastic spot, there was a beautiful castle.

Grandfather: But in the castle lived a terrible ogre! Then...

Legend: Jack vs. the Ogre!!

Grandson: And what happened next? Jack won, didn't he?!

Grandfather: Well, he did win, but...

Grandfather: ...he was charged with breaking and entering, and he had to pay the ogre for medical expenses, damages, and so on.

New elements 新しい部首

重 robot

免 pretty journalist 

曲 closed pentagram

辰 primitive man 

业 clothesline 

羊 tree of abundance 

Lesson 26
第二十六課

289 (3級)

ジュウ
体重(たいじゅう) body weight
重要(じゅうよう) important

チョウ
貴重(きちょう) valuable

おも(い)
重(おも)い heavy

かさ(なる/ねる)
重(かさ)なる to pile up

HEAVY

(9 strokes)

重	重	重	重
重	重	重	重

注 車 (32)
乗 (368)

 A big and *heavy* robot.

290 (3級)

ドウ
自動(じどう) automatic
活動(かつどう) activity
動物(どうぶつ) animal
行動(こうどう) behavior

うご(く/かす)
動(うご)く to move
心(こころ)を動(うご)かす to affect one's emotions, to move one's heart

TO MOVE

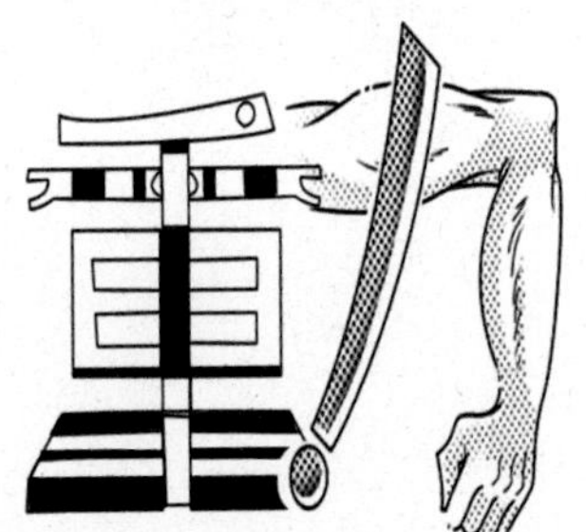

(11 strokes)

動	動	動	動
動	動	動	動

 働 (461)

 *To move* a heavy robot, you need strength.

 动 (simp)

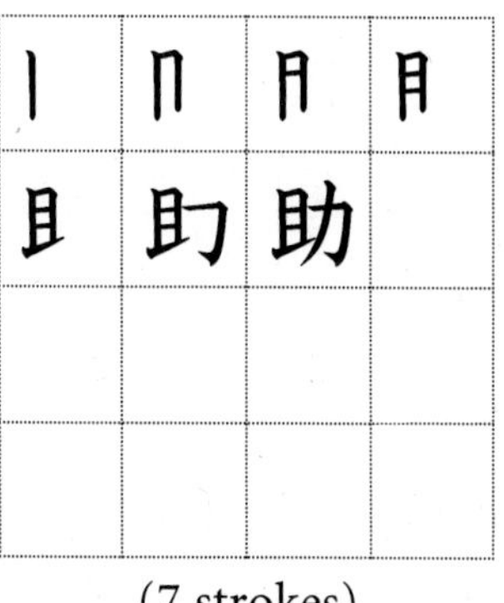

(7 strokes)

291 HELP

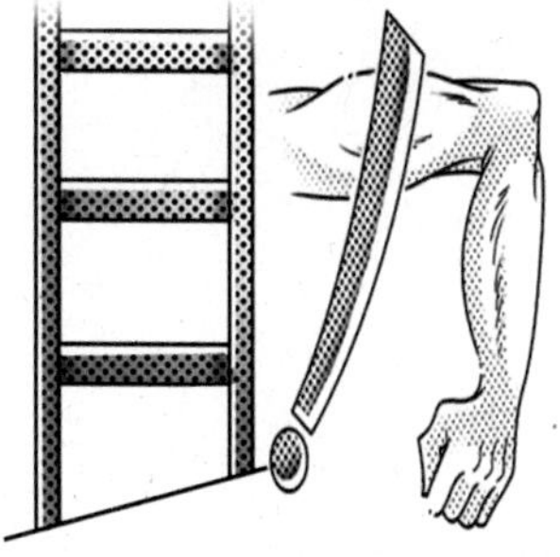

(2級)

ジョ

助力(じょりょく) help

援助(えんじょ) (financial) help

すけ

助平(すけべい) pervert

たす(ける/かる)

人(ひと)を助(たす)ける to help someone

助(たす)かる to be of help

 Here is the emergency ladder, and a strong arm which *helps* you to climb it.

注 加 (463)

組 (121)

292 EFFORT, HARD WORK

ノ ㇒ 㑒 ... 免 勉

(10 strokes)

(3級)

ベン

勉強(べんきょう) to study

勤勉(きんべん) diligent, hard-working

つと(める)

勉(つと)める to try hard

 A pretty journalist needs strength to *work hard.*

 起 (309)

293 (2級)

ジャク

今昔（こんじゃく） present and past

セキ

昔年（せきねん） years ago

昔日（せきじつ） old times

むかし

昔（むかし） in the past

昔々（むかしむかし） once upon a time...

昔話（むかしばなし） legend story

FORMER TIMES

昔

(8 strokes)

注 音 (43)
者 (262)

The sun remembers *former times* of when he was able to relax in his hammock as a happy little star.

294 (1級)

ショウ

昭和（しょうわ） Shōwa era (from 1926 to 1989)

CLEAR, BRIGHT

昭

(9 strokes)

明 (227)
脂 (Jōyō)

See how the sun reflects the *bright* shine of the katana on the sadist's mouth.

(13 strokes)

暗	暗	暗	暗
暗	暗	暗	暗

DARK

(3級)

295

アン

暗夜（あんや） dark night
明暗（めいあん） light and darkness, contrast
暗号（あんごう） secret number, code
暗殺（あんさつ） murder

くら(い)

暗い（くらい） dark, depressed
暗い過去（くらいかこ） shadowy past

特

学 Even on a sunny day, the sound of the vulture is a *dark* omen.

 晴 (228)
噴 (Jōyō)

(6 strokes)

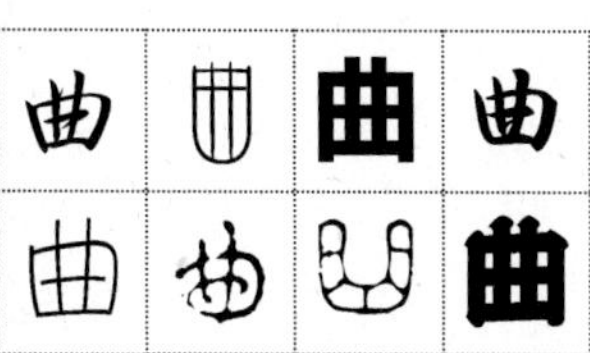

MUSIC, CURVE

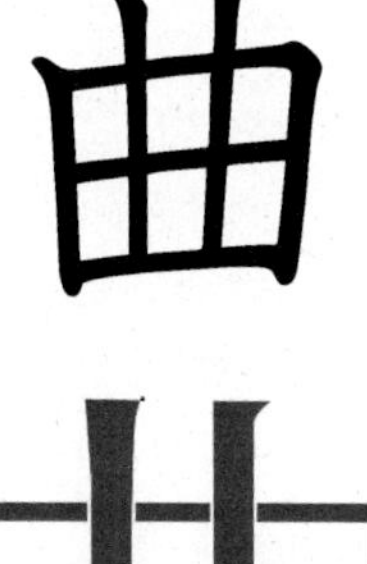

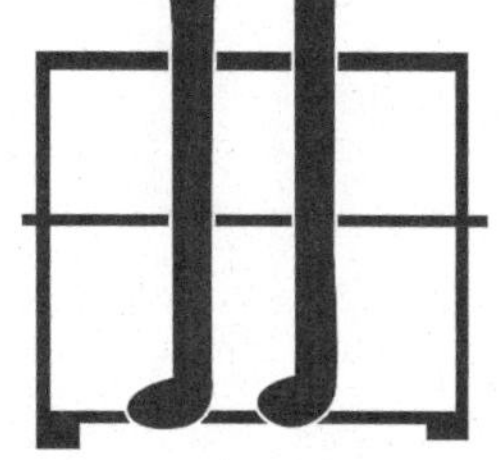

(2級)

296

キョク

名曲（めいきょく） famous song
新曲（しんきょく） new song
作曲家（さっきょくか） composer
曲線（きょくせん） curved line
曲折（きょくせつ） curve, zigzag, complications

ま(がる/げる)

曲がる（まがる） to turn (left or right)

 The kanji for *music* is a score of music with two nodes on it.

 由 (339)
血 (338)

297 (2級)

SURFACE

表

ヒョウ
- 表紙（ひょうし） book cover
- 表現（ひょうげん） expression, set phrase
- 代表（だいひょう） to represent
- 表題（ひょうだい） title

おもて
- 表（おもて） front

あらわ(す/れる)
- 表す（あらわす） to express, to show
- 表れる（あらわれる） to be expressed

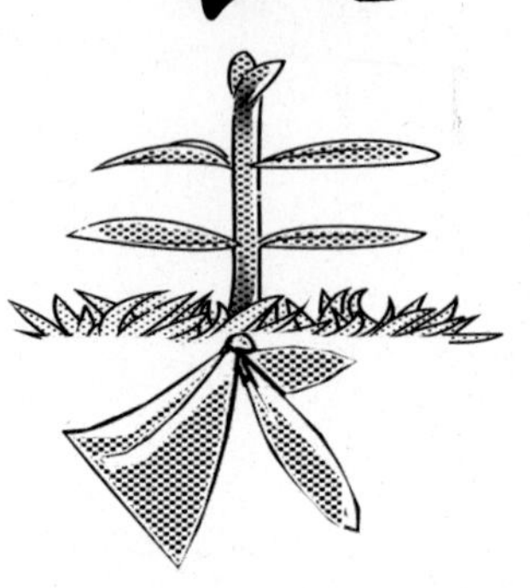

一 十 キ 主 声 耒 耒 表

(8 strokes)

表 表 表 表 表 表 表 表

注 麦 (150) 衣 (511)

学 A plant will grow if you plant a cowboy scarf. The secret is in the *surface* of the ground.

特

298 (2級)

AGRICULTURE

農

ノウ
- 農業（のうぎょう） agriculture
- 農村（のうそん） agricultural village
- 農民（のうみん） peasants
- 農家（のうか） farmer
- 農作（のうさく） farming

丨 冂 巾 巾 曲 曲 曲 芦 芦 芦 農 農 農

(13 strokes)

農 農 農 農 農 農 農 農

注 豊 (5th) 雲 (Jōyō)

学 Music and *agriculture* are the primitive man's passions (under a cliff, with two slices of bread, and a few letters).

特

(11 strokes)

NOTEBOOK

(1級)

299

チョウ

手帳（てちょう） pocket notebook, one's daily planner

通帳（つうちょう） bankbook

学 The housewife with an apron has a *notebook* full of long shopping lists.

鳴 (232)

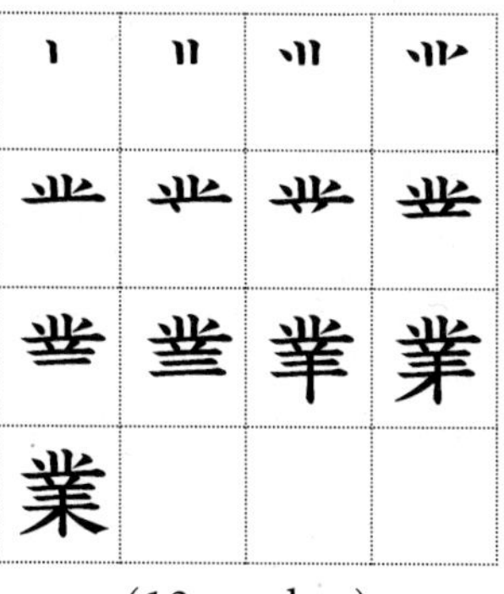

(13 strokes)

BUSINESS, WORK, KARMA

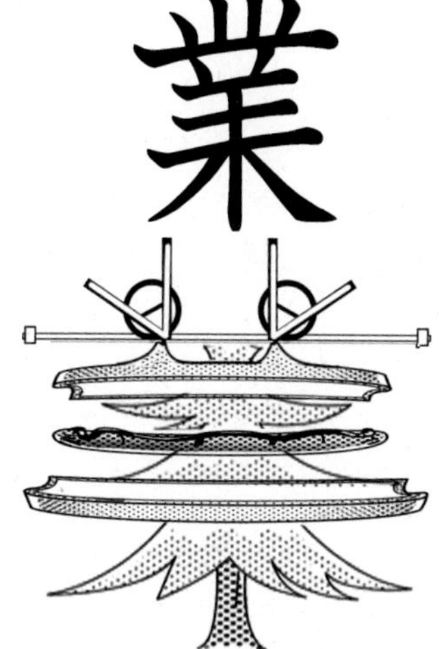

(3級)

300

ギョウ

業界（ぎょうかい） business work

企業（きぎょう） enterprise

営業時間（えいぎょうじかん） business hours

ゴウ

業（ごう） karma

悪業（あくごう） bad karma

わざ

仕業（しわざ） act, deed

If you hang the tree of abundance (a tree from which sandwiches grow) and it dries, *business* will be in dire straits.

集 (250)
美 (405)
僕 (Jōyō)

重いいい！
全然動かないよ！

あの…手伝いましょうか？
あっ…ありがたい！助かるぞ！

失礼ですけど…その手帳に書いているのは、音楽ですか？

するどいね、きみ！いや、わしは作曲家や。たった今オペラを書いている。

表題は「昔の農業人の暗い生活」。昭和時代までの農民についてのオペラや。

そうですか？
それで、インスピレーションをえるために田舎に来られたのですね。

その通り！具体的に、本物の農家を持っていく。いやあ、勉強になるな！
助けて!!誰か!!!

Exercises 練習

1. Develop the stroke order of the following kanji.

重												
曲												
農												
業												

2. Choose the correct reading for each kanji or kanji combination.

a) この暗殺はね... あのあやしい行動をした助平の仕業だと思うよ。

This murder... I think it was the deed of that pervert with the strange behavior.

暗殺:　1．くらさ　2．くらさつ　3．あんさ　4．あんさつ

行動:　1．こどう　2．こうど　3．こど　4．こうどう

助平:　1．すかぺい　2．すけぺい　3．すかべい　4．すけべい

仕業:　1．しわざ　2．しごう　3．しぎょ　4．しぎょう

b) 気分が重い時は、心を動かす音楽を聞くと助かります。

When I'm depressed, listening to moving music helps me.

重:　1．しゅう　2．ちょう　3．おも　4．かさ

動かす:　1．う　2．うご　3．どう　4．うぐ

助かり:　1．じょかり　2．すけかり　3．たすかり　4．たかり

c) 昭和時代と比(く)べれば、農業に従事(じゅうじ)している人は少ない。

Compared with the Shōwa era, there are less people who are engaged in agriculture.

昭和　1．しょうわ　2．しょわ　3．へいわ　4．みわ

農業:　1．きょくごう　2．のうぎょう　3．のぎょう　4．のうわざ

3. Write the kanji (one or more) and the meaning of the following words.

たいじゅう ______ ______　あんごう ______ ______

じどう ______ ______　おもて ______ ______

むかしばなし ______ ______　えいぎょう 営______ ______

4. Correct either the reading or the writing mistakes in the following words.

重る　かさなる　免強　べんきょう　曲る　まがる

援助　えんじょう　暗らい　くらい　手長　てちょう

Answers to exercises 練習解答

1. (Check them in the corresponding kanji table: #289, #296, #298, and #300)

2. a) 暗殺: 4 | 行動: 4 | 助平: 4 | 仕業: 1 / b) 重い: 3 | 動かす: 2 | 助かり: 3 / c) 昭和: 1 | 農業: 2

3. たいじゅう: 体重, body weight | じどう: 自動, automatic | むかしばなし: 昔話, legend, story | あんごう: 暗号, key, secret number | おもて: 表, front | えいぎょう: 営業, working, open to the public

4. 重なる かさなる | 勉強 べんきょう | 曲がる まがる | 援助 えんじょ | 暗~~ち~~い くらい | 手帳 てちょう

Manga translation マンガ翻訳

Old man: This sure is heavy! I can't move it!

Young man: Hi, may I help you?

Old man: Oh, thank you very much. You have saved me!

Young man: Excuse me, but… that thing you are writing in that notebook, is it music?

Old man: You are a keen observer, lad. Yes, I'm a composer. Right now I'm writing an opera.

Old man: Its title is: "The Dark Life of Farmers in Old Times." It's about farmers until the Shōwa era.

Young man: Really? Oh, so that's why you've come to the country, to get some inspiration, right?

Old man: Exactly. Concretely (speaking), I'm taking this genuine farmer with me. Studying him will be very useful!

Farmer: Help! Help me, please!

Onomatopoeia clapping: Clap, clap

Onomatopoeia chest: Clatter clatter

New elements 新しい部首

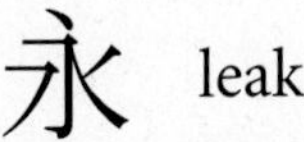
永 leak

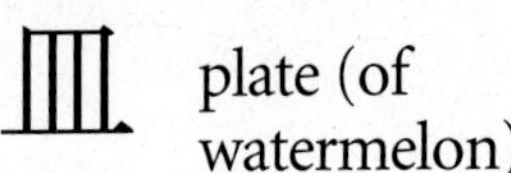
皿 plate (of watermelon)

冗 cabaret

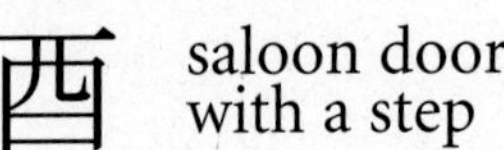
西 saloon doors with a step

Lesson 27
第二十七課

301

(2級)

ヒョウ

氷点（ひょうてん） freezing point

氷山（ひょうざん） iceberg

氷塊（ひょうかい） block of ice

こおり

氷（こおり） ice

かき氷（ごおり） flavored crushed ice

ICE

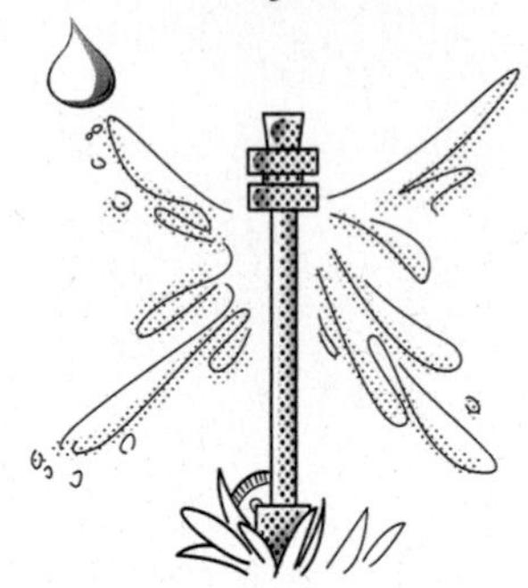

(5 strokes)

注 水 (53)
永 (5th)

A drop is enough to transform water into *ice*. (When it functions as a radical, it takes the 冫 form.)

冰 (alt)

302

(2級)

エイ

水泳（すいえい） swimming

水泳大会（すいえいたいかい） swim meet/competition

水泳選手（すいえいせんしゅ） swimmer

背泳（はいえい） backstroke

およ(ぐ)

泳ぐ（およぐ） to swim

TO SWIM

(8 strokes)

注 永 (5th)
派 (6th)
流 (307)

You can't *swim*, there's no water! There has been a leak!

荥 (alt)

丶	冫	氵	氵
汁	汁	汼	注

(8 strokes)

注	注	注	注
注	注	注	注

TO POUR, TO PAY ATTENTION

注

(3級)

303

チュウ

注入(ちゅうにゅう) to pour

注射(ちゅうしゃ) injection

注意(ちゅうい) (to pay) attention

注目(ちゅうもく) to take notice of

そそ(ぐ)

注ぐ(そそぐ) to pour

 注 (alt)

 Magic water: the magician king *pours* it.

注 柱 (267)

丶	冫	氵	氵
氵	氵	氵	氵
温	温	温	温

(12 strokes)

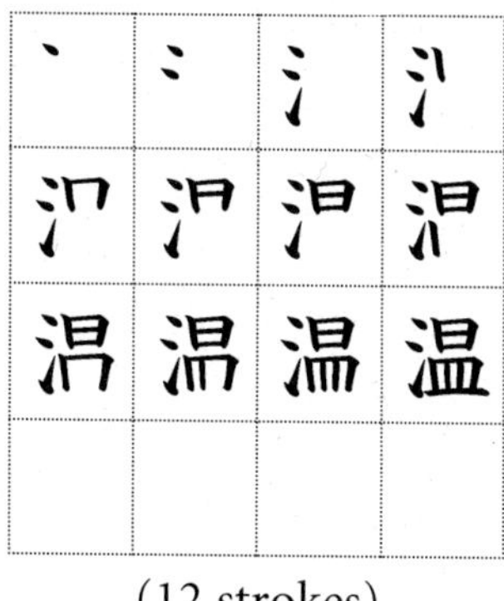

WARM

温

(2級)

304

オン

温泉(おんせん) *onsen* (hot spring)

温和(おんわ) warm weather

気温(きおん) temperature

保温(ほおん) maintained temperature

あたた(かい/める/まる)

温(あたた)かいスープ hot soup

スープを温(あたた)める to warm up soup

 溫 (alt)

 Water and sun... and a plate of fresh watermelon: the keys to a *warm* summer.

注 漫 (Jōyō)

305 (2級)

LAKE

湖

コ

湖面（こめん） surface of a lake
湖岸（こがん） shore of a lake
のじり湖（こ） Nojiri lake

みずうみ

湖（みずうみ） lake

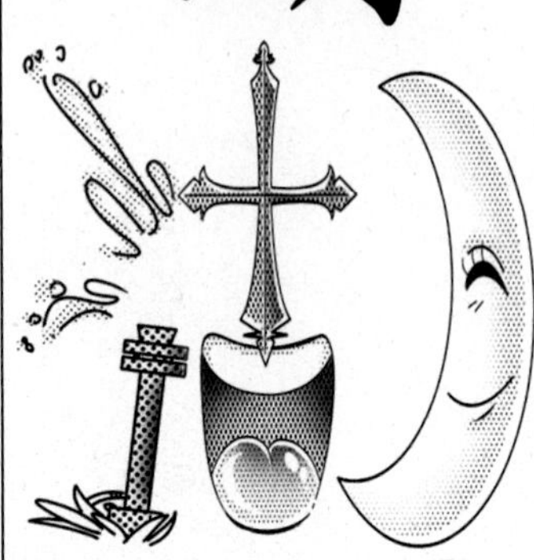

丶	冫	氵	汁
汁	汁	沽	沽
湖	湖	湖	湖

(12 strokes)

湖	湖	湖	湖
湖	湖	湖	湖

注 潮 (6th)

 The *waters* of the lake reflect the face of the old moon.

306 (2級)

DEEP

シン

深海（しんかい） sea depths
深夜（しんや） dead of night
深刻（しんこく） serious, grave

ふか(い/める/まる)

深い（ふかい） deep
興味深い（きょうみぶかい） interesting
知識を深め（ちしきをふかめ） to deepen one's knowledge

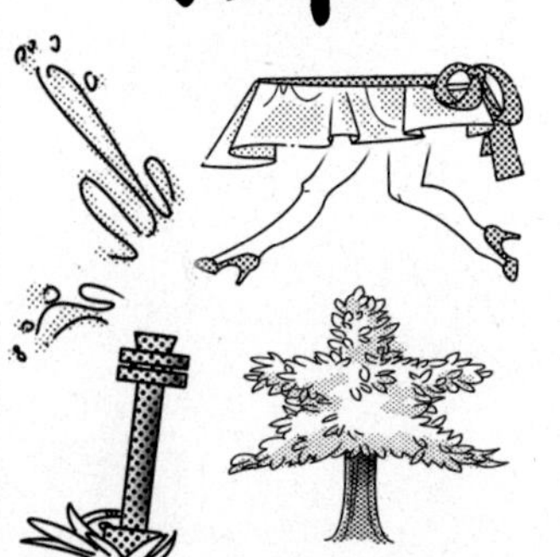

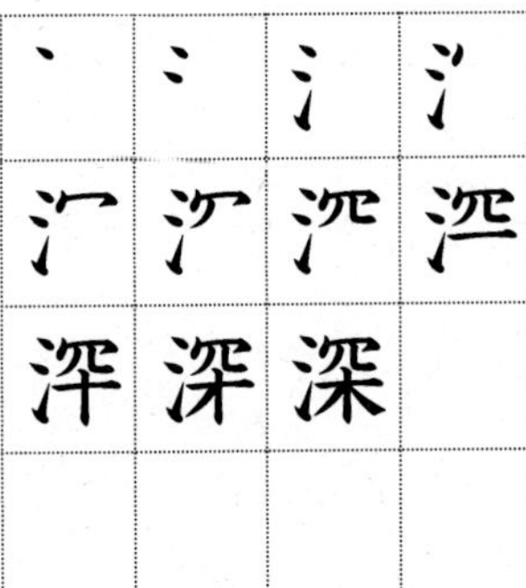

(11 strokes)

深	深	深	深
深	深	深	深

注 探 (6th)
浮 (Jōyō)

 In the *depths* of the water, a cabaret and a magic tree are hiding.

307 CURRENT, FLOW

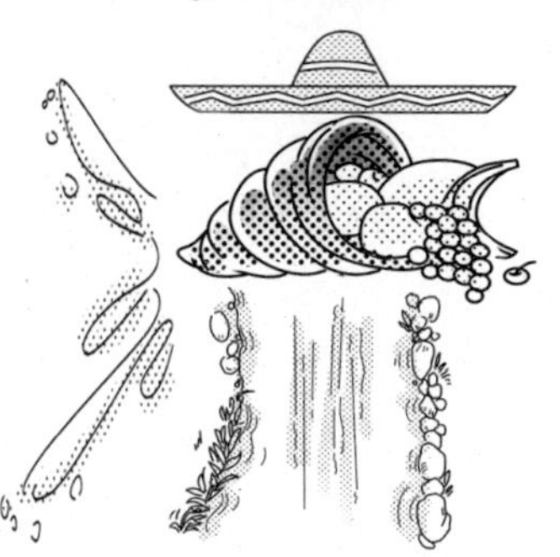

(10 strokes)

(2級)

リュウ

- 流血 (りゅうけつ) bloodshed
- 中流 (ちゅうりゅう) middle class
- 交流 (こうりゅう) exchange

なが(れる/す)

- 流れる (ながれる) to flow
- 流れ星 (ながれぼし) shooting star
- 流れ込む (ながれこむ) to flow into, absorb
- 情報を流す (じょうほうをながす) to spread information

 Besides water, the *current* of the river carries other delicacies with which we can fill our pantry.

 派 (6th) 済 (6th)

308 HARBOR

(12 strokes)

(2級)

コウ

- 港内 (こうない) in the harbor
- 空港 (くうこう) airport
- 入港 (にゅうこう) to enter a port

みなと

- 港 (みなと) harbor, port
- 港町 (みなとまち) port town

 港 (alt)

 Every sailor loves the water, lives at a *port*, sleeps in a hammock, and fishes with worms.

 満 (492) 済 (6th)

309 (3級)

TO WAKE UP, TO HAPPEN

キ

- 起草（きそう） (written) draft
- 縁起（えんぎ） luck

お(きる/こる/こす)

- 起（お）きる to wake up
- 早起（はやお）き to get up early
- 起（お）こる to happen
- 起（お）こす to cause

一	十	土	丰
丰	赱	走	起
起	起		

(10 strokes)

注 逃 (Jōyō)
超 (Jōyō)
勉 (292)

学 *Wake up* and run, Little Worm, something terrible has happened!

特  起 (alt)

310 (3級)

SUBJECT

ダイ

- 話題（わだい） conversation subject
- 問題（もんだい） problem
- 主題（しゅだい） subject matter
- 宿題（しゅくだい） homework
- 題名（だいめい） title
- 題（だい） subject (e.g., of an essay)

日	旦	早	早
是	是	是	是
是	題	題	題
題	題	題	

(18 strokes)

注 超 (Jōyō)
勉 (292)

学 The *subject* of this meeting is that the sun wants to learn how to take photos. He has lost his head!

特

(10 strokes)

SAKE, ALCOHOLIC DRINK

(2級) **311**

シュ

日本酒(にほんしゅ) sake, Japanese liquor

洋酒(ようしゅ) Western liquor

さけ

お酒(さけ) sake, (rice wine)

酒癖(さけぐせ) (good/bad) drunk

甘酒(あまざけ) sweet sake

 Look at the water puddle where the *sake* drunkard falls in when he leaves the pub with the saloon doors and misses the step!

 活 (166)

西 (200)

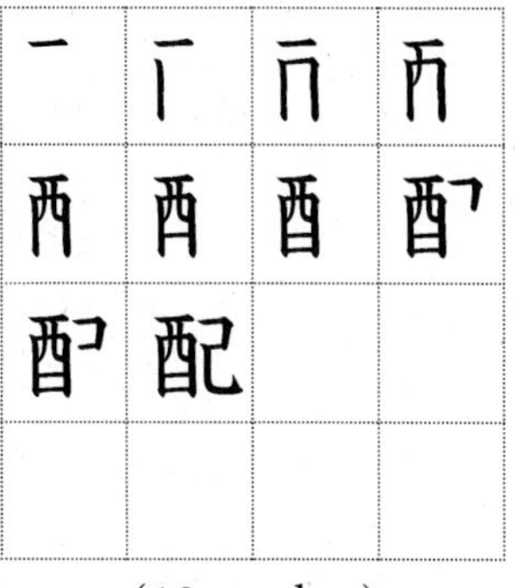

(10 strokes)

TO DISTRIBUTE, TO WORRY

(2級) **312**

ハイ

配送(はいそう) (mail) delivery

配達(はいたつ) (parcels) delivery

心配(しんぱい) worry

手配(てはい) arrangements

くば(る)

配る(くばる) to distribute

 On the step before the saloon doors of houses, Little Worm *distributes* newspapers.

 酒 (311)

酌 (Jōyō)

深宇宙研究所
その夜…
…暑かったので、湖で泳いでいた。
突然、空港の上にピカピカする光が現れた。飛行機か流れ星かしらと思ったけど…
そしたら、起きると、UFOの中にいた!!
いよいよこれは主題だぞ！注意しろ!!!
するとね… きゃあ！恐ろしかったわよ！
酒やジュースを配られたけど、氷がなかったから、あたしのコーラが温まってて、まずかったよ！
……

Exercises 練習

1. Develop the stroke order of the following kanji.

泳												
港												
起												
配												

2. Choose the correct reading for each kanji or kanji combination.

a) 深夜、酒飲んで、湖で泳いで... あなたのことを忘(わす)れようとしていた。

In the dead of night, I drank alcohol and swam in the lake... trying to forget you.

深夜: 1. しんよる 2. しんや 3. ふかよる 4. ふかや

酒: 1. しゅ 2. じゅ 3. さけ 4. さか

湖: 1. みずみ 2. みずうみ 3. みすみ 4. みすうみ

泳: 1. えい 2. およぐ 3. およ 4. およい

b) とけて湖岸に寄(よ)せられた氷塊が、川に流れ込みはじめた。

The block of ice approaching the shore of the lake, half melted, was absorbed by the river.

湖岸: 1. みずかん 2. みずうかん 3. こうかん 4. こがん

氷塊: 1. こおりかい 2. こりかい 3. ひょかい 4. ひょうかい

c) 空港には、必ずパスポートを持っていくように注意してください。

Make sure you take your passport with you at the airport.

空港 1. くうこう 2. くこ 3. くうこ 4. くこう

注意: 1. そそい 2. そぞい 3. ちゅうい 4. ちゅい

3. Write the kanji (one or more) and the meaning of the following words.

ちゅうもく ______ ______ すいえい ______ ______

おんせん ______ ______ こうりゅう ______ ______

きおん ______ ______ みなとまち ______ ______

4. Correct either the reading or the writing mistakes in the following words.

水山	ひょうざん	興味深い	きょうみふかい	早起き	はやいき
注そぐ	そそぐ	起る	おこる	門題	もんだい
舌題	わだい	日本西	にほんしゅ	心酒	しんぱい

Answers to exercises 練習解答

1. (Check them in the corresponding kanji table: #302, #308, #309, and #312)

2. a) 深夜: 2 | 酒: 3 | 湖: 2 | 泳: 3 / b) 湖岸: 4 | 氷塊: 4 / c) 空港: 1 | 注意: 3

3. ちゅうもく: 注目, to take notice of | おんせん: 温泉, *onsen* (spa) | きおん: 気温, temperature | すいえい: 水泳, swimming | こうりゅう: 交流, exchange | みなとまち: 港町, port town

4. 氷山　ひょうざん | 興味深い　きょうみぶかい | 早起き　はやおき | 注~~そ~~ぐ　そそぐ | 起こる　おこる | 問題　もんだい | 話題　わだい | 日本酒　にほんしゅ | 心配　しんぱい

Manga translation マンガ翻訳

Sign: Deep Space Research Institute.

Girl: That night...

Girl: ...it was hot, so I was swimming in the lake.

Girl: Suddenly, there was a bright light over the airport. I thought it might be an airplane or a shooting star, but...

Girl: Then, when I woke up, I was inside a UFO!

Investigator: We are getting to the main point! Pay attention!

Girl: Then... Aahhh! It was horrible!

Girl: They served alcohol and juice, but since they had no ice, my cola drink warmed up and it was disgusting!

Investigator: ...

New elements 新しい部首

平 revolving plates 

羊 ox 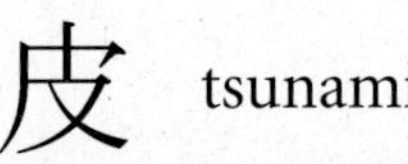

ュ guillotine 

夫 husband 

皮 tsunami 

勿 giant comb 

Lesson 28
第二十八課

313 (1級)

SHEEP, LAMB

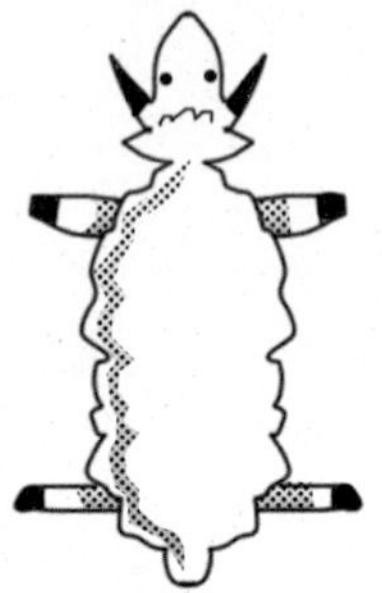

ヨウ

- 羊毛（ようもう） wool
- 羊肉（ようにく） mutton
- 牧羊（ぼくよう） sheep breeding
- 牧羊犬（ぼくようけん） sheep dog

ひつじ

- 羊（ひつじ） sheep
- 子羊（こひつじ） lamb
- 牡羊座（おひつじざ） Aries (the Ram)

(6 strokes)

手 (18)
美 (405)
半 (210)

A flat *sheep*, hit by a car.

314 (3級)

OCEAN, THE WEST

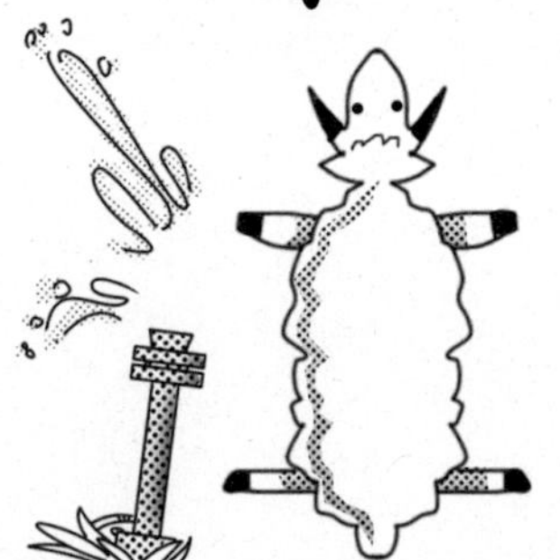

ヨウ

- 洋服（ようふく） Western clothes
- 太平洋（たいへいよう） Pacific ocean
- 東洋（とうよう） The East (Orient)
- 西洋（せいよう） The West (Occident)
- 大西洋（たいせいよう） Atlantic Ocean
- 南氷洋（なんぴょうよう） Antartic Ocean
- インド洋（よう） Indian Ocean
- 洋風（ようふう） Western style

(9 strokes)

注 (303)
浅 (494)

Look at these two elements in Western symbology: with the *ocean* water, the sheep is baptized.

315 FLAT, PLAIN

(2級)

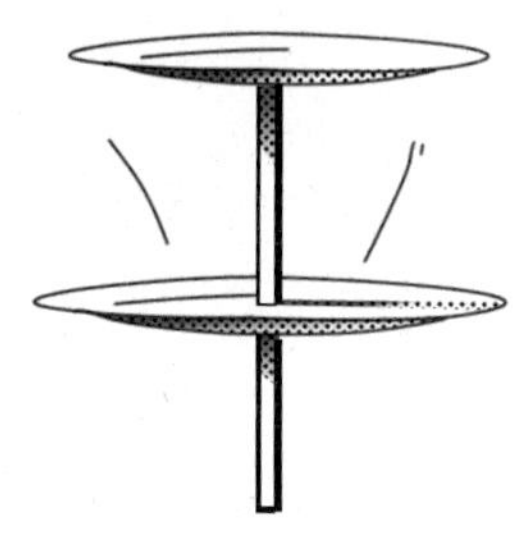

(5 strokes)

ヘイ
平気（へいき） calm
平野（へいや） plain, prairie
平凡（へいぼん） ordinary, mediocre

ビョウ
平等（びょうどう） equality

ひら / たい(ら)
平泳ぎ（ひらおよ） breaststroke
平地（ひらち） flatland
平ら（たい） flat, level

 乎 (alt)

 The secret of revolving plates: they must stay level and *flat*!

 半 (210)
羊 (313)

316 HAPPINESS

(2級)

(8 strokes)

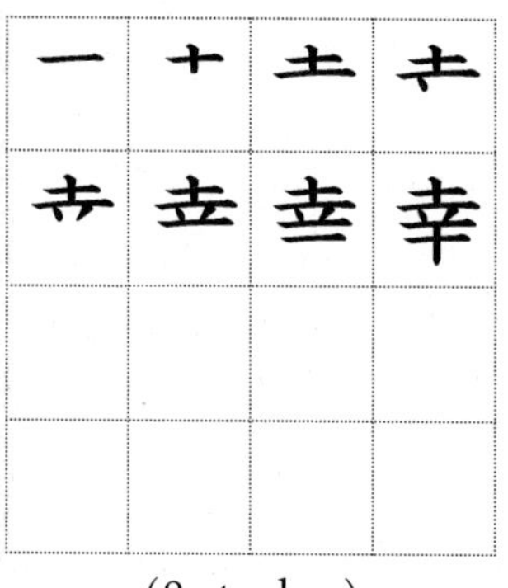

コウ
幸福（こうふく） bliss, happiness
幸運（こううん） good fortune, luck
不幸（ふこう） unhappiness, misfortune
多幸（たこう） happiness, fortune

さいわ(い)
幸い（さいわ） good fortune, bliss

しあわ(せ)
幸せ（しあわ） happiness
不幸せ（ふしあわ） misfortune

 Fertile land and an ox to work it meant *happiness* for the man of yesteryear.

 羊 (313)
美 (405)
辛 (Jōyō)

317 (2級)

TO DECIDE

ケツ

- 決定（けってい） decision
- 判決（はんけつ） (judicial) sentence
- 決勝（けっしょう） final match
- 決して（けっ） never
- 決心（けっしん） resolution, determination
- 評決（ひょうけつ） veredict

き(める/まる)

- 決める（き） to decide
- 決まる（き） to be decided

丶	冫	氵	氵
氵	氵	決	

(7 strokes)

決	決	決	決
決	決	決	決

注 洗 (6th)
法 (491)

学 Kim must *decide*: he either drowns in the water or dies under the guillotine.

特 決 (alt)

318 (3級)

CHINA, OF CHINESE ORIGIN

カン

- 漢字（かんじ） kanji
- 漢文（かんぶん） Chinese literature
- 巨漢（きょかん） giant
- 暴漢（ぼうかん） ruffian, thug, rowdy
- 漢語（かんご） Chinese word
- 漢和辞典（かんわじてん） Chinese/Japanese dictionary

丶	冫	氵	氵
氵	氵	氵	氵
氵	氵	氵	漢
漢			

(13 strokes)

漢	漢	漢	漢
漢	漢	漢	漢

注 漂 (6th)
落 (432)
清 (487)

 The *Chinese* woman adores water: she waters the plants with it and quenches her big-mouthed husband's thirst. (Check the explanation of kanji #436.)

 漢 (alt)

319

(10 strokes)

消 消 消 消
消 消 消 消

TO TURN OFF, TO CONSUME

消

(2級)

ショウ

- 消費 (しょうひ) spending, consumption
- 解消 (かいしょう) cancellation
- 消火器 (しょうかき) fire extinguisher
- 消防士 (しょうぼうし) fireman
- 消極性 (しょうきょくせい) passive, pessimistic

き(える)

- 消える (きえる) to get out, to die out

け(す)

- 消す (けす) to erase, to turn off

 消 (alt)

 Look at how much water the dwarf on the moon is *consuming.*

 清 (487) 油 (340) 泊 (Jōyō)

320

ノ 厂 广 皮 皮

(5 strokes)

皮 皮 皮 皮
皮 皮 皮 皮

SKIN

皮

(2級)

ヒ

- 木皮 (もくひ) bark
- 果皮 (かひ) rind
- 皮膚 (ひふ) skin
- 皮革 (ひかく) leather
- 皮肉 (ひにく) irony

かわ

- 皮 (かわ) skin, leather
- 甘皮 (あまかわ) cuticle

 After the tsunami, the director is all *skin* and bones, and all he has left are the clapperboard and his chair.

 友 (151) 反 (361)

321 (2級)

WAVE

波

ハ

- でんぱ 電波 electromagnetic wave
- のうは 脳波 brain wave
- よは 余波 influence, aftereffect
- はちょう 波長 wavelenght
- かんぱ 寒波 cold wave

なみ

- なみ 波 wave
- つなみ 津波 tsunami

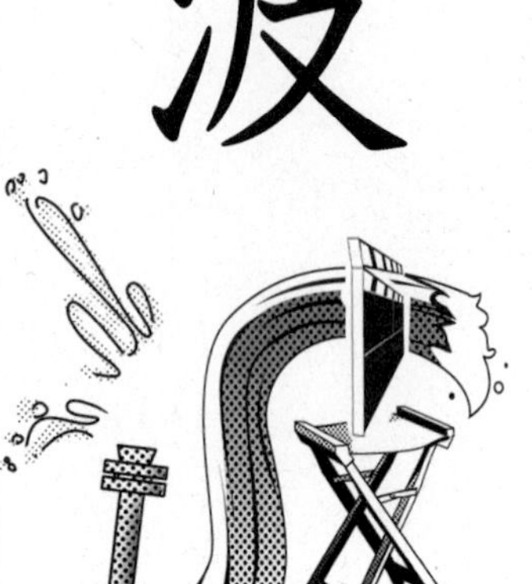

丶	冫	氵	氵
氵	汇	涉	波

(8 strokes)

波	波	波	波
波	波	波	波

注 彼 (Jōyō) 渡 (Jōyō) 済 (6th)

 Water in the form of a *wave* that drenches the skin is surely a tsunami.

322 (2級)

HOT WATER

湯

トウ

- せんとう 銭湯 public bath
- ねっとう 熱湯 boiling water
- にゅうとう 入湯する to take a bath

ゆ

- ゆ お湯 hot water
- ゆげ 湯気 steam
- ゆぶね 湯船 bathtub
- ちゃのゆ 茶の湯 tea ceremony

丶	冫	氵	氵
沪	沪	沪	浬
浧	湯	湯	湯

(12 strokes)

湯	湯	湯	湯
湯	湯	湯	湯

注 温 (304) 漫 (Jōyō)

 *Hot water* is what the farmer bathes himself in after working in the sun with the plough.

(12 strokes)

POSITIVE, SUNLIGHT

(2級)

323

ヨウ

太陽(たいよう) the Sun
陽子(ようし) proton
陽性(ようせい) positive, optimistic
陰陽(いんよう) positive and negative; yin and yang
陽極(ようきょく) positive pole, anode

ひ

陽(ひ) sunlight
陽射(ひざ)し rays of the sun
夕陽(ゆうひ) setting sun

特

学 A knife reflects the *sunlight* on the plough.

注 場 (170)
湯 (322)
傷 (6th)

(8 strokes)

(MATERIAL) THING

(3級)

324

ブツ

動物(どうぶつ) animal
物価(ぶっか) price
物理学(ぶつりがく) physivs

モツ

荷物(にもつ) luggage, load
食物(しょくもつ) food

もの

本物(ほんもの) genuine, authentic
建物(たてもの) building

 The only (material) *thing* this coquettish cow can't live without is her comb.

 揚 (Jōyō)
場 (170)
易 (5th)

へ～いいバッグだね。その洋服にぴったり!! 本物なの？
もちろんよ！羊の皮だよ。
!
この…くそ鳥め！バカヤロウ！暴漢！
まあ、まあ、平気。落ち着いてね。
平気じゃないわよ。こんなこと起こったら幸せになるワケないじゃない、決まってるでしょ。
消極的だね。お湯でなんとかきれいにしてあげるから、大丈夫。
能天気だね、あんた…陽性すぎるわ！
ね？シミがとれたよ！
本当？あっ、よかった…
RIP…
ほら、何もないよ。少しシミの余波がのこってるんだけど…

Exercises 練習

1. Develop the stroke order of the following kanji.

羊											
幸											
漢											
波											

2. Choose the correct reading for each kanji or kanji combination.

a) 動物はだいたい太陽の下でゆっくりできると幸せだね。

Animals, generally speaking, are happy as long as they can laze in the sun.

動物:	1．どうふつ	2．どうぶつ	3．どうもつ	4．どうもの
太陽:	1．たいとう	2．たいゆ	3．たいよ	4．たいよう
幸せ:	1．さいわいせ	2．さいわせ	3．しあせ	4．しあわせ

b) 物価が上がってしまうと、消費も落(お)ち込(こ)んでしまう。

As soon as prices go up, consumption goes down.

物価:	1．ぶつか	2．もつか	3．ぶっか	4．ものか
消費:	1．きひ	2．けひ	3．しょうひ	4．しょひ

c) 皮肉なことに、消防士は燃(も)えていた建物の中に死んでしまった。

Ironically, the fireman died inside a burning building.

皮肉:	1．かわにく	2．かわうち	3．ひにく	4．ひうち
消防士:	1．きぼうし	2．けぼうし	3．しょぼうし	4．しょうぼうし
建物:	1．たてもの	2．たてもつ	3．たてぶつ	4．たてふつ

. Write the kanji (one or more) and the meaning of the following words.

ようもう	______	______	せいよう	______	______
ひつじ	______	______	けっしん	______	______
とうよう	______	______	かんじ	______	______

. Correct either the reading or the writing mistakes in the following words.

平等	ひらどう	津皮	つなみ	陽射し	ひさし
辛福	こうふく	銭陽	せんとう	荷物	にぶつ
決る	きめる	お陽	おゆ	本物	ほんもつ

Answers to exercises 練習解答

1. (Check them in the corresponding kanji table: #313, #316, #318, and #321)

2. a) 動物: 2 | 太陽: 4 | 幸せ: 4 / b) 物価: 3 | 消費: 3

c) 皮肉: 3 | 消防士: 4 | 建物: 1

3. ようもう: 羊毛, wool | ひつじ: 羊, sheep | とうよう: 東洋, the East | せいよう: 西洋, the West | けっしん: 決心, resolution, determination | かんじ: 漢字, kanji

4. 平等 びょうどう | 津波 つなみ | 陽射し ひざし | 幸福 こうふく | 銭湯 せんとう | 荷物 にもつ | 決める きめる | お湯 おゆ | 本物 ほんもの

Manga translation マンガ翻訳

Friend B: Wow, that's a cool handbag! And it suits your dress perfectly. Is it genuine?

Friend A: Of course. It's sheepskin.

Friend A, B: !

Friend A: Damn bird! You wretched ruffian!

Friend B: Hey, hey, calm down.

Friend A: I can't calm down. You'll understand this does not make me happy.

Friend B: You sure are being negative. I'll wash it in hot water, it'll be alright.

Friend A: No kidding. She's too optimistic.

Friend B: There, the spot is gone.

Friend A: Really? Oh, thank God.

Friend B: Look, no trace at all. There are a few aftereffects, though...

News elements 新しい部首

事	skewer		及	pigeon	
比	cowboys and Indians		求	complaining roots	

Lesson 29
第二十九課

325 (3級)

THING, MATTER, EMPLOYEE

ジ
事件（じけん） case, matter
事故（じこ） accident
家事（かじ） housework
返事（へんじ） answer
私事（しじ） personal affairs

こと
事（こと） (abstract) thing
仕事（しごと） work
見事（みごと） excellent, superb
出来事（できごと） incident

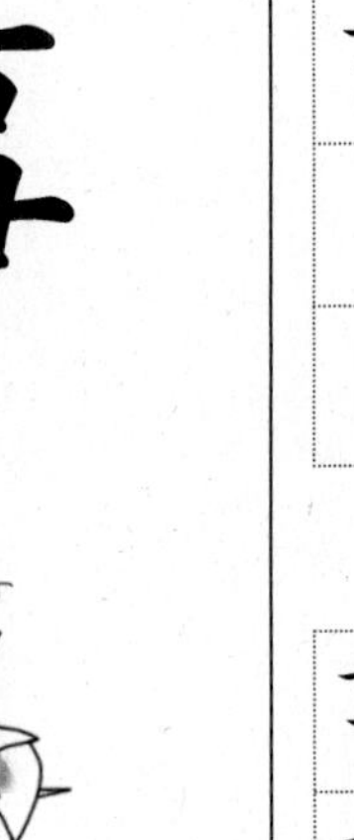

(8 strokes)

注 書 (113)

学 An *employee* decides important matters, such as which skewer he will eat first!

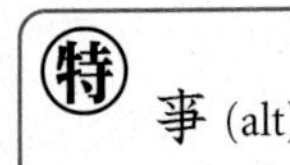

特 亊 (alt)

326 (3級)

INSTITUTION, CENTER

イン
病院（びょういん） hospital
入院（にゅういん） to be admitted to hospital
退院（たいいん） to leave the hospital
大学院（だいがくいん） postgraduate course
僧院（そういん） monastery
美容院（びよういん） beauty salon
書院（しょいん） study, drawing room

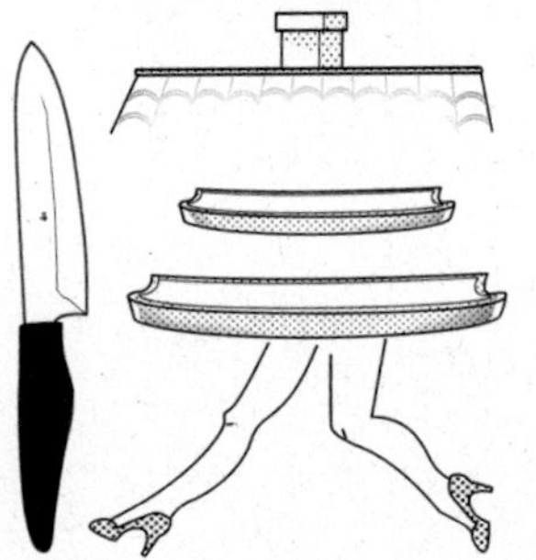

(10 strokes)

注 際 (5th)
険 (5th)

学 The place where a knife is used under a roof is the medical *center*: the origin of life.

特

327 FLOOR (OF A BUILDING)

(2級)

階

(12 strokes)

カイ

一階 (いっかい) first/ground floor
三階 (さんがい) third fllor
階段 (かいだん) stairs
階級 (かいきゅう) grade, rank
音階 (おんかい) musical scale
階層 (かいそう) social class, social stratum

特

学 What about this knife? It fell from the *floor* where cowboys and Indians confront each other with this white weapon.

注 混 (Jōyō)
混 (5th)

328 TO LEARN, HABIT, CUSTOM

(3級)

習

(11 strokes)

シュウ

練習 (れんしゅう) exercise, practice
復習 (ふくしゅう) review
習慣 (しゅうかん) custom
実習 (じっしゅう) practice/ drill
演習 (えんしゅう) rehearsal, tactical, exercises, training maneuvers

なら(う)

習う (ならう) to learn
見習う (みならう) to follow another's example

特  (alt)

学 The bird *learned* to fly thanks to its feathers of white; now it's a habit.

注 混 (Jōyō)
翌 (6º)

329 (2級)

PREVIOUSLY, BEFOREHAND

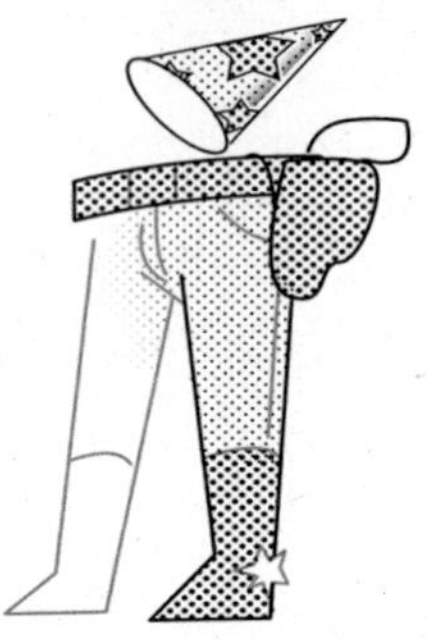

ヨ

- 予定(よてい) plan, program
- 予感(よかん) premonition
- 予約(よやく) reservation, booking
- 予防(よぼう) to prevent, to take precautionary measures
- 予想(よそう) to anticipate, to expect
- 予知(よち) to foretell, to predict

あらかじ(め)

- 予め(あらかじめ) previously

(4 strokes)

注 子 (76)
序 (5th)
矛 (Jōyō)

学 In a duel, the magician cowboy always attacks his rival *beforehand* (look at his holster).

特 豫 (ant)

330 (2級)

CHAPTER, BADGE

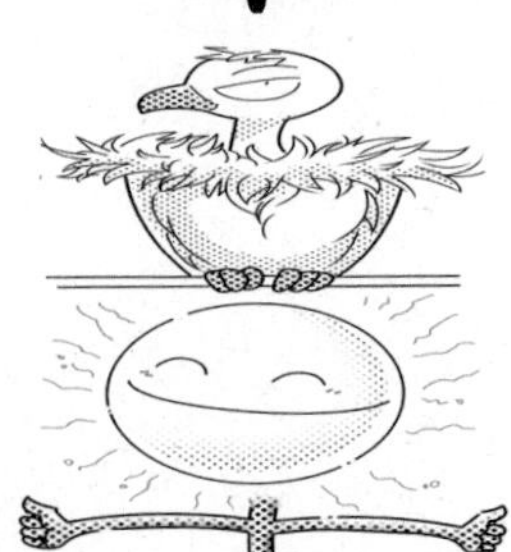

ショウ

- 第一章(だいいっしょう) first chapter
- 文章(ぶんしょう) sentence, composition
- 序章(じょしょう) preface
- 詞章(ししょう) poetry and prose
- 紋章(もんしょう) coat of arms, crest
- 記章(きしょう) badge, medal
- 印章(いんしょう) seal, emblem
- 腕章(わんしょう) armband

(11 strokes)

注 草 (69)
童 (331)

学 This is how the *chapter* starts: "The vulture arrived there very early."

特

331

(12 strokes)

CHILD, CHILDREN

(2級)

ドウ

童話（どうわ） children's story
童画（どうが） pictures for children
童子（どうじ） child
童心（どうしん） innocence
天童（てんどう） cherub

Special

かっぱ/こわっぱ

河童（かっぱ） *kappa* (mythological being, half turtle and half frog)

 The vulture in this village is the *children's* storyteller.

注 章 (330)
黄 (225)

332

(11 strokes)

END, TO FINISH

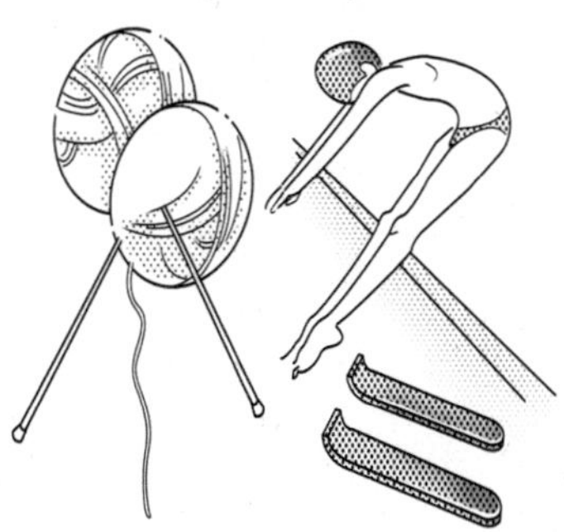

(3級)

シュウ

終点（しゅうてん） final stop, terminus
終始（しゅうし） from beginning to end
終了（しゅうりょう） completion
終戦（しゅうせん） end of the war
終止（しゅうし） termination, stop

お(わる/える)

終（お）わる to come to an end

つい(に)

終（つい）に finally

  (alt)

学 When the thread doesn't freeze, winter has *finished.*

 約 (525)
級 (333)
絡 (Jōyō)

333 (2級)

RANK, CLASS

級

キュウ

- 一級（いっきゅう） first class, top rank
- 初級（しょきゅう） beginner's class
- 中級（ちゅうきゅう） intermediate class
- 上級（じょうきゅう） upper class
- 高級（こうきゅう） high-grade, high-class
- 学級（がっきゅう） school class
- 同級生（どうきゅうせい） classmate
- 等級（とうきゅう） rank, category

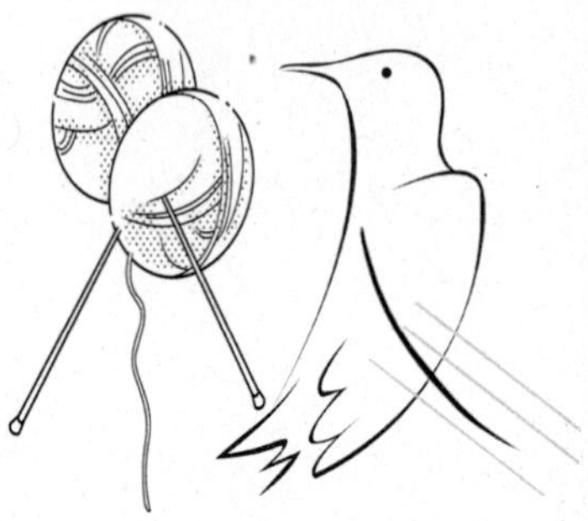

(9 strokes)

注 終 (332)
絡 (Jōyō)

 To be promoted to a higher *rank*, the pigeon must take the thread as high as it can.

 級 (alt)

334 (2級)

TO PRACTICE

レン

- 練習（れんしゅう） practice
- 訓練（くんれん） exercise, training
- 鍛練（たんれん） to train, to forge
- 水練（すいれん） swimming practice
- 手練（しゅれん） dexterity, skill
- 修練（しゅうれん） training, drill
- 練兵（れんぺい） military drill

ね(る)

- 練る（ねる） to knead, to refine, to polish up

(14 strokes)

注 錬 (Jōyō)
緒 (Jōyō)

 Such a luxury for the seamstress *to practice* with thread from the East.

 練 (alt)

335

(14 strokes)

GREEN

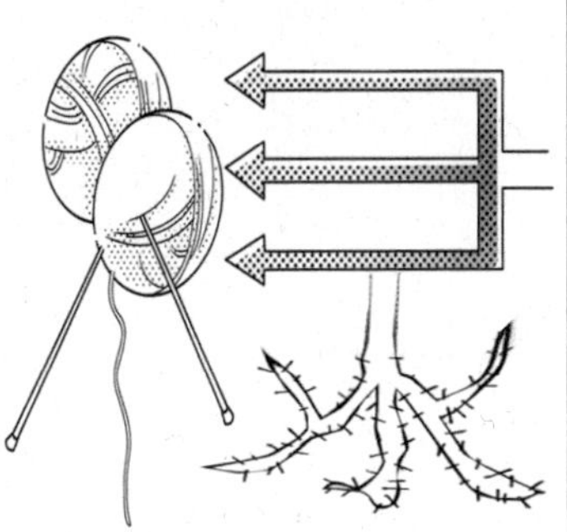

(2級)

リョク

葉緑素（ようりょくそ） chlorophyll

緑化（りょっか） tree planting

常緑（じょうりょく） evergreen

緑茶（りょくちゃ） green tea, Japanese tea

みどり

緑（みどり） green

緑色（みどりいろ） green color

黄緑（きみどり） yellowish green

特 綠 (alt)

学 With thread, you will tie the trident to the ground until it takes root and becomes part of the *green* flora.

注 線 (119)

336

(11 strokes)

BALL, SPHERE

(2級)

キュウ

電球（でんきゅう） light bulb

野球（やきゅう） baseball

地球（ちきゅう） the Earth

天球（てんきゅう） firmament, celestial sphere

半球（はんきゅう） hemisphere

球根（きゅうこん） (plant) bulb

たま

球（たま） ball

特

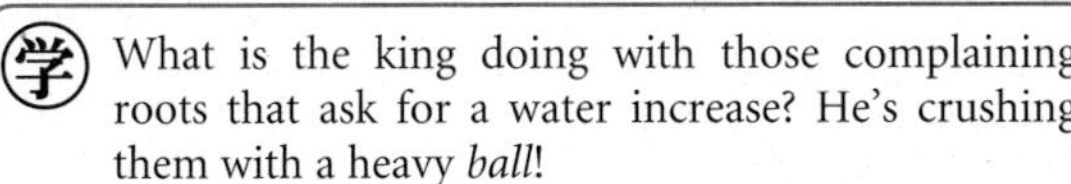

学 What is the king doing with those complaining roots that ask for a water increase? He's crushing them with a heavy *ball*!

注 救 (482)

求 (481)

大学や練習を終えてから、卒業し、医者になった。
病院での仕事、これがはじめて…
二階、緑のドア…ここだろう、小児科。
問題は…この顔。
一級の医者であっても、子どもがこわかったら何にもならない。
よし！しょうがないなぁ。
おはよ、ちびっこのみんな〜!! 球遊びが好き？それとも、童話の一章でも読んであげようか？
!
あっ、先生。探していました。予定が変りました、ごめんなさい。これから老人医学科を任せることになりましたので…

Exercises 練習

1. Develop the stroke order of the following kanji.

事											
予											
終											
緑											

2. Choose the correct reading for each kanji or kanji combination.

a) 地球 緑化センターへの見学のおかげで色々なことを習いました。

Thanks to the visit to the Earth Tree Planting center, I learned a few things.

地球: 1. じきゅう 2. ちきゅう 3. じたま 4. ちたま

緑化: 1. りょくか 2. りょか 3. りょっか 4. りょうか

習い: 1. ならうい 2. ない 3. らない 4. ならい

b) 練習と復習したら、大学院に入れるに違(ちが)いない。

If you do the exercises and review, I'm sure you'll be able to enter gradschool.

練習: 1. れんしゅう 2. れんしゅ 3. ねなら 4. ねらな

復習: 1. ふしゅう 2. ふくしゅう 3. ふなら 4. ふなら

大学院: 1. たいがくいん 2. だいがくいん 3. たいがっきん 4. だいがっきん

c) 入院したから、仕事ができなくなった。だから、メールの返事もしないの。

Since I was admitted to hospital, I have not been able to work. That is why I haven't been able to answer those emails either.

入院: 1. にゅいん 2. にゅういん 3. いりん 4. いりん

仕事: 1. しじ 2. じし 3. じこと 4. しごと

返事: 1. へんし 2. へんじ 3. へんこと 4. へんごと

3. Write the kanji (one or more) and the meaning of the following words.

かじ ______ ________ よてい ______ ________

できごと ______ ________ ぶんしょう ______ ________

いっかい ______ ________ どうわ ______ ________

4. Correct either the reading or the writing mistakes in the following words.

皆段	かいだん	終点	しゅてん	同終生	どうきゅうせい
予約	ようやく	終る	おわる	緑り	みどり

Answers to exercises 練習解答

1. (Check them in the corresponding kanji table: #325, #329, #332, and #335)

2. a) 地球: 2 | 緑化: 3 | 習い: 4 / b) 練習: 1 | 復習: 2 | 大学院: 1 / c) 入院: 2 | 仕事: 4 | 返事: 2

3. かじ: 家事, housework | できごと: 出来事, incident | いっかい: 一階, first floor | よてい: 予定, plan, program | ぶんしょう: 文章, sentence, composition | どうわ: 童話, children´s story

4. 階段 かいだん | 終点 しゅうてん | 同級生 どうきゅうせい | 予約 よ~~亍~~やく | 終わる おわる | 緑~~井~~ みどり

Manga translation マンガ翻訳

Young doctor: Once I finished university and my internship, I graduated, and became a doctor.

Young doctor: This is the first time I've worked in a hospital...

Young doctor: Second floor, a green door... It must be here, pediatrics...

Young doctor: My problem is... my face.

Young doctor: Even though I'm a first-class doctor, if I frighten the children, we will get nowhere...

Young doctor: Well, it can't be helped.

Young doctor: Hi, little ones! Do you like playing ball? Or would you prefer me to read you a chapter of a story?

Doctor: Oh, doctor. I was looking for you. I'm sorry, but there has been a change of plans. It's been decided that you will take care of geriatrics instead.

News elements 新しい部首

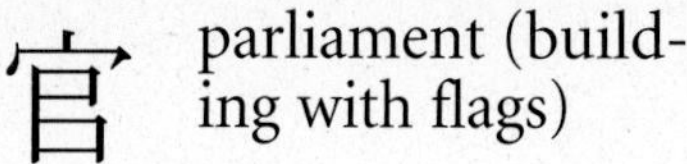
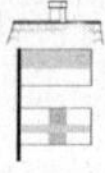

Lesson 30
第三十課

337 (2級)

PLATE

さら

- 皿 (さら) plate
- 平皿 (ひらざら) flat (dinner) plate
- 小皿 (こざら) saucer
- 大皿 (おおざら) platter, serving dish
- 皿洗い (さらあらい) washing the dishes
- 皿洗い機 (さらあらいき) dishwasher
- 灰皿 (はいざら) ashtray

(5 strokes)

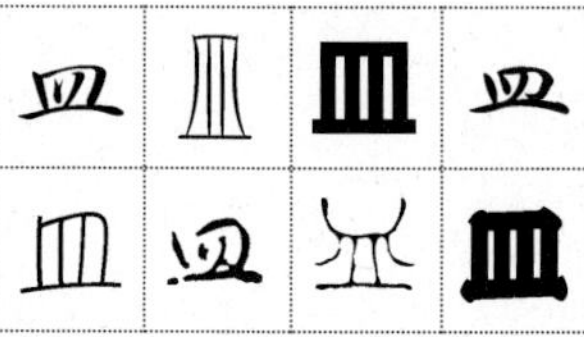

 血 (338)
目 (22)

 A *plate* of fresh watermelon...

338 (2級)

BLOOD, LINEAGE

ケツ

- 血圧 (けつあつ) blood pressure
- 血管 (けっかん) blood vessel, vein
- 貧血 (ひんけつ) anemia
- 献血 (けんけつ) blood donation
- 血液型 (けつえきがた) blood type

ち

- 血 (ち) blood
- 鼻血 (はなぢ) nosebleed

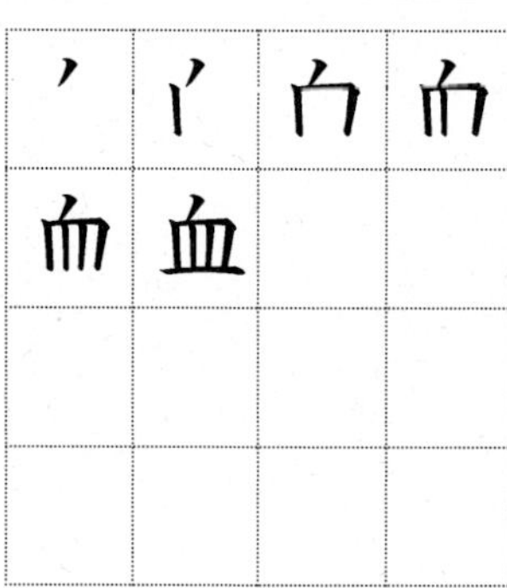

(6 strokes)

 皿 (337)
自 (173)

 ...With *blood* sauce.

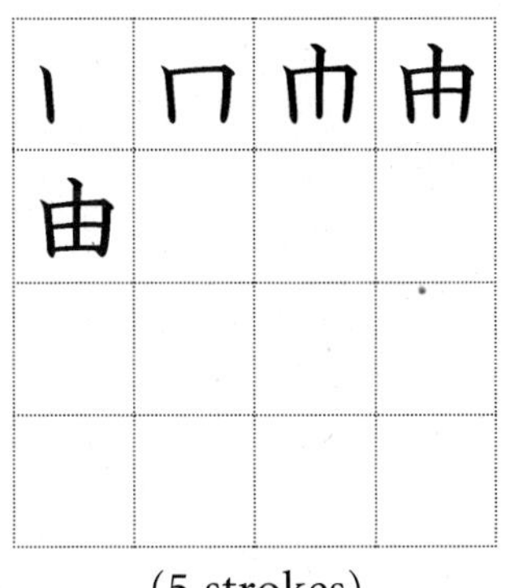

(5 strokes)

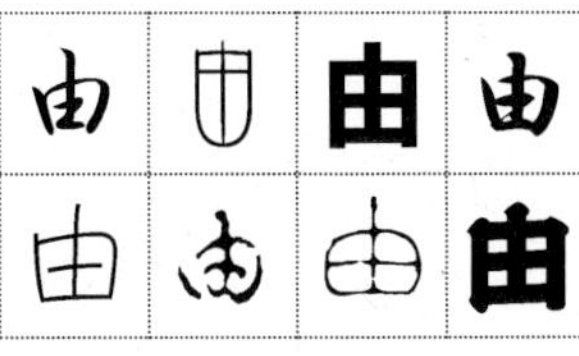

REASON, CAUSE

由

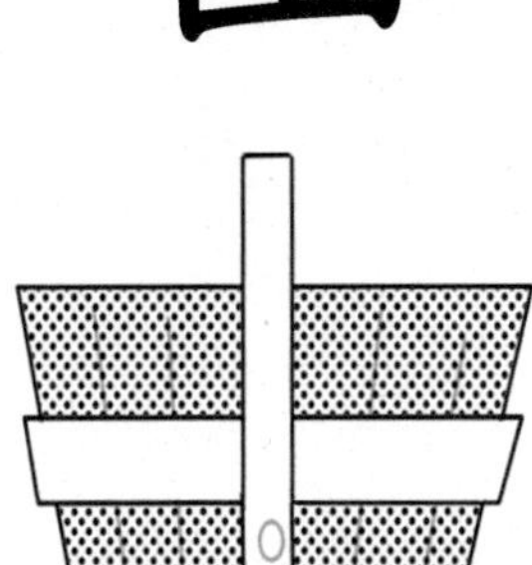

(2級) 339

ユウ

理由(りゆう) reason, cause
自由(じゆう) freedom

ユ/ユイ

因由(いんゆ) cause, origin
由来(ゆらい) origin, cause
由緒(ゆいしょ) background, history

よし/よ(る)

由(よし) reason, way
由(よ)る due to, depending on

 The bucket, come to think of it, is the *reason* for the well to exist.

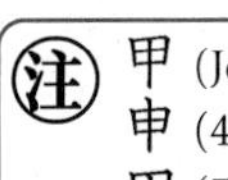

甲 (Jōyō)
申 (417)
田 (72)

(8 strokes)

OIL, PETROLEUM

油

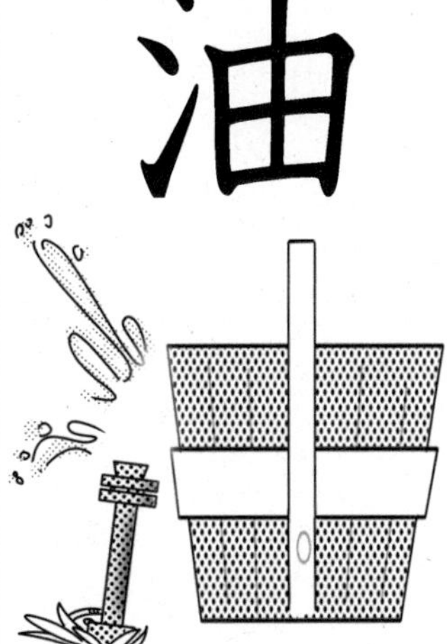

(1級) 340

ユ

石油(せきゆ) oil, petroleum
油断(ゆだん) negligence, inattention
軽油(けいゆ) gas oil
製油所(せいゆじょ) oil refinery

あぶら

油(あぶら) oil
油(あぶら)を売(う)る to loaf away one's time
油絵(あぶらえ) oil painting

 The water you take out with the bucket, with a bit of luck, could be *petroleum*.

 泊 (Jōyō)
清 (319)

341 (1級)

WHISTLE, FLUTE

笛

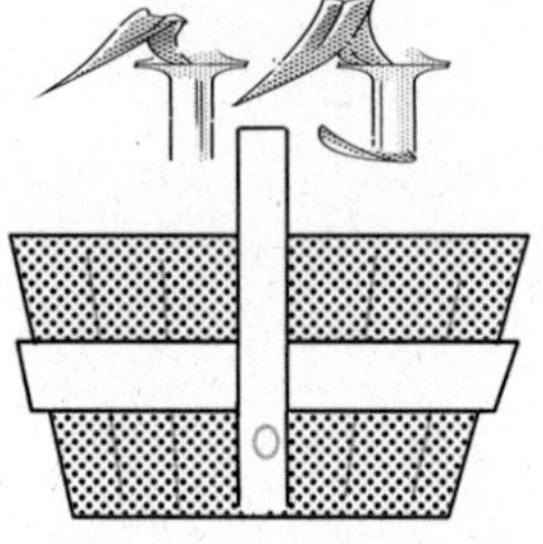

テキ

- 号笛（ごうてき） horn, alarm
- 警笛（けいてき） horn, siren
- 霧笛（むてき） fog horn

ふえ

- 笛（ふえ） whistle, Japanese flute
- 口笛（くちぶえ） to whistle (with the mouth)
- 横笛（よこぶえ） transverse flute, fife

(11 strokes)

注 算 (207)
筒 (Jōyō)

 Can you imagine a bamboo *whistle* you could use to call the bucket and make it rise up out of the well on its own?

342 (2級)

ORDINAL

第

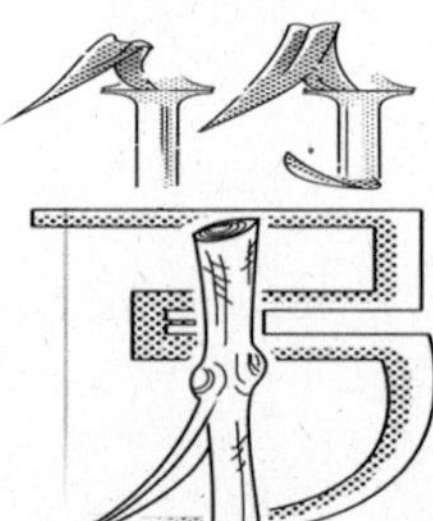

ダイ

- 第一（だいいち） the first, the main
- 第一歩（だいいっぽ） the first step
- 第一章（だいいちしょう） first chapter
- 第一線（だいいっせん） first line
- 第二次世界大戦（だいにじせかいたいせん） Second World War
- 第三者（だいさんしゃ） third person

(11 strokes)

注 弟 (239)
策 (6th)

学 Arranging bamboo shoots by *ordinal* numbers is my younger brother's favorite hobby. (Watch out: this "brother" has "bamboo shoots," not "horns." Refer to "younger brother," kanji #239, in KIM1.)

 才 (simp)

(12 strokes)

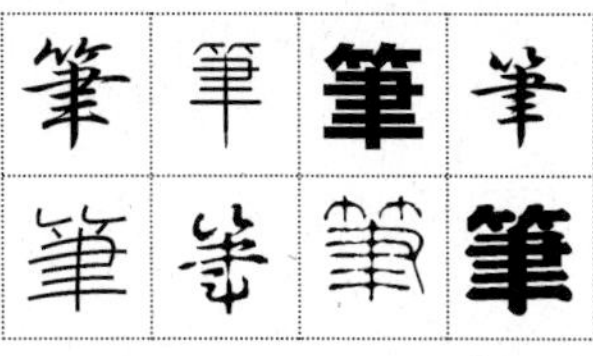

WRITING BRUSH

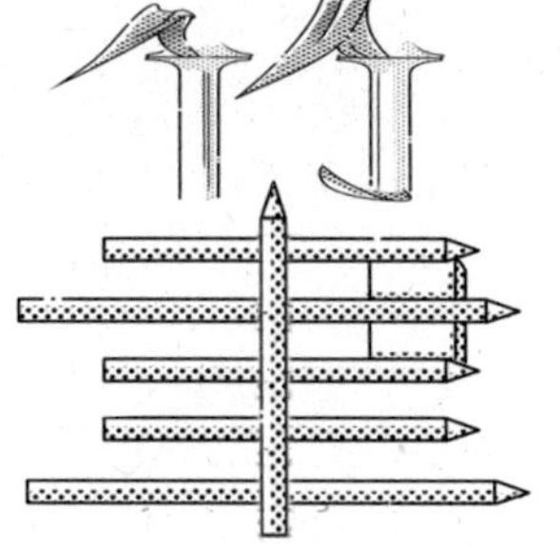

(2級) **343**

ヒツ

筆者（ひっしゃ） author
筆記（ひっき）する to take notes
万年筆（まんねんひつ） fountain pen
鉛筆（えんぴつ） pencil
筆名（ひつめい） pseudonym, stage name

ふで

筆（ふで） writing brush

 To draw bamboo, all a true artist really needs are a few color pencils and a *writing brush.*

 書 (113)
律 (6th)

(12 strokes)

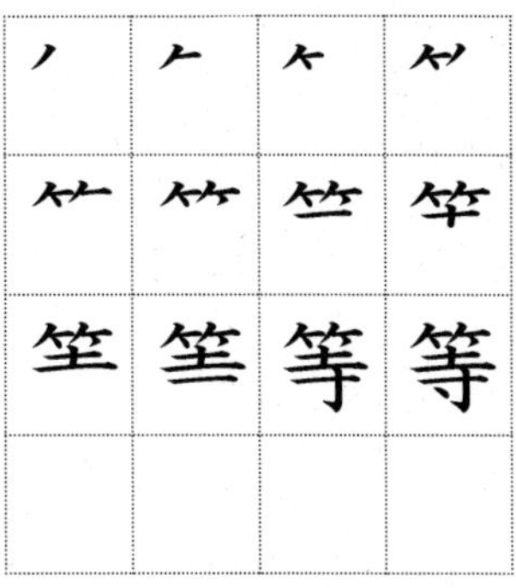

CLASS, KIND, EQUAL, ETCETERA

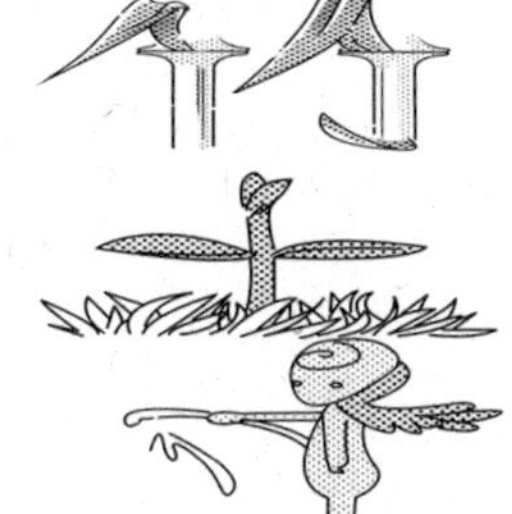

(2級) **344**

トウ

高等（こうとう） high, advanced
均等（きんとう） equality, average
平等（びょうどう） equality
等価（とうか） equivalent
劣等感（れっとうかん） inferiority complex

ひと(しい)

等（ひと）しい same, equal

など

等（など） etcetera

 Some are long, some short, some have been cut, *etc...* Depending on the bamboo you find around it, you'll know what *kind* of temple it is.

 第 (342)
筆 (343)
待 (248)

345 (2級)

BOX

箱

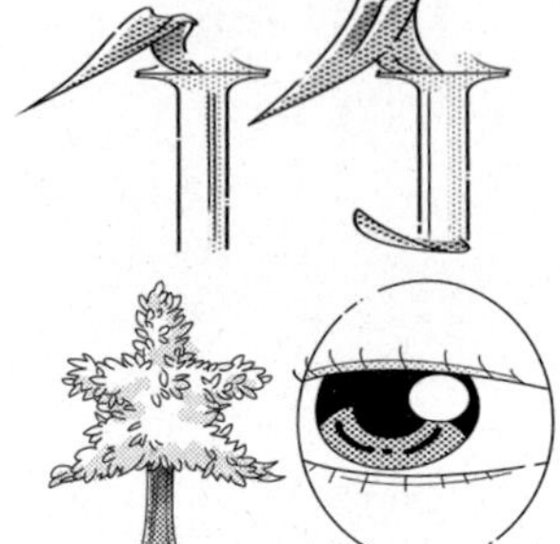

はこ

- 箱（はこ） box
- ごみ箱（ばこ） trash can
- 郵便箱（ゆうびんばこ） mailbox (at home)
- 靴箱（くつばこ） shoe box
- 宝石箱（ほうせきばこ） jewelry box
- 空き箱（あきばこ） empty box
- 弁当箱（べんとうばこ） lunch box

(15 strokes)

注 想 (392)
相 (391)
籍 (Jōyō)

Sssh... A bamboo forest is a box full of surprises: the trees have eyes.

346 (2級)

NEXT, FOLLOWING, SUCCESSION

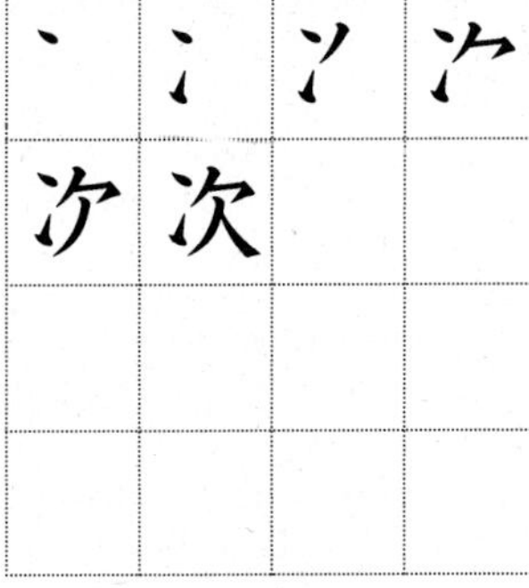

ジ/シ

- 次回（じかい） next time
- 三次元（さんじげん） three dimensions
- 次代（じだい） the coming era
- 目次（もくじ） index
- 次第（しだい） according to, depending on

つぎ/つ(ぐ)

- 次ぐ（つぐ） comes after
- 次（つぎ） next
- 次々（つぎつぎ） one after another

(6 strokes)

注 欠 (582)

Sucking on ice cubes and taking a seat, helped the drunken Kim to sober up. Remember this technique, because you could be *next*.

347 (4級)

TO DRINK

(12 strokes)

イン

飲酒[いんしゅ]する to drink alcohol
飲用水[いんようすい] drinking water
飲食[いんしょく] food and drink

の(む)

飲[の]む to drink
飲[の]み物[もの] drink, beverage
大酒飲[おおさけの]み heavy drinker

 飲 (ant)

 If Kim is drunk after the lavish meal at home, that's because he *drank* something else besides water.

 飯 (579)

348 (3級)

PUBLIC BUILDING, HOTEL, MANSION

(16 strokes)

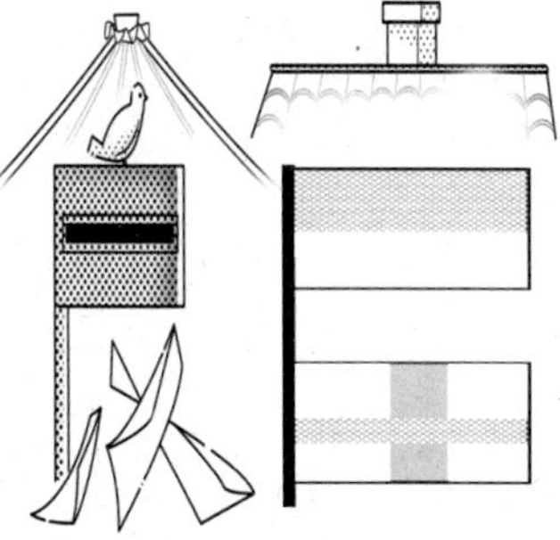

カン

映画館[えいがかん] movie theater
大使館[たいしかん] embassy
旅館[りょかん] traditional Japanese hotel
美術館[びじゅつかん] art gallery
図書館[としょかん] library
水族館[すいぞくかん] aquarium

やかた

館[やかた] mansion, palace

 舘 (alt)

 If we could have lunch in parliament, it would go from being called a *public building* to a hotel.

 飾 (Jōyō)

今夜、美術館より、いつもの居酒屋へ行こうか？
まあ…またそこへ？

え？何、その返事？がっかりしているみたいだね。
だって、くつ箱のようなせまい店でしょ。あたし、やっぱりきれいなレストランやホテル等へ行きたいのに…

理由を数えてあげよう。第一：私たちの大好きな飲み物がある店、非常に少ないだろ？第二：朝が来ると号笛で知らせるから、安全な場所だ。第三…
まあ、いいわ。でも、次回、あたしが店を選ぶからね。

おい、何油売っとる？お客様がいるぞ。鉛筆を持って注文をとるんだ。

いらっしゃいませ！お飲み物は何にしましょうか？

血で、お願いします。
何、その皿のような目？ドラクラ様だよ！知らなかった？早く、急いで！

Exercises 練習

1. Develop the stroke order of the following kanji.

血												
第												
筆												
館												

2. Choose the correct reading for each kanji or kanji combination.

a) 図書館には飲み物を持ち込みしてはいけません。映画館であるまいし。

You can't bring drinks into the library. It's not a movie theater.

図書館: 1．としょっかん 2．としょかん 3．とうしょかん 4．としょうかん

飲み物: 1．いんみぶつ 2．いんみもつ 3．のみみもの 4．のみもの

映画館: 1．えいがっかん 2．えいがくかん 3．えいがかん 4．えいががん

b) 私は、侵略(しんりゃく)の第一の理由は石油だったと考えています。

I think oil was the main reason for the invasion.

第一: 1．だいいち 2．だいち 3．たいち 4．たいい

理由: 1．りゆ 2．りゆう 3．りゆい 4．りよる

石油: 1．いしぶら 2．いしあぶら 3．せっきゅ 4．せきゆ

c) 昨日、飲酒後、貧血のように歩けなくなった。次回は、ジュースを飲みます。

Yesterday, after drinking alcohol, I couldn't walk, as if I had anemia. Next time, I'll drink juice.

飲酒: 1．のみざけ 2．のみさけ 3．いんしゅ 4．いんざけ

貧血: 1．ひんけつ 2．ひんげつ 3．ひんち 4．ひんぢ

次回: 1．しかい 2．しがい 3．じかい 4．じがい

3. Write the kanji (one or more) and the meaning of the following words.

ひらざら ______ ______ ひっしゃ ______ ______

くちぶえ ______ ______ びょうどう ______ ______

だいいっしょう ______ ______ もくじ ______ ______

4. Correct either the reading or the writing mistakes in the following words.

火皿 はいざら 第三者 だいさんしゃ 弁当箱 べんとうはこ

油絵 うきよえ 律 ふで 次 つじ

Answers to exercises 練習解答

1. (Check them in the corresponding kanji table: #338, #342, #343, and #348)

2. a) 図書館: 2 | 飲み物: 4 | 映画館: 3 / b) 第一: 1 | 理由: 2 | 石油: 4

c) 飲酒: 3 | 貧血: 1 | 次回: 3

3. ひらざら: 平皿, dinner plate | くちぶえ: 口笛, to whistle | だいいっしょう: 第一章, first chapter | ひっしゃ: 筆者, author | びょうどう: 平等, equality | もくじ: 目次, index

4. 灰皿 はいざら | 第三者 だいさんしゃ | 弁当箱 べんとうばこ | 油絵 あぶらえ | 筆 ふで | 次 つぎ

Manga translation マンガ翻訳

Count: Tonight, instead of going to the art museum, shall we go to our usual pub?

Countess: What? There again?

Count: What kind of answer is that? You look disappointed.

Countess: It's just that the place is small as a shoe box. I'd rather go to a beautiful restaurant, a hotel, or something like that.

Count: Shall I number the reasons? First, there are very few pubs that serve our favorite drink. Second, they warn you with a whistle before dawn, so we are safe there. Third…

Countess: Okay, okay. But I'll choose next time.

Owner: You, stop loafing over there, we have clients. Take a pencil and go and take their order.

Waitress: Welcome. What would like to drink?

Count and countess: Blood, please.

Owner: What's with the eyes as big as saucers? They are Mr. and Mrs. Dracula! Didn't you know? Come on now, get moving!

New elements 新しい部首

尹	fork with fish	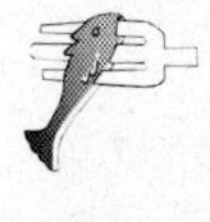	至	inexhaustible fountain of food	
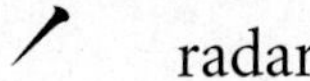	radar				

Lesson 31
第三十一課

349 (2級)

NUMBER

号

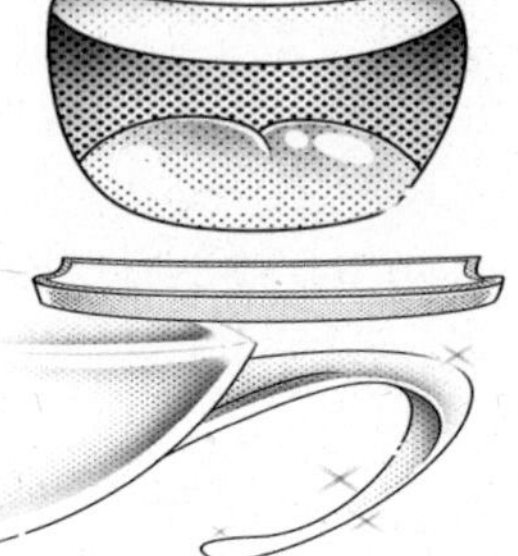

ゴウ

- 番号（ばんごう） number
- 電話番号（でんわばんごう） telephone number
- 暗号（あんごう） key number, secret number
- 記号（きごう） symbol, sign
- 信号（しんごう） traffic light
- 号令（ごうれい） order
- 号外（ごうがい） extra edition (newspaper)

(5 strokes)

号	号	号	号
号	号	号	号

注 考 (83)
五 (6)
呈 (Jōyō)

学 Imagine if you had to feed a *number* of mouths such as ten thousand.

特 號 (ant)

350 (2級)

YOU, NOUN SUFFIX (INFORMAL)

君

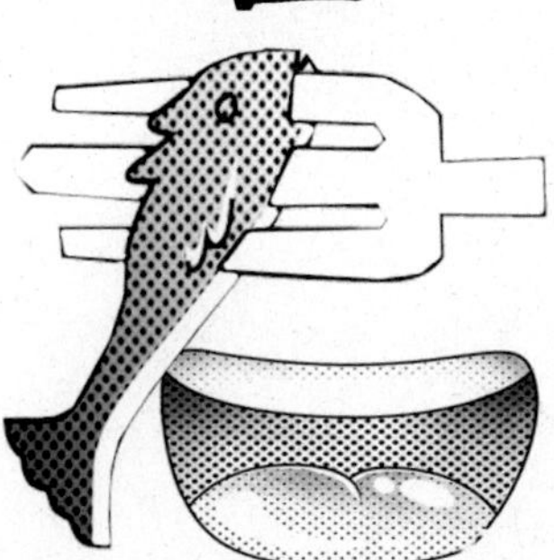

クン

- アキラ君（くん） (young) Akira
- 君主（くんしゅ） lord, monarch
- 君主国（くんしゅこく） monarchy
- 君子（くんし） man of virtue, wise man
- 諸君（しょくん） Ladies and gentlemen

きみ

- 君（きみ） you

(7 strokes)

君	君	君	君
君	君	君	君

注 伊 (no Jōyō)
若 (6th)
争 (485)

学 *You* feed yourself with fish through your mouth.

特

351 TASTE, SUBSTANCE, MEANING

(3級)

(8 strokes)

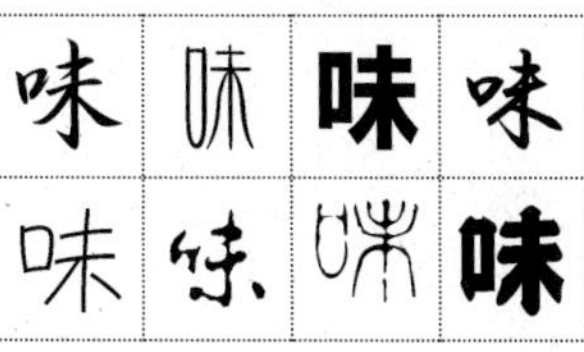

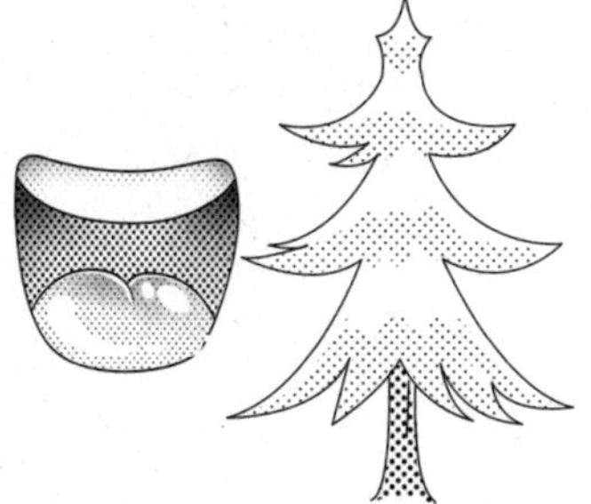

ミ

- 興味（きょうみ） interest
- 趣味（しゅみ） hobby, interest
- 意味（いみ） meaning, sense
- 味噌（みそ） miso (fermented soybean paste)

あじ（わう）

- 味（あじ） taste, flavor
- 味（あじ）わう to taste, to relish
- 味付（あじつ）けする to season

学 True *substance* is found when your mouth *tastes* something somewhere even higher.

注 妹 (211) 和 (397) 知 (234)

352 LIFE, ORDER

(2級)

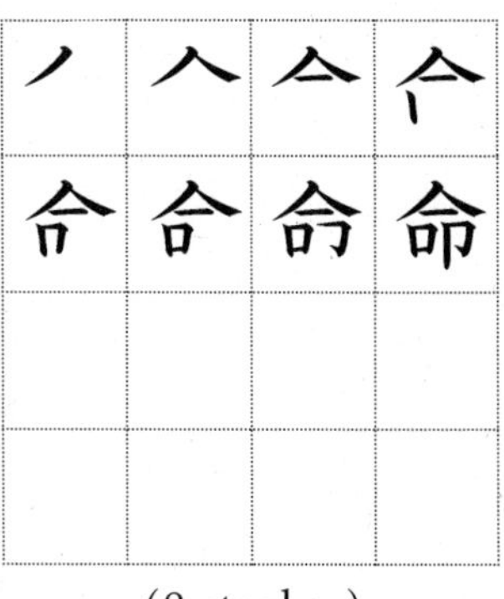

(8 strokes)

命

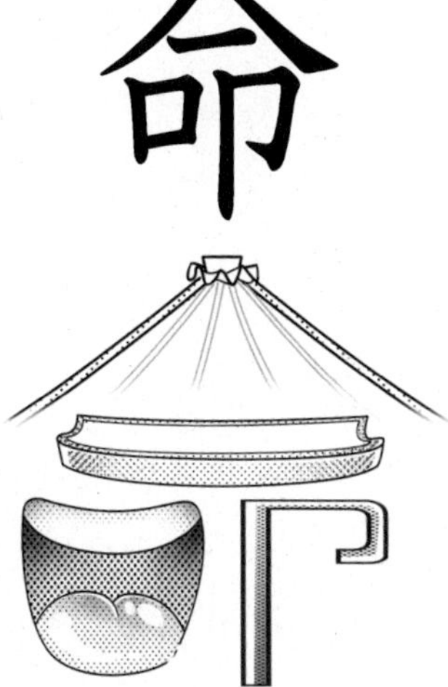

メイ

- 命令（めいれい） order
- 革命（かくめい） revolution
- 運命（うんめい） fate
- 一所懸命（いっしょけんめい） w/all one's might

ミョウ

- 寿命（じゅみょう） lifespan

いのち

- 命（いのち） life, existence
- 命拾（いのちびろ）いする to escape from death

学 Essential things in *life*: an umbrella for shelter, bread to eat with your mouth, and a cane for support when your legs fail you.

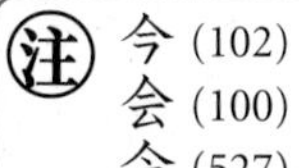

注 今 (102) 会 (100) 令 (527)

353 (2級)

ALL, COMPLETE

ゼン

- 全然（ぜんぜん） nothing, not at all
- 全国（ぜんこく） the whole country
- 安全（あんぜん） security
- 不全（ふぜん） incomplete
- 全集（ぜんしゅう） complete works

まった(く)

- 全く（まったく） completely

すべ(て)

- 全て（すべて） all

(6 strokes)

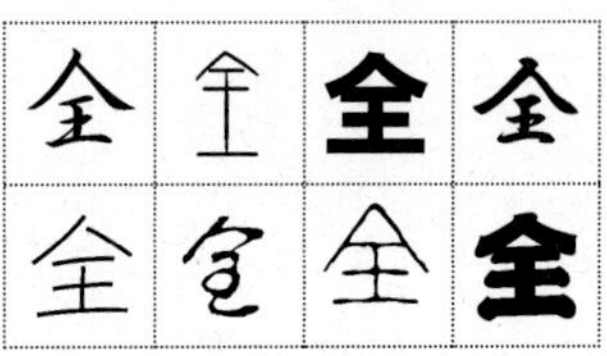

注 金 (17)
宝 (6th)

学 Under his umbrella, the king is the ruler of *all* things.

仝 (alt)

354 (3級)

ARTICLE

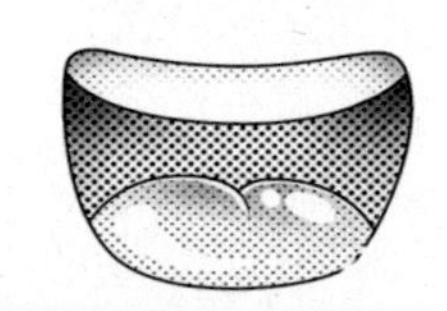

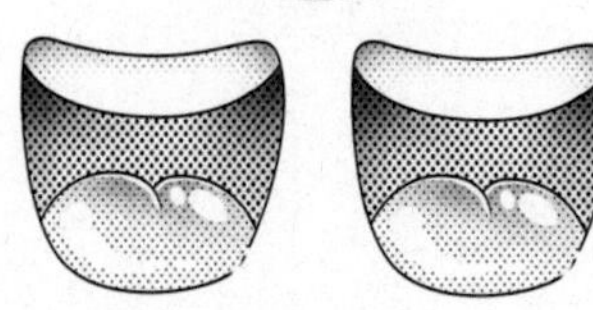

ヒン

- 日用品（にちようひん） articles for daily use
- 電気製品（でんきせいひん） electrical appliances
- 作品（さくひん） a work
- 商品（しょうひん） article of commerce
- 食品（しょくひん） food goods

しな

- 品（しな） goods
- 品物（しなもの） products, goods

(9 strokes)

晶 (Jōyō)

A quality *article* is tasted by at least three mouths.

355 MEMBER, EMPLOYEE

(10 strokes)

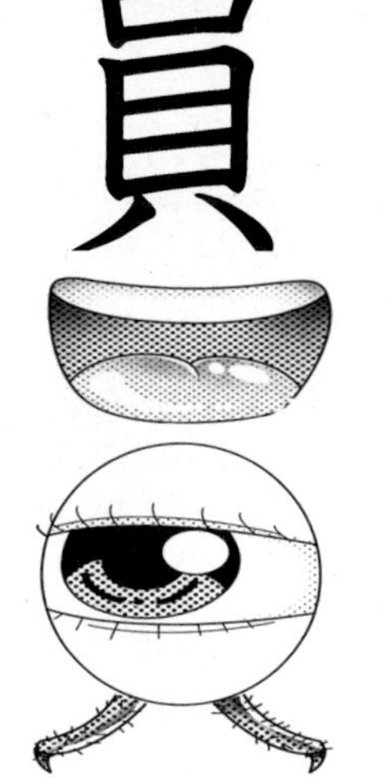

(3級)

イン

- 店員 (てんいん) clerk
- 満員 (まんいん) crowded, full of people
- 減員 (げんいん) staff reduction
- 事務員 (じむいん) office worker
- 工作員 (こうさくいん) worker, laborer
- 課員 (かいん) section staff
- 乗員 (じょういん) crew member

 The *members* of a committee are the mouths, eyes, and legs of any operation.

 貝 (23)
貴 (6th)

356 TO HEAD (TOWARD)

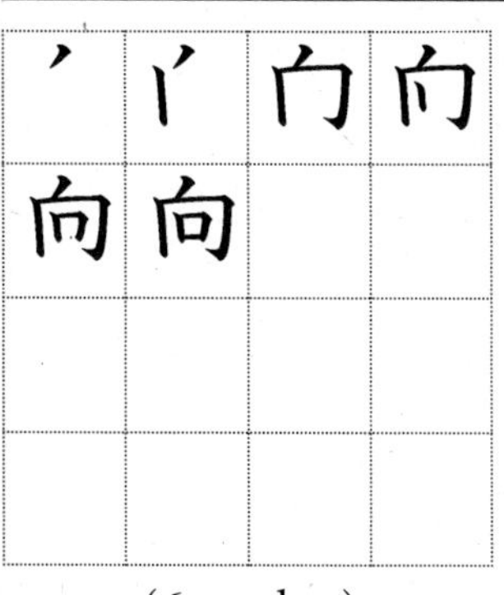

(6 strokes)

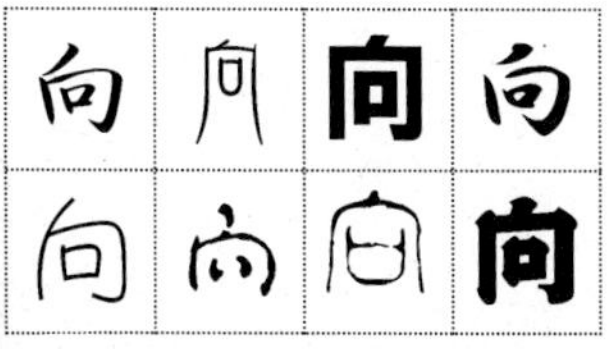

(2級)

コウ

- 方向 (ほうこう) direction
- 意向 (いこう) purpose, intention
- 偏向 (へんこう) tendency, propensity
- 内向 (ないこう) introverted

む(く/かう)

- 向く (むく) towards, facing toward
- 向かう (むかう) headed for
- 風向き (かざむき) wind direction

 This woman uses her radar *to head* towards the direction she wants.

 同 (194)
句 (5th)
何 (196)

357 (2級)

TRADE, BUSINESS

ショウ

- 商売（しょうばい） sale, trade
- 商人（しょうにん） merchant
- 商会（しょうかい） commercial company
- 商工（しょうこう） commerce and industry
- 商店街（しょうてんがい） shopping area, outdoor promenade

あきな(う)

- 商う（あきなう） to trade in, to deal in

(11 strokes)

注 南 (198)
昔 (293)

学 Things a good *business* cannot lack: a security guard (the vulture), something nice behind the shop window (slender legs), and a smooth- talking salesclerk.

特

358 (2級)

OFFICE, DEPARTAMENT

キョク

- 薬局（やっきょく） pharmacy
- 郵便局（ゆうびんきょく） post office
- 支局（しきょく） branch office
- 部局（ぶきょく） department
- 難局（なんきょく） crisis, difficult situation
- 結局（けっきょく） in the end, finally

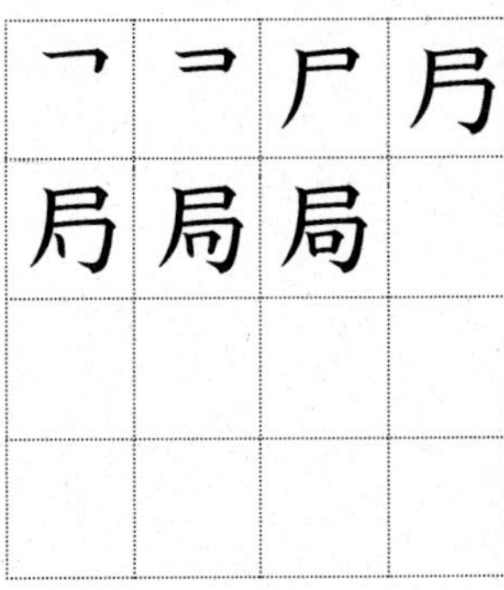

(7 strokes)

注 向 (356)
昜 (5th)
包 (559)

学 Going to a public *office* is always an adventure: one feels like an explorer, battling with the civil servants.

特

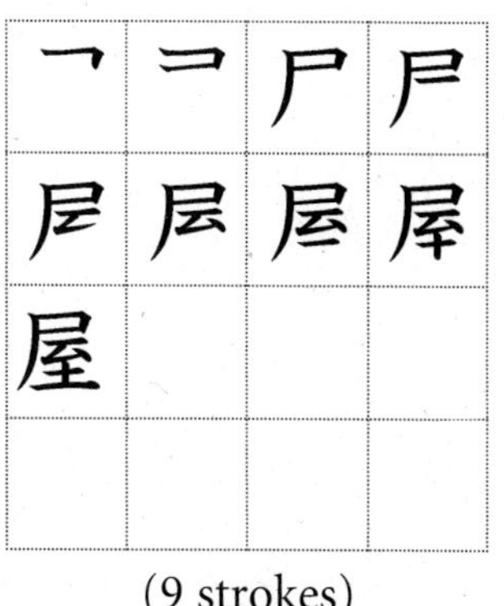

(9 strokes)

SHOP, BUILDING

(3級) **359**

オク

家屋（かおく） house, building
屋外（おくがい） outdoors

や

部屋（へや） room
屋根（やね） roof
酒屋（さかや） liquor store
肉屋（にくや） butcher shop
問屋（とんや） warehouse, wholesaler

特

学 A *shop* is an inexhaustible fountain of food (this is how we will call this collection of elements which appeared in #126: bread, cornucopia, and fertile land).

室 (126)
展 (6th)
属 (5th)

(5 strokes)

TO LEAVE, PASSING OF TIME

(3級) **360**

キョ

去年（きょねん） last year
死去（しきょ） death

コ

過去（かこ） the past

さ(る)

去る（さる） to leave, to depart from
連れ去る（つれさる） to take someone away

学 If one finds a plot of fertile land under which food in abundance lies hiding, one will never *leave* for anywhere, despite the *passing of time.*

会 (100)
公 (97)
走 (191)

いらっしゃいませ！何でございましょうか。
え～と…

じゃ、この店でこのミルクビンを買ったけど、味がちょっと変だが…
ああ、そうですか。うん…実をいうと、あたしはどうすればいいか全くわりませんから、店長に相談させていただき、あとでご連絡いたします。お電話番号を聞かせてくだされば…

おい、君!!この商売の基本はお客様のために一所懸命働くことだ！お客様に向かって「わからない」とは言えないぞ!!!

600¥
もうしわけございません。いまどきの若者は有能そうですが、結局だれでもいい店員になれません。
55¥

しかし、おかしいですね。毎日、問屋から新鮮な食品がとどくのですが…いつお買いあげになりましたか？きのうですか？
あ…ううん、違う…

それは、去年だったっけ…一昨年かな？

Exercises 練習

1. Develop the stroke order of the following kanji.

君												
品												
商												
局												

2. Choose the correct reading for each kanji or kanji combination.

a) あの商店街は安全な場所じゃない。命があぶないかもしれないよ！

That shopping area is not a safe place. Your life could be in danger!

商店街:	1．しょうてんがい	2．しょてんがい	3．あきてんがい	4．あてんがい
安全:	1．やすべ	2．やずべ	3．あんせん	4．あんぜん
命:	1．めい	2．みょう	3．いのち	4．いちの

b) 仕事に全然 興味のない店員だね。「ありがとう」さえ言わないなんて…

That clerk has not interest at all in his job. He doesn't even say thank you.

全然:	1．せんぜん	2．ぜんせん	3．せんせん	4．ぜんぜん
興味:	1．きょうんい	2．きょうみ	3．きょみ	4．きょうあじ
店員:	1．みせいん	2．てんにん	3．てにん	4．てんいん

c) 酒屋の方向へ歩いている、不気味(ぶきみ)な人を見た。

I saw a suspicious man walking towards the liquor store.

酒屋:	1．さかいあ	2．さかや	3．さおく	4．さかおく
方向:	1．ほうこう	2．ほこう	3．ほうこ	4．ほこ

3. Write the kanji (one or more) and the meaning of the following words.

しんごう ______ ______　　ないこう ______ ______

きみ ______ ______　　しょうばい ______ ______

しょくひん ______ ______　　きょねん ______ ______

4. Correct either the reading or the writing mistakes in the following words.

番号	ばんご	意味	みい	作品	さくしな
カノ伊	かのくん	令命	めいれい	郵便局	ゆうびんきょ
趣味	しゅうみ	運令	うんめい	屋外	やがい

Answers to exercises 練習解答

1. (Check them in the corresponding kanji table: #350, #354, #357, and #358)

2. a) 商店街: 1 | 安全: 4 | 命: 3
b) 全然: 4 | 興味: 2 | 店員: 4 / c) 酒屋: 2 | 方向: 1

3. しんごう: 信号, traffic light | きみ: 君, you | しょくひん: 食品, food | ないこう: 内向, introverted | しょうばい: 商売, sale, trade | きょねん: 去年, last year

4. 番号 ばんごう | 意味 いみ | 作品 さくひん | カノ君 かのくん | 命令 めいれい | 郵便局 ゆうびんきょく | 趣味 しゅ~~う~~み | 運命 うんめい | 屋外 おくがい

Manga translation マンガ翻訳

Sales clerk: Good morning, may I help you?

Client: Well... I bought this bottle of milk in this shop, but it tastes a little bit strange.

Sales clerk: Oh, I see. Well, to tell you the truth, I don't know what to do in a case like this, so I'll consult my boss, and then I'll call you. May I have your telephone number?

Boss: Hey, you! The basis of our trade is to work body and soul for our clients! Before a client, you can't say "I don't know!"

Boss: Please, excuse her. Young people nowadays seem very able, but, in the end, not everybody can be a good sales clerk.

Boss: However, this is weird. We receive fresh products from the wholesaler every day. Tell me, when did you buy it? Was it yesterday?

Client: Oh, no, not at all.

Client: I think it was last year. Or was it the year before that?

New elements 新しい部首

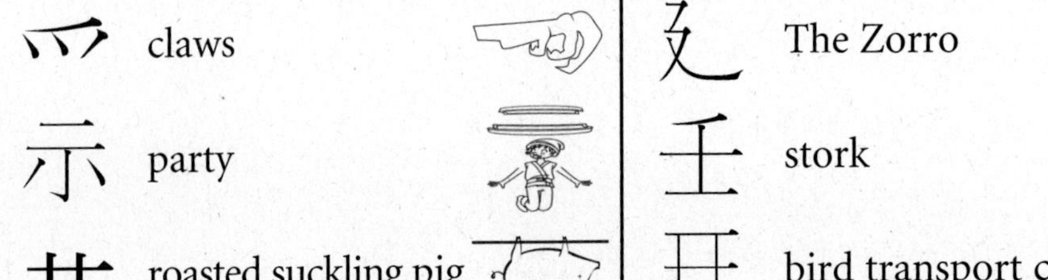

Lesson 32
第三十二課

361 (2級)

ANTI-, AGAINST; TO REACT

ハン

- 反応（はんのう） reaction
- 反対（はんたい） opposite
- 違反（いはん） violation
- 反省（はんせい）する to reflect on, to soul-search
- 反乱（はんらん） rebellion, mutiny

そ(る/らす)

- 反（そ）る to bow, to bend back

かえ(る/す)

- 反（かえ）す to return / to overturn

一	厂	历	反

(4 strokes)

反	反	反	反
反	反	反	反

注 友 (151)
支 (5th)
危 (6th)

学 Hiding a metal chair under a slope is not an *anti*-rust measure, because it´s still not good *against* the rain.

362 (2級)

TO TAKE, TO SEIZE, TO OBTAIN

シュ

- 取得（しゅとく） to acquire, to obtain

と(る)

- 取（と）る to seize, to obtain
- 取引（とりひき） business, transaction
- 取（と）り消（け）し cancellation
- 取（と）り扱（あつか）い treatment, handling
- 相撲（すもう）取（と）り sumo wrestler
- 書（か）き取（と）り dictation

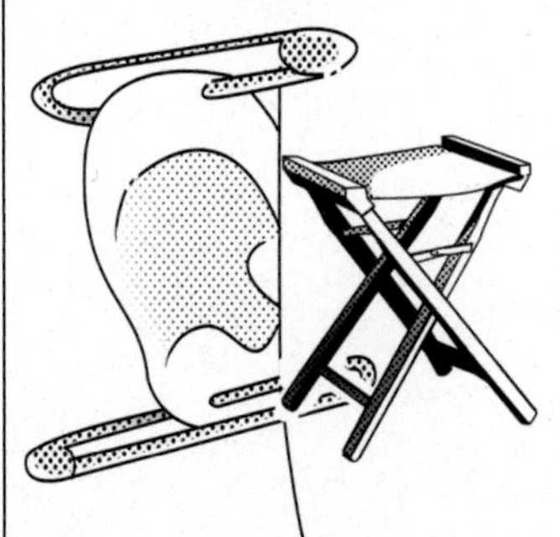

一	厂	F	F
下	耳	耴	取

(8 strokes)

取	取	取	取
取	取	取	取

注 消 (319)
恥 (Jōyō)
敢 (Jōyō)

学 If you see a pierced ear on a chair, *take* it; it surely doesn´t belong there.

363 受 — TO RECEIVE

(8 strokes)

(2級)

ジュ

受信 (じゅしん) reception (of radio, electronic messages)

受賞 (じゅしょう) to receive a prize

う(ける/かる)

受ける (う) to receive

受付 (うけつけ) reception desk

受け入れ (う・い) acceptance

受取 (うけとり) receipt

受身 (うけみ) passive voice (gram.)

学 Look at the ballerina, with her claws dug into her tutu; she sits on a chair, waiting *to receive* her prize.

愛 (518)
学 (78)
売 (110)

364 祭 — FESTIVAL

(11 strokes)

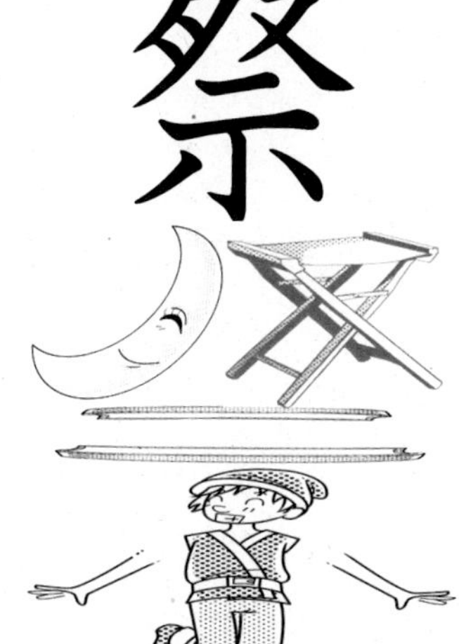

(2級)

サイ

祭日 (さいじつ) holiday

文化祭 (ぶんかさい) cultural festival

祝祭日 (しゅくさいじつ) national holiday

まつり

祭 (まつり) festival, feast day

お盆祭り (ぼんまつ) Obon festival

七夕祭り (たなばたまつ) Tanabata festival (7th of July)

A *festival* is a party celebrated under a reclined moon, either sitting on chairs or dancing in the street with dwarves while eating slices of bread.

発 (280)
茶 (205)

365 (3級) DEGREE, MEASURE, TIME

度

ド / ト

- 高度（こうど） altitude
- 温度（おんど） temperature
- 角度（かくど） angle
- 密度（みつど） density
- 態度（たいど） attitude
- 法度（はっと） prohibition

たび

- 度々（たびたび） frequently
- この度（たび） this time

(9 strokes)

度 度 **度** 度 度 度 度 **度**

注 席 (583)
店 (222)
庭 (366)

At how many *degrees* should a cave be so we can roast a suckling pig on a chair?

366 (2級) GARDEN, FAMILY

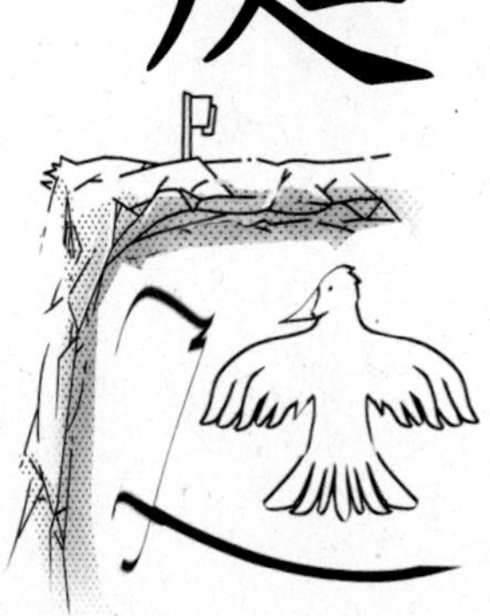

テイ

- 家庭（かてい） family, home
- 家庭用（かていよう） domestic use
- 庭園（ていえん） garden, park
- 校庭（こうてい） playground, schoolyard

にわ

- 庭（にわ） garden
- 庭師（にわし） gardener

(10 strokes)

庭 庭 **庭** 庭 庭 庭 庭 **庭**

注 健 (475)
廷 (6th)

The cave where Zorro lives is a little dwelling with a *garden*, shared only with his stork and marked by his Z.

庭 (alt)

(10 strokes)

WAREHOUSE

(2級)

367

コ

車庫（しゃこ） garage
公庫（こうこ） finance corporation
宝庫（ほうこ） treasury, hoard
国庫（こっこ） national treasury
冷蔵庫（れいぞうこ） refrigerator, fridge

くら

庫入れ（くらいれ） storage

学 Used as *warehouses*, these caves store cars.

軍 (561)
連 (560)
康 (477)

(9 strokes)

TO RIDE, TO GET ON

(3級)

368

ジョウ

搭乗する（とうじょうする） to board
乗車する（じょうしゃする） to get on a train
乗客（じょうきゃく） passenger
乗用車（じょうようしゃ） small car

の(る/せる)

乗る（のる） to ride / to get on
乗り物（のりもの） vehicle, (amusement park) ride

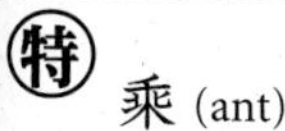
乘 (ant)

The weeping willow is the official stop for the bird transport cage, which birds *ride* just before they migrate.

業 (300)
重 (289)

369 (3級)

LIGHT, SLIGHT, EASY

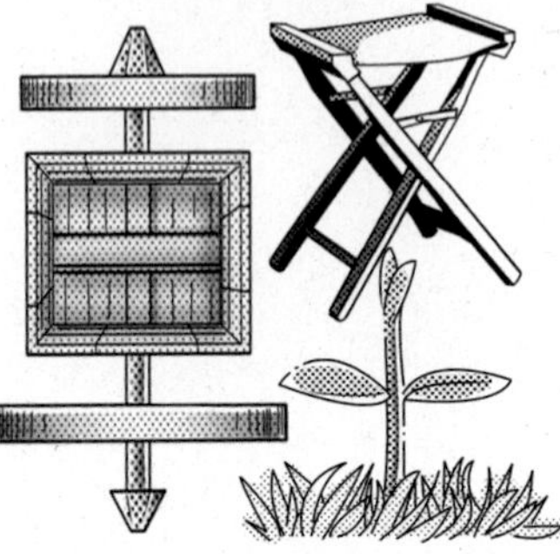

ケイ

軽傷（けいしょう） minor injuries
軽食（けいしょく） light meal
軽音楽（けいおんがく） light music
軽薄（けいはく） frivolous

かる(い)

軽い（かるい） light
軽々と（かるがると） easily, effortlessly

(11 strokes)

注 転 (370)
経 (5th)
較 (Jōyō)

学 Traveling by car is *easy* if you have a chair to sit on when you want to take a break in fertile land.

特 輕 (ant)

370 (3級)

TO TURN, TO ROTATE, TO FALL DOWN

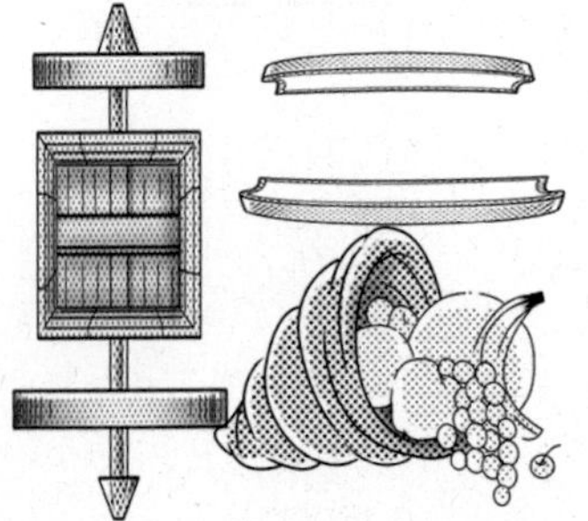

テン

自転車（じてんしゃ） bicycle
運転（うんてん） to drive
転職（てんしょく） to change jobs
回転（かいてん） to revolve, to rotate
転校（てんこう） to change schools
転落（てんらく） fall, downfall

ころ(ぶ)

転ぶ（ころぶ） to fall down, to tumble

(11 strokes)

注 軽 (369)

学 If you get on the car after a great feast, you had better not tumble, *fall*, and start *rotating* down a hill.

特 轉 (ant)

(13 strokes)

ROAD

路

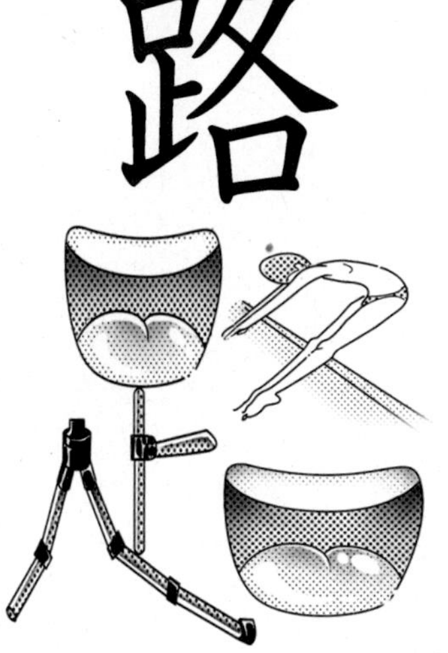

(2級) **371**

ロ

道路（どうろ） path, road
線路（せんろ） railroad
海路（かいろ） ocean route
迷路（めいろ） labyrinth

じ

山路（やまじ） mountain trail
小路（こうじ） narrow street

 When he puts his foot on the *road*, the swimmer shuts his mouth, because he´s not in his habitat.

 跡 (Jōyō)
踏 (Jōyō)

(9 strokes)

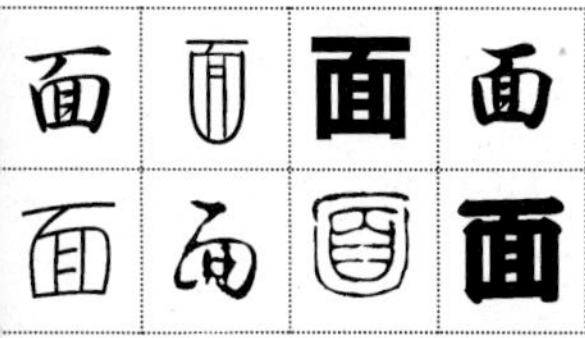

FACE, MASK, ASPECT

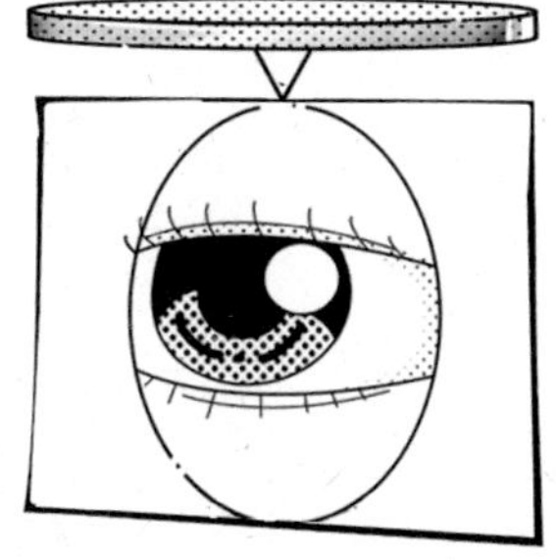

(2級) **372**

メン

外面（がいめん） aspect, appearance
面倒（めんどう） difficulty, trouble
一面（いちめん） the whole surface
表面（ひょうめん） face, surface

つら

面（つら） face, mug

おも/おもて

面（おもて） face, front part
面白い（おもしろい） interesting

 Look at the *face* of this home-made mask: a paper stuck with a thumbtack, and only one eye drawn in the middle.

 百 (38)
首 (174)

家庭用道具フェア・受付
あっ！見て、見て！ここだ！
わー にぎやかだね。フェアというより祭りみたいだね。
すいません、やせるためのいい物なんかありませんか？
この自転車はいかがですか。軽いし、45度の山路も登れます。自転車に乗るのはやせるのにはピッタリです。
そうかしら…でも、あたしは運動がちょっと…
それなら、この冷蔵庫をおすすめします。
ええ？冷蔵庫でやせる？
そうです。外面は普通ですが、特別なしかけがあり、だれかが近づくと、反応し、何も取れないように逃げるのです。

Exercises 練習

1. Develop the stroke order of the following kanji.

受												
庭												
乗												
面												

2. Choose the correct reading for each kanji or kanji combination.

a) 酔(よ)っ払(ばら)い運転は違反ですよ！部屋に行って、少し反省しなさい。

Drunk driving is a violation of the law! Go to your room and reflect on it.

運転:	1．うんでん	2．うんてん	3．はこごろ	4．はっころ
違反:	1．いは	2．いそ	3．いがえ	4．いはん
反省:	1．そせい	2．かえせい	3．はんせい	4．かえせい

b) 道路で転んでから、隣(となり)の人の面倒を見ているよ。面白い人ですね...

Since she fell on the street, I've been taking care of my neighbor. She's an interesting person...

道路:	1．どうろう	2．どろ	3．どろう	4．どうろ
面倒:	1．おもとう	2．おもどう	3．めんどう	4．つらどう
面白い:	1．めんしろい	2．つらしろい	3．おもてろい	4．おもしろい

c) 家庭を離(はな)れるに反対している私は、家の近くに転職しました。

Because I object to being far from home, I've looked for a job near my house.

家庭:	1．やてい	2．かてい	3．いえにわ	4．いちにわ
反対:	1．はんたい	2．はたい	3．そたい	4．かえたい
転職:	1．ころしょく	2．こしょく	3．てしょく	4．てんしょく

3. Write the kanji (one or more) and the meaning of the following words.

こうど	______	______	まつり	______	______
にわ	______	______	かるい	____い	______
じょうしゃ	______	______	かいてん	______	______

4. Correct either the reading or the writing mistakes in the following words.

温度	おんどう	乗り物	のりもな	取り消	とりけし
冷蔵車	れいぞうこ	取引	とりびき	受信	うけしん

Answers to exercises 練習解答

1. (Check them in the corresponding kanji table: #363, #366, #368, and #372)

2. a) 運転: 2 | 違反: 4 | 反省: 3 / b) 道路: 4 | 面倒: 3 | 面白い: 4
c) 家庭: 2 | 反対: 1 | 転職: 4

3. こうど: 高度, altitude | にわ: 庭, garden | じょうしゃ: 乗車, to get on a train | まつり: 祭, festival, feast day | かるい: 軽い, light | かいてん: 回転, to revolve, to rotate.

4. 温度 おんど~~う~~ | 乗り物 のりもの | 取り消し とりけし | 冷蔵庫 れいぞうこ | 取引 とりひき | 受信 じゅしん

Manga translation マンガ翻訳

Sign: Household Article Trade Fair? Reception desk.

Boy: Oh, look, it´s here.

Girl: Wow! It´s very lively! Rather than a trade fair, it looks like a festival.

Girl: Excuse me, do you have anything good for losing weight?

Hostess: How about this bicycle? It´s very light, and you can climb mountain trails with an inclination of up to 45 degrees. Riding a bicycle is an ideal exercise to lose weight.

Girl: Yes, sure, but I´m not that keen on excercise...

Hostess: In that case, I recommend to you this fridge.

Girl: Huh? Can you lose weight with a fridge?

Hostess: That´s right. It may look normal, but it has a special device: when somebody approaches it, it reacts, escaping so you can´t take anything.

New elements 新しい部首

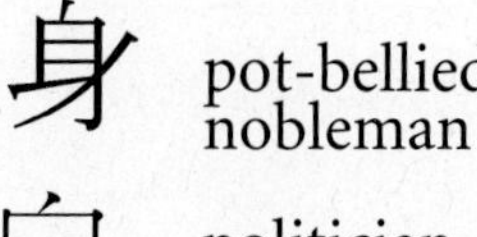

身 pot-bellied nobleman 

自 politician

关 hell

束 wise sequoia 

Lesson 33
第三十三課

373 (2級)

BODY, PERSON, SOCIAL STRATUM

シン

身長（しんちょう） height

出身（しゅっしん） originally from

自分自身（じぶんじしん） oneself

み

身（み） body

身近（みぢか） close, familiar

身分（みぶん） social standing, marital status

刺身（さしみ） *sashimi* (sliced raw fish)

(7 strokes)

 射 (6th)

 Look at the *body* of this pot-bellied nobleman; the bigger the belly, the higher the social status.

374 (3級)

TO TRANSPORT

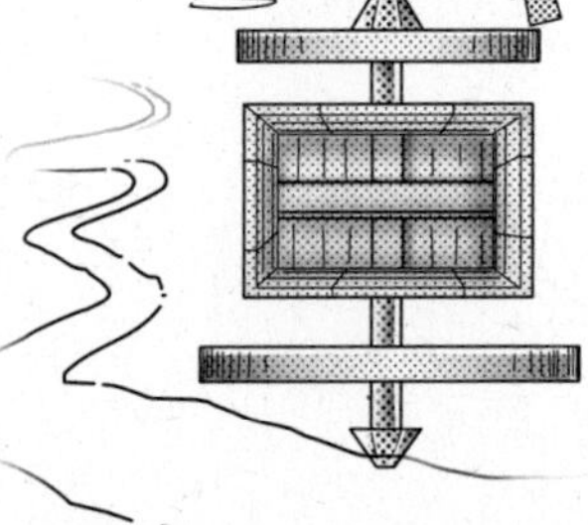

ウン

運動（うんどう） exercise, sport

運転（うんてん）する to drive

運命（うんめい） fate, destiny

運営（うんえい）する to administrate, to manage

運輸省（うんゆしょう） Ministry of Transport

はこ(ぶ)

運（はこ）ぶ to transport, to carry

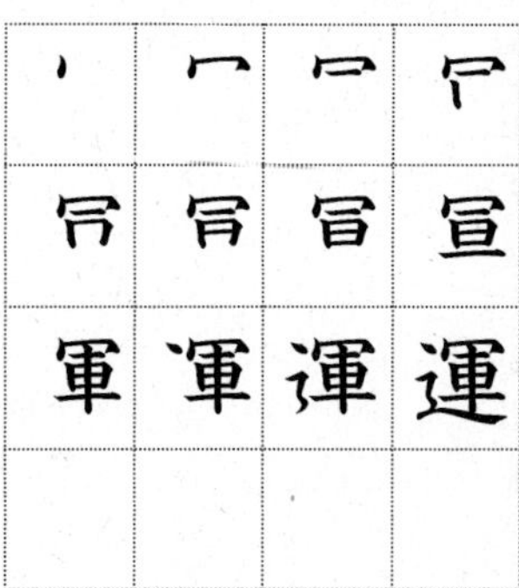

(12 strokes)

 連 (560)
達 (563)
速 (378)

 Along the road comes the queen´s tutu being *transported* by a car.

 運 (alt)

375 — TO RETURN

(2級)

一 厂 万 反 ˋ反 ì反 返

(7 strokes)

ヘン

返事 (へんじ) answer
返済 (へんさい) refund, repayment
返還 (へんかん) repayment

かえ(す/る)

返る (かえる) to return
返す (かえす) to give back (something borrowed)
取り返す (とりかえす) to pick up, to recover
繰り返し (くりかえし) repetition

特 返 (alt)

 The road goes up and down the slope; thus, it *returns* the traveler to his starting point.

 近 (178)
辺 (558)

376 — TO PURSUE, ADDITION

(2級)

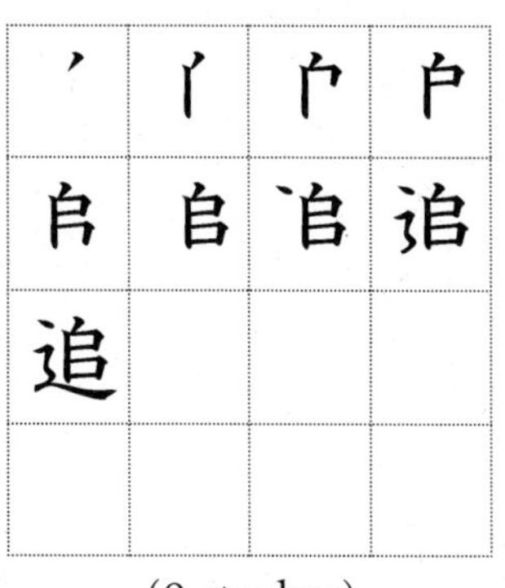

(9 strokes)

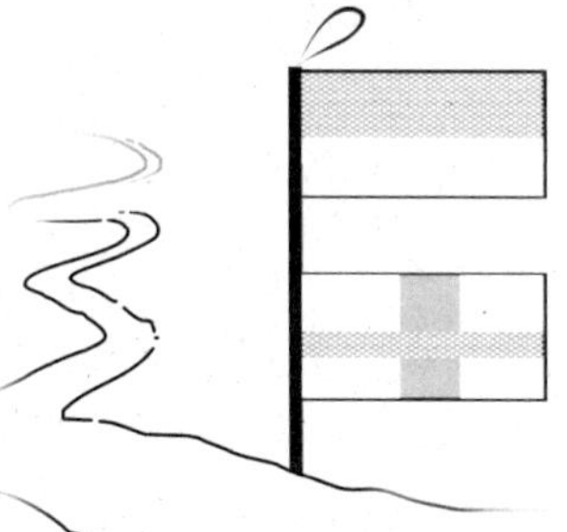

ツイ

追跡 (ついせき) pursuit
追放 (ついほう) exile, banishment
追加 (ついか) addition
追徴金 (ついちょうきん) supplementary charge

お(う)

追う (おう) to pursue
追い出す (おいだす) to kick out, to chase away

追 (alt)

 The road of the politician involves a large addition of promises and the *pursuit* of them.

 退 (5th)
造 (5th)

377 (3級)

TO SEND

ソウ

送別会（そうべつかい） farewell party
送信（そうしん） transmission
郵送（ゆうそう） mailing
送電（そうでん） transmission of electricity
送還（そうかん） repatriation, deportation (to one´s home country)

おく(る)

送る（おくる） to send

(9 strokes)

注 逃 (Jōyō)
迷 (5th)

 This is how the road that *sends* you to hell looks like: paradise with horns.

 送 (alt)

378 (2級)

FAST

ソク

早速（さっそく） immediately
速度（そくど） speed
高速道路（こうそくどうろ） expressway, freeway
速報（そくほう） news flash
加速（かそく） acceleration

はや(い/める)

速い（はやい） fast, quick

すみ(やか)

速やか（すみやか） quickly

(10 strokes)

注 遠 (177)
途 (Jōyō)
送 (377)

 To know the *fastest* road to achieving your goal, ask the wise talking sequoia.

 速 (alt)

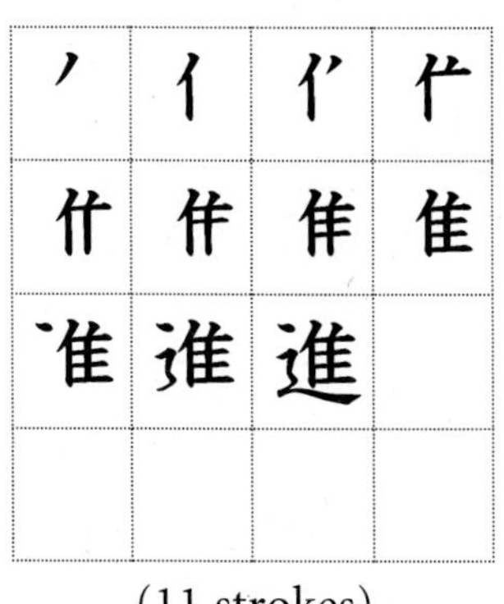

(11 strokes)

TO ADVANCE, TO PROGRESS

(3級)

379

シン

- 先進（せんしん） avant-garde
- 行進（こうしん） march, parade
- 進物（しんもつ） gift (sent by mail)
- 進化（しんか） evolution
- 進入（しんにゅう） approach, entry

すす(む/める)

- 進む（すすむ） to advance

 (alt)

学 *To progress*, follow “the swan’s road.”

注 推 (6th)

通 (186)

TO PLAY, TO HAVE A GOOD TIME

(12 strokes)

遊

(2級)

380

ユウ

- 遊園地（ゆうえんち） amusement park
- 遊休（ゆうきゅう） idle, unemployed
- 遊覧（ゆうらん） excursion, pleasure (trip)
- 遊戯（ゆうぎ） game, amusement
- 遊牧（ゆうぼく） nomadism

あそ(ぶ)

- 遊ぶ（あそぶ） to play, to amuse oneself, to visit

 (alt)

学 The person who *has a good time, playing* like a boy in a shed, is following the road to happiness.

 通 (186)

透 (Jōyō)

381 (3級)

ゾク

家族(かぞく) family

親族(しんぞく) relatives

民族(みんぞく) people, race

貴族(きぞく) aristocracy

皇族(こうぞく) imperial family

RELATIVES, TRIBE

族

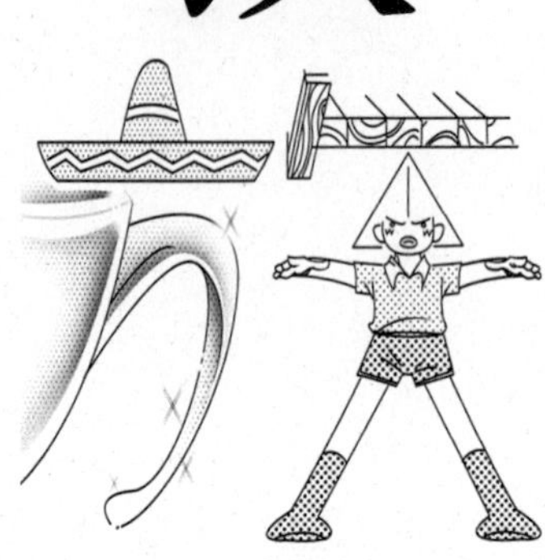

丶 亠 方 方 方' 方ㇰ 方ㇷ 方ㇷ 方ㇷ 方ㇷ 族

(11 strokes)

族 族 族 族 族 族 族 族

注 旅 (384)
放 (362)

学 Before the *relatives* (person) of the *tribe* come, in the shed they leave an arrow to announce their visit.

特

382 (2級)

ホウ

放送(ほうそう) broadcast (TV, radio)

解放(かいほう) releasing

放出(ほうしゅつ) emission (of energy)

放射能(ほうしゃのう) radioactivity

はな(す/れる)

放(はな)す to release, to set free

ほう(る)

放(ほう)る to throw, to rule out

TO RELEASE, TO EMIT, TO NEGLECT

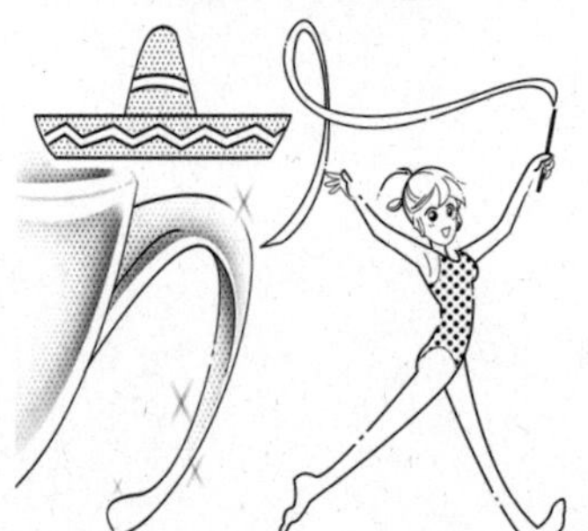

丶 亠 方 方 方' 方ㇰ 放 放

(8 strokes)

放 放 放 放 放 放 放 放

注 牧 (483)
防 (5th)
旅 (384)

学 The person who becomes an athlete is *released* from intellectual tasks.

特

(16 strokes)

TO ARRANGE, TO ADJUST

整

(2級) **383**

セイ

整理する (せいり) to arrange, to tidy up

整列する (せいれつ) to line up

均整 (きんせい) proportion, symmetry

整合 (せいごう) adjustment, coherence

不整脈 (ふせいみゃく) arrhythmia, irregular pulse

ととの(える/う)

整える (ととの) to put in place, to put in order, to arrange

特

学 The wise sequoia always *adjusts* and tidies up the athlete's behavior, since it always advises just the right thing.

 塾 (Jōyō)

製 (5th)

(10 strokes)

TO TRAVEL, TO TRIP

旅

(3級) **384**

リョ

旅行 (りょこう) trip

旅館 (りょかん) traditional Japanese hotel

旅費 (りょひ) traveling expenses

修学旅行 (しゅうがくりょこう) school trip / a trip for educational purposes

たび

旅 (たび) trip

旅人 (たびびと) traveler

 旅 (alt)

 A person who hides in sheds and covers himself with a scarf is *traveling* incognito.

 族 (381)

派 (6th)

ふわぁー!! やっと開放された！

やっぱり…このケチな家族……

いいんじゃない？飛行機なんかより自分自身が運ばれるのは安くて速いでしょ!?

いらなければ返していただいてもよろしいです。なお、人間なら追加料金がかかるんですよ。

Exercises 練習

1. Develop the stroke order of the following kanji.

身												
追												
進												
旅												

2. Choose the correct reading for each kanji or kanji combination.

a) 自分自身に決着がついていない時に、彼女(かのじょ)にどう返事すればいいでしょうか。

If I, myself, haven't reached a conclusion yet, how am I going to answer her?

自分自身: 1．じぶんじじん　2．じぶんじしん　3．じぶんじじん　4．しぶんししん

返事:　1．へんじ　2．へんし　3．かえごと　4．かえこと

b) 犯人(はんにん)は早速 遊園地に入って、追跡の手を逃(のが)れた。

The criminal quickly went into an amusement park and escaped from the pursuit.

早速:　1．はやばや　2．はやぞく　3．さつぞく　4．さっそく

遊園地: 1．ゆえんち　2．ゆうえんち　3．うえんち　4．あそえんち

追跡:　1．おぜき　2．おせき　3．ついせき　4．つっせき

c) 家族で旅行する時は必ず温泉付(おんせんづ)き旅館にする。

When we travel with the family, we stay at a traditional hotel with a hot spring.

家族:　1．かそく　2．かぞく　3．やそく　4．かぞぐ

旅行:　1．たびいく　2．たびく　3．りょこう　4．りょこ

旅館:　1．りょうかん　2．りょかん　3．たびかん　4．りかん

3. Write the kanji (one or more) and the meaning of the following words.

しゅっしん ______ ______　しんか ______ ______

うんてん ______ ______　ほうそう ______ ______

こうそくどうろ ______ ______　せいり ______ ______

4. Correct either the reading or the writing mistakes in the following words.

取り反す	とりかえす	早やい	はやい	親族	しんそく
送別会	おっべつかい	先無	せんしん	整える	ととのる
送信	そしん	遊そぶ	あそぶ	旅人	りょにん

Answes to exercises 練習解答

1. (Check them in the corresponding kanji table: #373, #376, #379, and #384)

2. a) 自分自身: 2 | 返事: 1 / b) 早速: 4 | 遊園地: 2 | 追跡: 3 / c) 家族: 2 | 旅行: 3 | 旅館: 2

3. しゅっしん: 出身, originally from | うんてん: 運転, to drive | こうそくどうろ: 高速道路, expressway | しんか: 進化, evolution | ほうそう: 放送, broadcast | せいり: 整理, to arrange, to tidy up.

4. 取り返す　とりかえす | 早~~や~~い　はやい | 親族　しんぞく | 送別会　そうべつかい | 先進　せんしん | 整える　ととのえる | 送信　そうしん | 遊~~そ~~ぶ　あそぶ | 旅人　たびびと

Manga translation マンガ翻訳

Mother: Come on, tidy up your room, we are about to leave.

Son: Huh? Where are we going?

Mother: The whole family is going to visit grandfather and grandmother in Okinawa.

Son: Yippee!! We are going on a trip!

Grandfather: Oh, well this is a big box.

Delivery man: Hi, here's a special delivery parcel.

Grandfather: How strange... I wonder who sent it? Could it be a gift?

Mother: Ufff, we've been released at last!

Grandfather: I should have expected it. What a stingy family...

Father: Why not? To mail oneself is much faster and cheaper than going by plane.

Delivery man: If you don't want it, you can return it. However, I warn you parcels with people inside come with a surcharge.

New elements 新しい部首

亍　hanger

非　armed coat

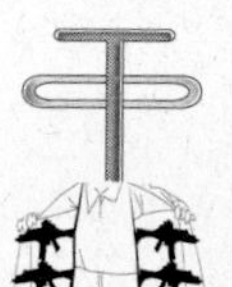

亜　prison cell

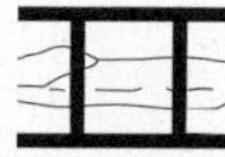

Lesson 34
第三十四課

385 (2級)

SHORE, COAST, BEACH

岸

ガン

海岸（かいがん） coast, beach
岸壁（がんぺき） cliff
対岸（たいがん） the opposite shore

きし

岸（きし） shore, coast
岸辺（きしべ） shore
岸本（きしもと） Kishimoto (surname)

(8 strokes)

注 岩 (160)

Climb the mountain and, before you jump from the cliff to the *coast*, hang your clothes on the hanger.

386 (2級)

TWO, BOTH

両

リョウ

両方（りょうほう） both
両親（りょうしん） parents
両手（りょうて） both hands
両腕（りょううで） both arms
両足（りょうあし） both legs
両雄（りょうゆう） two great rivals
車両（しゃりょう） vehicle, wagon
両替（りょうがえ） money exchange
一両（いちりょう） one *ryō* (old Japanese coin)

(6 strokes)

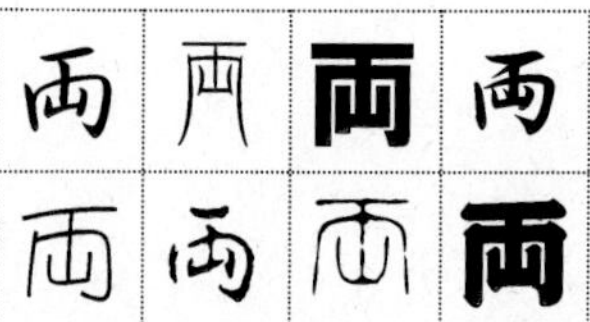

注 丙 (Jōyō)
同 (194)

The woman (wig) has hung her lover's portrait with a thumbtack; they *both* loved each other so much.

兩 (ant)

387 炭 — COAL, CHARCOAL

(2級)

(9 strokes)

炭 (alt)

タン

- 石炭 (せきたん) coal
- 木炭 (もくたん) charcoal
- 炭素 (たんそ) carbon
- 炭酸 (たんさん) carbonic acid
- 炭酸飲料 (たんさんいんりょう) carbonated drink, soda

すみ

- 炭 (すみ) coal
- 炭火 (すみび) coal fire
- 炭焼き (すみや) roasted in a charcoal (kiln)

At the foot of the mountain, hidden under a cliff, someone uses *charcoal* to light a fire.

注 岩 (160)
災 (5th)

388 島 — ISLAND

(2級)

(10 strokes)

トウ

- 諸島 (しょとう) archipelago
- 島民 (とうみん) islanders
- 半島 (はんとう) peninsula
- グアム島 (とう) Guam island

しま

- 島 (しま) island
- 島国 (しまぐに) island country
- 広島 (ひろしま) Hiroshima
- 硫黄島 (いおうじま) Iwo Jima

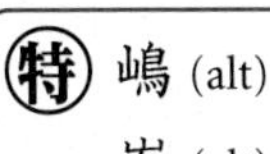
嵐 (alt)

When the bird alights on a sprouting mountain, it discovers an *island*.

烏 (231)
馬 (230)

389 (2級)

TO LOSE, TO CARRY

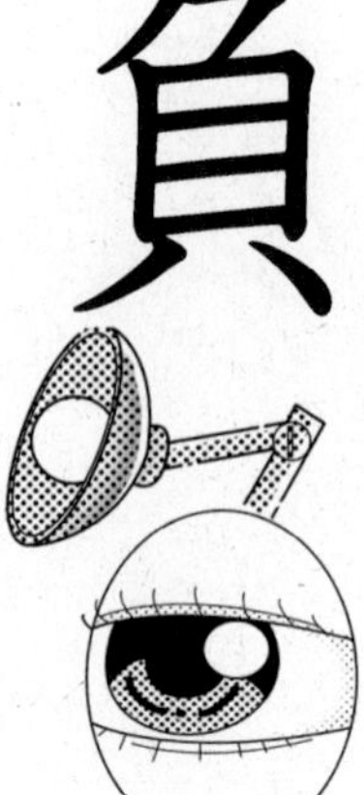

フ

負荷（ふか） burden (physical)
負担（ふたん） burden, responsibility
勝負（しょうぶ） fight, duel

ま(ける)

負（ま）ける to lose
勝（か）ち負（ま）け to win and lose
負（ま）け惜（お）しむ to be a bad loser

お(う)

背負（せお）う to carry on one's back

(9 strokes)

注 貝 (23)
息 (390)

 Look at the shellfish *carrying* a flash on its back; yes, it has lost its head.

 負 (alt)

390 (3級)

URGENT, TO HURRY

キュウ

急（きゅう）に suddenly
急行（きゅうこう） express train
急速（きゅうそく） fast, quick
救急車（きゅうきゅうしゃ） ambulance
急死（きゅうし） sudden death

いそ(ぐ)

急（いそ）ぐ to hurry
大急（おおいそ）ぎ in a big rush

(9 strokes)

注 争 (485)
負 (389)
思 (221)

学 *Hurry up*, turn the flash on! Someone is driving a trident into the president's heart!

 急 (alt)

一	十	才	木
札	机	相	相
相			

(9 strokes)

相	相	相	相
相	相	相	相

MUTUAL, MINISTER

相

(2級)

391

ソウ

しんそう
真相 the truth

てそう
手相 lines of the palm

そうご
相互 mutual, reciprocal

そうだん
相談 consultation

ショウ

しゅしょう
首相 prime minister

あい

あいしょう
相性 affinity

あいて
相手 rival, partner

学 The tree is the *minister* of the forest: with its omnipotent eye, it looks after the mutual interest of plants and animals.

査 (5th)
植 (268)
根 (274)

一	十	才	木
札	机	相	相
相	相	想	想
想			

(13 strokes)

想	想	想	想
想	想	想	想

THOUGHT, TO CONCEIVE

想

(2級)

392

ソウ

そうぞう
想像 imagination

かんそう
感想 impression

かいそう
回想 memory, flashback

よそう
予想 prediction

れんそう
連想 association of ideas

おも(う)

おも
想う to think (with love) of something or somebody

A minister with a heart thinks noble *thoughts*.

箱 (435)
息 (393)

393 (2級)

BREATH, SON

ソク

- 休息（きゅうそく） rest
- 窒息（ちっそく） asphyxiation
- 利息（りそく） (bank) interest

いき

- 息（いき） breath
- 息切れする（いきぎれする） to be short of breath
- 溜息（ためいき） sigh

Special

- 息子（むすこ） son

(10 strokes)

注 思 (221)
忘 (6th)

 My son is everything to me: he is the very *breath* of my life and of my heart.

394 (3級)

INTENTION, MEANING

イ

- 意（い） intention
- 意味（いみ） meaning
- 真意（しんい） true meaning
- 意識（いしき） conscience
- 意見（いけん） opinion
- 意外（いがい） unexpected
- 注意（ちゅうい） attention, care
- 意思（いし） thought
- 意志（いし） will, wish

(13 strokes)

注 恵 (Jōyō)

学 The sound of my heart reveals my *intentions* with you.

特

(12 strokes)

SAD(NESS)

悲

(2級)

395

ヒ

- 悲劇（ひげき） tragedy
- 悲惨（ひさん）な wretched, tragic
- 悲鳴（ひめい） scream
- 慈悲（じひ） compassion, mercy

かな（しい / しむ）

- 悲（かな）しい sad
- 悲（かな）しむ to be sad

特

When I see you with that armed coat, my heart is *sad.*

悪 (396)

(11 strokes)

BAD, EVIL

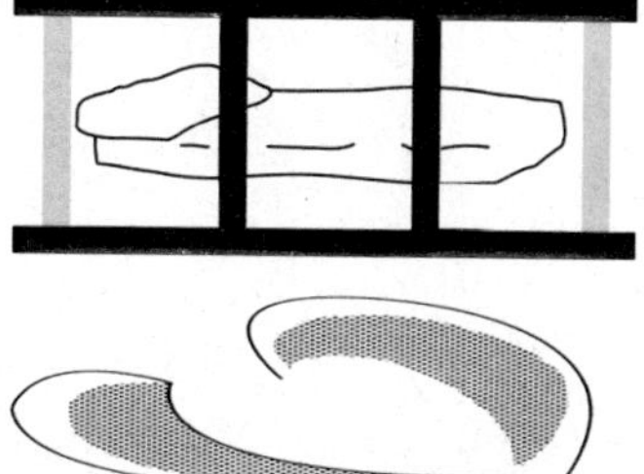

(3級)

396

アク

- 悪夢（あくむ） nightmare
- 最悪（さいあく） the worst
- 悪化（あっか）する to worsen
- 悪臭（あくしゅう） bad smell, stench
- 悪魔（あくま） devil, demon

わる（い）

- 悪（わる）い bad
- 頭（あたま）が悪（わる）い silly, fool
- 悪（わる）かった sorry, (it was my fault)

悪 (ant)

The cell where they imprison men with *evil* hearts.

悲 (395)
思 (221)
恐 (Jōyō)

この島には火山がないのに、どうして海岸は灰だらけなのかな？
それは悲しい話だ…
大昔、わしの先祖がこの島についた時…
急に火の息の恐ろしい悪魔があらわれた。
そんな相手では負けるだろうと思ったので、部族の魔術師と相談することにした…で、彼の意見は…
わしにまかせてくれ!!
でも、両雄が出会った時…
いや…すごく仲良くなって、一日中でっかい葉巻をすいつづけた…
あっ！想像できます…あの化け物を灰にしてしまったでしょう？

Exercises 練習

1. Develop the stroke order of the following kanji.

岸												
島												
悲												
悪												

2. Choose the correct reading for each kanji or kanji combination.

a) これだ！この島の海岸はこれから書きたい悲劇の舞台（ぶたい）になる。

Here it is! The coast of this island will be the scenery for the next tragedy I write.

島:	1．とう	2．しま	3．どう	4．じま
海岸:	1．うみきし	2．うみぎし	3．かいかん	4．かいがん
悲劇:	1．ひげき	2．びげき	3．かなげき	4．かげき

b) 息子とはどうも相性が悪い。彼（かれ）がボクと勝負しているような気がします。

My son and I don't get along well. I feel like he's always trying to compete with me.

息子:	1．そくこ	2．いきこ	3．いきっこ	4．むすこ
相性:	1．あいしょう	2．しょうしょう	3．そうしょう	4．そしょう
勝負:	1．しょうふ	2．しょうぶ	3．しょうま	4．しょうお

c) 美里（みさと）は悲鳴を上げて、急死した。悪夢を見ていたんだろう。それとも...

Misato let out a scream, and died suddenly. I guess she was having a nightmare. Or...

悲鳴:	1．ひめい	2．びめい	3．かなめい	4．かめい
急死:	1．いそし	2．きゅし	3．きゅうし	4．きゅっし
悪夢:	1．わるゆめ	2．あくゆめ	3．わるむ	4．あくむ

3. Write the kanji (one or more) and the meaning of the following words.

りょうて	______	______	しゅしょう	______	______
すみ	______	______	いけん	______	______
ひろしま	______	______	ちゅうい	______	______

4. Correct either the reading or the writing mistakes in the following words.

半島	はんとう	両新	りょうしん	負る	まける
岩辺	きしべ	石灰	せきたん	像想	そうぞう

Answers to exercises 練習解答

1. (Check them in the corresponding kanji table: #385, #388, #395, and #396)

2. a) 島: 2 | 海岸: 4 | 悲劇: 1 / b) 息子: 4 | 相性: 1 | 勝負: 2

c) 悲鳴: 1 | 急死: 3 | 悪夢: 4

3. りょうて: 両手, both hands | すみ: 炭, coal | ひろしま: 広島, Hiroshima | しゅしょう: 首相, prime minister | いけん: 意見, opinion | ちゅうい: 注意, to pay attention, to be careful of

4. 半島 はんとう | 両親 りょうしん | 負ける まける | 岸辺 きしべ | 石炭 せきたん | 想像 そうぞう

Manga translation マンガ翻訳

Explorer: Why is it that the beaches on this island are full of ash and coal, even though there are no volcanoes?

Native: That's a sad story...

Native: A long, long time ago, when my ancestors arrived on this island...

Native: ...a terrible fire-breathing monster suddenly appeared.

Native: Because they thought they would probably lose against such an opponent, they decided to consult the witch doctor of the tribe... And his opinion was that...

Witch doctor: I'll take care of it!!

Native: But when both great rivals met...

Woman explorer: Oh, I can imagine. He reduced it to ashes, didn't he?

Native: Not at all! They became friends and they spent all day smoking huge cigars...

Explorers: ...

New elements 新しい部首

呂 mouth-to-mouth 

Lesson 35
第三十五課

397 (3級)

PEACE, HARMONY, JAPAN

和

ワ

- 和(わ) harmony
- 調和(ちょうわ) harmonize (with)
- 平和(へいわ) peace
- 和服(わふく) Japanese clothing
- 和室(わしつ) Japanese style room

なご(む)

- 和(なご)む to relax, to be comfortable

Special

- 大和(やまと) Yamato (the ancient name for Japan)

(8 strokes)

 私 (6th)
知 (234)

 A pigeon, who gathers the tears of the weeping willow in its mouth, is a symbol of *peace.*

398 (2級)

SECONDS

秒

ビョウ

- 一秒(いちびょう) one second
- 十秒(じゅうびょう) ten seconds
- 秒速(びょうそく) speed per second

(9 strokes)

 利 (458)
秘 (6th)

 It takes a *second* for a tear to fall from the weeping willow, which is very little time indeed.

399

(2級)

一	二	千	禾
禾	秂	秊	委

(8 strokes)

COMMITTEE, TO DELEGATE

委

イ

委員会 (いいんかい) committee

委託する (いたくする) to entrust, to charge someone (with a task)

委任する (いにんする) to delegate, to trust

ゆだ(ねる)

委ねる (ゆだねる) to delegate, to entrust

学 The gathering of the tears of the weeping willow has traditionally been *delegated* to women.

 季 (546)

400

(3級)

く	𠂉	女	女𠂉
女厶	女台	始	始

(8 strokes)

TO START, TO BEGIN

始

シ

始発 (しはつ) the first train

年始 (ねんし) beginning of the year

始動する (しどうする) to start (machine)

開始する (かいしする) to start

終始 (しゅうし) from beginning to end

はじ(める/まる)

始める (はじめる) to start, to begin

始めて (はじめて) for the first time

始まり (はじまり) beginning, start

 When a beautiful woman brings the cornucopia to your mouth, then the party is about *to begin!*

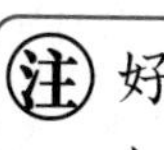 好 (545)

如 (Jōyō)

401 (4級)

CHEAP, EASY, PEACEFUL

安

アン

- 安心（あんしん） peace of mind
- 不安（ふあん） uneasiness
- 安定（あんてい） stability
- 安全（あんぜん） security
- 安易（あんい） easy, simple
- 安価（あんか） low price

やす(い/らか)

- 安い（やすい） cheap
- 安らか（やすらか） peaceful

(6 strokes)

安 安 安 安
安 安 安 安

注 家 (125)
妥 (Jōyō)

 What happens when you put a woman under a roof? Everything is *easier* and *cheaper*. Or so you wish...

402 (2級)

TO PROTECT

シュ

- 守備（しゅび） defense
- 守護（しゅご） protection, security
- 攻守（こうしゅ） attack and defense
- 守護神（しゅごしん） guardian deity
- 保守（ほしゅ） maintenance

まも(る)

- 守る（まもる） to protect
- お守り（おまもり） protective charm, amulet

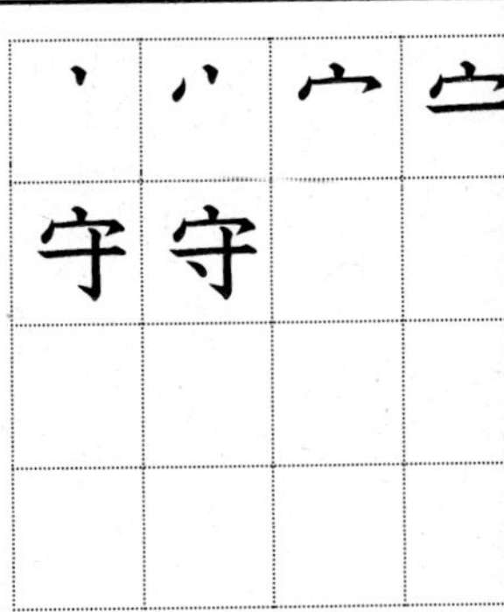

(6 strokes)

守 守 守 守
守 守 守 守

注 字 (77)
村 (64)
寺 (123)

 The way *to protect* a watering alien is having him under a roof, so the authorities won't discover him.

(8 strokes)

TO ESTABLISH, TO DETERMINE

定

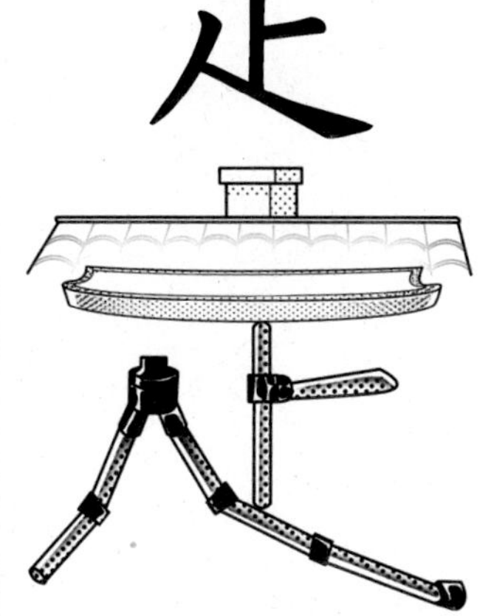

(2級)

403

テイ

- 安定 (あんてい) stability
- 決定 (けってい) decision
- 予定 (よてい) plan
- 定価 (ていか) fixed price

ジョウ

- 定規 (じょうぎ) ruler (for measurement)
- 案の定 (あんのじょう) just as I expected

さだ(める/まる)

- 定める (さだめる) to establish

特

学 If someone puts a tripod under his roof and *establishes* the rules of the house around it, then he must be a photographer.

注 正 (44)
庭 (366)

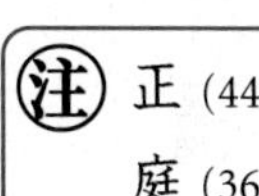

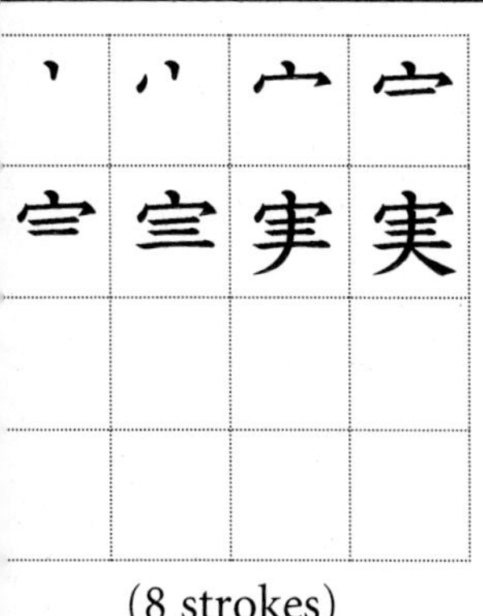

(8 strokes)

TRUE

実

(2級)

404

ジツ

- 実は (じつは) the truth is...
- 実験 (じっけん) experiment
- 真実 (しんじつ) the truth
- 実力 (じつりょく) real power
- 現実 (げんじつ) actuality, reality
- 果実 (かじつ) fruit

み/みの(る)

- 木の実 (このみ) fruit from a tree
- 実る (みのる) to bear fruit

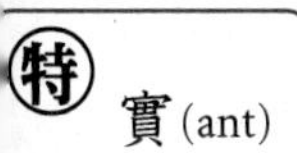

特 實 (ant)

学 The *true* Kim only reveals himself under the roof of his house: a fruit eating glutton.

注 美 (405)
参 (611)

405 (2級)

BEAUTIFUL

ビ

- 美術（びじゅつ） art
- 美人（びじん） beautiful woman
- 美少年（びしょうねん） beautiful boy
- 美味（びみ） good flavor
- 美容院（びよういん） beauty salon
- 優美（ゆうび） grace, elegance

うつく(しい)

- 美しい（うつくしい） beautiful, pretty

(9 strokes)

注 実 (404)

学 Isn't a sheep that is really big *beautiful?*

特

406 (2級)

CLIENT, GUEST

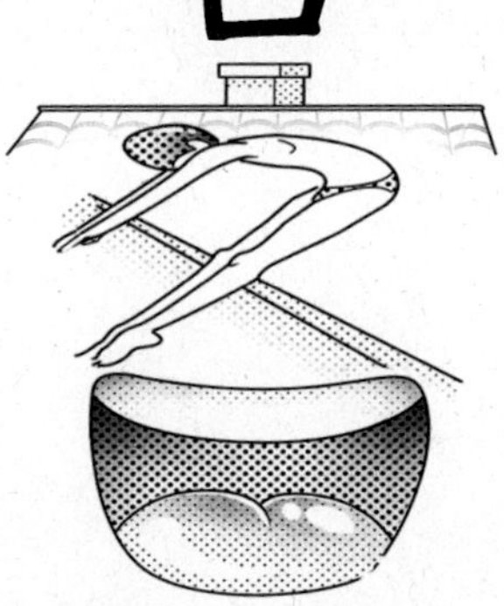

カク

- 刺客（しかく） murderer
- 客年（かくねん） last year

キャク

- 客（きゃく） client
- お客様（おきゃくさま） Mr. client
- 客室（きゃくしつ） guest room
- 来客（らいきゃく） visitor
- 観光客（かんこうきゃく） tourist
- 客観的な（きゃっかんてきな） objective

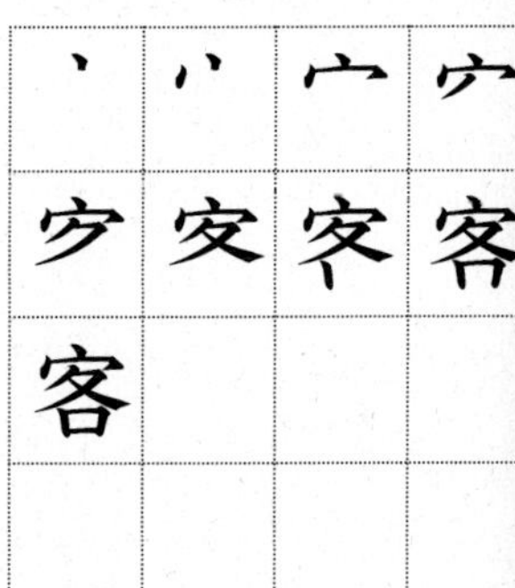

(9 strokes)

注 名 (46)
害 (540)
案 (569)

学 If you receive a swimming *guest* under your roof, win his favor through his mouth... He's sure to be hungry!

特

(10 strokes)

407

SHINTO SHRINE, PRINCE

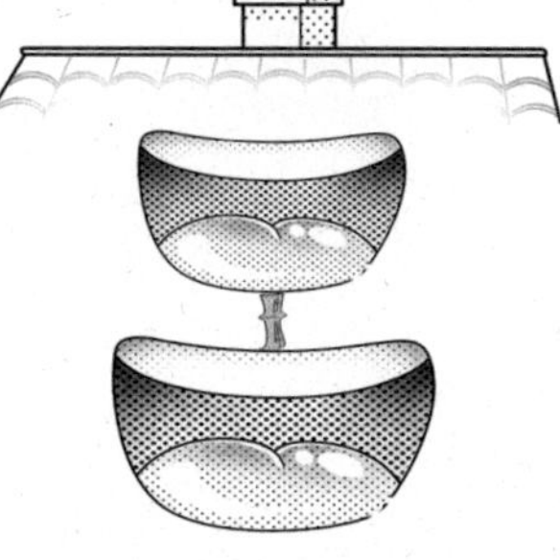

(1級)

キュウ

宮殿(きゅうでん) palace
迷宮(めいきゅう) labyrinth
宮廷(きゅうてい) imperial court
子宮(しきゅう) womb

グウ

神宮(じんぐう) Shinto shrine

みや

宮(みや) shrine
宮参り(みやまいり) visit to the shrine

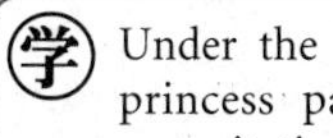

特

学 Under the roof of the *shrine*, the *prince* and the princess passionately practice mouth-to-mouth resuscitation.

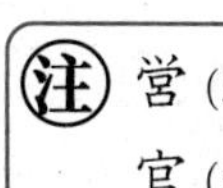

注 営 (5th)
官 (538)

408

LODGING, TO TAKE SHELTER

(11 strokes)

(2級)

シュク

宿泊(しゅくはく) lodging
宿題(しゅくだい) (school) homework
宿命(しゅくめい) fate
新宿(しんじゅく) Shinjuku (Tokyo)

やど

宿屋(やどや) inn, lodging house
宿無し(やどなし) homeless, vagrant

やど(る/す)

宿る(やどる) to take / give shelter

 特

 学 The ideal *lodging* for Kev is a roof under which he can take shelter for 100 yen.

 注 宣 (6th)
富 (5th)

宿屋
いらっしゃいませ、お客様！
はあ…こんばんは。お部屋はありますか？
怪しいやつだね。全く宇宙人みたいだ！
ダーン
やっぱり！一秒で真実に気がついたぞ！そのレザー銃を投げすてろ！
い…いたっ！
た…ただのヘアドライヤーだが…
何やってんの？このバカ息子!?
オ…オレ、地球の平和を守っていたのに…
宇宙宮廷委員長、地球との協定の交渉をもう始めましたか。
ふん…美しい惑星ですが、まだ少し不安定かもしれません…

Exercises 練習

1. Develop the stroke order of the following kanji.

委												
実												
美												
宮												

2. Choose the correct reading for each kanji or kanji combination.

a) 私(わたし)は宿泊なら、和室がいい。安心するから。

Whenever I take up lodging, I always choose a Japanese style room. It relaxes me.

宿泊:　1．やどと　2．やどど　3．しゅくはく　4．しゅくぱく

和室:　1．わや　2．わしつ　3．なごや　4．なごしつ

安心:　1．あんしん　2．あんごころ　3．やすしん　4．やすごころ

b) 日本の神宮や寺、美術などに興味(きょうみ)のある観光客が多いです。

There are many tourists interested in shrines, temples, and Japanese art.

神宮:　1．しんぐう　2．じんぐう　3．かみみや　4．しんきゅう

美術:　1．ひじゅつ　2．びじゅつ　3．みじゅつ　4．うつわざ

観光客:　1．かんこうきゃく　2．かんこうかく　3．かんこうかん　4．かんこうがん

c) この国の平和と安定を守るためには、委員会が協力(きょうりょく)しなければなりません。

To keep the peace and the stability of the country, the committee must cooperate.

平和:　1．ひらわ　2．ひらなご　3．へいわ　4．へいなご

安定:　1．やすてい　2．やすじょう　3．あんじょう　4．あんてい

委員会:　1．ゆだいんかい　2．ゆいんかい　3．ゆいんがい　4．いいんかい

3. Write the kanji (one or more) and the meaning of the following words.

いちびょう　______　______　　おまもり　お____り　______

ねんし　______　______　　よてい　______　______

あんぜん　______　______　　じつりょく　______　______

4. Correct either the reading or the writing mistakes in the following words.

実人	びじん	お各様	おきゃくさま	女い	やすい
美くしい	うつくしい	宿題	やどだい	始めて	はしめて

Answers to exercises 練習解答

1. (Check them in the corresponding kanji table: #399, #404, #405, and #407)

2. a) 宿泊: 3 | 和室: 2 | 安心: 1 / b) 神宮: 2 | 美術: 2 | 観光客: 1
c) 平和: 3 | 安定: 4 | 委員会: 4

3. いちびょう: 一秒, a second | ねんし: 年始, beginning of the year | あんぜん: 安全, security | おまもり: お守り, protective charm | よてい: 予定, plan | じつりょく: 実力, real power

4. 美人 びじん | お客様 おきゃくさま | 安い やすい | 美しい うつくしい | 宿題 しゅくだい | 始めて はじめて

Manga translation マンガ翻訳

Sign: Inn.

Landlady: Welcome, sir!

Traveler: Buff... Good evening, are there any rooms available?

Landlady's son: That guy looks very suspicious. I'm sure he's an alien!

Onomatopoeia: Slip

Landlady's son: I knew it! It took me a second to realize the truth! Throw that ray gun away!

Landlady's son: Ouch! Ouch!

Traveler: I-it's only a hairdryer.

Landlady: What are you doing?! Gosh, that son of mine is a fool!

Son: I-I was protecting peace on Earth...

Informer: Mr. Commissioner from the Galactic Imperial Court, have you already started negotiating for the alliance with Earth?

Commissioner: Hum, I'm not sure. This planet is beautiful, but it might be somewhat unstable yet...

New elements 新しい部首

龷 iron mask 

与 lookout sitting on a bathtub 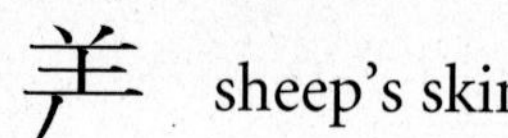

六 stool with spider legs 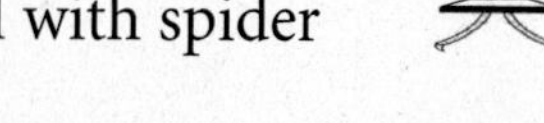

⺶ sheep's skin 

Lesson 36
第三十六課

409 (3級)

カン

- 寒波（かんぱ） cold wave
- 寒気（かんき） cold atmosphere
- 寒流（かんりゅう） cold current
- 大寒（だいかん） harsh winter

さむ(い)

- 寒い（さむい） cold
- 寒空（さむぞら） winter sky

COLD

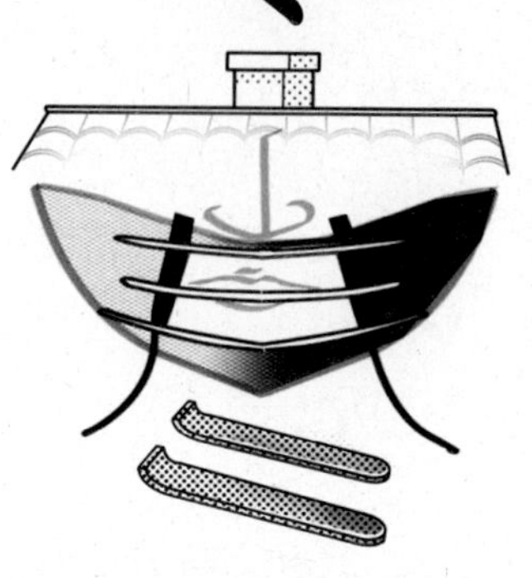

(12 strokes)

寒	寒	寒	寒
寒	寒	寒	寒

注 実 (404)

学 Under the roof of my house, it's *cold!* We must put on an iron mask, and move with our skis forming a wedge.

特  (alt)

410 (3級)

キュウ

- 研究（けんきゅう） research
- 究明（きゅうめい） study, clarification
- 追究（ついきゅう） exhaustive investigation
- 学究（がっきゅう） student

きわ(める)

- 究める（きわめる） to study thoroughly, to master

INVESTIGATION

(7 strokes)

究	究	究	究
究	究	究	究

注 空 (67)
突 (Jōyō)

 On a roof with slender legs, the scientist *investigates* the nine revelations.

(9 strokes)

TO POLISH, TO SHARPEN

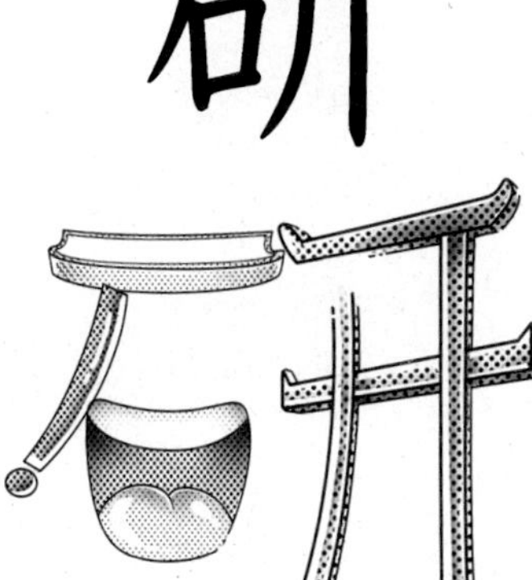

(3級)

411

ケン

研究(けんきゅう) research

研修(けんしゅう) course, training

研磨(けんま) to grind, to study hard

と(ぐ)

研(と)ぐ to polish, to sharpen

研(と)ぎ石(いし) grinding stone

 Made of *polished* stone is the temple torii.

 破 (5th)
拓 (Jōyō)

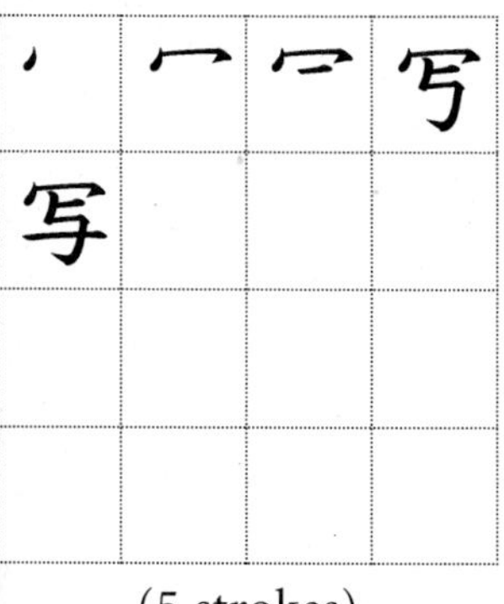

(5 strokes)

COPY, REPRODUCTION

(3級)

412

シャ

写真(しゃしん) photography

複写(ふくしゃ) copy, duplicate

書写(しょしゃ) transcription

描写(びょうしゃ) description, drawing

試写(ししゃ) private showing

写(しゃ)メール photograph taken and sent by cell phone

うつ(す/る)

写(うつ)す to reflect

写(うつ)る to be reflected

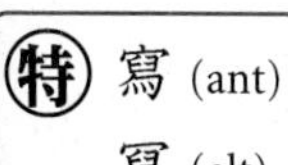 寫 (ant)
冩 (alt)

 With drawn tutu curtains, the crouching lookout hides in the bathtub, and *copies* everything he sees in the bedroom.

 考 (83)
号 (349)

413 (2級)

TOOL

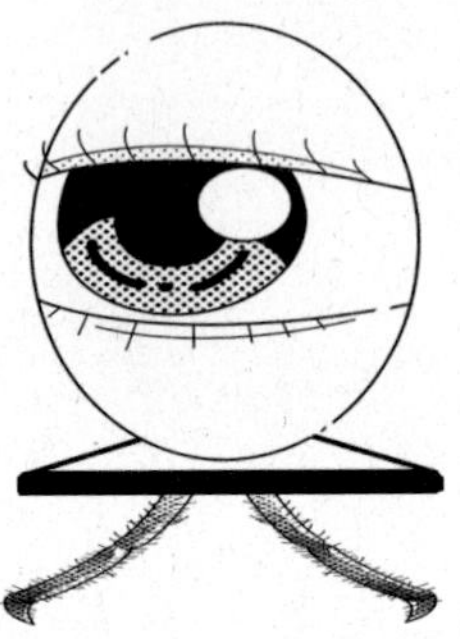

グ

- 道具（どうぐ） tool
- 器具（きぐ） utensil
- 家具（かぐ） furniture
- 具体的（ぐたいてき） concrete, specific
- 具合（ぐあい） condition
- 絵の具（えのぐ） paints (art)
- 文房具（ぶんぼうぐ） stationery

(8 strokes)

注 貝 (23)
首 (174)
真 (414)

学 Eyes are like removable *tools*, just like glasses. When you take them off, you leave them on a stool with legs.

特  具 (alt)

414 (3級)

TRUE

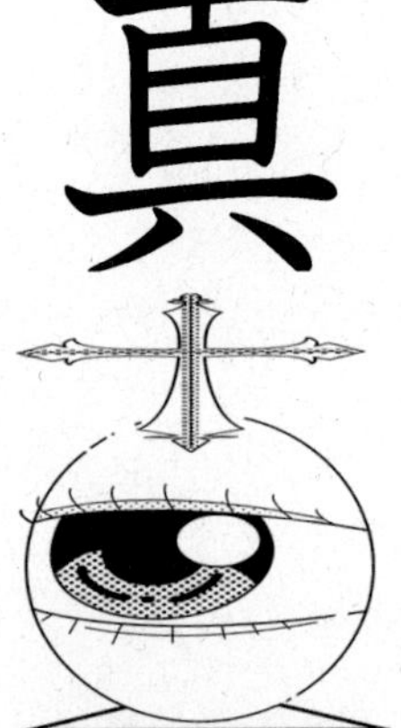

シン

- 真実（しんじつ） truth
- 真意（しんい） true intention
- 真剣（しんけん） real sword

ま

- 真ん中（まんなか） the center
- 真冬（まふゆ） midwinter
- 真夏（まなつ） midsummer

まこと

- 真に（まことに） really, truly

(10 strokes)

 具 (413)
章 (330)

 The cross on the removable eye tells you this is God's *true* eye.

 眞 (ant)

415 — PREFECTURE

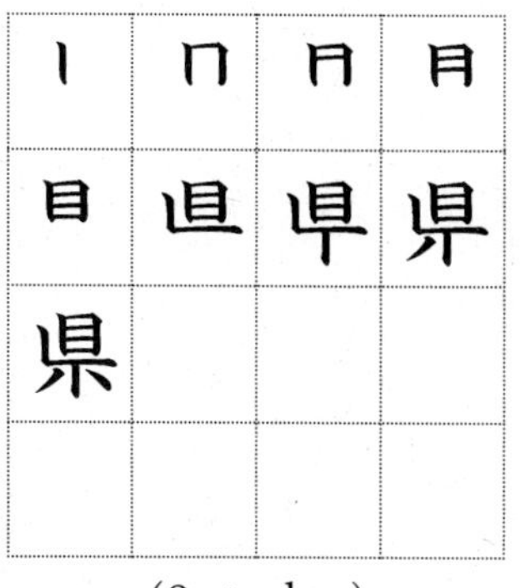

(9 strokes)

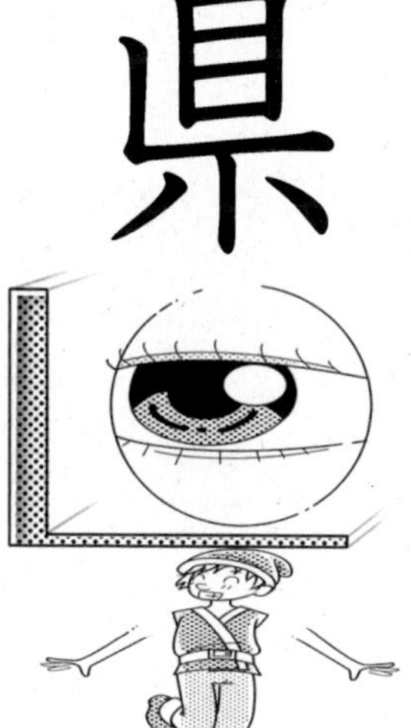

(3級)

ケン

県(けん) prefecture
県庁(けんちょう) prefectural government
県警(けんけい) prefectural police
県民(けんみん) citizens of a prefecture
群馬県(ぐんまけん) Gunma prefecture
佐賀県(さがけん) Saga prefecture

 縣 (ant)

学 Keep an eye on *prefectures*: they are divided with bookends made by Japanese dwarves, who had neither rulers nor squares.

 直 (104)
具 (413)

416 — TO WEAR, TO ARRIVE

(12 strokes)

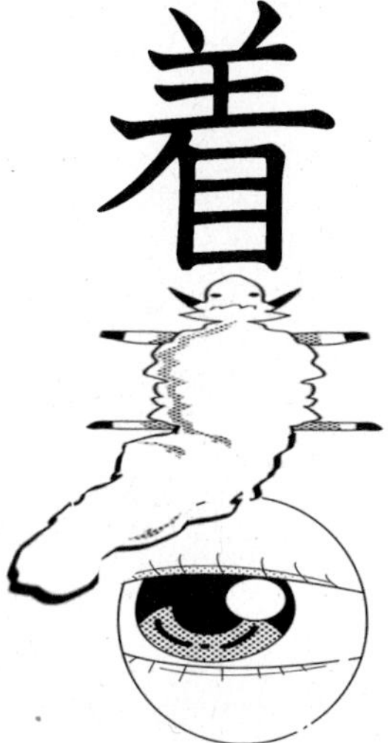

(3級)

チャク

決着(けっちゃく) settling (of a matter)
到着(とうちゃく) arrival
着信(ちゃくしん) received call
着(ちゃく)メロ cell phone ringtone

き(る/せる)

着(き)る to wear
着物(きもの) kimono

つ(く/ける)

着(つ)く to arrive

 If you *arrive* wearing a sheep's skin, all eyes will be on you.

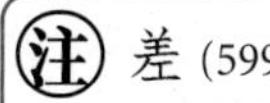 差 (599)
基 (5th)

隊長、スパイ衛星がとった最新の写真です。
ふん
これが新しい日本の「低温度研究所」か…
でも、具体的にどんな研究だろう？
超電導合金!?
絶対零度装置？
一方…
日本埼玉県
低温度研究所
ご注意ください！
シミュレーション始動！
なるほど!!!
寒い日には毛糸の服を着るのが一番です。
わぁ…
す…
すばらしい…

Exercises 練習

1. Develop the stroke order of the following kanji.

寒												
究												
県												
着												

2. Choose the correct reading for each kanji or kanji combination.

a) 到着した時、真冬じゃなかったのに、寒波がやってきたから、大変だった。
When I arrived, even though it wasn't winter, there was a cold wave and it was awful.

到着:	1．とうちく	2．とうちゃく	3．とうき	4．とうつ
真冬:	1．まふゆ	2．しんふゆ	3．まぶゆ	4．しんぶゆ
寒波:	1．かんは	2．かんば	3．かんぱ	4．さむは

b) 研究を進めた上で、お母さんの死の真実が明確（めいかく）になりました。
Since I proceeded with the investigation, I was able to clarify the truth about my mother's death.

研究:	1．ときわ	2．けんきゅう	3．けんきゅ	4．きわと
真実:	1．まじつ	2．まみ	3．しんじつ	4．しんみ

c) 彼女（かのじょ）の真意は分からないけど、着物姿（すがた）の写真を送ってくれた。
I don't know what her intentions are, but she sent me a photo of herself wearing traditional clothes.

真意:	1．まい	2．しんい	3．まことい	4．まこと
着物:	1．ちゃくぶつ	2．ちゃくもの	3．きぶつ	4．きもの
写真:	1．うつま	2．しゃま	3．うつしん	4．しゃしん

3. Write the kanji (one or more) and the meaning of the following words.

かぐ	______	______	ちゃくしん	______	______
まなつ	______	______	ぐあい	______	______
けん	______	______	さむぞら	______	______

4. Correct either the reading or the writing mistakes in the following words.

空明	きゅうめい	写す	うるす	道真	どうぐ
究研	けんきゅう	極る	きわめる	真とに	まことに
差る	きる	直民	けんみん	分房具	ぶんぼうぐ

Answers to exercises 練習解答

1. (Check them in the corresponding kanji table: #409, #410, #415, and #416)

2. a) 到着: 2 | 真冬: 1 | 寒波: 3 / b) 研究: 2 | 真実: 3
c) 真意: 2 | 着物: 4 | 写真: 4

3. かぐ: 家具, furniture | まなつ: 真夏, midsummer | けん: 県, prefecture | ちゃくしん: 着信, received call | ぐあい: 具合, condition | さむぞら: 寒空, winter sky

4. 究明 きゅうめい | 写す うつす | 道具 どうぐ | 研究 けんきゅう | 極める きわめる | 真~~そ~~に まことに | 着る きる | 県民 けんみん | 文房具 ぶんぼうぐ

Manga translation マンガ翻訳

Subordinate: Sir, here are the latest photos taken by the spy satellite.

Boss: Hummm...

Boss: The new “Low Temperature Research Institute” in Japan...

Boss: But, what are they researching specifically? Super conducting alloys? Some kind of device for the absolute zero?

Text panel: Meanwhile...

Sign: Japan, Saitama prefecture - Low Temperature Research Institute.

Loudspeaker: Your attention, please! The simulation is about to start.

Scientist: Wow! Fa-fascinating...

Scientist: Yes, indeed! On cold days, the best thing is to wear wool garments.

New elements 新しい部首

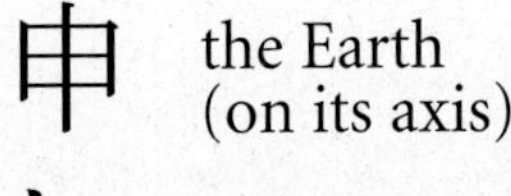
申 the Earth (on its axis)

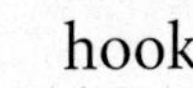
乚 hook

介 house

戈 fake Robin Hood

Lesson 37
第三十七課

417 (2級)

TO SAY (HUMBLY)

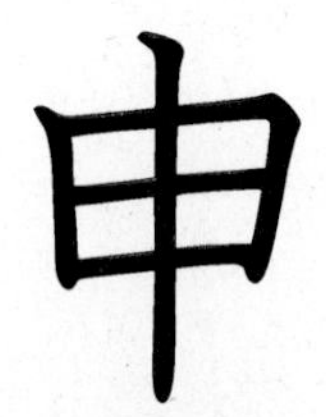

シン

- 申告（しんこく） report, notification
- 申請（しんせい） petition
- 追伸（ついしん） P.S. (postscript)

もう(す)

- 申す（もうす） to say (humbly)
- 申し訳ない（もうしわけない） I'm very sorry
- 申し上げる（もうしあげる） to talk (humble form)

(5 strokes)

注 甲 (Jōyō)
由 (339)

The Earth *humbly* requests permission to stop and rest on its axis for a bit.

418 (2級)

GOD, DEITY

シン/ジン

- 神父（しんぷ） Catholic priest
- 神道（しんとう） Shintoism
- 神話（しんわ） myth
- 神経（しんけい） nerve
- 精神（せいしん） mind, mentality
- 神社（じんじゃ） Shinto shrine

かみ

- 神（かみ） god(s)
- 神風（かみかぜ） *kamikaze* (divine wind)

(9 strokes)

注 社 (206)
初 (557)
紳 (Jōyō)

A *deity*: a business woman who rules the Earth.

神 (alt)

419

(2級)

CORTEOUS, TO THANK, BOW

丶	ラ	ネ	ネ
礼			

(5 strokes)

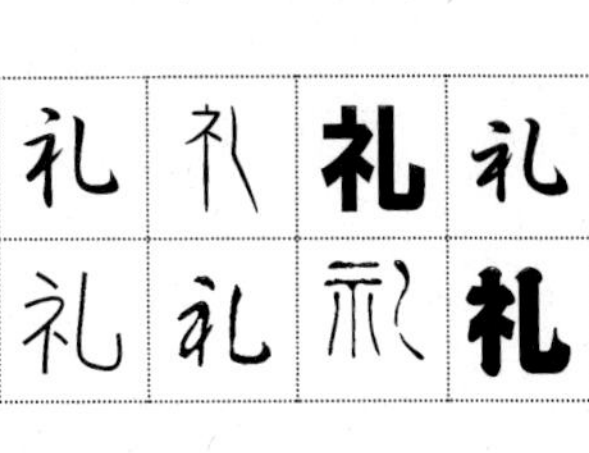

レイ

- 礼（れい） greeting, bow
- 礼金（れいきん） reward
- 謝礼（しゃれい） remuneration
- 失礼（しつれい） rudeness
- 礼儀（れいぎ） etiquette
- 礼服（れいふく） formal dress
- 洗礼（せんれい） baptism

 禮 (ant)

学 A good business woman can be *courteous* and bow to get herself off the hook.

 札 (565)

420

(2級)

FORTUNE

丶	ラ	ネ	ネ
礻	礻	福	福
福	福	福	福
福			

(13 strokes)

福	福	福	福
福	福	福	福

フク

- 福（ふく） happiness, fortune
- 祝福（しゅくふく） blessing
- 幸福（こうふく） happiness
- 大福（だいふく） great happiness, stuffed rice cake
- 福祉（ふくし） well-being

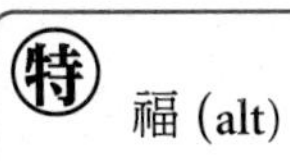 (alt)

 *Fortune* smiles on the business woman who has managed to gain bread to fill the mouths of all her workers on the rice field.

増 (5th)
塩 (581)
幅 (Jōyō)

421 (3級)

AGE, WORLD, GENERATION

セ/セイ

- 世界(せかい) world
- 世代(せだい) generation
- 世論(せろん) public opinion
- 世話(せわ)する to take care of somebody
- 世紀(せいき) century
- 近世(きんせい) modern age

よ

- あの世(よ) the "other" world
- 世(よ)の中(なか) (in) the world

(5 strokes)

注 他 (256)
也 (no Jōyō)

In another *age*, gymnasts invested their physical strength in carrying suckling pigs ready to be roasted.

丗 (alt)

422 (3級)

WORLD, BOUNDARY

カイ

- 世界(せかい) world
- 他界(たかい)する to die
- 限界(げんかい) limit, boundary
- 境界(きょうかい) border
- 視界(しかい) field of vision
- 電界(でんかい) electric field
- 政界(せいかい) political world
- 学界(がっかい) academic world
- マンガ界(かい) manga world

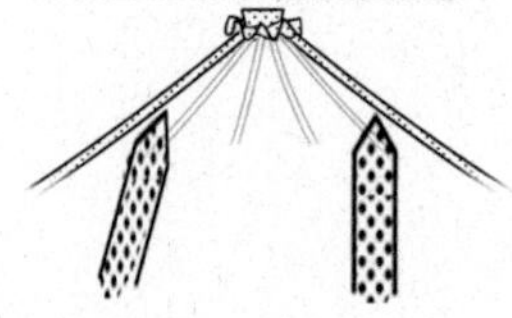

(9 strokes)

注 異 (6th)
男 (74)
果 (500)

A *world* of fields and houses.

畍 (alt)
堺 (alt)

(14 strokes)

NOSE

(2級)

423

ビ

耳鼻科(じびか) otorhinologist
鼻炎(びえん) nasal inflammation
鼻音(びおん) nasal sound

はな

鼻(はな) nose
鼻水(はなみず) runny nose
鼻糞(はなくそ) snot
鼻毛(はなげ) nostril hair
鼻血(はなぢ) nosebleed

特 鼻 (alt)

学 In days gone by, pointing at your *nose* was the equivalent to saying "I" for the Japanese man who lived in the country, by his field surrounded by a wooden fence. This gesture is still used today.

注  (207)

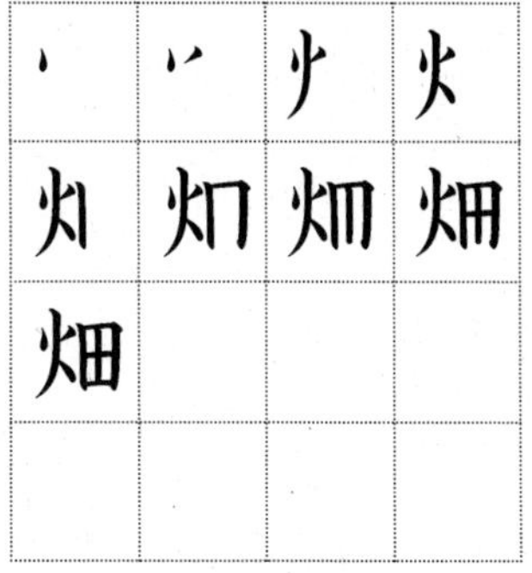

(9 strokes)

FIELD

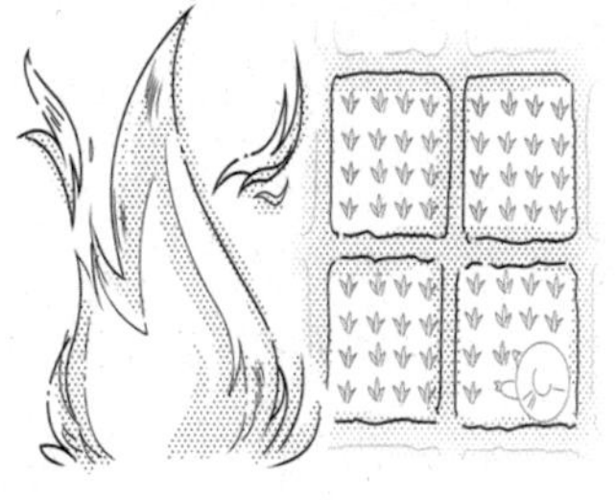

(2級)

424

はた

畑地(はたち) farmland
田畑(たはた) rice paddies and fields

はたけ

畑(はたけ) field, kitchen garden
花畑(はなばたけ) flower garden

特  (alt)

学 Fire in the rice field: that´s the way to fertilize it.

注 町 (73)
 (122)

425 (3級)

QUESTION

問

モン

質問（しつもん） question
難問（なんもん） difficult question
尋問（じんもん） interrogation
問題（もんだい） problem
訪問（ほうもん） visit
問責（もんせき） reprimand

と(う)

問（と）う to ask
問（と）い合（あ）わせ inquiry

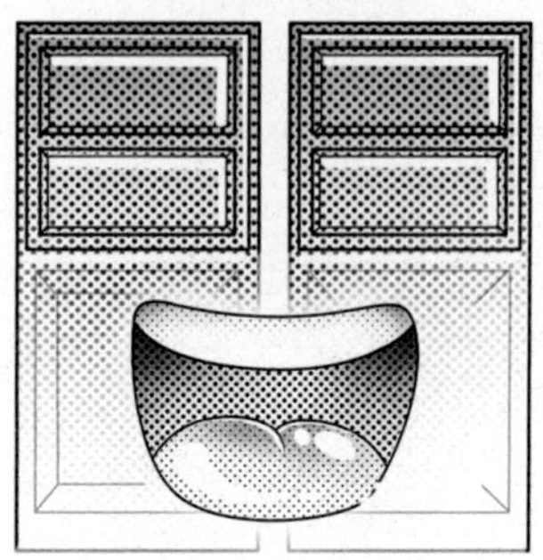

(11 strokes)

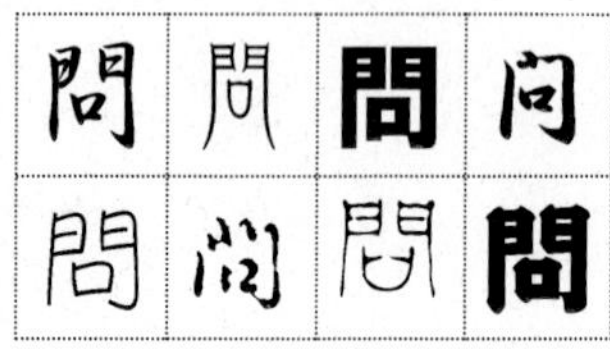

注 間 (133)
門 (132)

学 A mouth approaches the gate and asks a *question*: May I come in?

426 (3級)

TO OPEN, TO INAUGURATE

開

カイ

開門（かいもん）する to open a gate
開閉（かいへい）する to open and close
開始（かいし）する to start
公開（こうかい） opening to the public
展開（てんかい） development

ひら(く/ける)

開（ひら）く to open, to inaugurate

あ(く/ける)

開（あ）ける to open

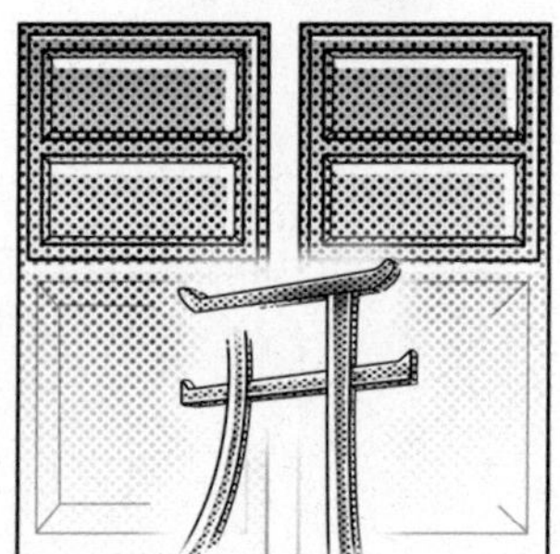

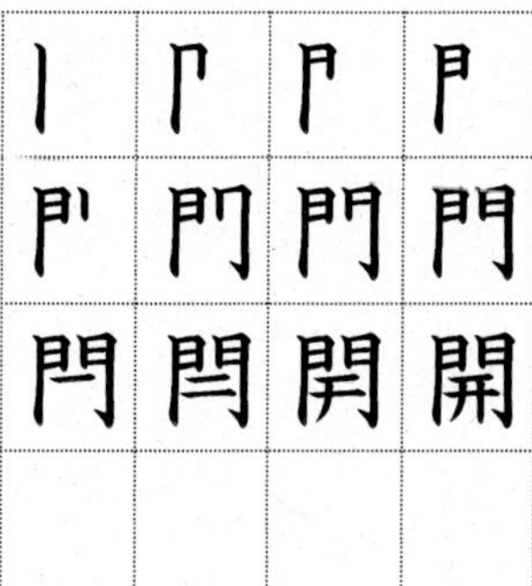

(12 strokes)

注 閉 (6th)
関 (586)

学 A gate in the shape of a torii *opens* the road to a temple.

开 (simp)

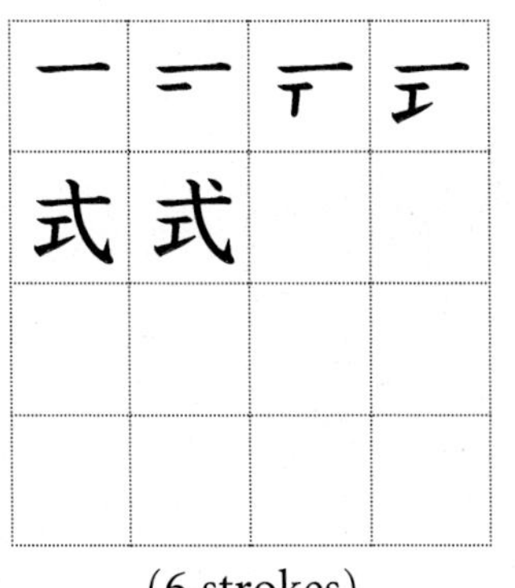

(6 strokes)

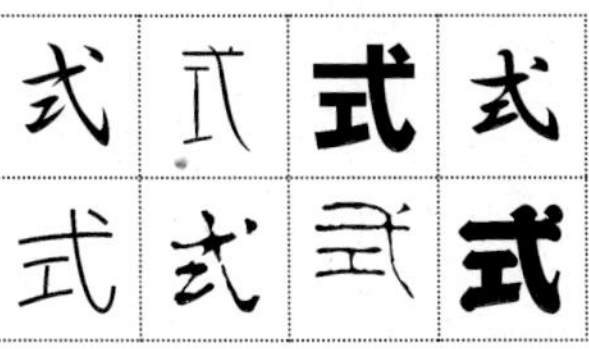

STYLE, CEREMONY

(2級)

427

シキ
- 儀式（ぎしき） ceremony, rite
- 式典（しきてん） ceremony
- 結婚式（けっこんしき） wedding
- 開会式（かいかいしき） opening ceremony
- 正式に（せいしきに） officially
- 和式（わしき） Japanese style
- 旧式（きゅうしき） old style
- 方式（ほうしき） form, method
- 方程式（ほうていしき） equation

特

学 A wedding in style: a *ceremony* officiated by Robin Hood, with an iron beam as an altar.

注 左 (30)
代 (257)

(13 strokes)

TO FEEL, FEELING

(2級)

428

カン
- 感情（かんじょう） feelings
- 感激（かんげき） deep emotion
- 感想（かんそう） impression, feeling
- 五感（ごかん） the five senses
- 感覚（かんかく） sense
- 感動（かんどう） emotion
- 感心（かんしん） admiration

かん(じる/ずる)
- 感じる（かんじる） to feel, to experience

 Under a cliff full of bread-hungry mouths, a fake Robin Hood *feels* his heart has become noble.

 盛 (6th)

静かに！儀式を開始する！
世界を支配なさるツルル神様よ！五羽のキジをご奉納いたしますから、ぶどう畑が幸福の太陽にめぐまれますように！
あ、何か来ます！それを感じるよ！
ツルル神様の力だ！
お礼を申し上げます、神様！
どどどどど
か…神様！なぜ鼻にもひっかけませんか？
サァァァー
こ…これは問責ですか…？
よそでは、一時間前に…
世界を支配なさるツルル神様よ！十羽のキジをご奉納いたしますから、田んぼが幸福の雨にめぐまれますように！

Exercises 練習

1. Develop the stroke order of the following kanji.

世												
鼻												
式												
感												

2. Choose the correct reading for each kanji or kanji combination..

a) 神社で家族の幸福と世界の平和を祈(いの)りました。

In the temple, I prayed for the happiness of my family and for peace in the world.

神社:　1．しんしゃ　2．じんしゃ　3．しんじゃ　4．じんじゃ

幸福:　1．こふく　2．こうふく　3．しあふく　4．しあわふく

世界:　1．よかい　2．ようかい　3．せかい　4．せいかい

b) 失礼ですが、視界をさえぎっているから、結婚式が見えないです。

Excuse my rudeness, but you are blocking my field of vision, and I can't see the wedding.

失礼:　1．しつれい　2．しつれ　3．しっれい　4．しっれ

視界:　1．しっかい　2．しゃっかい　3．しかい　4．しゃかい

結婚式:　1．けっこんじき　2．けつこんじき　3．けっこんしき　4．けつこんしき

c)「お世話になりました。少なくて申し訳ないですが、礼金を受(う)け取(と)ってください。」

"Thanks for everything. I'm afraid it's not much, but please accept this reward (for your efforts)."

世話:　1．よわ　2．ようわ　3．せわ　4．せいわ

申し訳:　1．もしわけ　2．もうしわけ　3．しんしわけ　4．じんしわけ

礼金:　1．しゃきん　2．じゃきん　3．れいきん　4．れきん

3. Write the kanji (one or more) and the meaning of the following words.

しんわ　______ ______　がっかい　______ ______

ふく　______ ______　はなみず　______ ______

せいき　______ ______　はなばたけ　______ ______

4. Correct either the reading or the writing mistakes in the following words.

質門　しつもん　開問　かいもん　開らく　ひらく

和代　わしき　憾激　かんげき　社風　かみかぜ

Answers to exercises 練習解答

1. (Check them in the corresponding kanji table: #421, #423, #427, and #428)

2. a) 神社: 4 | 幸福: 2 | 世界: 3 / b) 失礼: 1 | 視界: 3 | 結婚式: 3
c) 世話: 3 | 申し訳: 2 | 礼金: 3

3. しんわ: 神話, myth | ふく: 福, happiness, fortune | せいき: 世紀, century | がっかい: 学界, academic world | はなみず: 鼻水, runny nose | はなばたけ: 花畑, flower garden

4. 質問 しつもん | 開門 かいもん | 開~~ら~~く ひらく | 和式 わしき | 感激 かんげき | 神風 かみかぜ

Manga translation マンガ翻訳

Priest: Silence! The ceremony is about to start!

Priest: O great god Tsururu, ruler of the world! We have already offered you five pheasants; please bless our vineyard with the sun of fortune!

Faithful follower 1: Oh! I feel something is coming!

Faithful follower 2: It's the power of our god Tsururu!

Faithful follower 3: We are eternally grateful, lord!

Background sound: rumble rumble

Priest: O Lord, why do you ignore us?

Faithful follower 4: I-is this some kind of reprimand?

Rain: splash

Text panel: An hour earlier, somewhere else...

Priest 2: O great god Tsururu, ruler of the world! We have already offered you ten pheasants; please bless our rice fields with the rain of fortune!

New elements 新しい部首

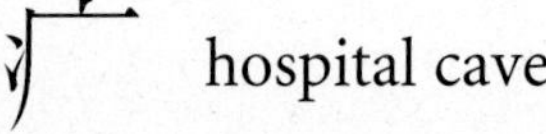
广 hospital cave

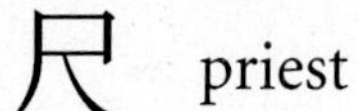
尺 priest

歹 moon pendant

州 land between rivers

Lesson 38
第三十八課

429 (2級)

ILLNESS

病

ビョウ

病気(びょうき) illness
病院(びょういん) hospital
病死(びょうし) death from illness
病人(びょうにん) sick person
病室(びょうしつ) sickroom

や(む/まい)

病(や)む to get sick
病(や)み付(つ)く to be addicted to
病(やまい) illness

(10 strokes)

注 医 (281) 疾 (Jōyō) 疲 (Jōyō)

学 The first public cave was the hospital cave, where *illness* was fought against, and where Kim is unwilling to go inside.

特

430 (2級)

TEETH

歯

シ

歯科(しか) dentistry
義歯(ぎし) false tooth
抜歯(ばっし) extraction of a tooth

は

歯(は) tooth
奥歯(おくば) molar
虫歯(むしば) decayed tooth, cavity
歯医者(はいしゃ) dentist
歯(は)ブラシ toothbrush
歯車(はぐるま) cogwheel

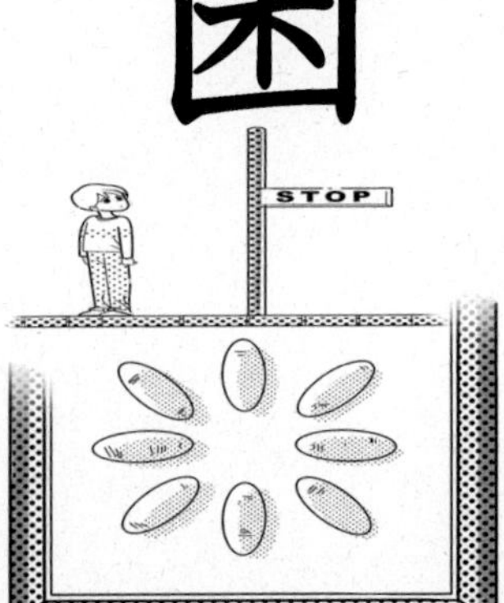

(12 strokes)

注 奥 (Jōyō) 歩 (88)

学 When your *teeth* say stop, you had better put the rest of your rice in a picture because you won't be able to eat it.

特 齒 (ant)

431 PAINFUL, BITTER, SUFFERING

苦

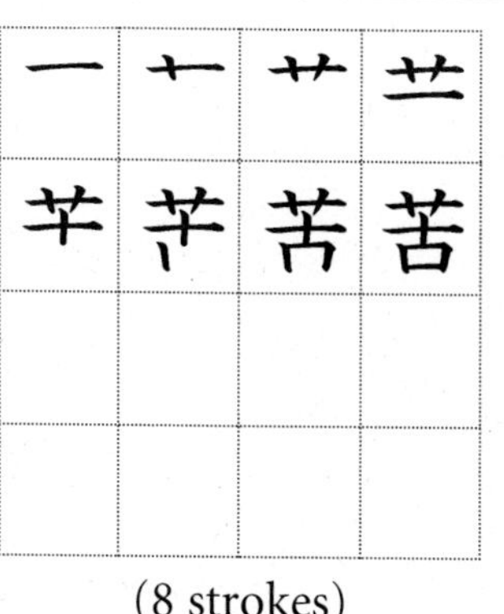

(8 strokes)

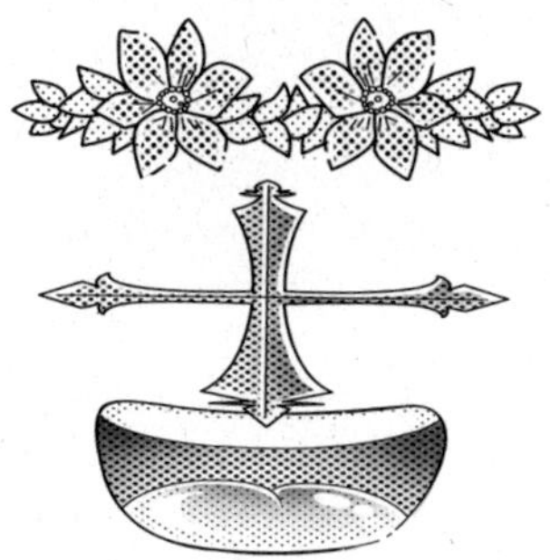

(2級)

ク

苦痛(くつう) pain
苦労(くろう) hardship
苦学生(くがくせい) poor student

くる(しい/しむ/しめる)

苦(くる)しい painful
苦(くる)しむ to suffer

にが(い/る)

苦(にが)い bitter
苦手(にがて) not good at / with

特 苦 (alt)

学 Even a crown of flowers can be the cause of *suffering* for the old man who carries it.

注 若 (6th)
舌 (5th)

432 TO FALL, TO DROP

落

(12 strokes)

(2級)

ラク

落雷(らくらい) falling of a thunderbolt
落下(らっか)する to fall, to descend
低落(ていらく) fall, decline
落語(らくご) rakugo (comedic Japanese) monologue

お(ちる/とす)

落(お)ちる to fall
落(お)とす to drop, to lose
落(お)ち葉(ば) fallen leaves

学 The crown of flowers *has fallen* into the water; but the swimmer has dived in, and he's coming back with it in his mouth.

注 漢 (Jōyō)

433 (2級)

LEAF (TREE OR PAPER)

葉

ヨウ

- 紅葉（こうよう） red leaves
- 落葉（らくよう） fallen leaf
- 前頭葉（ぜんとうよう） frontal lobe (of the brain)

は

- 葉（は） / 葉っぱ（はっぱ） leaf
- 松葉（まつば） pine needle
- 葉書き（はがき） postcard

Special

- 紅葉（もみじ） red leaves

(12 strokes)

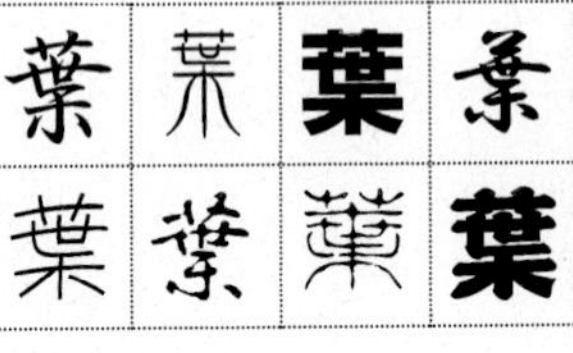

注 集 (250)
某 (Jōyō)
薬 (434)

学 To make a good crown of flowers, you will need to wait for the right world to adorn it with the *leaves* of a tree.

特

434 (3級)

MEDICINE, PHARMACY

薬

ヤク

- 薬局（やっきょく） pharmacy
- 薬草（やくそう） medicinal herb
- 薬品（やくひん） medicine
- 麻薬（まやく） drug
- 麻酔薬（ますいやく） anesthesia
- 火薬（かやく） gunpowder

くすり

- 薬（くすり） medicine
- 風邪薬（かぜぐすり） medicine for a cold

(16 strokes)

注 楽 (144)
葉 (433)

学 Flowers and music are simple *medicine* for the soul.

特  (ant)

435 LOAD, BAGGAGE

(2級)

一 十 艹 艹 芢 芢 荷 荷 荷 荷

(10 strokes)

カ

- 荷重（かじゅう） load
- 集荷（しゅうか） collection of cargo
- 電荷（でんか） electrical charge
- 負荷（ふか） burden, worry
- 入荷（にゅうか） arrival of new goods

に

- 荷物（にもつ） baggage
- 荷造り（にづくり） to pack
- 重荷（おもに） heavy burden

 What nicer *load* to carry than a crown of flowers?

 花 (70)
司 (Jōyō)

436 HUSBAND, WORKER

(2級)

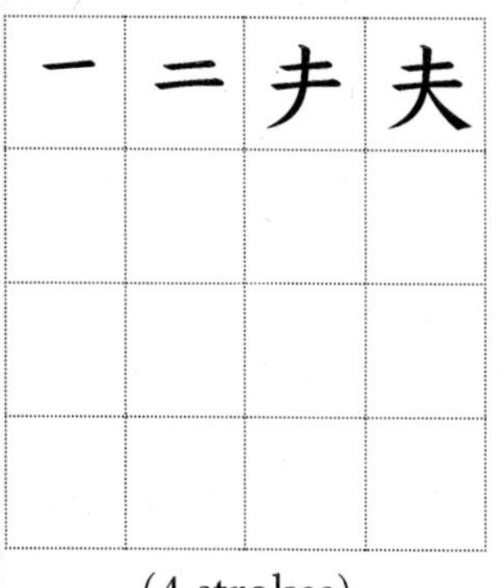

一 二 ナ 夫

(4 strokes)

夫

フ

- 夫妻（ふさい） husband and wife
- 夫人（ふじん） Mrs...
- 大丈夫（だいじょうぶ） all right, OK
- 農夫（のうふ） farmer

フウ

- 夫婦（ふうふ） married couple
- 工夫（くふう） ingenuity, invention / device / contraption

おっと

- 夫（おっと） husband

 They say behind every great husband, there's always an even greater wife.

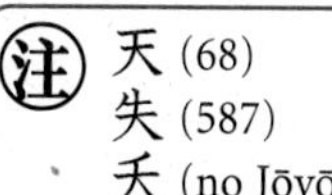
天 (68)
失 (587)
夭 (no Jōyō)

437 (4級)

STATION

駅

エキ

- 駅(えき) station
- 駅前(えきまえ) in front of the station
- 駅長(えきちょう) stationmaster
- 各駅(かくえき) every station
- 駅員(えきいん) station employee
- 駅弁(えきべん) box lunch sold at stations and on trains
- 大江駅(おおええき) Ōe station

(14 strokes)

駅	駅	駅	駅
駅	駅	駅	駅

注 験 (496)
訳 (6th)
駆 (Jōyō)

学 In front of the *station*, the horse of the priest is tied up.

特 驛 (ant)

438 (3級)

PLACE, OFFICE

ショ

- 場所(ばしょ) place
- 住所(じゅうしょ) address
- 名所(めいしょ) famous place
- 便所(べんじょ) toilet
- 近所(きんじょ) neighborhood

ところ

- 所(ところ) place, spot
- 所構わず(ところかまわず) anywhere
- 台所(だいどころ) kitchen

(8 strokes)

所	所	所	所
所	所	所	所

注 祈 (Jōyō)
匠 (Jōyō)
哲 (Jōyō)

The *office* is a place where you can't go through the door without having done some ironing.

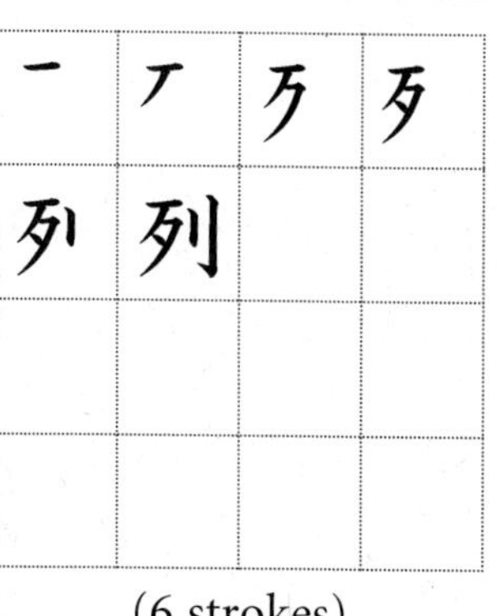

(6 strokes)

列 列 列 列
列 列 列 列

LINE, ARRANGEMENT

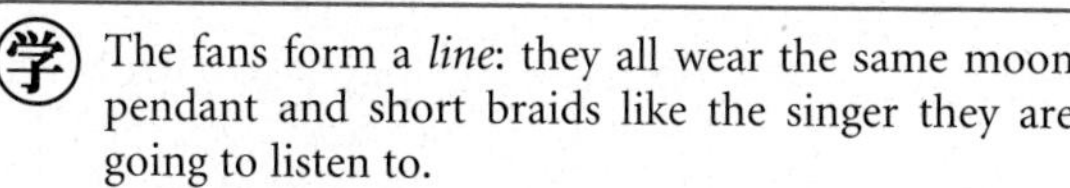

(2級) **439**

レツ

- 列 (れつ) row, line
- 行列 (ぎょうれつ) line, queue
- 系列 (けいれつ) series, association
- 列島 (れっとう) archipelago
- 列車 (れっしゃ) train, train cars
- 陳列する (ちんれつ) to lay out

特

学 The fans form a *line*: they all wear the same moon pendant and short braids like the singer they are going to listen to.

注 外 (128)
例 (452)

丶 丿 少 州
州 州

(6 strokes)

州 州 州 州
州 州 州 州

PROVINCE, STATE, SANDBANK

州

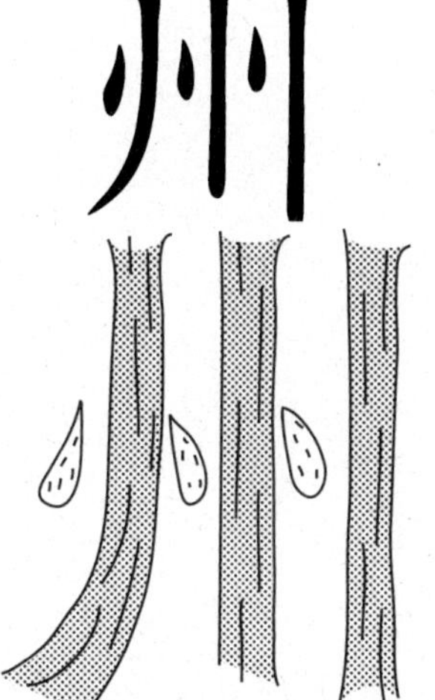

(2級) **440**

シュウ

- 州都 (しゅうと) state capital
- 本州 (ほんしゅう) Honshū island
- ミネソタ州 (しゅう) state of Minnesota
- 豪州 (ごうしゅう) Australia

す

- 三角州 (さんかくす) delta (of a river)
- 砂州 (さす) sandbank

 In the old times, the *states* were nothing but the land between rivers.

 川 (51)
巡 (Jōyō)

やはり、虫歯です。抜歯するほかありません。
んげげ…
だ…だめ!!絶対だめぇー!!
どうもすみません。夫は病院や歯医者さんが苦手なのです。
ちょっと！ その虫歯は葉のように自然に落ちないでしょ！
じゃ、麻酔薬を使わないから、これからは少しいたくなるかもしれません…
あっ!! いなくなった！
?
とりあえず、場所をかえたほうがいい。
間もなく、アーカンソー州行きの列車が駅にまいります。
ああ!! 荷物が…!!
だ…大丈夫ですか？
ラ…ラッキー………

Exercises 練習

1. Develop the stroke order of the following kanji.

病												
歯												
薬												
州												

2. Choose the correct reading for each kanji or kanji combination.

a) 病人が行列して待っていたから、先生は苦痛のひどい人を先にみてあげていた。

With so many sick people in the line, the doctor first saw those who suffered the most pain.

病人:	1．びょにん	2．びょんいん	3．びょうにん	4．びょんにん
行列:	1．ぎょれつ	2．ぎょうれつ	3．こうれつ	4．くれつ
苦痛:	1．くるつ	2．くるつう	3．くつ	4．くつう

b) 秋田(あきた)婦人が駅前の薬局で夫の薬を買いました。

Mrs. Akita bought the medicines for her husband at the pharmacy in front of the station.

婦人:	1．ふにん	2．ふうにん	3．ふじん	4．ふうじん
駅前:	1．えきせん	2．えきぜん	3．えきまえ	4．えきめ
薬局:	1．くすりきょく	2．くすりや	3．やきょく	4．やっきょく

c)「京都の紅葉を見に来ちゃったよ」という葉書が届(とど)きました。いいな…

A postcard arrived for me saying, "I've come to see the red leaves in Kyoto." Lucky you...

紅葉:	1．こよ	2．こうよう	3．もみよう	4．もみじ
葉書:	1．はしょ	2．はしょう	3．はがき	4．はかき

. Write the kanji (one or more) and the meaning of the following words.

びょうき ______ ______ にもつ ______ ______

むしば ______ ______ えきちょう ______ ______

にがて ______ ______ だいどころ ______ ______

. Correct either the reading or the writing mistakes in the following words.

病院	びょうにん	古しむ	くるしむ	川都	しゅうと
歯医者	いはしゃ	場所	ばしょう	古学生	くがくせい
落す	おとす	列島	れつとう	各語	らくご

Answers to exercises 練習解答

1. (Check them in the corresponding kanji table: #429, #430, #433, and #440)

2. a) 病人: 3 | 行列: 2 | 苦痛: 4 / b) 婦人: 3 |駅前: 3 | 薬局: 4 / c) 紅葉: 2 y 4 |葉書: 3

3. びょうき: 病気, illness | むしば: 虫歯, cavity | にがて: 苦手, not good at | にもつ: 荷物, baggage | えきちょう: 駅長, stationmaster | だいどころ: 台所, kitchen.

4. 病院 びょういん (o 病人 びょうにん) | 苦しむ くるしむ | 州都 しゅうと | 歯医者 はいしゃ | 場所 ばしょ~~う~~ | 苦学生 くがくせい | 落とす おとす | 列島 れっとう | 落語 らくご

Manga translation マンガ翻訳

Dentist: Just as I thought, it's a cavity. I must extract it.

Patient: Uggh...

Patient: N-no, you won´t! Absolutely not!

Patient´s wife: Excuse my husband; he doesn't do well with hospitals and dentists.

Wife: That's enough! You can't expect the tooth to fall out on its own, like the leaf of a tree, can you?!

Dentist: Well... This might hurt a little, because I won´t use anesthesia...

Dentist: Oh! He's disappeared!

Patient: For the time being, the best thing will be to emigrate...

Loudspeaker: Shortly, the train bound for Arkansas will enter the station.

Passenger: Oh, no! Damn suitcase!

Blow: baaang

Passenger: A-are you OK?

Patient: T-that was lucky...

Review of Grade 3

小学校三年生まとめ問題

Review of Grade 3 三年生・まとめ問題

1. Link the kanji with their corresponding *kun'yomi* and *on'yomi* readings.

1.	よこ	勝	シン
2.	の(む)	係	コン
3.	ね	決	トウ
4.	なみ	島	シン
5.	ととの(える)	進	セイ
6.	たび	深	リョ
7.	ふか(い)	旅	オウ
8.	すす(む)	整	ケイ
9.	しま	波	ショウ
10.	き(める)	根	ケツ
11.	かか(わる)	飲	ハ
12.	か(つ)	横	イン

2. Write the missing kanji in the following text.

何で______(やくしゃ)になったのかね... 本当はあこがれじゃなかった。______(りょうしん)は______(のうぎょう)の______(しごと)をしていて、____(ひつじ)を____(はじ)め、______(どうぶつ)がいっぱいいる村で____(そだ)った。小さいころに好きだったのは______(やきゅう)と______(すいえい)だけ。そして、家の近くに____(ふか)い____(みずうみ)があったので、プロになるために一所懸(いっしょけん)____(めい) ______(すいえい)の______(れんしゅう)をした。

Why did I become an actor? The truth is that it wasn't my greatest ambition. My parents worked on a farm and I grew up in a village where, starting with sheep, there were animals of all kinds. The only things I liked a a kid were baseball and swimming. And, since there was a deep lake near our house, I used to train with deter mination to become a swimmer.

ある日、______(かぞく)で________(たいへいよう)へ行って、____(およ)いでみました。____(なみ)になれていなかった僕(ぼく)は、なぜか怖(こわ)くなって____(うご)けなくなった。____(はな)から____(ち)が出はじめて、気を失(うしな)った。______(びょういん)は遠かったから、______(あんぜん)な____(ところ)まで____(はこ)ばれて、______(いしゃ)にチェックされたけど、あれからお父さんは______(すいえい)に______(はんたい)した。そして、僕も______(しんぱい)させてはいけないと思って、______(やくしゃ)のことを考え____(はじ)めた。

One day, I went with my family to the Pacific Ocean, and I tried to swim. But I wasn't used to the waves, an somehow I got frightened and I couldn't move. I had a nosebleed and I lost consciousness. The hospital was fa away, so they took me to a safe place, and a doctor came. Since then, my father was opposed to swimming. An not wanting to worry him, I began to think about becoming an actor.

3. Choose the correct reading for each kanji or kanji combination.

a) 本の第三章を書き終わってから、居酒屋で枝豆を食べながらワイワイしよう。
When I finish the third chapter of the book, we will celebrate it by eating edamame at the pub.

第三章:	1．ださんしょう	2．だいさんしょ	3．ださんしょ	4．だいさんしょう
終:	1．おわ	2．お	3．しゅう	4．しゅ
居酒屋:	1．いさけや	2．いざけや	3．いざかや	4．いさかや
枝豆:	1．えだまめ	2．えだず	3．えだとう	4．えとう

b) 美人だからこそ、注意した方がいい。世界には悪い人もいるんだから。
Precisely because you are beautiful, you should be careful. There are bad people in the world.

美人:	1．びじにん	2．びじん	3．うつじん	4．うつくじん
注意:	1．ちゅうい	2．ちゅい	3．ちゅいい	4．ちゅいう
世界:	1．よかい	2．せいかい	3．せかい	4．かいせい

c) 荷物が発送されたのは昨日(きのう)ですが、受取はまだです。
The baggage was sent yesterday, but it hasn't been picked up yet.

荷物:	1．かもの	2．かもつ	3．にもの	4．にもつ
発送:	1．はつそう	2．はっそう	3．はつおく	4．はおく
受取:	1．じゅうじゅ	2．じゅうじゅ	3．うけとり	4．うけと

4. Choose the correct kanji for each reading.

a) おきゃくさまのよさん しだいで、買えるしょうひんが違(ちが)うんですよ。
Depending on the client's budget, the product he can buy will change.

きゃくさま:	1．各様	2．宮様	3．古様	4．客様
よさん:	1．予算	2．矛算	3．代算	4．子算
しだい:	1．飲第	2．次第	3．飲弟	4．次弟
しょうひん:	1．南品	2．商品	3．西品	4．産品

b) たんきですが、とざんしたことがある。そうだんにのってほしいなら...
It was for a short period, but I have done some climbing. If I can give you any advice...

たんき:	1．知期	2．短期	3．豆期	4．学期
とざん:	1．発出	2．登山	3．登出	4．発山
そうだん:	1．想談	2．想炎	3．相談	4．相炎
のって:	1．載って	2．乗って	3．重って	4．動って

c) 宮沢賢治(みやざわけんじ)の有名な「銀河てつどう」を知らない? 彼(かれ)はしとどうわも書いていた。
Don't you know the famous "Night Train to the Milky Way" by Kenji Miyazawa? He also wrote poetry and children's stories.

てつどう:	1．矢道	2．失道	3．族道	4．鉄道
し:	1．寺	2．詩	3．持	4．待
どうわ:	1．童話	2．章話	3．童和	4．章和

Answers to exercises 練習解答

1.

か(つ)	勝	ショウ
かか(わる)	係	ケイ
き(める)	決	ケツ
しま	島	トウ
すす(む)	進	シン
ふか(い)	深	シン
たび	旅	リョ
ととの(える)	整	セイ
なみ	波	ハ
ね	根	コン
の(む)	飲	イン
よこ	横	オウ

2. 何で役者になったのかね... 本当はあこがれじゃなかった。両親は農業の仕事をしていて、羊を始め、動物がいっぱいいる村で育った。小さいころに好きだったのは野球と水泳だけ。そして、家の近くに深い湖があったので、プロになるために一所懸命水泳の練習をした。

ある日、家族で太平洋へ行って、泳いでみました。波になれていなかった僕は、なぜか怖くなって動けなくなった。鼻から血が出はじめて、気を失った。病院は遠かったから、安全な所まで運ばれて、医者にチェックされたけど、あれからお父さんは水泳に反対した。そして、僕も心配させてはいけないと思って、役者のことを考え始めた。

3. a) 第三章: 4 | 終: 2 | 居酒屋: 3| 枝豆: 1
b) 美人: 2 | 注意: 1 | 世界: 3
c) 荷物: 4| 発送: 2| 受取: 3

4. a) きゃくさま: 4 | よさん: 1 | しだい: 2 | しょうひん: 2
b) たんき: 2 | とざん: 2 | そうだん: 3 | のって: 2
c) てつどう: 4 | し: 2 | どうわ: 1

New elements 新しい部首

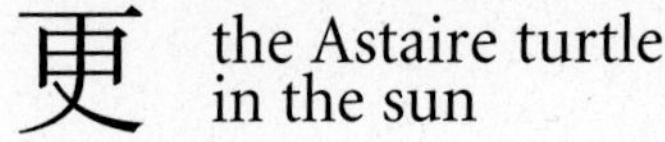

Lesson 39
第三十九課

441 (2級)

TO STICK TO, TO ATTACH

フ

- 付録（ふろく） supplement, appendix
- 付着（ふちゃく）する to stick to
- 寄付（きふ） donation
- 付近（ふきん） neighborhood

つ（く/ける）

- 付（つ）く to attach, to stick to
- 着付（きつ）けする to get dressed
- 気（き）を付（つ）ける to be careful
- 元気付（げんきづ）く to cheer up

ノ	イ	仁	付
付			

(5 strokes)

注 村 (64)
侍 (Jōyō)

Kim is a special being because aliens *stick* to him.

442 (2級)

GOVERNMENT, PREFECTURE

フ

- 政府（せいふ） government
- 幕府（ばくふ） bakufu, shogunate
- 府立（ふりつ） prefecture
- 府警（ふけい） prefectural police
- 京都府（きょうとふ） Kyoto prefecture

丶	亠	广	广
广	庁	府	府

(8 strokes)

府	府	府	府
府	府	府	府

注 庁 (6th)
店 (222)
守 (402)

The *government* is like a cave: a place where its inhabitants feel stuck to one to another.

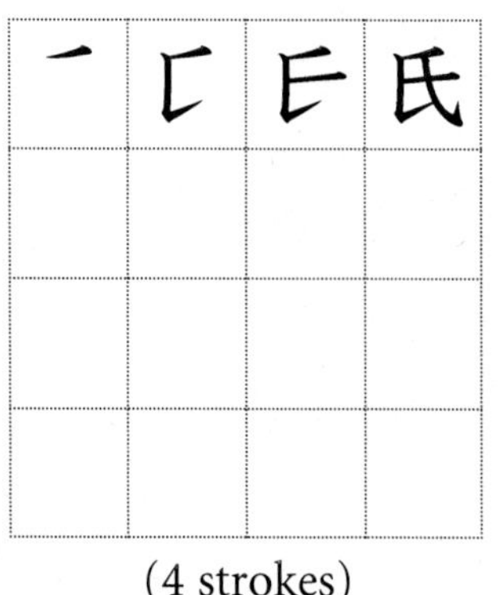

(4 strokes)

MR., CLAN

(1級)

443

シ

スミス氏(し) Mr. Smith
某氏(ぼうし) a certain person
氏名(しめい) full name
彼氏(かれし) boyfriend
源氏(げんじ) the Genji (the Minamoto clan)

うじ

氏(うじ) clan
氏神(うじがみ) clan deity

 A certain *Mr.* X needs a manuscript to certify that he is the boss of his own *clan*.

 民 (514)
代 (257)

(8 strokes)

BOTTOM, BASIS

(2級)

444

テイ

海底(かいてい) bottom of the sea
心底(しんてい) bottom of one's heart
基底(きてい) basis, foundation

そこ

底(そこ) bottom
底値(そこね) lowest price
どん底(ぞこ) slum
厚底靴(あつぞこぐつ) platform shoes

 At the *bottom* end of the cave, the manuscript you are looking for and a slice of bread are waiting for you.

 庭 (366)
座 (6th)

445 (3級)

LOW

テイ

- 低空(ていくう) low altitude
- 低温(ていおん) low temperature
- 最低(さいてい) the lowest, despicable
- 低下(ていか)する to go down, to fall
- 低価(ていか) low price
- 低血圧(ていけつあつ) low blood pressure

ひく(い)

- 低(ひく)い low
- 背(せ)が低(ひく)い low (body height)

ノ 亻 亻 仛 仾 低 低

(7 strokes)

低 低 低 低 低 低 低 低

 底 (444) 供 (6th) 依 (Jōyō)

 Kim has fallen very *low*: he has stolen the manuscript and the bread.

446 (2級)

MEDIATOR, RELATIONSHIP

なか

- 仲(なか)がいい to get along well
- 仲(なか)が悪(わる)い to be on bad terms
- 仲間(なかま) friend, mate, peer
- 仲直(なかなお)りする to reconcile
- 恋仲(こいなか) love relationship
- 仲居(なかい) ryokan maid

Special

- 仲人(なこうど) matchmaker

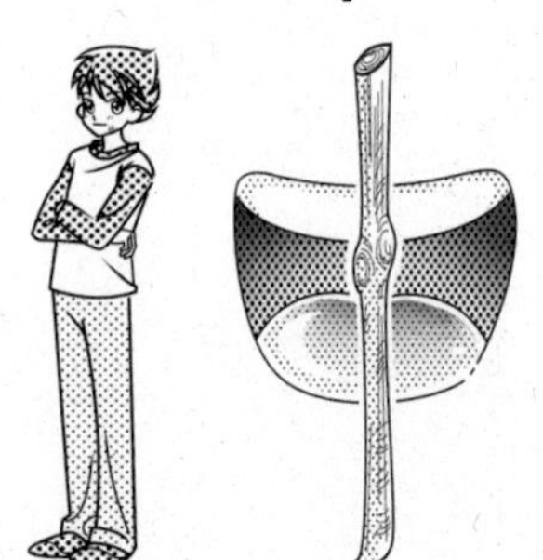

ノ 亻 亻 仲 仲 仲

(6 strokes)

仲 仲 仲 仲 仲 仲 仲 仲

 伸 (Jōyō) 仏 (5th) 使 (258)

 Kim is a born *mediator*: he studies the problem inside and out.

ノ 亻 仁 伝
伝 伝

(6 strokes)

TO TRANSMIT

(2級)

447

デン

伝達(でんたつ)する to transmit
伝染(でんせん) infection, contagion
伝統(でんとう) tradition
宣伝(せんでん) advertising
遺伝子(いでんし) genes
伝説(でんせつ) legend

つた(える/わる)

伝(つた)える to transmit
言(い)い伝(つた)え legend, myth

傳 (ant)

Kim *transmits* happiness when he has stuffed himself with food.

位 (448)
信 (449)
転 (370)

ノ 亻 亻 仁
什 竹 位

(7 strokes)

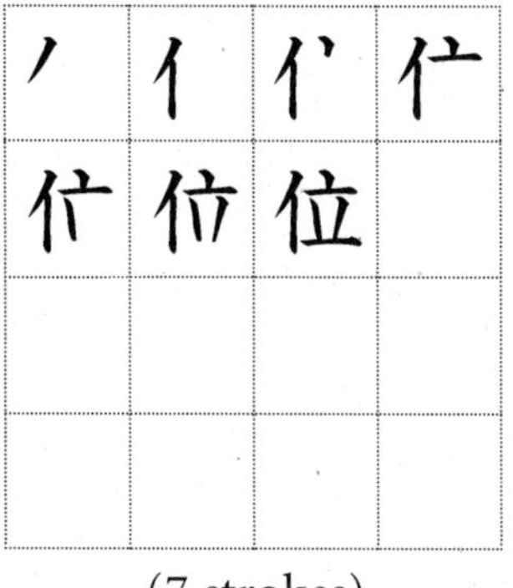

RANK, APPROXIMATION

(2級)

448

イ

一位(いちい) the first place
首位(しゅい) leading position
地位(ちい) position, rank
順位(じゅんい) order, ranking
学位(がくい) academic degree
位置(いち) position
水位(すいい) water level

くらい

二分位(にふんぐらい) about two minutes

Kim (the hero) and the vulture (the proud one) are the highest-*ranking* characters in this book.

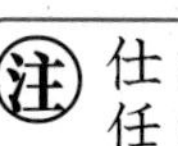
仕 (255)
任 (5th)
件 (5th)

449 (2級)

TRUST

シン

- 信頼（しんらい） to trust someone
- 自信（じしん） self-confidence
- 確信（かくしん） firm conviction
- 信者（しんじゃ） believer
- 信号（しんごう） signal (e.g., traffic)
- 通信（つうしん） communication
- 返信（へんしん） answer

しん(じる)

- 信（しん）じる to believe in, to trust

(9 strokes)

信	信	信	信
信	信	信	信

 伝 (447)
計 (6th)

 Kim *trusts* words and speaks up to obtain what he wants.

450 (3級)

TO BORROW, TO GET A LOAN

借

シャク

- 借金（しゃっきん） debt
- 借用（しゃくよう） loan
- 拝借（はいしゃく）する to borrow
- 借家（しゃくや） rented house

か(りる)

- 借（か）りる to borrow
- 借（か）りを返（かえ）す to return a favor

(10 strokes)

借	借	借	借
借	借	借	借

 倍 (260)
僧 (Jōyō)
価 (5th)

 Kim had *to get a loan*, because he lazed around so much in the past.

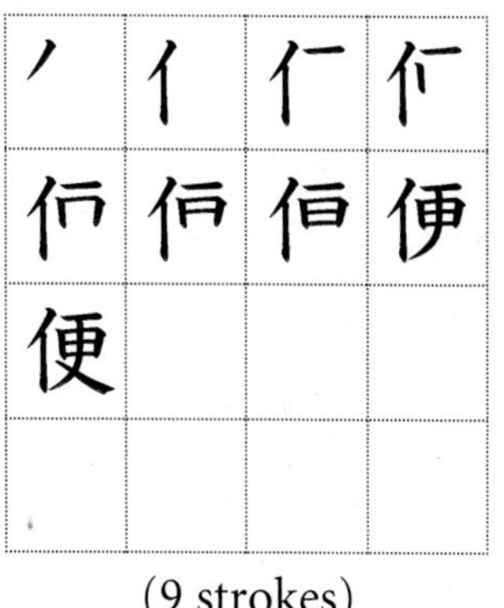

(9 strokes)

CONVENIENT, MAIL, FECES

(3級)

451

ベン

便利（べんり） practical, convenient
不便（ふべん） uncomfortable
便所（べんじょ） toilet
小便（しょうべん） urine
大便（だいべん） feces

ビン

郵便（ゆうびん） mail
郵便局（ゆうびんきょく） post office
航空便（こうくうびん） air mail

便 (alt)

Taking a look at the Astaire turtle in the sun would be very *convenient* for Kim; it's more practical than studying a *mail* correspondence course.

使 (258)
更 (Jōyō)

(8 strokes)

EXAMPLE

(2級)

452

レイ

例（れい） example
例文（れいぶん） example sentence
実例（じつれい） practical example
例外（れいがい） exception
恒例（こうれい） established custom
条例（じょうれい） rules, regulations

たと(える)

例（たと）える to give examples of
例（たと）えば for example

An *example* of Kim's feminine side is his obsession with putting on moon pendants and braiding his hair when nobody is looking.

列 (439)
倒 (Jōyō)

ラーメン
いらっしゃい…
あっ！
君らは…！
おい、
じじい！
例の金、
どこだ？
あ、あっ、
「保護の料金」
っすね？
まだないんだけど、
もうすぐ払うさ！
信じてくれ！
何言ってんだ？
政府の収税官に
みえるか？
自分の位置、
わかる⁉
石を付けて、
川の底まで潜って
みたいか、
じじい⁉？
なんでふるえている？小便したく
なったかな
へへへ？
そこまでだ‼
や…やめて
ください…
おお！
正義の
仲間、
伝説の
六反田氏
だ‼
ちょっと背が
低いけどな…
あの…お金を
借りてもいい？

Exercises 練習

1. Develop the stroke order of the following kanji.

底												
借												
使												
例												

2. Choose the correct reading for each kanji or kanji combination.

a) 地位の高い人は信頼できないよ。気を付けた方がいいと思う。

You can't trust people with a high social position. You had better be careful.

地位:	1. しい	2. ちい	3. じい	4. ぢい
信頼:	1. しんらい	2. じんらい	3. しんじらい	4. じんしらい
気を付けた:	1. きをつけた	2. きをすけた	3. きをふけた	4. きをぶけた

b) 彼氏と仲直りって？できないよ。あの人は最低だよ。

Reconcile myself with my boyfriend? I can't do that. He is the worst kind of man.

彼氏:	1. かるじ	2. かれうじ	3. かれし	4. かれうし
仲直り:	1. かななおり	2. かなのり	3. なかのり	4. なかなおり
最低:	1. さいてぃ	2. さいてい	3. さいし	4. さいじ

c) ここに来てから、仲間との伝達手段(しゅだん)は郵便だけだ。

Since I arrived, the only way I can transmit information to my friends is by mail.

仲間:	1. かなもん	2. かなま	3. なかもん	4. なかま
伝達:	1. つたつ	2. つたたつ	3. でんたつ	4. てんたつ
郵便:	1. ゆうべん	2. ゆうびん	3. ゆうへん	4. ゆうひん

3. Write the kanji (one or more) and the meaning of the following words.

しめい ______ ______ しゃっきん ______ ______

かいてい ______ ______ しょうべん ______ ______

じしん ______ ______ れいがい ______ ______

4. Correct either the reading or the writing mistakes in the following words.

政府	せいふう	伝統	つたとう	借る	かりる
厚低	あつぞこ	遺伝子	いてんし	京都付	きょうとふ

Answers to exercises 練習解答

1. (Check them in the corresponding kanji table: #444, #450, #451, and #452)

2. a) 地位: 2 | 信頼: 1 | 気を付けた: 1 / b) 彼氏: 3 | 仲直り: 4 | 最低: 2
c) 仲間: 4 | 伝達: 3 | 郵便: 2

3. しめい: 氏名, full name | かいてい: 海底, bottom of the sea | じしん: 自身, self-confidence | しゃっきん: 借金, debt | しょうべん: 小便, urine | れいがい: 例外, exception

4. 政府 せいふ~~う~~ | 伝統 でんとう | 借りる かりる | 厚底 あつぞこ | 遺伝子 いでんし | 京都府 きょうとふ

Manga translation マンガ翻訳

Sign: Ramen (noodles with soup)

Owner: Welco... Oh! It's you!

Thug 1: Hey, man, where's the money for you-know-what?

Owner: Oh, the protection fee, right? I don't have it yet, but I'll pay very soon, trust me.

Thug 1: What was that? Do we look like government money-collectors? Don't you understand the situation you are in?!

Thug 2: Do you want to sink to the bottom of the river, fastened to a rock, old man?

Thug 3: Why are you trembling? Are you dying for a piss or what? He, he, he.

Owner: L-leave me alone, please.

Voice (OFF): That's enough!

Owner (OFF): Oh! It's Mr. Rokutanda, the legendary companion of justice!

Owner: ...A pity he's so short.

Owner: Excuse me, could I borrow some money from you?

New elements 新しい部首

mark 

Lesson 40
第四十課

453 (2級)

SIDE, PART

側

ソク

- 側面（そくめん） lateral side
- 側壁（そくへき） side wall

そば

- 側（そば） beside (proximity)

がわ

- 北側（きたがわ） north side
- 両側（りょうがわ） both sides
- 内側（うちがわ） inside
- 政府側（せいふがわ） government side

(11 strokes)

側	側	側	側
側	側	側	側

 則 (5th)
測 (5th)

 Kim will let you be by his *side* on two conditions: you must like seashells, and you must braid your hair.

454 (3級)

SEPARATE, DIFFERENT

ベツ

- 別々（べつべつ） separately
- 別に（べつ） nothing particular
- 別冊（べっさつ） separate volume
- 差別（さべつ） discrimination
- 分別（ぶんべつ） classification
- 特別（とくべつ） special

わか(れる) / わ(ける)

- 別ける（わ） to separate
- 別れる（わか） to separate from, to bid farewell

(7 strokes)

別	別	別	別
別	別	別	別

 列 (439)
刑 (Jōyō)
剖 (Jōyō)

 This magic lamp is *different*, because it has a mouth, with which it asks for wishes: it wants braids.

(6 strokes)

STAMP, MARK

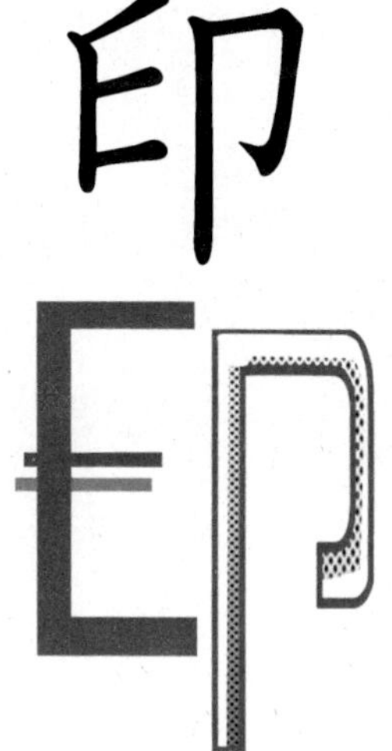

(2級)

455

イン

印刷（いんさつ）する to print
印税（いんぜい） royalties
印鑑（いんかん） seal (to use as signature)
印象（いんしょう） impression
封印（ふういん）する to stamp

しるし

印（しるし） mark, stamp
矢印（やじるし） arrow (graphic sign)
目印（めじるし） sign, visible marker

 The *mark* of the cane is the *stamp* of the crippled murderer.

 以 (510)
犯 (5th)
即 (Jōyō)

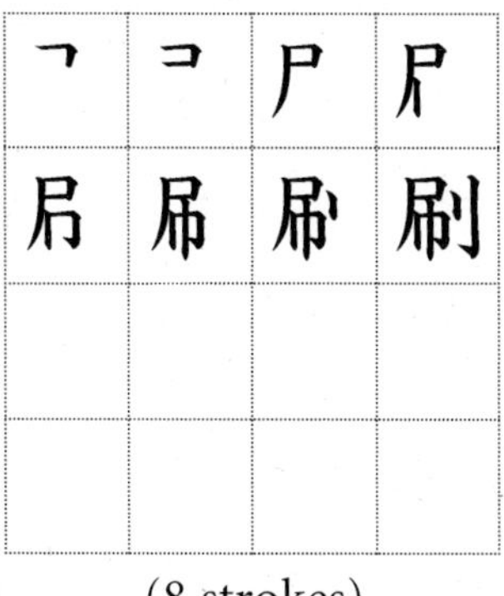

(8 strokes)

TO PRINT

(2級)

456

サツ

印刷（いんさつ）する to print
増刷（ぞうさつ） additional printing

す(る)

刷（す）る to print
刷（す）り上（あ）げる to finish printing
第二刷（だいにず）り second printing

 *Print* in your mind the image of an exploring housewife: the cap, the apron, and the braids.

 制 5th
剤 Jōyō

457

(2級)

VICE-

副

フク

副作用(ふくさよう) aftereffect

副詞(ふくし) adverb

副社長(ふくしゃちょう) vice-director

副大統領(ふくだいとうりょう) vice president (of a country)

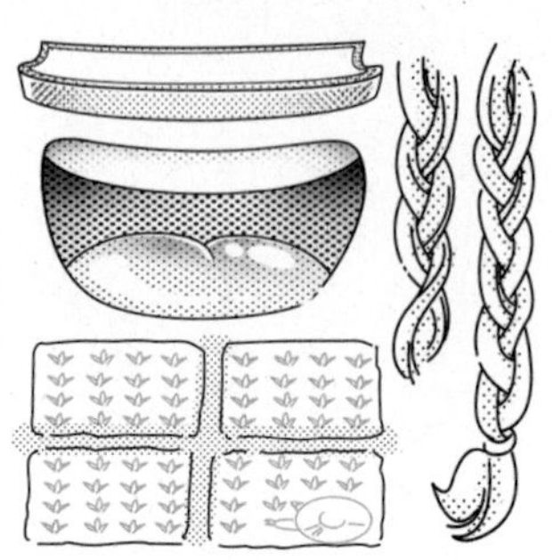

一 丅 丆 百
畐 畐 畐 畐
畐 畐 副

(11 strokes)

注 富 (5th)
福 (420)

学 For the *vice* president, putting bread in the mouths of all her workers in the rice fields is her priority before she does her braids.

特

458

(2級)

BENEFIT, TO FUNCTION (WELL)

利

リ

便利(べんり) convenient, practical

利用(りよう) usage (to use)

権利(けんり) right (to do something)

利子(りし) (bank) interest

利口(りこう) intelligent, smart

勝利(しょうり) victory

き(く)

左利き(ひだりき) left-handed

耳が利く(みみがきく) to be sharp-eared

一 二 千 禾
禾 利 利

(7 strokes)

注 科 (153)
秒 (398)
列 (349)

学 The weeping willow has been given braids with which to hang a swing from its branches for everybody's *benefit.*

特

一	二	千	禾
禾	𥝌	𥝌	秆
秳	秳	秳	種
種	種		

(14 strokes)

種	種	種	種
種	種	種	種

KIND, SPECIES, SEED

種

(2級)

459

シュ

種類（しゅるい） kind (of thing)
種目（しゅもく） item, event
各種（かくしゅ） every kind, various
人種（じんしゅ） (human) race

たね

種（たね） seed
柿（かき）の種（たね） persimmon seeds
種馬（たねうま） stallion, stud
特種（とくだね） scoop

特

学 The weeping willow and the robot get together to plant their seed and perpetuate the *species*.

注 動 (290)
稚 (Jōyō)
積 (460)

一	二	千	禾
禾	𥝌	秆	秆
秸	秸	積	積
積	積	積	積

(16 strokes)

積	積	積	積
積	積	積	積

TO ACCUMULATE, VOLUME

積

(2級)

460

セキ

面積（めんせき） surface
容積（ようせき） capacity, volume
積雪（せきせつ） fallen snow
積極的（せっきょくてき） positively

つ(む/もる)

積（つ）み上（あ）げる to pile up
積（つ）み込（こ）む to load up, to put on board
雪（ゆき）が積（つ）もる snow piles up

特

学 The weeping willow pours such an enormous volume of *accumulated* tears on the plants that even seashells come out.

注 績 (5th)
責 (5th)

副社長、
これが新しい
輪転機です。
書類はどんな種類でも
印刷ができますから、
とても
便利です。
一時間で二万部も印刷できますよ！
しかも、両側で同時に！
ふんん
それなら、
どうして倉庫に
空き箱だけを
積みいれて
いるんだ？
あ、それは
別の課の
関係ですが…
この装置は操作が
ちょ〜っとむずかしい
ので、まだ作動
させることが
できないそうです…

Exercises 練習

1. Develop the stroke order of the following kanji.

別												
印												
刷												
種												

2. Choose the correct reading for each kanji or kanji combination.

a) 1998年の試合(しあい)、私には印象に残(のこ)る特別な勝利でした。

The victory of the 1998 match was a very special one, and left a deep impression on me.

印象: 1．いしょう　2．いんしょう　3．いしょ　4．いんしょう

特別: 1．とくべつ　2．とくぺつ　3．とくわか　4．とくわ

勝利: 1．しょうき　2．しょき　3．しょうきく　4．しょうり

b) 今日は、適切(てきせつ)な住居(じゅうきょ)の権利にかかわる差別について語りたいと思います。

Today, I would like to talk about the discrimination concerning the right to a decent home.

権利: 1．けんき　2．けんきく　3．けんり　4．けり

差別: 1．さわか　2．さべ　3．さわ　4．さべつ

c) 便利な火の利用を発見してから、どの人種も発達し続(つづ)けました。

Since the discovery of the practical use of fire, all races have continued their development.

便利: 1．びんり　2．べんり　3．びんき　4．べんき

利用: 1．きよう　2．きよ　3．りよう　4．きよう

人種: 1．にんしゅ　2．ひとだね　3．ひとたね　4．じんしゅ

3. Write the kanji (one or more) and the meaning of the following words.

きたがわ ______ ________　ふくさよう ______ ________

ぶんべつ ______ ________　たね ______ ________

やじるし ______ ________　めんせき ______ ________

4. Correct either the reading or the writing mistakes in the following words.

則面	そくめん	目印	めしるし	列れる	わかれる
福社長	ふくしゃちょう	左科き	ひだりきき	積極的	せつきょくてき
刷印	いんさつ	種木	しゅもく	積もる	うもる

Answers to exercises 練習解答

1. (Check them in the corresponding kanji table: #454, #455, #456, and #459)

2. a) 印象: 2 | 特別: 1 | 勝利: 4 / b) 権利: 3 | 差別: 4 / c) 人種: 4 | 便利: 2 | 利用: 3

3. きたがわ: 北側, north side | ぶんべつ: 分別, to divide, to classify | やじるし: 矢印, arrow (graphic sign) | ふくさよう: 副作用, aftereffect | たね: 種, seed | めんせき: 面積, surface

4. **側面** そくめん | **目印** めじるし | **別れる** わかれる | **副社長** ふくしゃちょう | **左利き** ひだりきき | **積極的** せっきょくてき | **印刷** いんさつ | **種目** しゅもく | **積もる** つもる

Manga translation マンガ翻訳

Employee: Mr. Vice president, this is the new rotary press.

Employee: It's very convenient, because it allows you to make any kind of document.

Employee: It can print 20,000 copies per hour! Even both sides at the same time!

Vice president: Hmm.

Vice president: I see. Then, why are all those empty boxes piled up in the warehouse?

Employee: Well, that has to do with another section, but...

Employee (OFF): Apparently, this machinery is a little difficult to handle, and they still have not been able to start it.

New elements 新しい部首

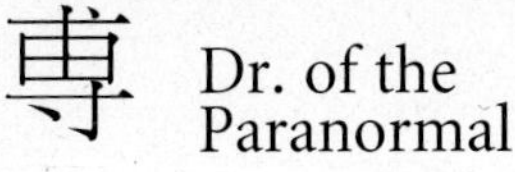

Lesson 41
第四十一課

461 (3級)

TO WORK

働

ドウ

- 労働（ろうどう） work
- 労働者（ろうどうしゃ） laborer
- 協働（きょうどう） cooperation

はたら(く)

- 働く（はたらく） to work
- ただ働き（ただばたらき） to work for nothing
- 共働き（ともばたらき） to work together for a living

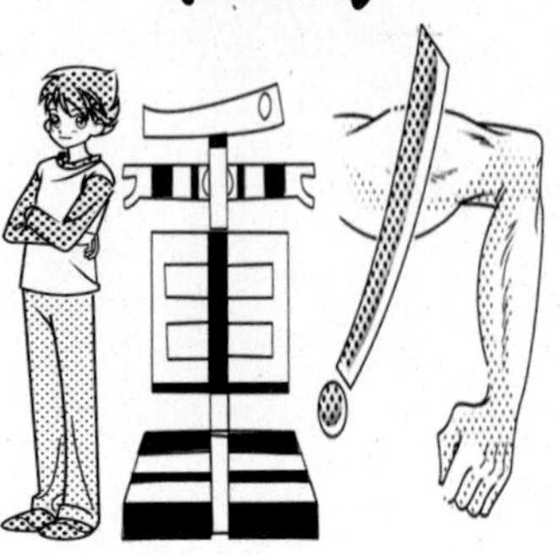

(13 strokes)

 動 (290)

 Kim has hired a robot who is strong to *work* for him.

 伪 (simp)

462 (1級)

RESULT, SUCCESS

コウ

- 成功（せいこう） success, good result
- 功績（こうせき） merits
- 功名（こうみょう） distinguished services
- 戦功（せんこう） distinguished war service

ク

- 功徳（くとく） virtue

(5 strokes)

 加 (463)
切 (94)

 Can you see the iron beam? If you have the strength to raise it, your *success* is guaranteed.

㇆	力	加	加
加			

(5 strokes)

加	加	加	加
加	加	加	加

TO ADD, TO INCREASE

加

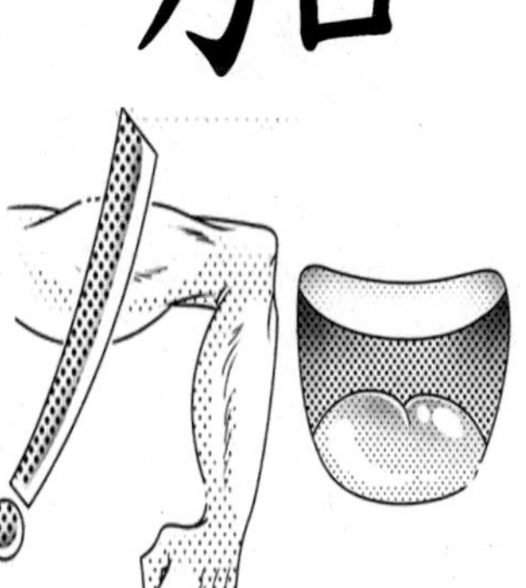

(2級)

463

カ

- 加速(かそく)する to accelerate
- 追加(ついか)する to add on
- 加算(かさん) addition (algebra)
- 参加(さんか)する to join in
- 増加(ぞうか) growth, increase
- いい加減(かげん)にしろ! That's enough! / Behave yourself!

くわ(える/わる)

- 加(くわ)える to add, to include
- 加(くわ)わる to join

 If you use your strong arm to hit someone in the mouth, you'll *add* on another enemy to your list.

 功 (462)
助 (291)

く	女	女	奴
奴	努	努	

(7 strokes)

努	努	努	努
努	努	努	努

EFFORT

努

(2級)

464

ド

- 努力(どりょく) effort
- 努力家(どりょくか) hardworking person

つと(める)

- 努(つと)める to make an effort

 The fruit of *effort* is seen by the woman who makes it to the director's chair through her strength.

 怒 (Jōyō)

465 (2級)

BRAVERY

勇

ユウ

- 勇気（ゆうき） bravery
- 勇者（ゆうしゃ） brave person
- 勇敢（ゆうかん）な valiant, brave
- 勇士（ゆうし） brave warrior

いさ(む/ましい)

- 勇（いさ）ましい brave
- 勇（いさ）む to be brave

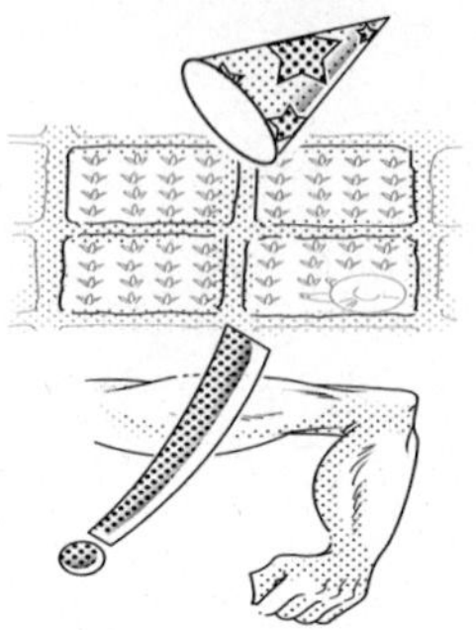

(9 strokes)

注 男 (74)

 A magician is a *brave* man who confronts supernatural beings.

466 (2級)

LABOR, TIREDNESS

労

ロウ

- 労働（ろうどう） work
- 功労（こうろう） distinguished services
- 労力（ろうりょく） effort, work
- 疲労（ひろう） fatigue, tiredness
- 労働組合（ろうどうくみあい） labor union
- 厚生労働省（こうせいろうどうしょう） Ministry of Health, Labor, and Welfare
- 勤労感謝の日（きんろうかんしゃのひ） Labor Thanksgiving Day (November, 23)

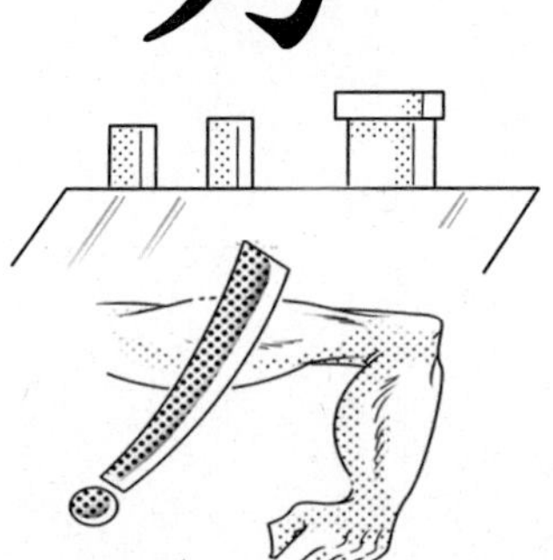

(7 strokes)

 努 (464)
学 (78)

 *Labor* is done under an industrial roof and it requires physical strength.

 労 (ant)

467 協 — COOPERATION

(2級)

(8 strokes)

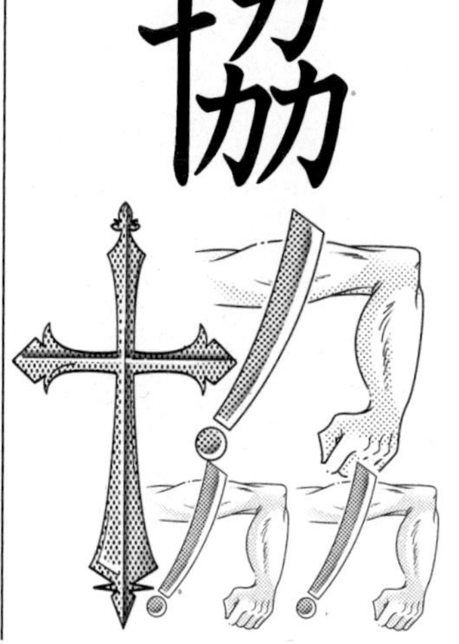

キョウ

- 協力（きょうりょく） collaboration
- 協同（きょうどう） combined effort
- 協会（きょうかい） association, group
- 生協（せいきょう） cooperative, co-op store (for food and goods)
- 協議（きょうぎ） conference
- 協定（きょうてい） treaty, agreement

 协 (simp)

学 The cross guides the union of strengths that are *cooperating* for the same goal.

 脅 (Jōyō)

468 博 — SPECIALIST, EXTENSIVE KNOWLEDGE

(1級)

(12 strokes)

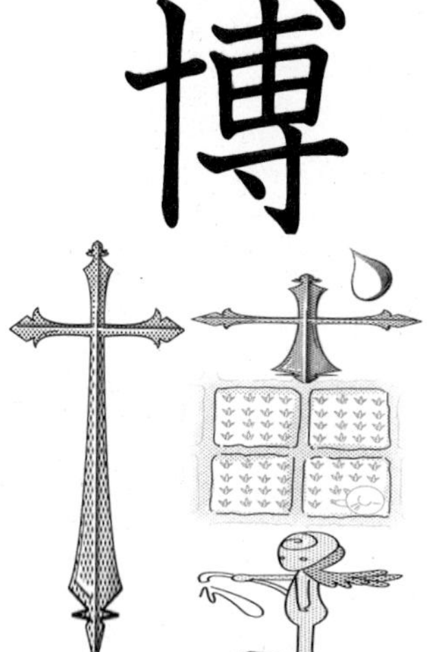

ハク

- 博士（はくし） Ph. D., doctor
- 博物館（はくぶつかん） museum
- 博覧会（はくらんかい） exhibition
- 万博（ばんぱく） World Fair

バク

- 博打（ばくち） gambling, bet
- 博徒（ばくと） gambler

Special

- 博士（はかせ） Ph.D., doctor

 愽 (alt)

 Before the cross, the *Dr.* of the Paranormal proves his theory: crosses are grown by aliens, who water them often.

 専 (Jōyō)
得 (583)

469 (2級)

PROSPERITY

(9 strokes)

エイ

繁栄（はんえい） prosperity
光栄（こうえい） honor
栄光（えいこう） glory
栄養（えいよう） nutrition

さか(える)

栄える（さかえる） to flourish

は(える)

栄える（はえる） becoming, flattering
見栄え（みばえ） vanity

注 労 (466)
床 (Jōyō)

A *prosperous* world is where industry can live with trees without harming them.

特 榮 (ant)

470 (3級)

HALL, TEMPLE

(11 strokes)

ドウ

食堂（しょくどう） dining room / hall, cafeteria
講堂（こうどう） auditorium
殿堂（でんどう） palace
音楽堂（おんがくどう） concert hall
本堂（ほんどう） main temple
国会議事堂（こっかいぎじどう） the Diet (Japanese parliament)
二月堂（にがつどう） Nigatsudō pavilion (in Nara)

常 (5th)
党 (6th)

The dinning *hall* where the generous queen receives visitors is a place where mouths are fed with produce from the land.

(12 strokes)

TO FEEL, TO REMEMBER, TO WAKE UP

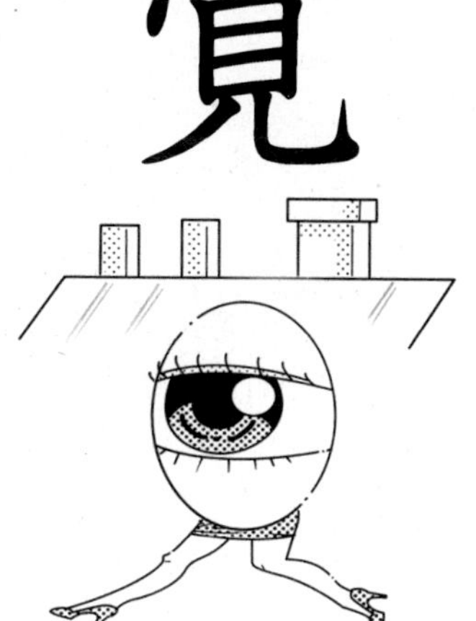

(2級)

471

カク
感覚（かんかく） sense, feeling
味覚（みかく） sense of taste
覚悟（かくご） mental preparation

おぼ(える)
覚（おぼ）える to remember

さ(める/ます)
覚（さ）める to awake tarse
目覚（めざ）める to wake up
目覚（めざ）まし時計（どけい） alarm clock

特 覺 (ant)

学 When you enter the industrial premises, you *feel* the eyes of everyone looking at you.

注 発 (280)
寛 (Jōyō)

(18 strokes)

TO LOOK, VIEW

(2級)

472

カン
観光（かんこう） tourism
観客（かんきゃく） audience, public
楽観（らっかん） optimism
観点（かんてん） point of view
観念（かんねん） concept, idea
世界観（せかいかん） world view

み(る)
観（み）る to look, to observe

特 觀 (ant)

学 People astonishingly *look* at the grotesque pair formed by the cow and the swan; they are worth observing, indeed.

注 勧 (Jōyō)
歓 (Jōyō)

アフリカから
来られたばかりの
ピピングストーン博士は、
国王軍隊と
協働して…

…疲労とたたかいながら、
その地方の新しい地図を作る
ことに参加されました。

彼の努力は
国家に
多大なる
貢献をはた
しました。

するどい
感覚、直観と
勇気の
おかげで、
他人が失敗
したところで
成功
しました。

Exercises 練習

1. Develop the stroke order of the following kanji.

働												
堂												
覚												
観												

2. Choose the correct reading for each kanji or kanji combination.

a) 労働者の皆さん！増加しているただ働きを終わりにしよう！
Laborers! Let's put an end to this increasing working for nothing!

労働者:	1．ろどしゃ	2．ろうどうしゃ	3．ろどうしゃ	4．ろうどしゃ
増加:	1．ぞうく	2．ぞうか	3．ぞうくわ	4．ぞうっか
ただ働き:	1．ただばらき	2．ただはらき	3．ただはたらき	4．ただばたらき

b) 大阪万博に協力できて光栄です。一生忘れられないことでした。
Having been able to collaborate at the World Fair in Osaka has been an honor. It was an unforgettable experience.

万博:	1．ばんぱく	2．ばんはく	3．まんぱく	4．まんはく
協力:	1．きょりょく	2．きょりく	3．きょうりょく	4．きょうりく
光栄:	1．こうさか	2．こうざか	3．こうはえ	4．こうえい

c) 栄養の観点から、食堂のサンドイッチは避(さ)けた方がいいですよ。
From the point of view of nutrition, you had better avoid the dining room sandwiches.

栄養:	1．さかよう	2．はえよう	3．えよう	4．えいよう
観点:	1．みてん	2．みってん	3．かてん	4．かんてん
食堂:	1．しょくどう	2．しょっどう	3．しょどう	4．たべどう

3. Write the kanji (one or more) and the meaning of the following words.

めざめる	______	______	ゆうき	______	______
らっかん	______	______	はかせ	______	______
どりょく	______	______	きょうかい	______	______

4. Correct either the reading or the writing mistakes in the following words.

労力	どりょく	成功	せいく	見える	おぼえる
勇しい	いさましい	追功	ついか	権光	かんこう

Answers to exercises 練習解答

2. (Check them in the corresponding kanji table: #461, #470, #471, and #472)

2. a) 労働者: 2 | 増加: 2 | ただ働き: 4 / b) 万博: 1 | 協力: 3 | 光栄: 4
c) 栄養: 4 | 観点: 4 | 食堂: 1

3. めざめる: 目覚める, to wake up | らっかん: 楽観, optimism | どりょく: 努力, effort | ゆうき: 勇気, bravery | はかせ: 博士, Ph.D., doctor | きょうかい: 教会, association, group.

4. 努力 どりょく | 成功 せいこう | 覚える おぼえる | 勇ましい いさましい | 追加 ついか | 観光 かんこう

Manga translation マンガ翻訳

Speaker: Dr. Pipingstone, who has just arrived from Africa, in collaboration with Her Majesty's army...

Speaker: ...fighting against fatigue, has contributed to the making of the new maps of the area. His effort has rendered a great service to the country.

Speaker (OFF): Thanks to his sharp senses, his instinct, and his bravery, he has succeeded where others had failed.

Speaker: Therefore, it's an honor to have with us today...

Speaker: Huh? Where's Dr. Pipingstone?

Audience (OFF): hum hum hum

Explorer: Where am I? I can't find the auditorium! I'm lost! Waah!

New elements 新しい部首

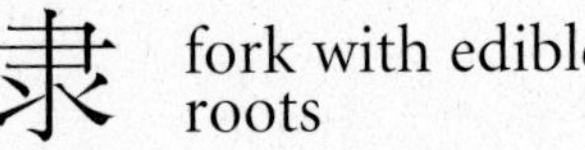

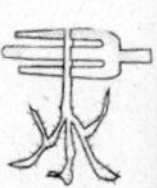

Lesson 42
第四十二課

473 (2級)

TO STOP, TO SUSPEND, PAUSE

停

テイ

停留所（ていりゅうじょ） stop (vehicle)
バス停（てい） bus stop
停止（ていし） suspension
停車（ていしゃ）する to stop (vehicle)
停学（ていがく）する to shelve one's studies
停電（ていでん） blackout
停戦（ていせん） armistice, cease-fire

と(める/まる)

停（と）まる to stop, to halt

(11 strokes)

停 停 停 停
停 停 停 停

 倍 (260)
僚 (Jōyō)
偉 (Jōyō)

 Kim *stops* that unreliable guy who, with a Mexican hat, a big mouth, and a tutu, wants to open another bottle to keep the party going.

474 (2級)

WEATHER

候

コウ

気候（きこう） weather, climate
時候（じこう） season
天候（てんこう） weather
候鳥（こうちょう） migratory bird
候補（こうほ） candidate
立候補（りっこうほ） candidacy

(10 strokes)

候 候 候 候
候 候 候 候

注 修 (5th)

学 This Kim, a countryman, uses a guillotine to cut an arrow; depending on how the arrow falls, he forecasts the *weather.*

特

(11 strokes)

HEALTHY, STRONG

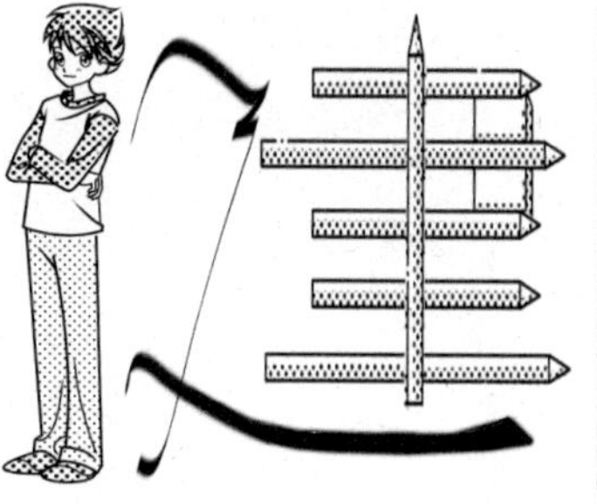

(2級) 475

ケン

健康(けんこう) health

健康保険(けんこうほけん) Health Insurance

健全(けんぜん) healthy

強健(きょうけん) strong, robust

健闘(けんとう)する to fight bravely

すこ(やか)

健(すこ)やか healthy, vigorous

 For Kim, the *healthiest* and strongest hero is the Zorro, who uses color pencils to leave his mark.

 建 (476)

修 (5th)

(9 strokes)

TO BUILD

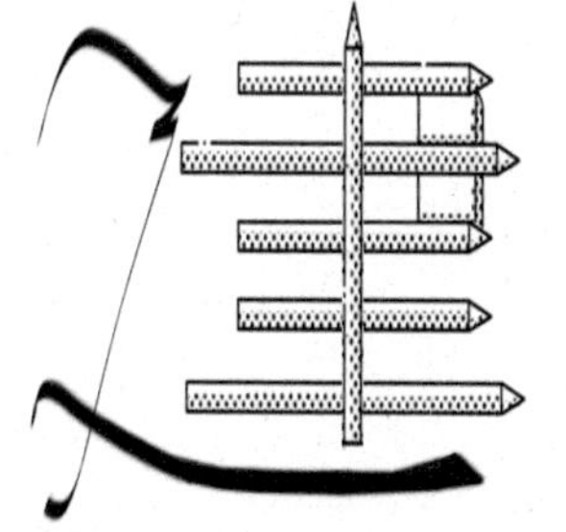

(3級) 476

ケン

建築(けんちく) architecture

建設(けんせつ) construction

再建(さいけん) reconstruction

建造(けんぞう) building

た(てる/つ)

建(た)てる to stand (something), to build

建物(たてもの) building

建(た)て直(なお)し to rebuild

特 建 (alt)

学 With colored pencils, the Zorro writes his name on the houses he *builds*.

注 健 (475)

延 (6th)

477 (2級)

HEALTHY

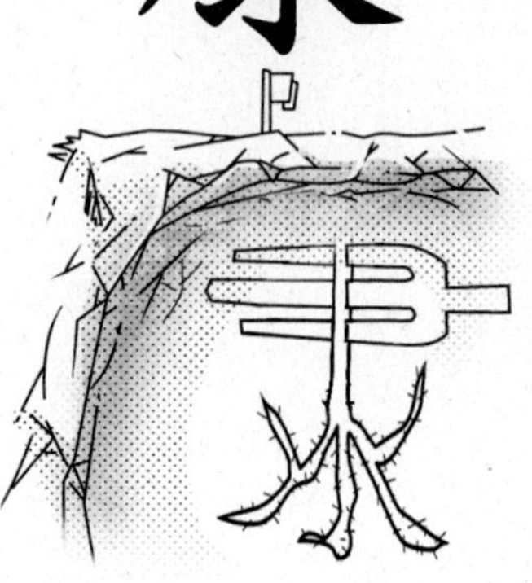

コウ

健康（けんこう） health

小康（しょうこう） respite, pause

不健康（ふけんこう） bad health

健康保険（けんこうほけん） health insurance

健康体（けんこうたい） robust body, healthy body

丶	亠	广	户
庐	庐	庚	庚
康	康	康	

(11 strokes)

 厚 (5th) 席 (583) 廉 (Jōyō)

学 For a *healthy* diet there is nothing like filling the inhabited cave with edible roots.

478 (2級)

FAILURE, DEFEAT

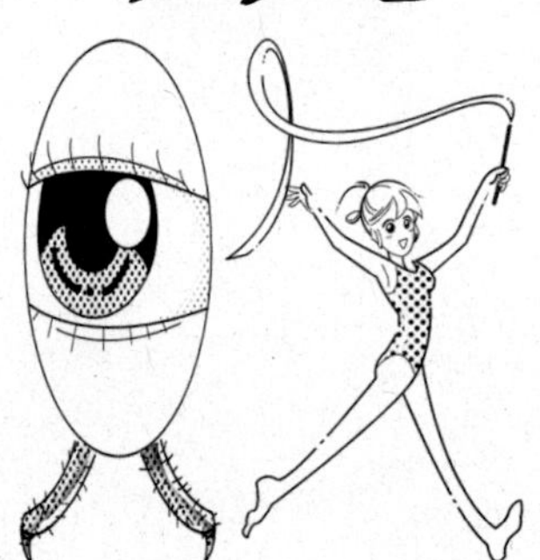

ハイ

敗北（はいぼく） defeat

勝敗（しょうはい） victory or defeat

完敗（かんぱい） complete defeat

敗戦（はいせん） defeat in a war

敗軍（はいぐん） defeated army

連敗（れんぱい） successive defeats

失敗（しっぱい） failure

やぶ(れる)

敗れる（やぶれる） to be defeated

丨	冂	月	目
目	貝	貝	貝
貯	敗	敗	

(11 strokes)

注 負 (389) 財 (5th) 資 (5th)

学 If a seashell wants to try its luck as an athlete, it will only find *failure.*

一	十	廾	共
艹	昔	昔	昔
背	背	散	散

(12 strokes)

散	散	散	散
散	散	散	散

TO SCATTER, DISPERSED

散

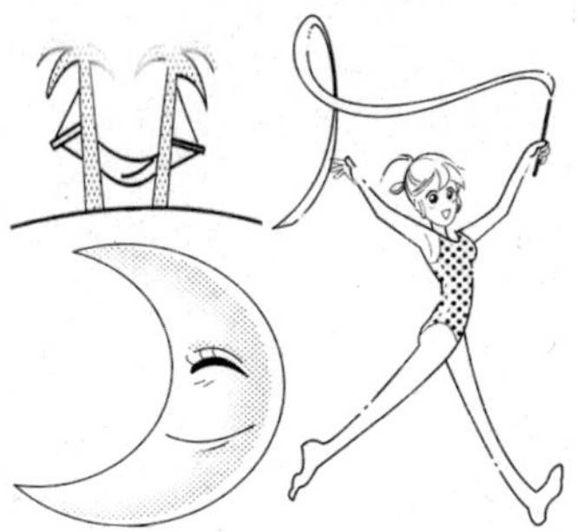

(2級) **479**

サン

散歩（さんぽ） a stroll, a walk

解散（かいさん） disbandment, break up, dismissal

散乱（さんらん） dispersion

散髪屋（さんぱつや） barber shop

ち(らす/らかす/る)

散（ち）らかす to scatter

散（ち）らし flier

(桜が)散（ち）る to fall (cherry blossom petals)

特

学 *Scattering* hammocks on the moon to lie down on is the dream of a retired athlete.

注 敬 (6th)
借 (450)

フ	コ	己	己'
己'	改	改	

(7 strokes)

改	改	改	改
改	改	改	改

TO REFORM

改

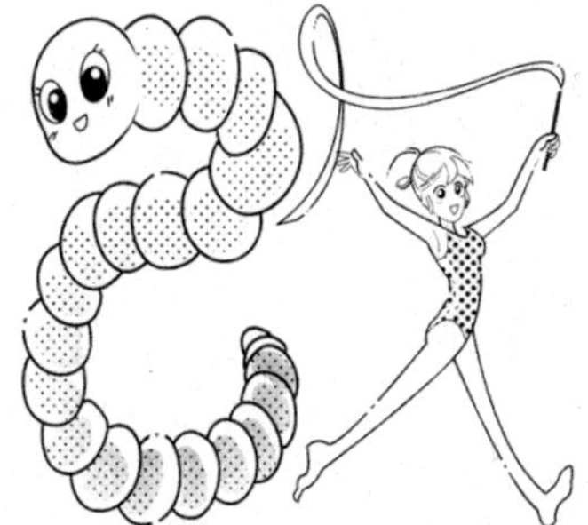

(2級) **480**

カイ

改革（かいかく） reform

改善（かいぜん） improvement

改名（かいめい） change of name

改札口（かいさつぐち） ticket gate

あらた(める/まる)

改（あらた）める to repeat, to renew

改（あらた）めて again, another time

改（あらた）まった挨拶（あいさつ） formal greeting, “snotty” greeting

 Little Worm is going *to reform* her body to become a great athlete.

 放 (382)
牧 (483)
攻 (Jōyō)

481 (2級)

TO ASK, TO WANT

(7 strokes)

求 求 求 求
求 求 求 求

キュウ

- 求人（きゅうじん） job vacancy
- 求職（きゅうしょく） job hunting
- 要求（ようきゅう） request
- 請求書（せいきゅうしょ） application form, order, bill

もと(める)

- 求める（もとめる） to ask for, to request
- 求め（もとめ） a request, a demand
- 買い求める（かいもとめる） to buy

注 氷 (301)
永 (5th)

 Complaining roots are those constantly *asking* for water, and even coming up to the surface to get it.

482 (2級)

TO SAVE, RESCUE

一 十 寸 才
才 求 求 求
求 救 救

(11 strokes)

救 救 救 救
救 救 救 救

キュウ

- 救助（きゅうじょ） help, rescue
- 救出（きゅうしゅつ） rescue, salvation, deliverance
- 救済（きゅうさい） relief (funds)
- 救急車（きゅうきゅうしゃ） ambulance
- 救命ボート（きゅうめいボート） lifeboat
- 救世主（きゅうせいしゅ） the Messiah

すく(う)

- 救う（すくう） to save, to rescue
- 救い主（すくいぬし） the Savior

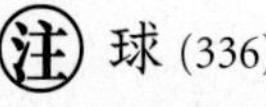
注 球 (336)
牧 (483)

学 Complaining roots know that, when they come up to the surface for water, their ally the athlete will come to *rescue* them.

ノ	𠂉	牛	牛
牜	牝	牧	牧

(8 strokes)

牧	牧	牧	牧
牧	牧	牧	牧

TO GRAZE, SHEPHERD

牧

(1級) **483**

ボク

牧人 (ぼくじん) shepherd
牧師 (ぼくし) pastor
牧羊 (ぼくよう) sheep raising
牧場 (ぼくじょう) stock farm
牧畜 (ぼくちく) livestock
遊牧 (ゆうぼく) nomadism
牧歌的 (ぼっかてき) bucolic, idyllic

まき

牧場 (まきば) pasture, grazing land

 While the cow *grazes*, her *shepherdess* trains for athletics.

 攻 (Jōyō)
放 (382)

ノ	𠂉	牛	牛
牛一	牛十	牛土	牛土
特	特		

(10 strokes)

特	特	特	特
特	特	特	特

SPECIAL

特

(3級) **484**

トク

特に (とくに) specially
特別 (とくべつ) special
特殊 (とくしゅ) special, peculiar
特徴 (とくちょう) characteristic
特集 (とくしゅう) special edition
特価 (とっか) special price
特大 (とくだい) extra large
特許 (とっきょ) patent
東京特許許可局 (とうきょうとっきょきょかきょく) Tokyo Patent and License Office

特

 If you ever see a cow in a temple, it means it's *special*: you must worship it.

 待 (248)
持 (247)

21世紀の牧場へようこそ！
こちらで、過去の失敗に学んで、動物の幸福を求める。
天候・停電にかかわらず、
この建物の中に改善した理想的な環境で生活しています。
健康のために、特別な設備がととのえており、
ジャクジー、サウナ、屋内プール…もちろん、緊急救命室もあります。
はっ！失礼ですが、散歩の時間になりまして…
へー！牧場の動物でも散歩に連れて行くの？
ちがうんですけど…私の散歩なのです。では、また来てくださいね。

Exercises 練習

1. Develop the stroke order of the following kanji.

候												
健												
康												
救												

2. Choose the correct reading for each kanji or kanji combination.

a) 求職しても、いつも失敗ばっかりです。不健康ですし...

No matter how much I hunt for a job, I do nothing but fail. With my bad health...

求職:　1．きしょく　2．きゅうしょく　3．きゅしょく　4．ろうどしゃ

失敗:　1．しつはい　2．しっはい　3．しつぱい　4．しっぱい

不健康:　1．ふけんこ　2．ふけこう　3．ふけんこう　4．ふけんこ

b) 建設の事故（じこ）で強健な山田（やまだ）さんは救急車で運ばれた。

Due to the accident in the construction, they took strong Yamada away in an ambulance.

建設:　1．けんせつ　2．けせつ　3．たんせつ　4．たせつ

強健:　1．きょうけん　2．つよけん　3．きょうけ　4．つよけん

救急車:　1．すくしゃ　2．すきゅうしゃ　3．きゅきゅうしゃ　4．きゅうきゅうしゃ

c) 特殊な牧人は、気候の厳（きび）しさになれている。

Peculiar shepherds are used to the harshness of the weather.

特殊:　1．とっしゅ　2．とっくしゅ　3．とくしゅう　4．とくしゅ

牧人:　1．ぼくにん　2．ほくにん　3．まきびと　4．ぼくじん

気候:　1．きこ　2．きっこう　3．きこう　4．きっこ

3. Write the kanji (one or more) and the meaning of the following words.

ていし　______　______　さんぽ　______　______

けんこう　______　______　あらためて　___めて　______

たてもの　______　______　とくべつ　______　______

4. Correct either the reading or the writing mistakes in the following words.

停電	てでん	改れる	やぶれる	待徴	とくちょう
健て直し	たてなおし	散す	ちらかす	水める	もとめる

Answers to exercises 練習解答

1. (Check them in the corresponding kanji table: #474, #475, #477, and #482)

2. a) 求職: 2 | 失敗: 4 | 不健康: 3 / b) 建設: 1 | 強健: 1 | 救急車: 4
c) 牧人: 4 | 特殊: 4 | 気候: 3

3. ていし: 停止, suspension | けんこう: 健康, health | たてもの: 建物, building | さんぽ: 散歩, a stroll, a walk | あらためて: 改めて, again, another time | とくべつ: 特別, special

4. 停電 ていでん | 敗れる やぶれる | 特徴 とくちょう | 建て直し たてなおし | 散らかす ちらかす | 求める もとめる

Manga translation マンガ翻訳

Guide: Welcome to the 21st century farm!

Guide: Here, we have learned from the mistakes of the past, and we want the animals to be happy.

Guide: In these buildings they live in an ideal and improved environment, regardless of the weather outside or of power outages.

Guide: We have special facilities keeping their health in mind: Jacuzzi, sauna, covered swimming pool... and, of course, we also have a first-aid room.

Guide: Oh! You'll excuse me, but it's now time for a stroll.

Visitor: What? You also take the farm animals out for a walk?

Guide: No, no. I´m the one who's taken out for a walk. See you soon, please come back whenever you'd like.

New elements 新しい部首

彐	fork with meat		山	moustache	
戋	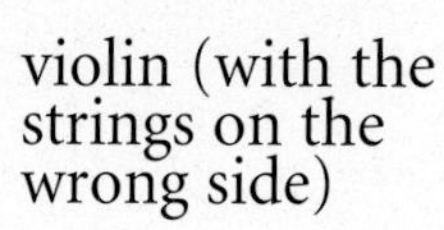 violin (with the strings on the wrong side)		矣	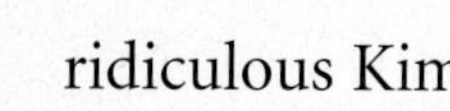 ridiculous Kim	

Lesson 43
第四十三課

485 (2級)

TO ARGUE, TO COMPETE

争

ソウ
戦争(せんそう) war
紛争(ふんそう) conflict
競争(きょうそう) competition
争議(そうぎ) dispute
論争(ろんそう) argument

あらそ(う)
争(あらそ)う to argue, to dispute
言(い)い争(あらそ)い quarrel

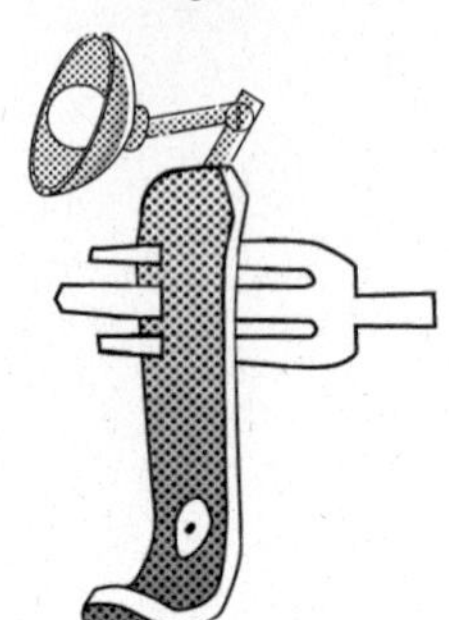

ノ ク 乌 乌 争 争

(6 strokes)

注 急 (390)
勇 (465)
隶 (no Jōyō)

学 Flashes *compete* to obtain the best shot of this beautiful steak speared with a meat fork.

特 爭 (ant)

486 (2級)

CALM, PEACE

静

セイ
冷静(れいせい) calm, cold blood
静寂(せいじゃく) silence, calm
静止(せいし) standstill
静電気(せいでんき) static electricity

ジョウ
静脈(じょうみゃく) vein

しず(か/まる/める)
静(しず)か calm, silent
静(しず)まる to calm down

一 十 キ 主 主 青 青 青 青 青 靜 靜 静 静

(14 strokes)

注 晴 (228)
精 (5th)
清 (487)

学 The moon's bluish light calms the flashes competing for the photograph of the meat.

特  靜 (ant)

487

(2級)

CLEAN, PURE

清

(11 strokes)

清	清	清	清
清	清	清	清

セイ

- 清掃 (せいそう) cleaning
- 清純 (せいじゅん) pure
- 清浄 (せいじょう) spotless
- 清水 (せいすい) pure water
- 清澄 (せいちょう) clear, crystal-clear

きよ(い/まる/める)

- 清い (きよい) pure, clean
- 清める (きよめる) to purify
- 清水寺 (きよみずでら) Kiyomizu (pure water) temple

淸 (alt)

Pure is the blue water with which we water the plants growing on the moon.

精 (5th)
晴 (228)
浦 (Jōyō)

488

(2級)

TO CRY, TO WEEP

泣

(8 strokes)

泣	泣	泣	泣
泣	泣	泣	泣

キュウ

- 号泣 (ごうきゅう) wail, bitter crying
- 感泣 (かんきゅう) tears of emotion

な(く)

- 泣く (なく) to cry, to weep
- 泣き虫 (なきむし) crybaby
- 泣き顔 (なきがお) tearful face

When they can't find water, vultures cry too.

法 (491)
注 (303)
沈 (Jōyō)

489 (2級)

TO GOVERN, TO CURE, TO CONTROL

治

チ

治安（ちあん） public order
治療（ちりょう） cure, treatment
自治（じち） self-government

ジ

政治（せいじ） politics

おさ(まる/める)

治まる（おさまる） to govern

なお(る/す)

治る（なおる） to be cured

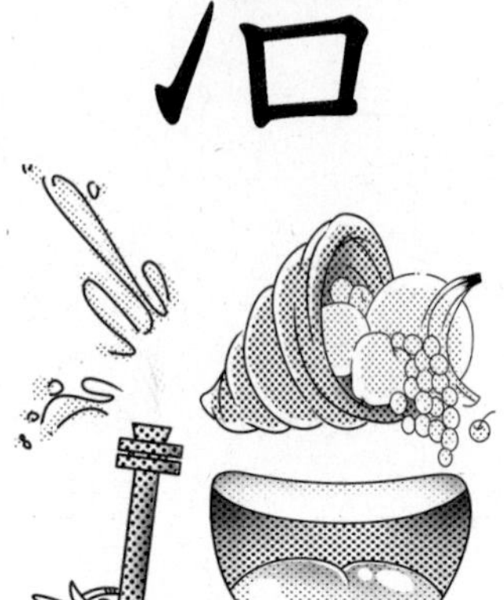

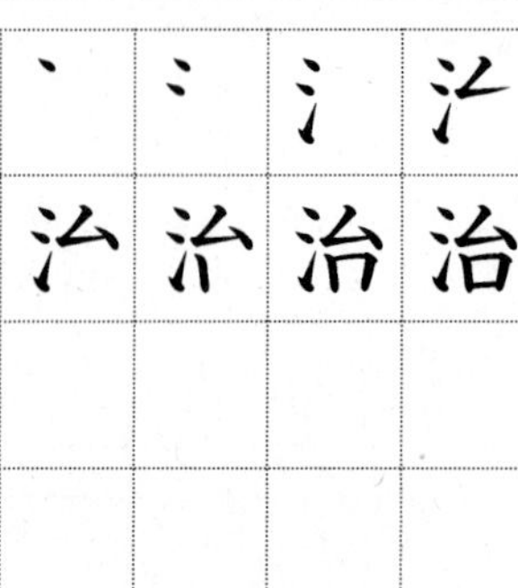

(8 strokes)

注 活 (166)
沿 (6th)
沼 (Jōyō)

Governing well is to ration the water and the food from the cornucopia among the mouths of the people.

490 (2級)

TO BATHE

浴

ヨク

入浴する（にゅうよくする） to bathe
浴室（よくしつ） bathroom
日光浴する（にっこうよくする） to sunbathe

あ(びる/びせる)

浴びる（あびる） to pour (water) on oneself, to bathe
シャワーを浴びる（あびる） to take a shower

Special

浴衣（ゆかた） *yukata* (summer kimono)

浴 (stroke order, 10 strokes)

(10 strokes)

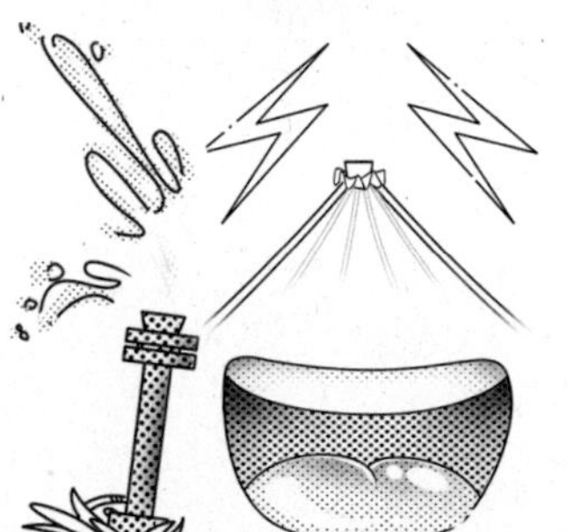

沿 (6th)
治 (469)
活 (166)

A storm *bathes* you in water and lightning, so you should use a tiny umbrella to cover your mouth while you eat.

(8 strokes)

LAW, METHOD, TECHNIQUE

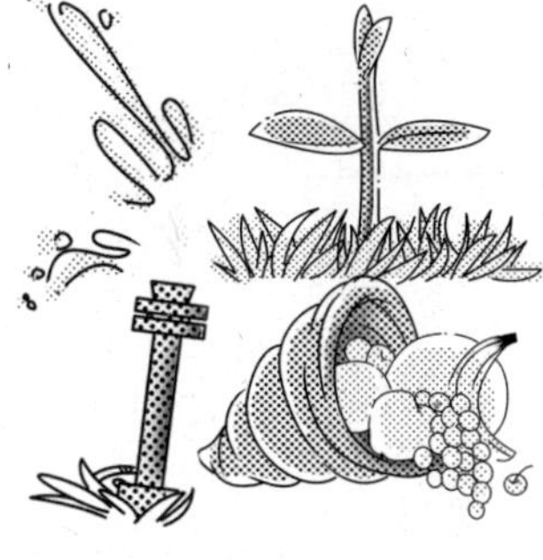

(2級) **491**

ホウ

- 法律（ほうりつ） legislation, laws
- 法学（ほうがく） law (study)
- 法廷（ほうてい） court
- 憲法（けんぽう） constitution
- 違法（いほう） crime, illegal
- 国際法（こくさいほう） international law
- 方法（ほうほう） method, way
- 法王（ほうおう） the Pope
- マーフィーの法則（ほうそく） Murphy's law

特

学 The *laws* of nature regulate water, making the land fertile; this, then, produces the food for the cornucopia.

注 洗 (6th) 決 (317) 流 (307)

(12 strokes)

FULL, TO FILL, TO SATISFY

満

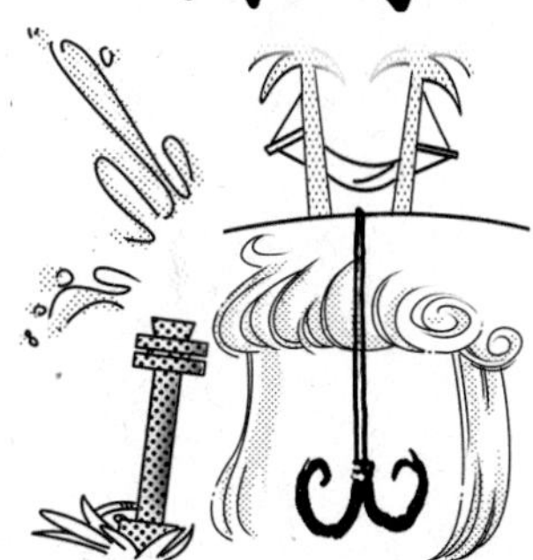

(2級) **492**

マン

- 満足（まんぞく） satisfaction
- 不満（ふまん） dissatisfaction
- 満員（まんいん） crowded
- 満月（まんげつ） full moon
- 未満（みまん） less than
- 充満（じゅうまん） to be full, to be brimming with

み(ちる/たす)

- 満（み）ちる to become full
- 満（み）たす to fill, to load

特 滿 (ant)

学 The fugitive's *satisfaction*: lying by a mountain lake, on a hammock, while wearing his wig and his false moustache so nobody recognizes him.

注 港 (308) 浦 (Jōyō)

493 (2級)

TO FISH

(14 strokes)

漁	漁	漁	漁
漁	漁	漁	漁

ギョ

漁業（ぎょぎょう） fishing industry
漁船（ぎょせん） fishing boat

リョウ

漁師（りょうし） fisherman
禁漁（きんりょう） prohibition of fishing
大漁（たいりょう） large catch, great benefit

注 魚 (229)

 Water is where one usually goes *fishing*. However, we took a photo of the rice field that we caught our fish in, which had been burnt by a fire.

494 (2級)

SHALLOW, SUPERFICIAL

(9 strokes)

浅	浅	浅	浅
浅	浅	浅	浅

セン

浅海（せんかい） shallow sea
浅学（せんがく） superficial knowledge
深浅（しんせん） depth

あさ(い)

浅い（あさい） shallow
考え（かんがえ）が浅い（あさい）
shallow-minded (thinking)

注 残 (495)

学 *Superficial* mermaids in shallow waters come out when they hear the notes from this peculiar violin

 浅 (ant)

495 — TO REMAIN, REMNANT

(10 strokes)

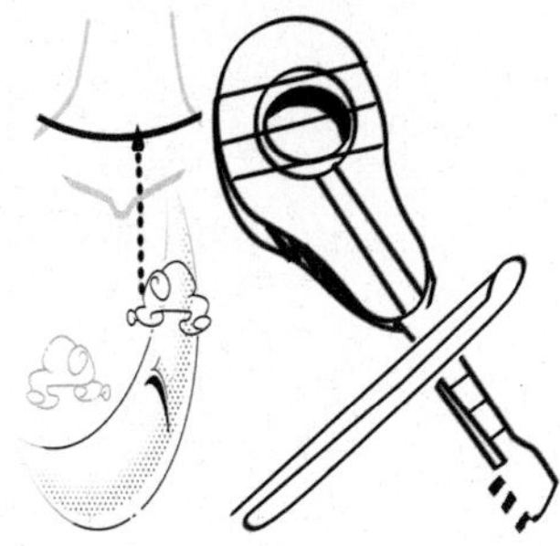

(2級)

ザン

- 残念（ざんねん） a pity, a shame
- 残高（ざんだか） (bank) balance
- 残業（ざんぎょう） overtime
- 残酷（ざんこく） cruelty
- 残骸（ざんがい） remains, carcass, ruins

のこ(る/す)

- 残る（のこる） to stay, to remain
- 残す（のこす） to leave behind
- 食べ残し（たべのこし） food leftovers

特 殘 (ant)

学 The moon pendant is all that *remains* of the remnants of the murdered violinist.

注 銭 (5th)
浅 (494)

496 — TEST, EXAM

(18 strokes)

(3級)

ケン

- 試験（しけん） exam, test
- 経験 experience
- 体験（たいけん） experience (physical)
- 実験（じっけん） experiment
- 受験（じゅけん）する to take an exam

特  驗 (ant)

学 To become a member of the knight club, Kim must pass a *test*: he must ride a horse looking as ridiculous as possible.

 注 駅 (437)
駆 (Jōyō)
騎 (Jōyō)

頭のかたい
政治家と
きびしい法律との
長い争いのすえ、
やっと漁業許可を
もらった!!

経験は浅い
けど、
一生懸命
がんばろう!!

静かな海、
清浄な空気、
あたたかい日光を浴びて…
なんて幸せだ!

グオオ!
大漁、
大漁!!

こんなに満載できる
なんて…あっ!
うれしくてたまらない!
泣いてしまうほど…

ゴオオオオ
?

残念…
やっぱり、
経験が
浅いね…
ゴポ
ゴポ

Exercises 練習

1. Develop the stroke order of the following kanji.

争												
満												
残												
験												

2. Choose the correct reading for each kanji or kanji combination.

a) 戦争を体験したオレは、あれほど残酷なものはないと分かっておる。
I have experienced war and I know there's nothing as cruel as that.

戦争: 1．せならそ　2．せんあらそ　3．せんあそ　4．せんそう
体験: 1．きゅうけん　2．たいけん　3．たんけ　4．たんま
残酷: 1．さんごく　2．ざんこく　3．さんこく　4．ざんごく

b) この紛争に関しては、冷静に解決(かいけつ)方法を考えるべきだ。
Concerning the conflict, we should think of ways to resolve it calmly.

紛争: 1．ふんらそ　2．ふんあそ　3．ふんそう　4．ふんあらそ
冷静: 1．れいせい　2．れいじょ　3．れいじょう　4．れいせ
方法: 1．ほほ　2．ほうほう　3．ほほう　4．ほうほ

c) 清掃のため入浴が不可能(ふかのう)なので、浴衣を着てお待ちください。
Since they are cleaning the bathroom and you can't go in, put on the summer yukata and wait, please.

清掃: 1．じょうそう　2．じょそう　3．せそう　4．せいそう
入浴: 1．にゅうよく　2．いりよく　3．いよく　4．いりあ
浴衣: 1．よくい　2．ゆかた　3．よっきの　4．よくきの

3. Write the kanji (one or more) and the meaning of the following words.

せいすい ______ ________　まんぞく ______ ________
きよみずでら ______ ________　ちあん ______ ________
なきがお ______ ________　あさい ______ ________

4. Correct either the reading or the writing mistakes in the following words.

静か	しすか	台療	ちりょう	満月	まんつき
立く	なく	法律	ほりつ	浅念	ざんねん

Answers to exercises 練習解答

1. (Check them in the corresponding kanji table: #485, #492, #495, and #496)

2. a) 戦争: 4 | 体験: 2 | 残酷: 2 / b) 紛争: 3 | 冷静: 1 | 方法: 2
c) 清掃: 4 | 入浴: 1 | 浴衣: 2

3. せいすい: 清水, pure water | みよみずでら: 清水寺, Kiyomizu temple | なきがお: 泣き顔, tearful face | まんぞく: 満足, satisfaction | ちあん: 治安, public order | あさい: 浅い, superficial, shallow

4. 静か しずか | 治療 ちりょう | 満月 まんげつ | 泣く なく | 法律 ほうりつ | 残念 ざんねん

Manga translation マンガ翻訳

Young fisherman: After a long battle with those hard-headed politicians and their strict laws, I have finally obtained my fishing license!

Young fisherman: I have little experience, but I will try as hard as I can!

Young fisherman: A calm sea, pure air, the warm sun's rays bathing me... Oh, this sure is happiness!!

Young fisherman: Wooow! What a catch, what a catch!

Young fisherman: I have filled the boat to the brim... Oh, I´m so happy... I could cry.

Noise: rumble

Young fisherman: ?

Young fisherman: What a shame... I guess I'm still lacking in experience...

Noise: gurgle gurgle

New elements 新しい部首

⺍ little birds

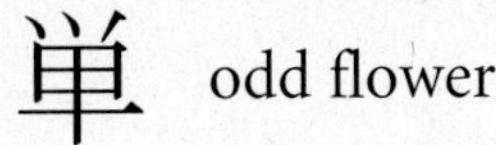
単 odd flower

果 fruit tree
(rice field + tree)

Lesson 44
第四十四課

497 (2級)

SINGLE, UNITY, SIMPLE

タン

- 単(たん)に simply
- 簡単(かんたん) simple, easy
- 単位(たんい) unit
- 単語(たんご) word
- 単純(たんじゅん) simple, simple-minded
- 単独(たんどく) independent, alone
- 単車(たんしゃ) motorcycle

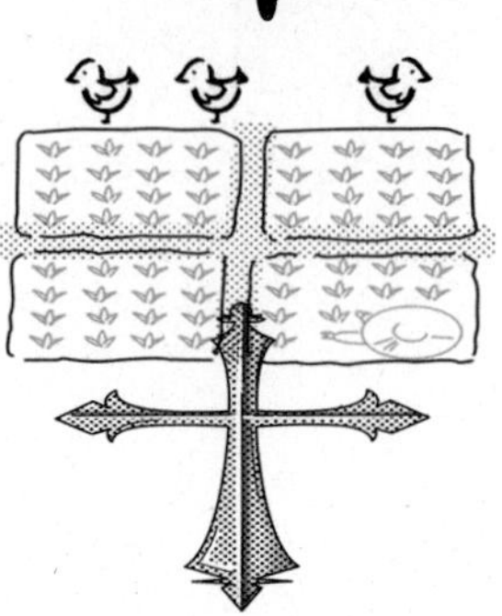

(9 strokes)

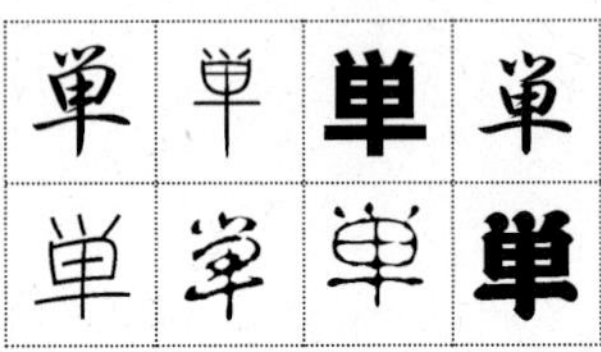

注 巣 (501)
草 (69)

学 Little birds alight on a *single* odd flower: it has a rice field for petals and a cross for the stem.

特  單 (ant)

498 (2級)

WAR, TO FIGHT

セン

- 戦争(そんそう) war
- 戦場(せんじょう) battle field
- 戦略(せんりゃく) war strategy
- 戦況(せんきょう) war situation
- 作戦(さくせん) tactics, plan

いくさ

- 戦(いくさ) war

たたか(う)

- 戦(たたか)う to wage war, to fight

(13 strokes)

注 誠 (6th)
載 (Jōyō)

学 Behind the simple odd flower a fake Robin Hood hides when he's called to *war*.

特 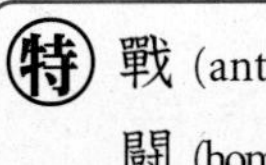 戰 (ant)
闘 (hom)

499 — TO BECOME, TO ACHIEVE

成

(2級)

(6 strokes)

セイ

- 成功 (せいこう) success, achievement
- 成績 (せいせき) academic results
- 成立する (せいりつ) to establish
- 構成 (こうせい) composition
- 成長する (せいちょう) to grow
- 成人 (せいじん) adult

な(る/す)

- 成る (な) to become, to achieve
- 成し遂げる (な・と) to accomplish

 When he gathers strength to jump from the cliff, the fake Robin Hood *becomes* a free man

 我 (6th) 戒 (Jōyō) 域 (6th)

500 — FRUIT, RESULT; TO ACHIEVE

果

(2級)

(8 strokes)

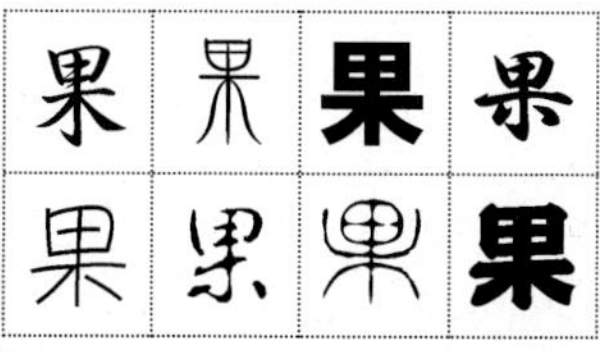

カ

- 果実 (かじつ) fruit
- 成果 (せいか) achievement
- 効果 (こうか) result, effect
- 戦果 (せんか) war results

は(たす/てる)

- 果たす (は) to accomplish
- 世界の果て (せかい・は) the end of the world

Special

- 果物 (くだもの) fruit

 "Rice field" is what we call the *fruit* of this tree.

 東 (199) 巣 (501)

501 (1級)

NEST, TO BUILD A NEST

ソウ

- 病巣（びょうそう） focus of an infection
- 卵巣（らんそう） ovary

す

- 巣（す） nest
- くもの巣（す） spider web
- 巣箱（すばこ） birdhouse
- 空き巣泥棒（あきすどろぼう） sneak thief, burglar

す（くう）

- 巣くう（すくう） to build a nest

(11 strokes)

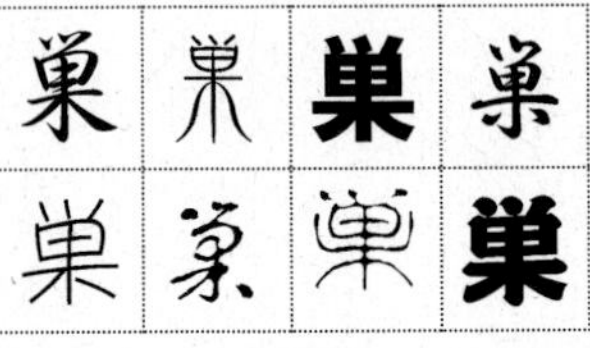

注 単 (497)
菓 (Jōyō)

To guarantee their sustenance, little birds build their *nest* on a fruit tree.

巣 (alt)

502 (2級)

LESSON, SECTION

カ

- 人事課（じんじか） lesson, section
- 会計課（かいけいか） accounts section
- 課長（かちょう） section chief
- 課題（かだい） task, assignment
- 日課（にっか） daily routine
- 放課後（ほうかご） after school

(15 strokes)

読 (114)
諜 (Jōyō)
練 (334)

学 The words you have learned are the fruit of a *lesson*.

(10 strokes)

訓	訓	訓	訓
訓	訓	訓	訓

INSTRUCTION

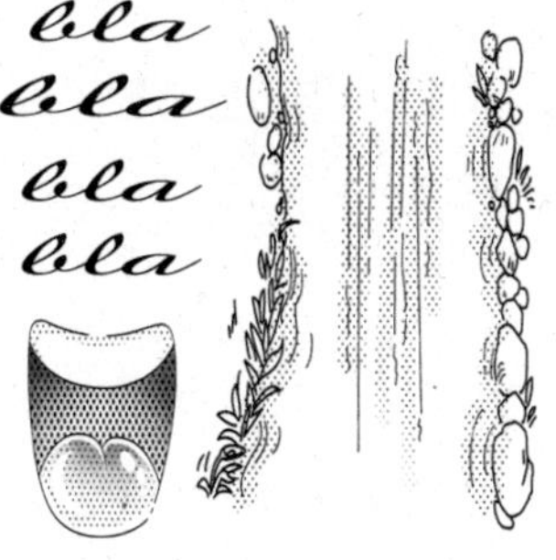

(2級)

503

クン

訓練(くんれん) training
特訓(とっくん) special training
教訓(きょうくん) moral lesson, precept
家訓(かくん) family morals / precepts
訓読み(くんよみ) *kun'yomi* reading (for kanji)

 You must give your word that you will follow the *instructions* taught to you by the river.

注 順 (530)
診 (Jōyō)

(13 strokes)

試	試	試	試
試	试	試	試

TO TRY, TO ATTEMPT

試

(3級)

504

シ

試験(しけん) exam
入試(にゅうし) entrance exam
試写(ししゃ) preview (film)
試食(ししょく) food sample, tasting
試行(しこう) trial (of a test)

こころ(みる)

試みる(こころみる) to attempt

ため(す)

試す(ためす) to try out, to taste

 *Trying* to use words to convince Robin Hood is like talking to an iron beam.

 討 (6th)
訴 (Jōyō)

505 (2級) DELIBERATION, LEGISLATIVE

議

ギ

- 議論(ぎろん) argument, debate
- 議題(ぎだい) topic for discussion
- 会議(かいぎ) meeting, conference
- 国会議事堂(こっかいぎじどう) Diet Building (parliament)
- 議員(ぎいん) deputy, member of parliament
- 決議(けつぎ) resolution, decision
- 異議(いぎ) complaint, objection against
- 不思議(ふしぎ) mysterious

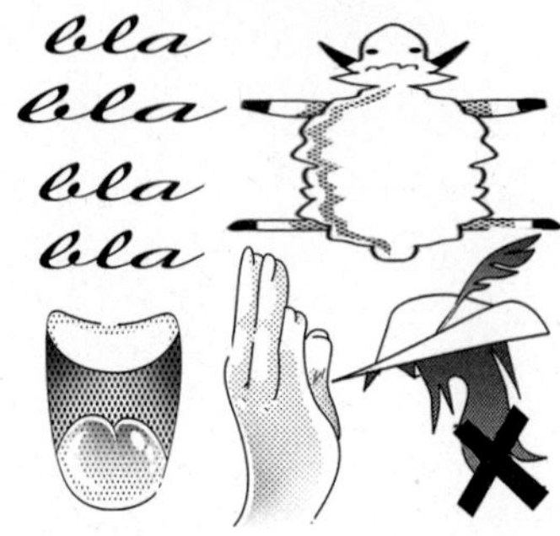

(20 strokes)

注 護 (5th) 譲 (Jōyō) 義 (5th)

学 Words are a tool for *deliberation*. The sheep tries to keep peace by holding up his hand among the fake Robin Hoods, who are debating over who is the real one.

特

506 (3級) THEORY, NARRATIVE, EXPLANATION

説

セツ

- 説(せつ) theory
- 説明(せつめい) explanation
- 解説(かいせつ) commentary
- 図説(ずせつ) diagram
- 序説(じょせつ) preface, introduction
- 仮説(かせつ) hypothesis
- 小説(しょうせつ) novel

と(く)

- 説(と)き明(あ)かす to explain
- 口説(くど)く to persuade

(14 strokes)

注 話 (107) 詰 (Jōyō) 鋭 (Jōyō)

学 The words in my *theory* about why horns have sprouted upon my brother are in vain, because he doesn't want to know.

特  (alt)

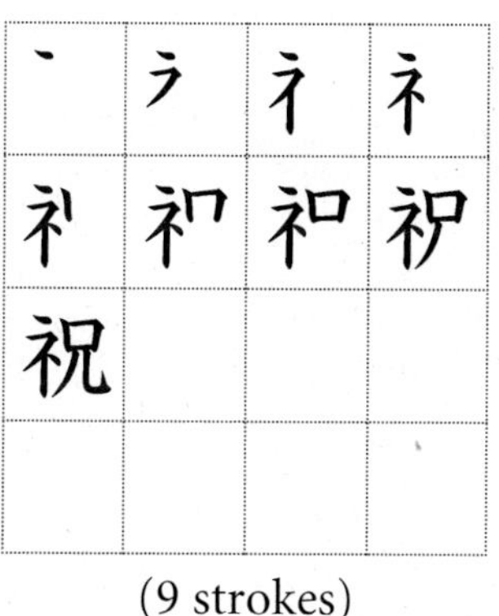

(9 strokes)

祝	祝	祝	祝
祝	祝	祝	祝

CELEBRATION

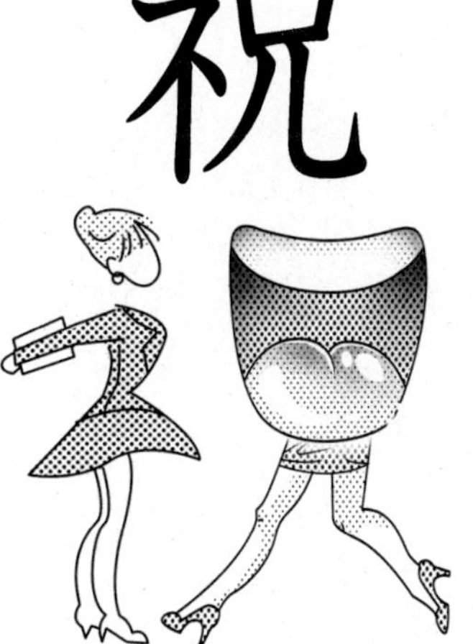

(2級)

507

シュク

祝日（しゅくじつ） holiday

祝福（しゅくふく） blessing, luck

シュウ

祝儀（しゅうぎ） celebration

祝言（しゅうげん） wedding ceremony

いわ(う)

祝う（いわう） to celebrate

祝い酒（いわいざけ） celebratory drink

 祝 (alt)

学 The business woman has invited my elder brother to her *celebration* (and not me, how annoying!)

 初 (567)

神 (418)

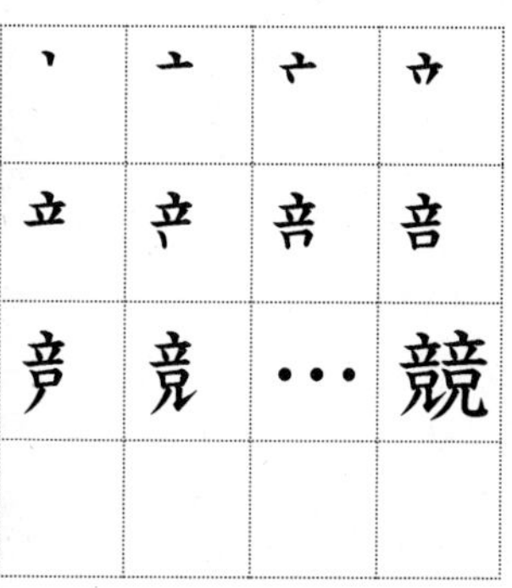

(20 strokes)

競	競	競	競
競	競	競	競

COMPETITION

(2級)

508

キョウ

競争（きょうそう） competition

競走（きょうそう） race

競技場（きょうぎじょう） athletics stadium

ケイ

競輪（けいりん） bicycle race

競馬（けいば） horse race

きそ(う)

競う（きそう） to compete, to vie for

 競 (alt)

 When two elder brothers *compete*, they become ruthless vultures.

 鏡 (605)

戦況は複雑だな…
図説を見てみよう。まず、「ワシの巣」という地点を占めること。そうすれば、もうすぐ成功を祝えるぞ！
スポーツの競技会じゃないぞ。
異議なし。
だが、簡単じゃないだろう。
作戦を果たす軍隊は圧倒的な戦力を持つべきだ。
それは軍事戦略の第一課の教訓。
じゃ、秘密兵器を試行しよう。ウルトラパンの出番だ!!
おおっ!! 名案!!
太郎君！ご飯ができたよ！
へぇー 今おもしろくなってきたのに…

Exercises 練習

1. Develop the stroke order of the following kanji.

成												
巣												
議												
祝												

2. Choose the correct reading for each kanji or kanji combination.

a) 毎日、放課後に訓練したら、効果が見えてきた。

After training every day after school, I began to see the results.

放課:	1．ほうか	2．ほか	3．ほうが	4．ほが
訓練:	1．くんれん	2．くれん	3．ぐんれん	4．ぐれん
効果:	1．こうくだ	2．こうは	3．こうが	4．こうか

b) 作戦もなく戦場に出るのは単純な若者(わかもの)だけさ。

The only ones to go onto the battle field without a plan are dumb young men.

作戦:	1．させん	2．さぜん	3．さくせん	4．さくぜん
戦場:	1．さじょう	2．いくさじょう	3．せんじょう	4．ぜんじょう
単純:	1．かじゅん	2．がじゅん	3．たんじゅん	4．たじゅん

c) 競争の激しい世界についていくため、試験の成績は大事です。

To survive in such a competitive world, exam results are important.

競争:	1．きょうそう	2．きようそう	3．けいそう	4．きそそう
試験:	1．こころみけん	2．じけん	3．しけん	4．ちけん
成績:	1．せいせき	2．せせき	3．しせき	4．しいせき

3. Write the kanji (one or more) and the meaning of the following words.

せいじん	______	______	くだもの	______	______
たんご	______	______	かいぎ	______	______
くんよみ	___み___	______	せつめい	______	______

4. Correct either the reading or the writing mistakes in the following words.

社日	しゅくじつ	小説	しょうぜつ	不思儀	ふしぎ
競馬	きょうば	祝わう	いわう	果長	かちょう

Answers to exercises 練習解答

1. (Check them in the corresponding kanji table: #499, #501, #505, and #507)

2. a) 放課: 1 | 訓練: 1 | 効果: 4 / b) 作戦: 3 | 戦場: 3 | 単純: 3 / c) 競争: 1 | 試験: 3 | 成績: 1

3. せいじん: 成人, adult | たんご: 単語, word | くんよみ: 訓読み, *kun'yomi* reading (for kanji) | くだもの: 果物, fruit | かいぎ: 会議, meeting, conference | せつめい: 説明, explanation

4. 祝日 しゅくじつ | 小説 しょうせつ | 不思議 ふしぎ | 競馬 けいば | 祝わう いわう | 課長 かちょう

Manga translation マンガ翻訳

General 1: The battle situation is difficult...

General 2 (OFF): Let's have a look at the diagram. First, we must occupy the "Eagle Nest." If we accomplish that, we will soon be able to celebrate our success.

General 1 (OFF): This is not a sports competition! No objections. But it won't be easy.

General 1: The troops executing the operation must have an overwhelming fighting power. This is a precept from the first chapter in military strategy.

General 2: Then, let's try out our secret weapon. It's Ultrapan's turn now!

General 1: Wow! What a great idea!

Mother (OFF): Tar?! Lunch is ready!

Child (general) 1: Gosh... Just when it was getting interesting...

New elements 新しい部首

 negative ear of wheat

 surfer

 handkerchief attached with a safety pin 

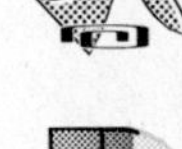

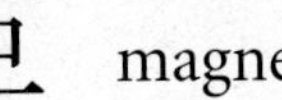 magnet

Lesson 45
第四十五課

509 (3級)

NON, UN-, DIS- (A NEGATIVE KANJI)

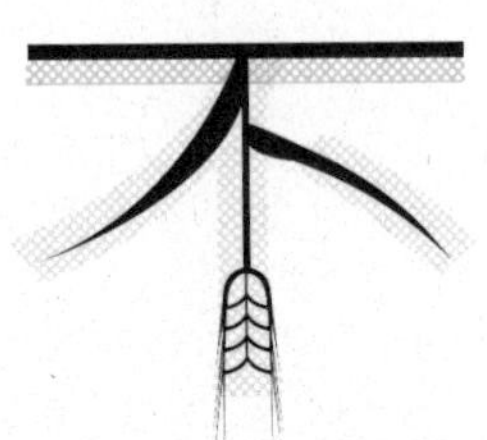

フ

- 不安（ふあん） uneasiness
- 不幸（ふこう） unhappiness
- 不満（ふまん） dissatisfaction
- 不運（ふうん） bad luck
- 不足（ふそく） deficiency, lack
- 不実（ふじつ） false, insincere

ブ

- 不気味（ぶきみ） uncanny, weird
- 不器用（ぶきよう） awkward, clumsy

一	フ	不	不

(4 strokes)

 木 (59)
午 (145)

 Look at that negative ear of wheat: it's growing incorrectly, and will only find *un*happiness and be *dis*satisfied.

510 (3級)

TO, TOWARDS; WITH

以

イ

- 以上（いじょう） the aforementioned, the end
- 以下（いか） the following, under, below
- 以外（いがい） except
- 以来（いらい） since then
- 以前（いぜん） before
- 以後（いご） after

も(って)

- 以（も）ってする to do something using something

ｌ	レ	レ丶	以
以			

(5 strokes)

以 以 以 以
以 以 以 以

 収 (6th)
外 (128)

 Since they became friends, the surfer always takes Kim *with* him *to* the sea.

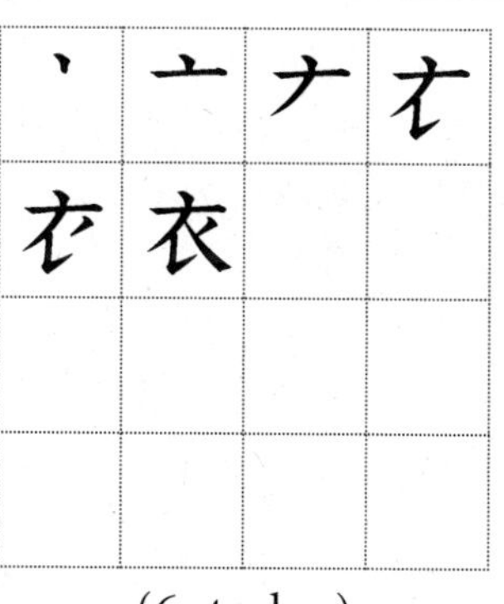

(6 strokes)

CLOTHING

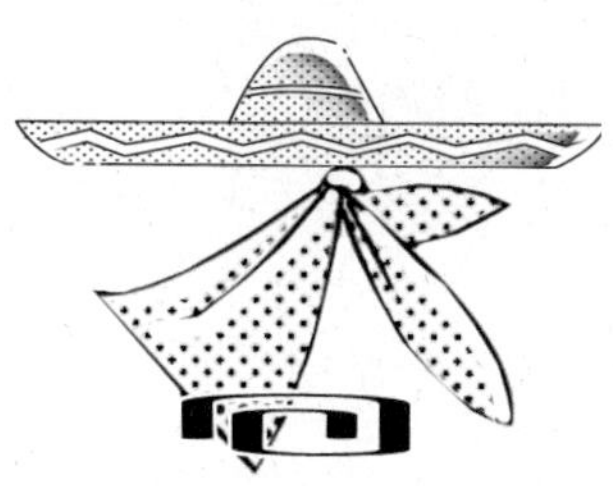

(2級)

511

イ

衣装（いしょう） dress, clothes
衣服（いふく） clothing, clothes
衣類（いるい） clothing
白衣（はくい） white robe

ころも

衣（ころも） clothes, robes
衣替え（ころもがえ） change of clothes (e.g., winter clothes to summer clothes)
羽衣（はごろも） robe of feathers

特

学 A Mexican hat and a scarf with a safety pin are sure to steal attention away from one's *clothing.*

注 表 (297)
立 (42)
哀 (Jōyō)

丶 亠 亣 亦 亦 亦 亦 卒

(8 strokes)

TO GRADUATE

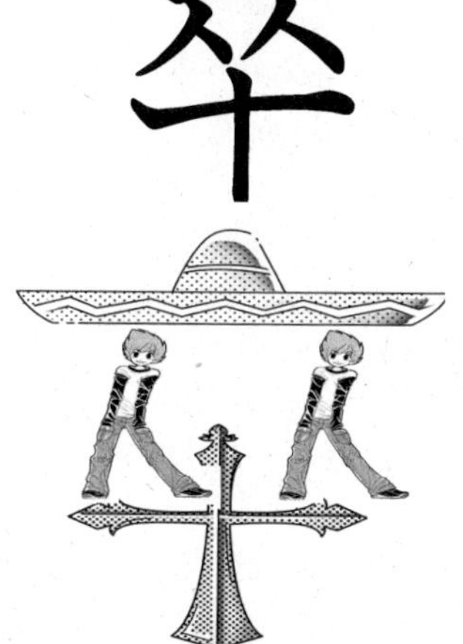

(2級)

512

ソツ

卒業する（そつぎょうする） to graduate
卒論（そつろん） graduation thesis
東大卒（とうだいそつ） Tokyo University graduate
卒中（そっちゅう） apoplexy, stroke
卒去する（そっきょする） to die

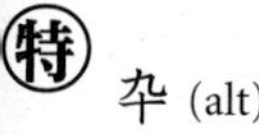

特 卆 (alt)

学 Under a Mexican hat, two Kims celebrate their *graduation* dancing the mariachi on both sides of the cross.

注 率 (5th)
傘 (Jōyō)

513 (2級)

SERVANT, VASSAL

シン

家臣（かしん） retainer (in a house)
臣民（しんみん） subjects
忠臣（ちゅうしん） loyal subject

ジン

大臣（だいじん） minister
総理大臣（そうりだいじん） Prime Minister

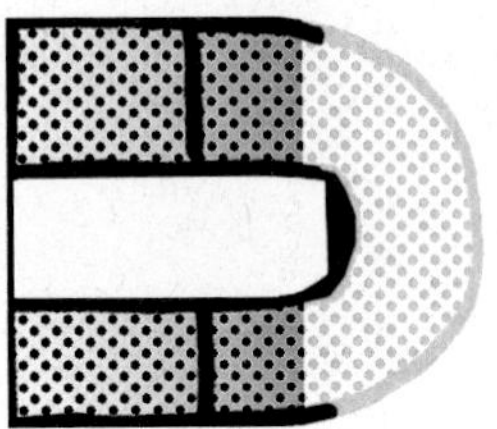

(7 strokes)

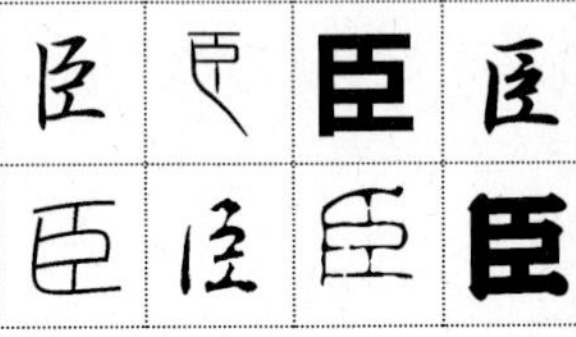

注 巨 (Jōyō)
官 (538)

 Look at the vassal's curious horseshoe: it's magnetic, which keeps him stuck to his master.

514 (3級)

THE PEOPLE, PEOPLE

ミン

民族（みんぞく） race, ethnic group
国民（こくみん） nationals
市民（しみん） citizens
住民（じゅうみん） inhabitants
民家（みんか） traditional house
民間（みんかん） civilian
民主主義（みんしゅしゅぎ） democracy

たみ

民（たみ） people, ethnic group

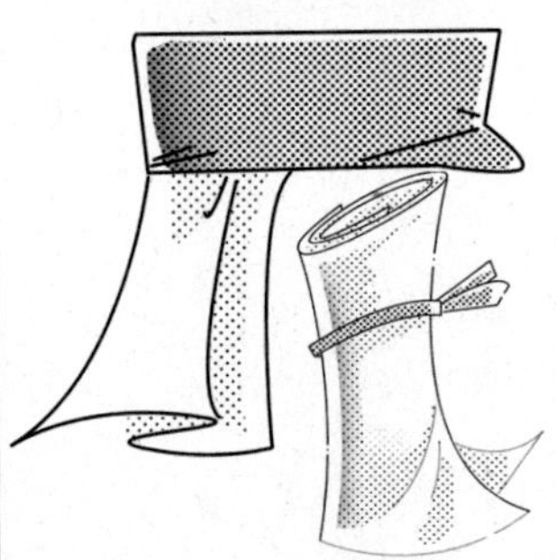

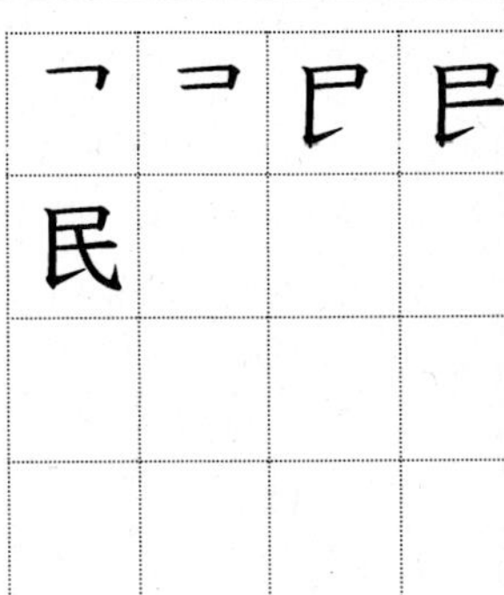

(5 strokes)

注 氏 (443)
尺 (6th)

 The explorer, acclaimed by the *people*, gives them the manuscript he has found.

(7 strokes)

TO ANNOUNCE, TO ADVISE, TO ACUSE

(2級) 515

コク

報告(ほうこく) report
通告(つうこく) announcement, notice
予告(よこく) advance notice
広告(こうこく) advertisement
忠告(ちゅうこく) advice
警告(けいこく) warning
告発(こくはつ) accusation

つ(げる)

告げる(つげる) to inform, to tell

特  (alt)

学 This cow is the big mouth of the herd: it *announces* the news and it *advises* everyone.

注 古 (103)
苦 (431)
否 (6th)

(6 strokes)

EACH, EVERY

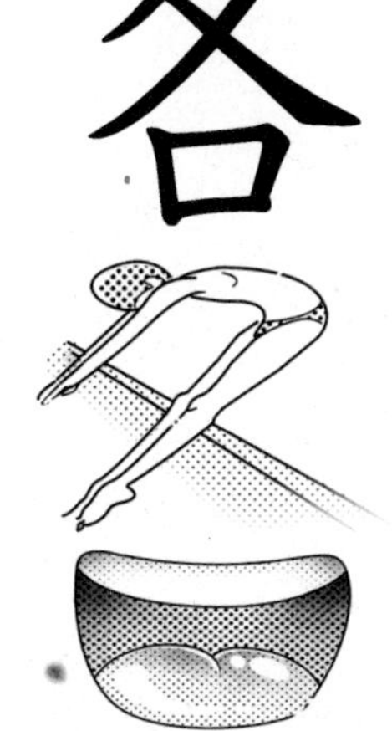

(2級) 516

カク

各自(かくじ) each person
各人(かくじん) each person, everyone
各地(かくち) every place
各国(かっこく) every country
各社(かくしゃ) every company

 *Every* swimmer dives from his mouth-shaped starting block.

 谷 (95)
名 (46)
客 (406)

517 (2級)

TO CHANGE, ABNORMAL, STRANGE

変

ヘン

変(へん) strange, weird
変化(へんか) change, evolution
変更(へんこう) change, variation
変身(へんしん) transformation
変人(へんじん) eccentric person
大変(たいへん) serious, tough
変態(へんたい) pervert

か(わる/える)

変(か)わる to change
変(か)える to change (stg.)

丶 亠 亣 亣 亦 亦 亦 変 変

(9 strokes)

注 恋 (Jōyō)
麦 (150)

学 Did you know that, smothered with a Mexican hat, fire *changes* into water so you can swim in it? *Strange*, but true.

特 變 (ant)

518 (2級)

LOVE

愛

アイ

愛(あい) love
愛情(あいじょう) affection
同性愛(どうせいあい) homosexual love
愛国心(あいこくしん) patriotism
愛車(あいしゃ) cherished car
愛人(あいじん) lover
愛嬌(あいきょう) charming

いと(しい)

愛(いと)しい dear, beloved

(13 strokes)

注 夢 (5th)
受 (363)

学 The claws of the ballerina in *love* dig into the heart of her swimming lover.

特

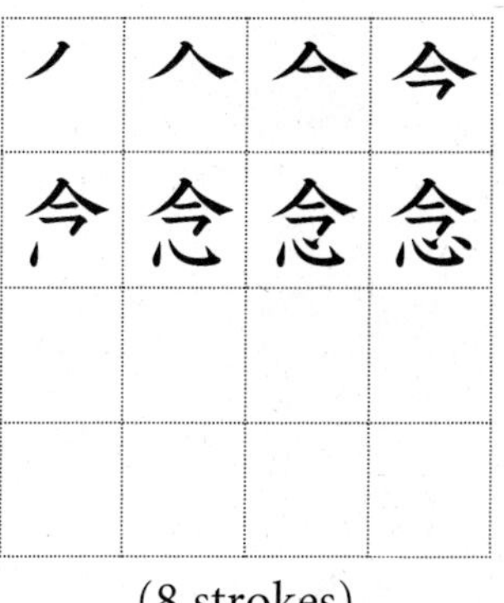

(8 strokes)

CONCEPT, THOUGHTS

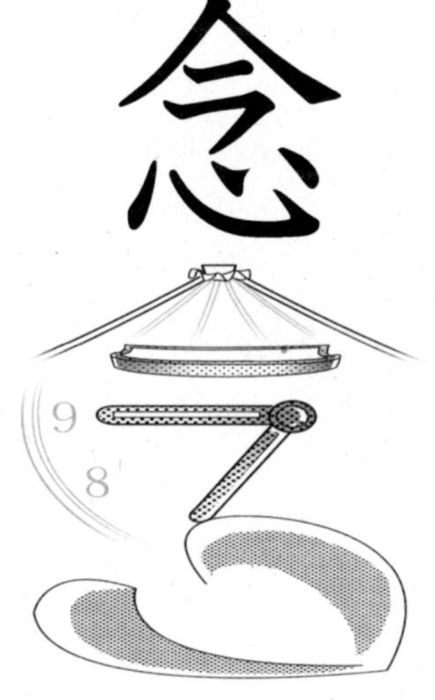

(2級) 519

ネン

- 一念（いちねん） determination, faith
- 概念（がいねん） concept
- 残念（ざんねん） a pity, a shame
- 信念（しんねん） belief
- 記念（きねん） commemoration, remembrance
- 執念（しゅうねん） tenacity
- 無念（むねん） helplessness, vexation
- 念仏（ねんぶつ） Buddhist prayer
- 念珠（ねんじゅ） Buddhist rosary

特

学 Now our heart's clock helps us understand the *concept* of time.

注 志 (5th) 忠 (6th) 怠 (Jōyō)

(5 strokes)

CERTAINLY, SURELY

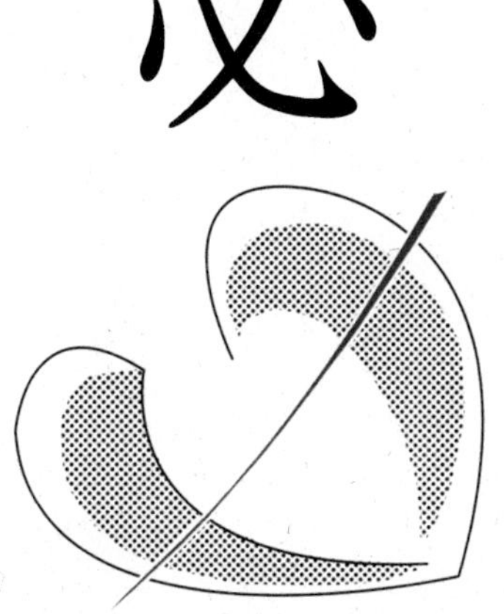

(2級) 520

ヒツ

- 必要（ひつよう） necessary
- 必然（ひつぜん） inevitable
- 必須（ひっす） indispensable
- 必死（ひっし） desperation
- 必勝（ひっしょう） sure victory

かなら(ず)

- 必ず（かならず） surely, without fail

特

学 A gash in the heart *surely* causes pain *without fail.*

注 心 (220)

国民の皆さん、
総理大臣に選ばれたら、
以後労働者のために
一念をこめて
がんばります！
VOTE
おい！
それじゃ、若者は
どうなる？
ご心配なく。
卒業した学生が
必ず就職できる
ことを
目指しています。
農家は？
もちろん、各人に
念頭におきます。ただの
広告ではありませんよ。
不実な
政治家は「すぐに
衣服を変える」と
言われている
けど、これは
ちょっと…
あっ、愛嬌
たっぷりの
主婦も…

Exercises 練習

1. Develop the stroke order of the following kanji.

以												
臣												
愛												
必												

2. Choose the correct reading for each kanji or kanji combination.

a) あの不気味な家臣を見た？あれは変態だ。

Have you seen that weird retainer? I'm sure he's a pervert.

不気味: 1．ふきみ　2．ぶきみ　3．ふきあじ　4．ぶきあじ

家臣: 1．かじん　2．かしん　3．やじん　4．やしん

変態: 1．へんたい　2．かたい　3．へんのう　4．かのう

b) あれ以来、市民であるかどうかは愛国心で決まると考えている。

Since then, I think people are citizens depending on their patriotism.

以来: 1．もっくる　2．もっらい　3．いぐる　4．いらい

市民: 1．しみん　2．じみん　3．したみ　4．じだみ

愛国心: 1．あいこくしん　2．いとこくしん　3．あいごくしん　4．いとごくしん

c) 愛人が東京大学の卒業生で不安です。彼女(かのじょ)はまだ若(わか)すぎます。

I'm worried about her lover being a Tokyo University graduate. She is too young.

愛人: 1．いとにん　2．いとじん　3．あいにん　4．あいじん

卒業: 1．そつぎょう　2．そっぎょう　3．そつぎょ　4．そっぎょ

不安: 1．ぶやす　2．ふやす　3．ぶあん　4．ふあん

3. Write the kanji (one or more) and the meaning of the following words.

ふこう　_______　_______　こうこく　_______　_______

いがい　_______　_______　かくち　_______　_______

こくみん　_______　_______　へんか　_______　_______

4. Correct either the reading or the writing mistakes in the following words.

受情	あいじょう	記今	きねん	衣装	いじょう
心要	ひつよう	大変	だいへん	衣	こども

Answers to exercises 練習解答

1. (Check them in the corresponding kanji table: #510, #513, #518, and #520)

2. a) 不気味: 2 | 家臣: 2 | 変態: 1 / b) 以来: 4 | 市民: 1 | 愛国心: 1
c) 愛人: 4 | 卒業: 1 | 不安: 4

3. ふこう: 不幸, unhappiness | いがい: 以外, except | こくみん: 国民, nationals | こうこく: 広告, advertisement | かくち: 各地, every place | へんか: 変化, evolution, change

4. 愛情 あいじょう | 記念 きねん | 衣装 いしょう | 必要 ひつよう | 大変 たいへん | 衣 ころも

Manga translation マンガ翻訳

Politician: People, if I'm elected for Prime Minister, I'll look after the workers with great determination.

Young man: Hey, and what about young people?

Politician: Don't worry. My aim is to make sure that all students find a job upon graduating.

Old man: And what about farmers?

Politician: I bear everyone in mind, of course. And this is not mere propaganda!

Boy: I'd heard lying politicians "change clothes quickly," but this is ridiculous...

Politician: Oh, and charming housewives too...

New elements 新しい部首

 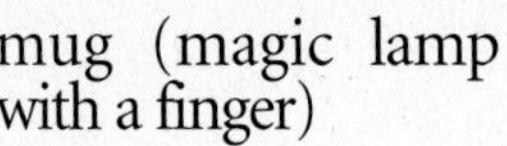 mug (magic lamp with a finger) 

 cast 

Lesson 46
第四十六課

521 (2級)

TO TIE, TO CLOSE (A SUBJECT), TO BIND

結

(12 strokes)

ケツ

- 結婚(けっこん) wedding, marriage
- 凍結(とうけつ) freezing
- 結構(けっこう) fine, correct, OK
- 結論(けつろん) conclusion
- 結局(けっきょく) after all
- 完結(かんけつ) finish
- 結果(けっか) result

むす(ぶ)

- 結(むす)ぶ to bind, to tie

 給 (522)
絡 (Jōyō)

 With thread, the frog will tie your mouth up *to close the subject.*

522 (2級)

WAGES, SUPPLY

給

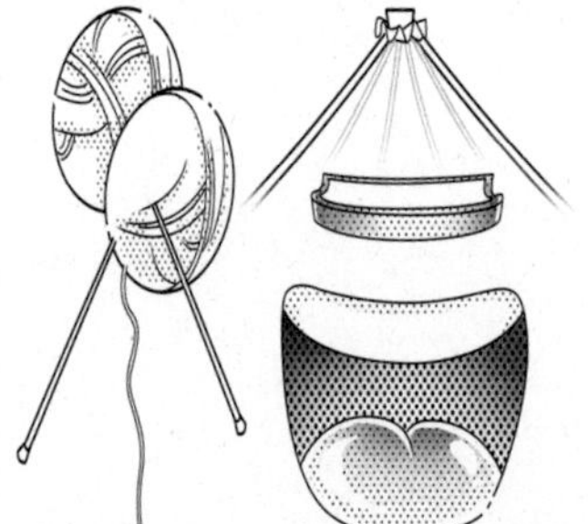

(12 strokes)

キュウ

- 給料(きゅうりょう) wages
- 月給(げっきゅう) monthly salary
- 給水(きゅうすい) water supply
- 給油(きゅうゆ) oil supply
- 補給(ほきゅう)する to stock up, to replenish
- 配給(はいきゅう) distribution
- 需給(じゅきゅう) supply and demand

たま(え)

- 行(い)き給(たま)え go (imperative)

 絡 (Jōyō)
詔 (Jōyō)
絵 (117)

 Thread binds the gathered wad of notes of your *wages.*

(9 strokes)

PERIOD, ERA, DISCIPLINE

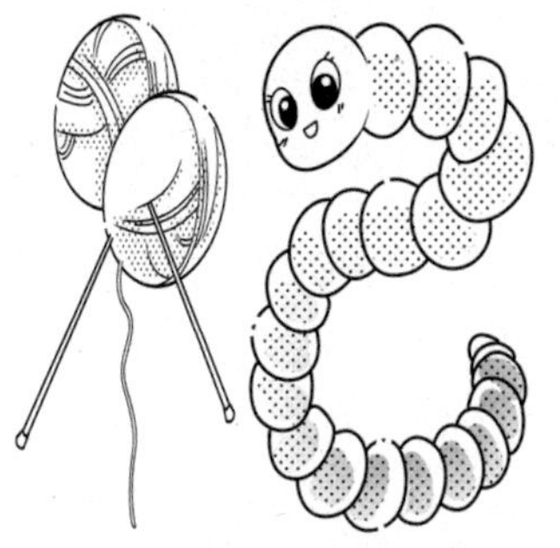

(1級)

523

キ

- 世紀（せいき） century
- 紀元（きげん） era
- 校紀（こうき） school discipline
- 風紀（ふうき） discipline
- 日本書紀（にほんしょき） Nihon Shoki (The Chronicles of Japan)

 The thread of infinite time is what Little Worm follows to visit other *eras*.

 約 (525)
記 (109)

(13 strokes)

TO CONTINUE

(2級)

524

ゾク

- 続行する（ぞっこうする） to continue
- 続編（ぞくへん） second part
- 連続（れんぞく） series, continuously
- 接続（せつぞく） connection

つづ(く/ける)

- 続く（つづく） to continue
- 手続き（てつづき） procedure
- 続き物（つづきもの） serial story
- 食べ続ける（たべつづける） to keep on eating

 續 (ant)

 The thread-vending frog will *continue* to sell tutus as long as people walk about wearing them.

 読 (114)
結 (521)

525 (2級)

PROMISE, AGREEMENT

約

ヤク
- 約束（やくそく） promise
- 契約（けいやく） contract
- 予約（よやく） reservation, booking
- 条約（じょうやく） treaty
- 婚約（こんやく） engagement (for a wedding)
- 節約する（せつやくする） to economize
- 制約（せいやく） restriction, limitation
- 要約（ようやく） summary

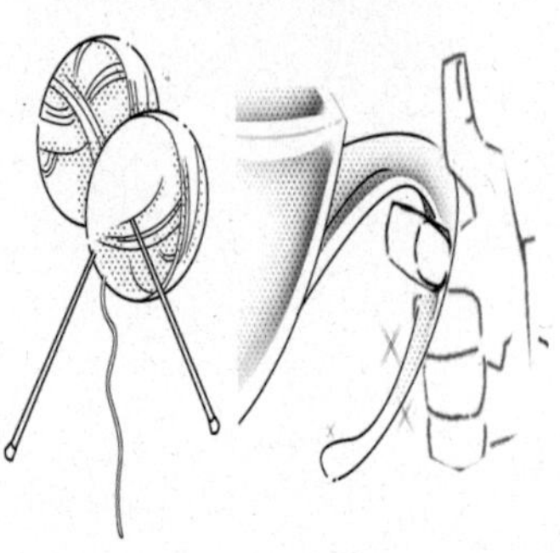

(9 strokes)

注 釣 (Jōyō)
的 (526)
紀 (523)

学 A *promise* of love is sealed with the thread that binds lovers who drink out of the same mug.

特 約 (alt)

526 (2級)

TARGET, SUFFIX FOR ADJECTIVES

的

テキ
- 的中（てきちゅう） bull's eye
- 標的（ひょうてき） target, mark
- 射的（しゃてき） target shooting
- 目的（もくてき） aim, goal, purpose
- 歴史的（れきしてき） historical
- 私的（してき） private
- 合理的（ごうりてき） rational

まと
- 的（まと） target, mark

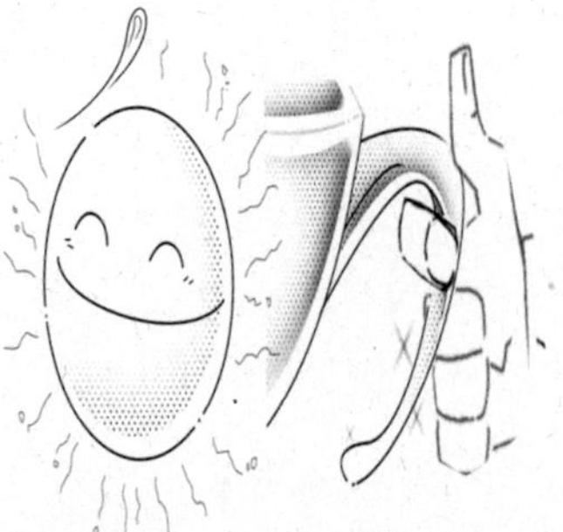

(8 strokes)

注 負 (389)
旬 (Jōyō)

学 To contain white milk is the *target* of every mug.

特 的 (alt)

527

(2級)

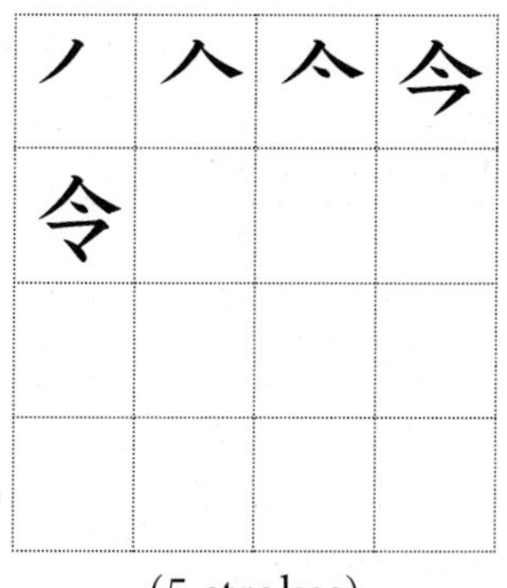

(5 strokes)

ORDER

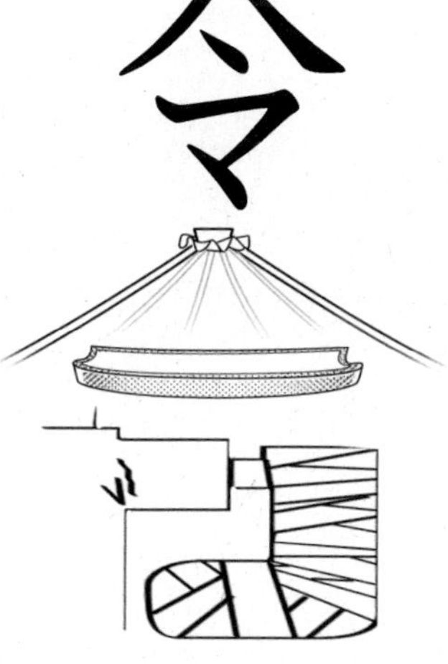

レイ

命令（めいれい） order
指令（しれい） assignment, order
司令（しれい） commander
辞令（じれい） written appointment
動員令（どういんれい） mobilization order
令嬢（れいじょう） young lady

特 令 (alt)

学 The *orders* come from the injured general, who is under the umbrella, chewing a slice of bread, with his arm in a cast.

注 今 (102)
会 (100)
命 (352)

528

(2級)

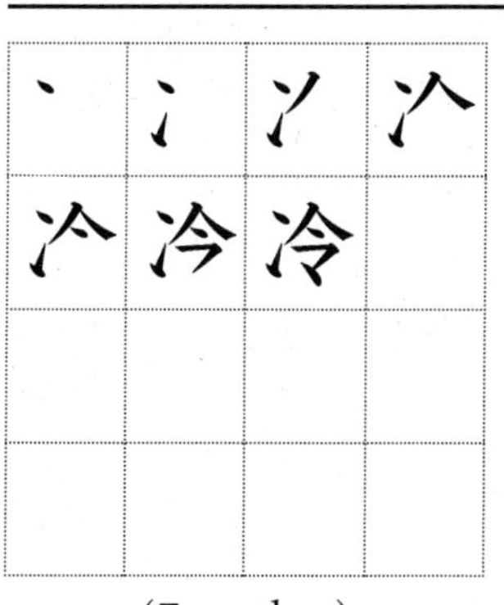

(7 strokes)

COLD, TO RESCUE, TO COOL

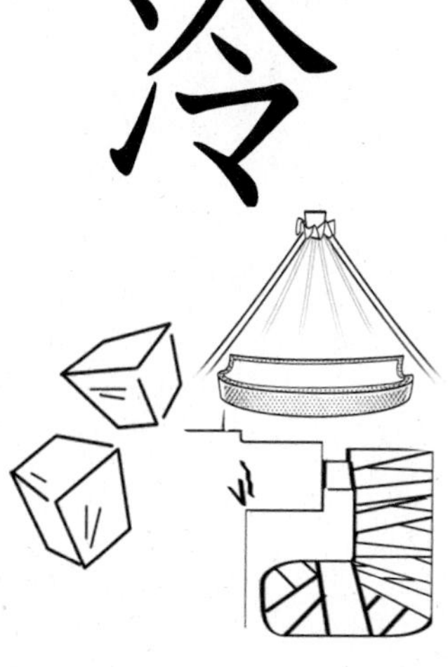

レイ

冷凍（れいとう） freezing
冷蔵庫（れいぞうこ） fridge

つめ(たい)

冷たい（つめたい） cold, cool

ひ(える/やす/やかす)

冷える（ひえる） to be cold
冷やす（ひやす） to cool

さ(める/ます)

冷める（さめる） to get cold

特 冷 (alt)

学 In spite of the *cold*, crushing ice is an order from the injured general.

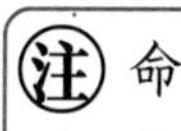

注 命 (352)
次 (346)

529 (1級)

WAREHOUSE

ソウ

- 倉庫 (そうこ) warehouse
- 穀倉 (こくそう) granary
- 船倉 (せんそう) ship's hold
- 倉卒 (そうそつ) very busy

くら

- 倉 (くら) warehouse

(10 strokes)

注 食 (130)

A *warehouse* can be improvised under an umbrella: you store the bread away and you leave the gate open for the mouth who hopes to eat it.

蔵 (alt)

530 (2級)

ORDER, TO OBEY

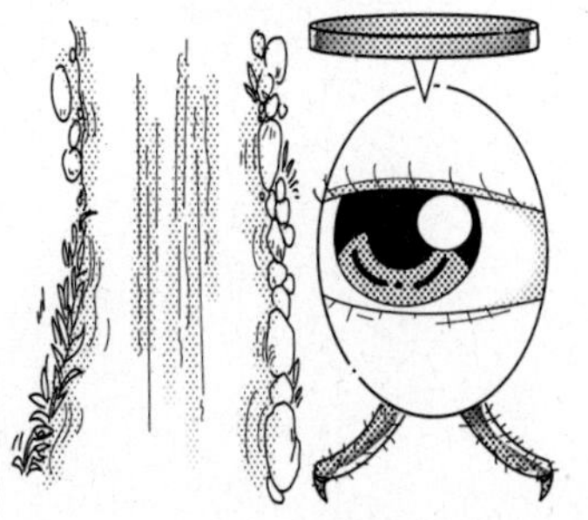

ジュン

- 順番 (じゅんばん) order
- 順調 (じゅんちょう) smooth (progress)
- 順位 (じゅんい) order, rank
- 従順 (じゅうじゅん) obedient, submissive
- 順序 (じゅんじょ) system, order
- 書き順 (かきじゅん) stroke order
- 手順 (てじゅん) procedure
- 先着順 (せんちゃくじゅん) by order of arrival

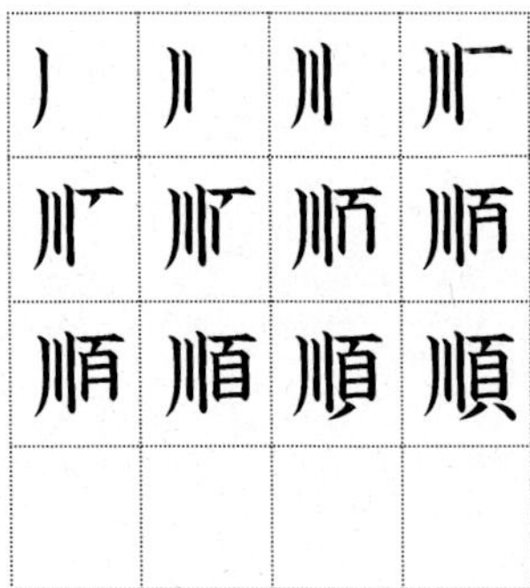

(12 strokes)

訓 (503)

Down the river floats a head: the one that did not obey the direct *order*... the poor thing.

531

TO WISH, TO ASK FOR A FAVOR

(2級)

(19 strokes)

ガン

- 願書 (がんしょ) written request
- 出願 (しゅつがん) request
- 願望 (がんぼう) wish, aspiration
- 念願 (ねんがん) wish, desire

ねが(う)

- 願い (ねがい) wish
- お願い (おねがい) please (when asking for a favor)

特

学 In Kim's world, those asking for a *wish* must go to a field and leave their head. Once the *wish* comes true, then they may retrieve it.

注 額 (5th)
頼 (Jōyō)

532

KIND, SPECIES, SIMILAR

(2級)

(18 strokes)

類	類	類	類
類	類	類	類

ルイ

- 種類 (しゅるい) species, kind of
- 人類 (じんるい) mankind
- 同類 (どうるい) similar, same kind
- 衣類 (いるい) clothing
- 分類 (ぶんるい) classification
- 類語 (るいご) synonym
- 親類 (しんるい) a relative

特 類 (alt)

学 Rice is the only *kind* of food there is for that gigantic *species* with a huge head.

注 頭 (171)
額 (5th)

…そして契約の
書類について、
手続きは…

お・
おいおい、
あの子、
誰なんだ？
ん？
雪子
ちゃん？

フ…目的が結婚なら、
他の相手を探した
ほうがいい。
冷たい女だ。雪姫。
ゆ…ユキ子
だって…

最初はどんなに
冷遇されても…
何歳？
まだ独身？
給料は？
…最後に世紀の
恋愛になる
にちがいない!!

彼女が従順じゃなくても
大丈夫だよ！紹介して
くれない？
うるさいなぁ…
今、倉卒なのだ。

お願い、紹介して
くれ！
お・ね・
が・い!!!
め・命令だよ、
それ！わ…わかった、
わかかった！
やった
!!!
じゃ、週末、
みんなでお茶でも飲みに
行くなら、いいって。

さ…
さぶい…
冷たい！
…言った
だろう。

Exercises 練習

1. Develop the stroke order of the following kanji.

紀												
冷												
倉												
類												

2. Choose the correct reading for each kanji or kanji combination.

a) 20世紀の人類の科学発展はめざましかった。

Mankind's scientific development in the 20th century is remarkable.

世紀:　1．せいぎ　2．せいき　3．よぎ　4．よき

人類:　1．にんるい　2．じんるい　3．にんうい　4．じんうい

b) 結局、順番予約とは、いわゆる「先着順」のことを意味します。

After all, "booking order" means "first come, first served."

結局:　1．けつきょく　2．けきょく　3．けっきょく　4．けきょく

順番:　1．じょんばん　2．じょんぱん　3．じゅんばん　4．じゆんばん

予約:　1．よてき　2．よまと　3．よいあく　4．よやく

先着順:　1．せんちゃくじょん　2．せんちゃくじゅん　3．せんちゃくじよん　4．せんちゃくじゆん

c) 給料のいい仕事は、私にとって優先(ゆうせん)順位が高い。はっきり言って、目的だ。

A well paid job is a priority for me. Frankly, that's my goal.

給料:　1．たまりょ　2．たまえりょ　3．きゅりょ　4．きゅうりょう

順位:　1．じゅんい　2．じょんい　3．じゅんりつ　4．じょんりつ

目的:　1．めまと　2．めてき　3．もくまと　4．もくてき

3. Write the kanji (one or more) and the meaning of the following words.

げっきゅう　______　______　　ひえる　______　______

つづく　____く　______　　おねがい　お____い　______

してき　______　______　　るいご　______　______

4. Correct either the reading or the writing mistakes in the following words.

鎌食	かまくら	連売	れんぞく	令命	めいれい
給ぶ	むすぶ	契的	けいやく	令蔵庫	れいぞうこ

Answers to exercises 練習解答

1. (Check them in the corresponding kanji table: #523, #528, #529, and #532)

2. a) 世紀: 2 | 人類: 2 / b) 結局: 3 | 順番: 3 | 予約: 4 | 先着順: 2

c) 給料: 4 | 順位: 1 | 目的: 4

3. げっきゅう: 月給, monthly salary | つづく: 続く, to continue | してき: 私的, private | ひえる: 冷える, to be cold | おねがい: お願い, please | るいご: 類語, synonym

4. **鎌倉** かまくら | **連続** れんぞく | **命令** めいれい | **結ぶ** むすぶ | **契約** けいやく | **冷蔵庫** れいぞうこ

Manga translation マンガ翻訳

Office worker 1: And concerning the documents for the contract, the procedure is...

Office worker 2: H-hey, who was that girl?

Office worker 1: Hm? Who, Yukiko?

Office worker 1: If your goal is to get married, you had better look for someone else. She is a very cold woman: The Snow Queen.

Office worker 2: H-her name is Yukiko.

Office worker 2: No matter how cold she is with me in the beginning...

Girl: How old are you? And you are still single? How much do you earn?

Office worker 2: ...in the end, I´m sure ours will be the romance of the century.

Office worker 2: I don't mind her not being submissive and obedient. Won't you introduce me to her?

Office worker 1: Don't be a pain. I´m very busy now.

Office worker 2: Please, introduce me to her! Pleeease!

Office worker 1: T-that sure is an order! OK, OK!

Office worker 1: Well, she says we can all go together for a drink this weekend.

Office worker 2: Yippeee!!

Office worker 2: S-she's cold! She's freezing!

Office worker 1: I told you so.

New elements 新しい部首

No new elements!

Lesson 47
第四十七課

533 (3級)

FEE, MATERIALS

料

リョウ

- 料金(りょうきん) price
- 無料(むりょう) free
- 給料(きゅうりょう) salary, wages
- 送料(そうりょう) shipping charges
- 資料(しりょう) document, material
- 料理(りょうり) cooking
- 材料(ざいりょう) ingredient
- 調味料(ちょうみりょう) seasoning
- 料亭(りょうてい) luxurious Japanese-style restaurant

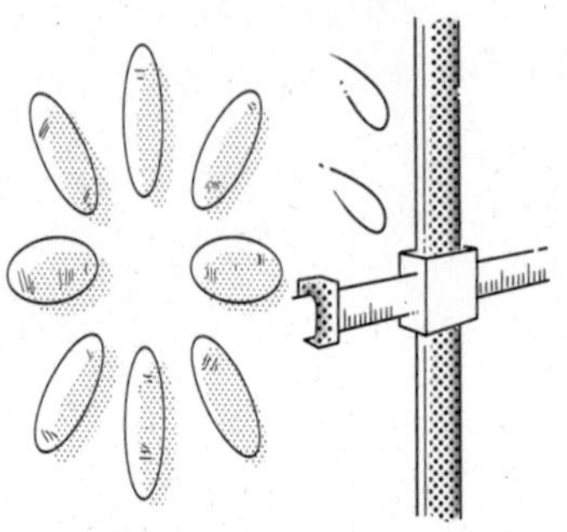

(10 strokes)

注 科 (153)
粒 (Jōyō)

学 Consider the *fees* as war rationings: handfuls of rice weighed on the scales.

特

534 (2級)

POWDER, FLOUR

粉

フン

- 粉砕(ふんさい) pulverization
- 花粉(かふん) pollen

こな

- 粉(こな) powder
- 粉薬(こなぐすり) powdered medicine
- 粉々(こなごな) pulverized

こ

- 小麦粉(こむぎこ) wheat flour

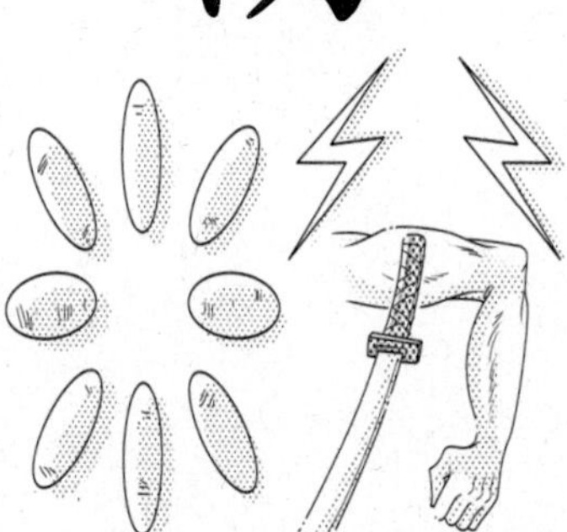

(10 strokes)

注 粧 (Jōyō)
初 (557)
粉 (Jōyō)

学 Rice, like *powder*, slips through fingers like the minutes of time.

特 粉 (alt)

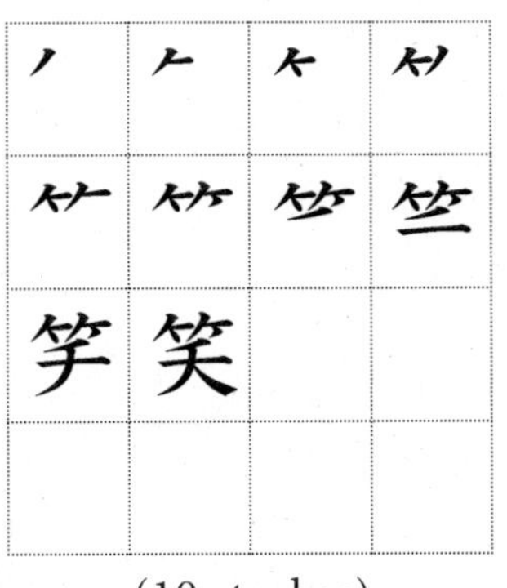

(10 strokes)

LAUGHTER

(2級)

535

ショウ

爆笑(ばくしょう) uproarious laugh
微笑(びしょう) smile
苦笑(くしょう) strained laugh
笑止(しょうし) absurd, "don't make me laugh"

わら(う)

笑(わら)う to laugh
笑(わら)い声(ごえ) laughter

Special

笑顔(えがお) smiling face

 A bamboo forest for Kim is the paradise of *laughter*.

注 策 (6th)
第 (342)
矢 (233)

(13 strokes)

SEASON, KNOT, SAVING

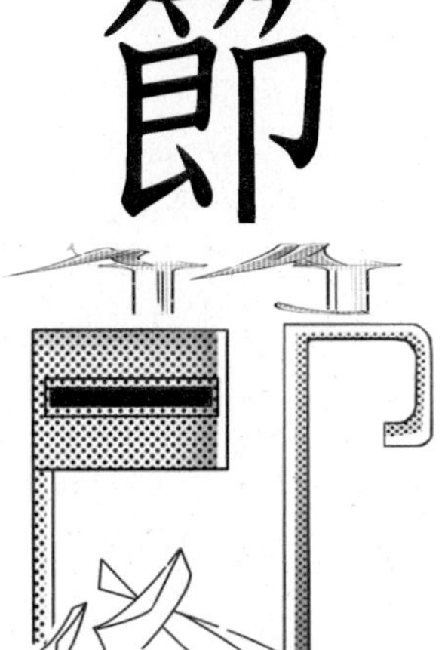

(2級)

536

セツ

関節(かんせつ) joint
節約(せつやく) saving
節水(せっすい) water saving
調節(ちょうせつ) adjustment, regulation
忠節(ちゅうせつ) loyalty, faithfulness
季節(きせつ) season
節分(せつぶん) Setsubun (festival)

ふし

節(ふし) knot, joint

 節 (alt)

 You can use bamboo to make both a mail box and a cane, because it lasts throughout all *seasons*.

 既 (Jōyō)
筋 (6th)
箱 (345)

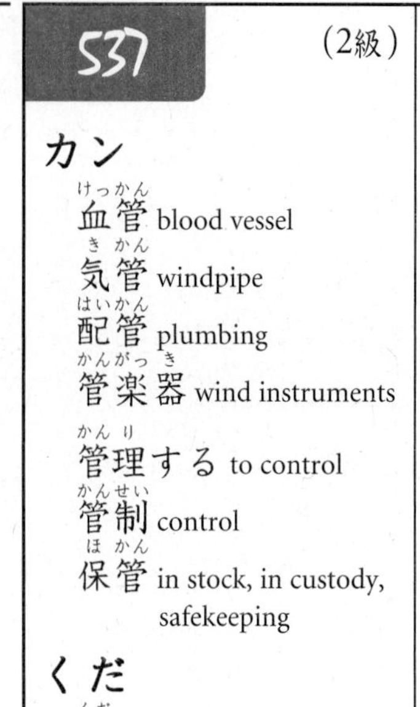

537 (2級)

カン

- 血管（けっかん） blood vessel
- 気管（きかん） windpipe
- 配管（はいかん） plumbing
- 管楽器（かんがっき） wind instruments
- 管理（かんり）する to control
- 管制（かんせい） control
- 保管（ほかん） in stock, in custody, safekeeping

くだ

- 管（くだ） tube, pipe

PIPE, TUBE, CONTROL

(14 strokes)

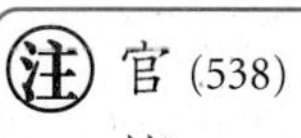
注 官 (538)
節 (536)

Bamboo is used by Parliament to make a peace *pipe* for maintaining control.

538 (2級)

カン

- 長官（ちょうかん） officer, director
- 警察官（けいさつかん） police officer
- 裁判官（さいばんかん） judge
- 官邸（かんてい） official residence
- 官庁（かんちょう） government office
- 任官（にんかん） appointment, commission

GOVERNMENT, OFFICER

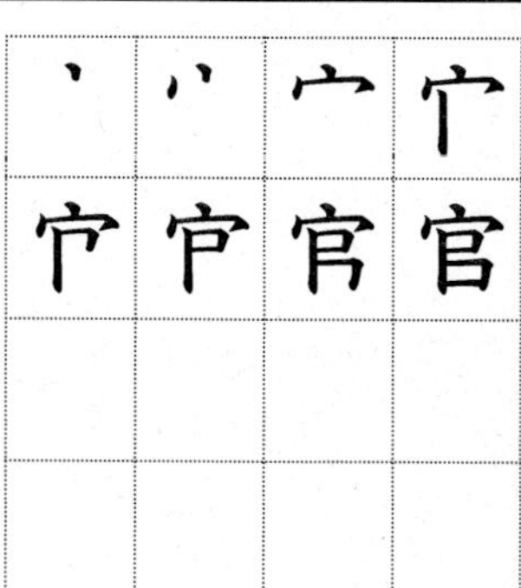

(8 strokes)

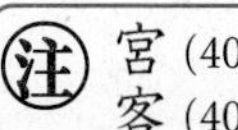
注 宮 (407)
客 (406)
館 (348)

The Parliament is the building (under a roof) for *government* officials with two flags: they use one or the other, depending on how it suits them.

539 COMPLETE

(2級)

(7 strokes)

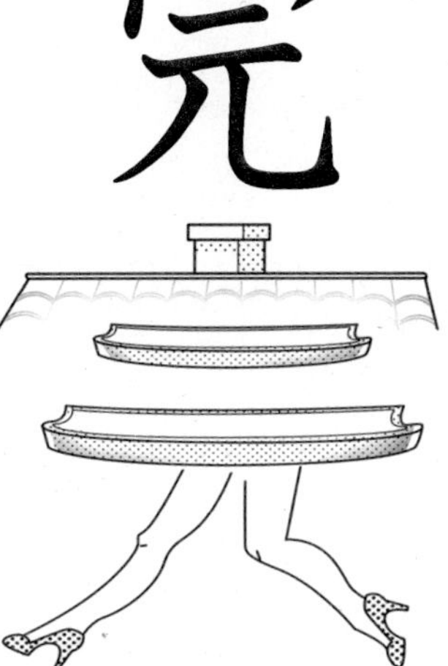

カン

- 完全 (かんぜん) complete, full
- 完璧 (かんぺき) perfect
- 完備 (かんび) fully equipped
- 完成 (かんせい) completed
- 完了 (かんりょう) finished
- 未完 (みかん) unfinished

特

学 The man who, under his roof, yields to the temptation of bread and slender legs is, curiously enough, a *complete* pervert.

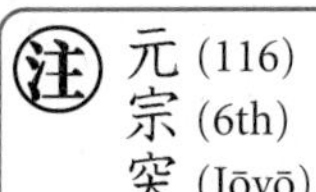

注 元 (116)
宗 (6th)
突 (Jōyō)

540 HARM, DAMAGE

(2級)

(10 strokes)

ガイ

- 害 (がい) harm
- 被害 (ひがい) damage
- 被害者 (ひがいしゃ) victim
- 有害 (ゆうがい) harmful
- 障害 (しょうがい) obstacle, hindrance, disability
- 公害 (こうがい) pollution
- 損害 (そんがい) casualty, loss
- 殺害 (さつがい) murder
- 害虫 (がいちゅう) harmful insect

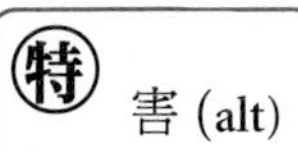

特  (alt)

学 A roof does nothing but *harm* the fertile land which feeds the mouths; after all, land needs to be in the open air.

注 容 (5th)
客 (406)

541 (2級)

ヒント:
サツ

- 偵察（ていさつ） reconnaissance
- 視察（しさつ） inspection
- 警察（けいさつ） police
- 警察官（けいさつかん） police officer
- 診察（しんさつ） medical examination
- 察知（さっち）する to gather, to understand

INSPECTION

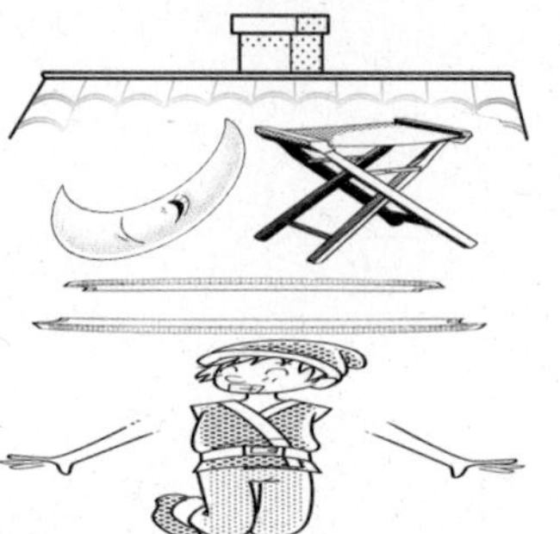

(14 strokes)

注 窒 (Jōyō)
祭 (364)
際 (5th)

学 If you *inspect* under the roofs of the people, you'll find that they are always in a festival mood.

542 (1級)

ヒョウ

- 一票（いっぴょう） one vote
- 投票（とうひょう）する to vote
- 白票（はくひょう） white vote
- 伝票（でんぴょう） a form
- 住民票（じゅうみんひょう） residence card
- 調査票（ちょうさひょう） questionnaire

VOTE

票

(11 strokes)

注 要 (544)
禁 (5th)
衆 (6th)

学 The convicts in prison have *voted* to organize a party, but the director has refused to show up.

(15 strokes)

MARK, SYMBOL

標

(2級)

543

ヒョウ

- 標識 (ひょうしき) signpost
- 商標 (しょうひょう) trademark
- 指標 (しひょう) index, indicator
- 音標 (おんぴょう) phonetic sign
- 座標 (ざひょう) the coordinates
- 標的 (ひょうてき) target, mark
- 標準 (ひょうじゅん) standard
- 目標 (もくひょう) goal, objective
- 標本 (ひょうほん) specimen

特

学 In Kim's world, a tree is where people place their votes, marking them with either the *symbol* √ or X on the trunk.

注 構 (5th) 様 (269) 横 (270)

(9 strokes)

NECESSARY

要

(2級)

544

ヨウ

- 必要 (ひつよう) necessary
- 要件 (ようけん) important matter
- 重要 (じゅうよう) important
- 概要 (がいよう) summary
- 要求 (ようきゅう) requirement
- 要請 (ようせい) request
- 要するに (よう) in sum...

い(る)

- 要る (い) to need

特  要 (alt)

学 When you imprison a woman in a cell, it's because it was absolutely *necessary*.

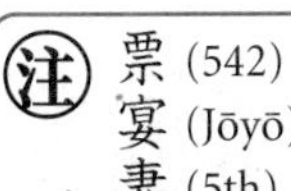

注 票 (542) 宴 (Jōyō) 妻 (5th)

シカゴ　1923年
警察だあああ!!
禁酒の特別査察官です。協力してくれ。
は・はい、よろこんで！ど・どうぞ！
そんな作り笑いは必要ありません。
酒は大損害の原因だ。だからこそ禁酒法が投票で決められた。そして、この僕の目標は節操を守ることだ。
おい!!何だい、その管だらけのボイラー。その材料、その粉、そのアルコールの匂い…
あ・あの…その…
やっぱり。この店で…
ち・ち・ちがう…
…手作り香水が完成するんですね。いいね。
…?

Exercises 練習

1. Develop the stroke order of the following kanji.

節												
官												
害												
票												

2. Choose the correct reading for each kanji or kanji combination.

a) 今年もいよいよ花粉の季節がやってきました。私(わたし)はその被害者の一人ですが...

This year, yet again, the pollen season has arrived. I'm one of its victims...

花粉: 1．かこ　2．かふん　3．かこな　4．かごな

季節: 1．きせっ　2．きせつ　3．きぶし　4．きふし

被害者: 1．ひがいしゃ　2．ひかいしゃ　3．ひがいもの　4．ひかいもの

b) 料理をする前に、材料をそろえる必要がある。

Before you start cooking, you need to gather the ingredients.

料理: 1．りより　2．りり　3．りょうり　4．りょっり

材料: 1．さいりょ　2．ざいりょ　3．さいりょう　4．ざいりょう

必要: 1．ひよう　2．ひつよう　3．ひっよう　4．ひつい

c) 「今、障害を乗り越(こ)えるのはただの目標です」と悲しい笑顔で言った。

"Now, overcoming this obstacle is my only goal," he said, with a sad smile.

障害: 1．しょうかい　2．しょうがい　3．しょかい　4．しょがい

目標: 1．めひょ　2．めひょう　3．もくひょ　4．もくひょう

笑顔: 1．えがお　2．えかお　3．しょうがお　4．しょうかお

3. Write the kanji (one or more) and the meaning of the following words.

りょうきん ______ ______　じゅうよう ______ ______

かんり ______ ______　はくひょう ______ ______

ちょうかん ______ ______　かんぜん ______ ______

4. Correct either the reading or the writing mistakes in the following words.

粉薬　ふんぐすり　元了　かんりょう　票準　ひょうじゅん

警祭管　けいさつかん　投要　とうひょう　要る　いる

Answers to exercises 練習解答

1. (Check them in the corresponding kanji table: #536, #538, #540, and #542)

2. a) 花粉: 2 | 季節: 2 | 被害者: 1 / b) 料理: 3 | 材料: 4 | 必要: 2
c) 障害: 2 | 目標: 4 | 笑顔: 1

3. りょうきん: 料金, price | かんり: 管理, to supervise | ちょうかん: 長官, officer | じゅうよう: 重要, important | はくひょう: 白票, white vote| かんぜん: 完全, complete

4. 粉薬 こなぐすり | 完了 かんりょう | 標準 ひょうじゅん | 警察管 けいさつかん | 投票 とうひょう | 要る いる (correct)

Manga translation マンガ翻訳

Text panel: Chicago, 1923.

Little boy: The police! Aaaah!

Police inspector: Special inspector against alcohol. Please, cooperate.

Barman: Y-yes, it will be a pleasure. Come in!

Inspector: There´s no need for that fake smile.

Inspector: Alcohol is the cause of much damage. That´s why the Prohibition was voted on and passed, and my aim is to uphold my principles.

Inspector (OFF): Hey!! What´s that cauldron full of pipes, those ingredients, that powder, that smell of alcohol...?

Barman: W-well, that is... Err...

Inspector: Yes, I knew it. In these premises...

Barman: N-no. You´re mistaken...

Inspector: ...perfumes are made using traditional methods. Well, that´s very good.

Barman: ...?

New elements 新しい部首

凵 birthday cake

牙 evil duke

Lesson 48
第四十八課

545 (3級)

TO LIKE

好

コウ

好物（こうぶつ） favorite dish
好意（こうい） good intention
好評（こうひょう） favorable criticism

この(む)

好み（このみ） (personal) preference
お好み焼き（おこのみやき） okonomi-yaki (Japanese-style pancake)

す(く)

好き（すき） liking
物好き（ものずき） eccentric

く 女 女 好 好 好

(6 strokes)

好 好 好 好 好 好 好 好

注 妙 (Jōyō)
妊 (Jōyō)

学 A woman *likes* her son above everything else.

特

546 (2級)

SEASON

キ

季節（きせつ） season
四季（しき） the four seasons
季刊（きかん） quarterly publication
夏季（かき） summer
春季（しゅんき） spring
雨季（うき） rainy season

(8 strokes)

季 季 季 季 季 季 季 季

注 委 (399)
秀 (Jōyō)
孝 (6th)

学 The leaves of the weeping willow show the boy the changes of the *seasons*.

特

(10 strokes)

GRANDCHILD

(2級)

547

ソン

子孫（しそん） descendant

天孫（てんそん） descendant of a god

孫悟空（そんごくう） Sun Wukong (Son Gokū, literary character)

まご

孫（まご） grandchild

孫娘（まごむすめ） granddaughter

 The *grandchild* is the boy with the golden thread binding him to his grandparents.

 係 (259)
孤 (Jōyō)
乳 (6th)

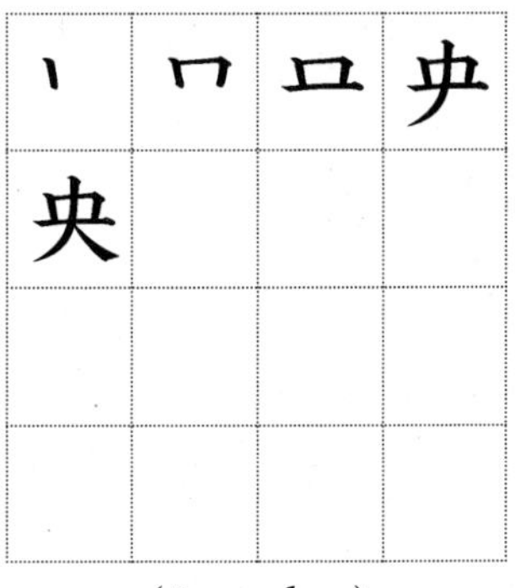

(5 strokes)

CENTER

央

(2級)

548

オウ

中央（ちゅうおう） center, central

中央アメリカ（ちゅうおう） Central America

中央口（ちゅうおうぐち） central exit

震央（しんおう） epicenter (in an earthquake)

 On his birthday, Kim feels the *center* of the universe.

 来 (135)
英 (549)
市 (203)

549 (3級)

TALENTED, ENGLISH

英

エイ

- 英雄（えいゆう） hero
- 英才（えいさい） talent, genius
- 英国（えいこく） England
- 英語（えいご） English (language)
- 英文学（えいぶんがく） English literature
- 英会話（えいかいわ） English conversation

一	十	廾	艹
艹	苎	英	英

(8 strokes)

英	英	英	英
英	英	英	英

注 栄 (469)
映 (6th)
芸 (550)

学 Kim has been given a flower crown on his birthday to celebrate his *talent*: he truly feels like a hero now.

特 英 (alt)

550 (2級)

ART

芸

ゲイ

- 芸術（げいじゅつ） art
- 手芸（しゅげい） handcraft
- 文芸（ぶんげい） literature
- 芸能人（げいのうじん） entertainer celebrity, star
- 芸者（げいしゃ） geisha
- 曲芸（きょくげい） acrobatics
- 無芸（むげい） artless, talentless

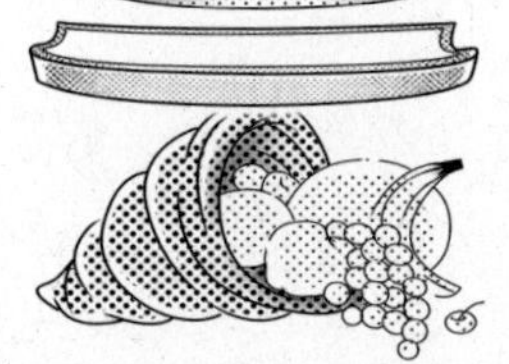

一	十	廾	艹
芏	芸	芸	

(7 strokes)

芸	芸	芸	芸
芸	芸	芸	芸

注 若 (6th)
苦 (431)

学 A nutritive form of *art* is to wear a crown of flowers and stuff oneself with food.

特 藝 (ant)

551 — SPROUT, SEED

(1級)

Stroke order: 一 十 廾 芏 芒 芉 芽 芽

(8 strokes)

芽

ガ

発芽(はつが)する to sprout, to germinate

芽胞(がほう) spore

め

芽(め) bud, sprout

芽生(めば)える to sprout

若芽(わかめ) young bud

  芽 (alt)

学 A crown of flowers on an evil duke helps the *seed* of goodness to *sprout* within him.

注 草 (69)
芝 (Jōyō)
茂 (Jōyō)

552 — VEGETABLE

(3級)

Stroke order: 一 十 廾 芏 芒 芓 芔 莁 苹 菜 菜

(11 strokes)

菜 菜 菜 菜 菜 菜 菜 菜

菜

サイ

野菜(やさい) vegetable

菜食主義(さいしょくしゅぎ) vegetarianism

白菜(はくさい) Chinese cabbage

前菜(ぜんさい) appetizer, starter

な

菜(な)っ葉(ぱ) vegetables, lettuce

青菜(あおな) vegetables

  菜 (alt)

学 Here is a tree holding tight to a crown of flowers: it doesn't want to cease being the king of *vegetables*.

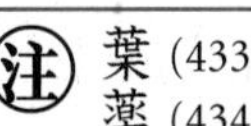

注 葉 (433)
薬 (434)
栄 (469)

553 (2級)

レキ

- 歴史（れきし） history
- 歴史的（れきしてき） historical
- 学歴（がくれき） academic background
- 病歴（びょうれき） medical history
- 逮捕歴（たいほれき） criminal history
- 履歴書（りれきしょ） personal history, résumé

CALENDAR

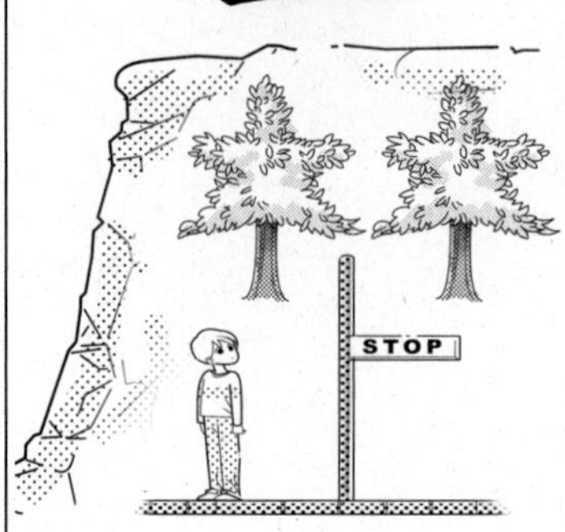

(14 strokes)

注 暦 (Jōyō)
禁 (5th)
磨 (Jōyō)

Under the cliff, shall we meet by the woods? Stop! Let me have a look at the *calendar*...

特  歷 (alt) 歴 (simp)

554 (2級)

シ

- 歴史（れきし） history
- 世界史（せかいし） world history
- 日本史（にほんし） Japanese history
- 史上（しじょう） in history
- 史書（ししょ） history book
- 史料（しりょう） historical document
- 史学者（しがくしゃ） historian

CHRONICLE, HISTORY

(5 strokes)

注 央 (548)
吏 (Jōyō)
虫 (14)

学 The dream of our Astaire Turtle, before losing his head, is to make *history* dancing.

555 (2級)

(12 strokes)

VIEW, SCENERY

景

ケイ

夜景 (やけい) night view
風景 (ふうけい) view, scenery
背景 (はいけい) background
絶景 (ぜっけい) striking view
全景 (ぜんけい) complete view
不景気 (ふけいき) recession
景品 (けいひん) free bonus gift

Special

景色 (けしき) scenery

 Look at the beautiful *view* of the capital under the sun.

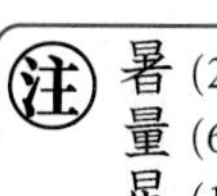 暑 (264) 量 (632) 星 (147)

556 (2級)

(12 strokes)

THE MOST, MAXIMUM

最

サイ

最新 (さいしん) the newest
最初 (さいしょ) the first
最悪 (さいあく) the worst
最大 (さいだい) the biggest
最低 (さいてい) the lowest, despicable
最高 (さいこう) the highest, great
最近 (さいきん) recently

もっと(も)

最も (もっとも) the most...

 The sun is responsible for *most* things. That's why he takes care of everything, from the greatest to the lowest, under his watchful eye.

 農 (298) 暴 (5th) 職 (5th)

こんな景色が大好きです。春季になると花が芽生えて、まるで絵画みたい。

絵画と言えば、孫は画家ですわ。今、歴史的な都市、京都で最新の作品を展示しています。
おお～
いらっしゃい！新鮮な野菜よ!!

歴史と言えば、家の孫は歴史と英語学を勉強して、今はね、東京大学で働いています。
おお おぉ～！
大学喫茶店
はい、コーヒーです。

社長、新しい中央処理装置のおかげで、今月の売り上げが30兆円に上がりました。
IBN
はあ？30兆だけ？まいったなあ…
いいわね…うちは無芸だな。パソコンの前に釘付けの日々が続いている。

Exercises 練習

1. Develop the stroke order of the following kanji.

央												
芽												
菜												
史												

2. Choose the correct reading for each kanji or kanji combination.

a) 僕(ぼく)の好物は季節によります。冬は野菜のお好み焼きなんだ。

My favorite dish depends on the season. In winter, it's a vegetable Japanese pancake.

好物:	1．こうもの	2．このもの	3．こうぶつ	4．このぶつ
野菜:	1．のな	2．のさい	3．やな	4．やさい
お好み焼き:	1．おこうみやき	2．おこのみやき	3．おこのみなき	4．おこのみさき

b) 最近の芸者は、芸術や文芸はともかく、英語も学びます。

Lately, geishas, besides art and literature, also study English.

最近:	1．さいきん	2．さきん	3．もときん	4．もっときん
芸者:	1．げえしゃ	2．げしゃ	3．げいしゃ	4．ぎいしゃ
芸術:	1．げいしゅつ	2．げいじゅつ	3．げえしゅつ	4．げじゅつ
文芸:	1．ぶんげえ	2．ぶんげい	3．ぶんけい	4．ぶんぎい
英語:	1．えいご	2．えご	3．えいごう	4．えごう

c) ９０年代の不景気がわかるには、歴史的な背景を知るべきだと思います。

In order to understand the 90's recession, I think we should know the historical background.

不景気:	1．ぶけいき	2．ぶけき	3．ふけいき	4．ぶけいき
歴史:	1．しれき	2．しきれ	3．れしき	4．れきし
背景:	1．けいはい	2．けはい	3．はいけい	4．はいけ

3. Write the kanji (one or more) and the meaning of the following words.

まご	______	______	はくさい	______	______
ちゅうおう	______	______	がくれき	______	______
きせつ	______	______	せかいし	______	______
えいかいわ	______	______	さいあく	______	______

Answers to exercises 練習解答

1. (Check them in the corresponding kanji table: #548, #551, #552, and #554)

2. a) 好物: 3 | 野菜: 4 | お好み焼き: 2 / b) 最近: 1 | 芸者: 3 | 芸術: 2 | 文芸: 2 | 英語: 1
c) 不景気: 3 | 歴史: 4 | 背景: 3

3. まご: 孫, grandchild | ちゅうおう: 中央, center, central | きせつ: 季節, season | えいかいわ: 英会話, English conversation | はくさい: 白菜, Chinese cabbage | がくれき: 学歴, academic background | せかいし: 世界史, world history | さいあく: 最悪, the worst

Manga translation マンガ翻訳

Grandmother 2: I love this view. As soon as spring arrives, flowers sprout, and it's just like a picture.

Grandmother 1: Speaking of pictures, my grandson is a painter. Right now his latest work is being exhibited in the historical city of Kyoto.

Grandson 1: Walk up! Fresh vegetables!

Grandmother 2/ Grandmother 3: Oooh

Grandmother 2: Speaking of history, my grandson studied History and English, and he now works at Tokyo University.

Sign: University Cafe

Grandson 2: Here's your coffee.

Grandmother 1/ Grandmother 3: Ooooh!

Grandmother 3: I'm so jealous... Mine is artless. He spends day after day in front of his computer.

Employee: Sir, thanks to the new central processing unit, this month's sales amount to 30 trillion yen.

Grandson 3: What? Only 30 trillion? That beats me.

New elements 新しい部首

 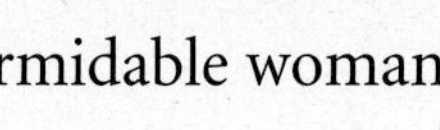 formidable woman  |  devil teeth 

Lesson 49
第四十九課

557 (2級)

FIRST, BEGINNING

初

シ ョ

初日(しょにち) the first day
初級(しょきゅう) beginner's level
初期(しょき) initial period
初対面(しょたいめん) first meeting

はじ(め/めて)

初め(はじめ) in the beginning

はつ

初恋(はつこい) one's first love
初の成功(はつのせいこう) one's first success

丶	ラ	ネ	ネ
ネ	初	初	

(7 strokes)

初	初	初	初
初	初	初	初

注 礼 (419)
切 (94)

学 The *first* woman in history was a formidable woman who wore a sword around the house. That's where women get their reputation from.

特

558 (2級)

OUTSKIRTS, VICINITY

辺

ヘン

この辺(へん) this area
周辺(しゅうへん) outskirts
近辺(きんぺん) vicinity
辺地(へんち) remote place

あた(り)

この辺り(あたり) around here

べ

海辺(うみべ) seaside
浜辺(はまべ) beach

フ	刀	刀	辺
辺			

(5 strokes)

辺	辺	辺	辺
辺	辺	辺	辺

注 切 (94)
近 (178)
迎 (Jōyō)

学 Be sure to carry a sword when you take to the road, because the *outskirts* are dangerous.

特 邊 (ant)
邉 (ant)

(5 strokes)

TO WRAP

(2級) **559**

ホウ

包装（ほうそう） wrapping
包帯（ほうたい） bandage
包容（ほうよう）する to accept, to embrace
包囲（ほうい）する to surround

つつ(む)

包（つつ）む to wrap
小包（こづつみ） (postal) parcel

 包 (alt)

 Don't forget *to wrap* the present: a mug with a little worm inside!

 句 (5th)
危 (6th)

(10 strokes)

TO LINK, TO CONTINUE, TO GO TOGETHER

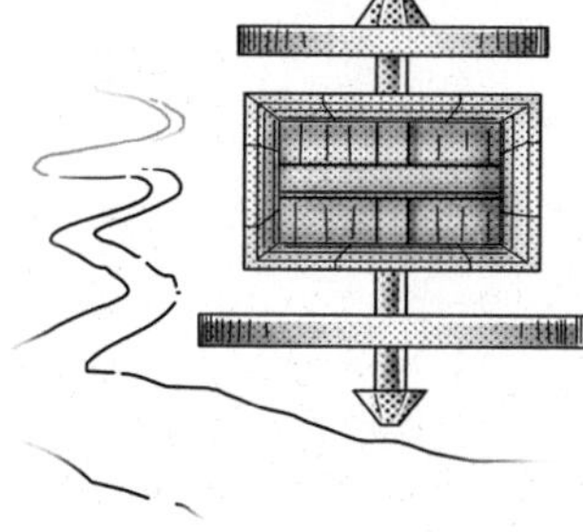

(2級) **560**

レン

連絡（れんらく） contact, call
関連（かんれん） relationship, connection
連中（れんちゅう） people, the crowd
国連（こくれん） United Nations

つ(れる)

連（つ）れ合（あ）い (your) partner, companion

つら(なる/ねる)

連（つら）なる to stand in a row

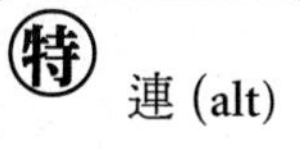 連 (alt)

 Without a car, the road needn't exist; without a road the car can't *continue*. These are two *linked* concepts that always go *together*.

 軍 (561)
運 (374)
道 (175)

561 (2級)

ARMY

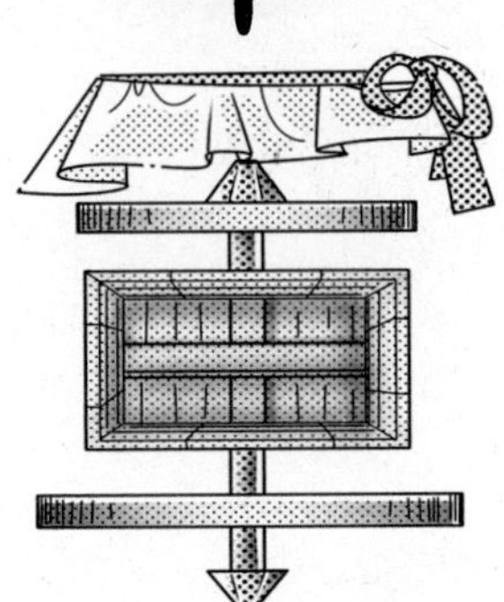

グン

- 軍隊（ぐんたい） army
- 軍人（ぐんじん） military person
- 空軍（くうぐん） air force
- 敵軍（てきぐん） enemy army
- 連合軍（れんごうぐん） allied armies
- アメリカ軍（ぐん） USA forces
- 将軍（しょうぐん） general, *shōgun*

丶 冖 冖 冖 冒 冒 冒 亘 軍

(9 strokes)

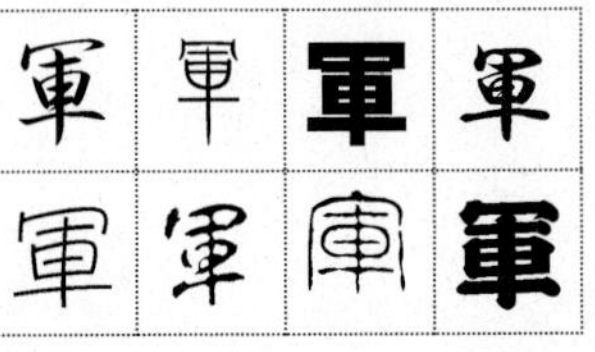

注 運 (374) 庫 (367)

学 Look at this old *army* tank: it was nothing but a tutu draped over a car so the enemy couldn't see inside.

特

562 (2級)

RING, WHEEL

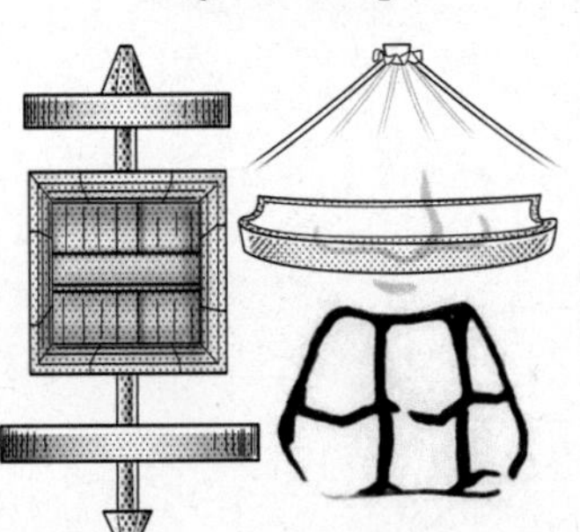

リン

- 車輪（しゃりん） wheel
- 前輪（ぜんりん） front wheel
- 二輪車（にりんしゃ） two-wheeled vehicle
- 競輪（けいりん） bicycle race
- 五輪（ごりん） Olympic rings; Olympic Games

わ

- 輪（わ） circle
- 指輪（ゆびわ） ring

一 厂 币 币 百 亘 車 軡 軡 軡 軡 輪 輪 輪 輪

(15 strokes)

輪 輪 輪 輪 輪 輪 輪 輪

注 輪 (5th) 論 (6th)

学 The car has a punctured *wheel*; beside it, under an umbrella, chewing bread, the devil wonders what to do next.

特

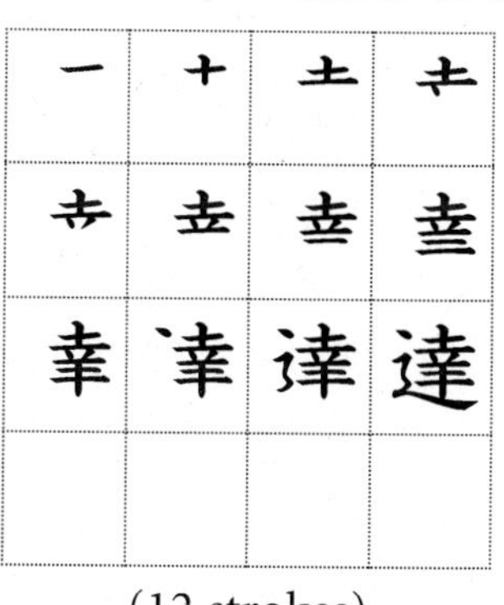

(12 strokes)

TO ATTAIN, SEVERAL, TO REACH

(2級)

563

タツ

到達（とうたつ） arrival, goal
達成（たっせい）する to achieve
配達（はいたつ） delivery
速達（そくたつ） express delivery
達人（たつじん） expert, master
上達（じょうたつ） improvement
達（たっ）する to arrive, to reach

たち

私達（わたしたち） we
ジン達（たち） Jin and the others

特 達 (alt)

学 *To reach* fertile land is the goal that the sheep wishes to attain; but, first, he must find the road there.

注 連 (560) 遅 (Jōyō)

(15 strokes)

TO CHOOSE

(2級)

564

セン

選挙（せんきょ） election
選出（せんしゅつ）する to choose
抽選（ちゅうせん） to draw lots
選択（せんたく） choice
選手（せんしゅ） player, athlete

えら(ぶ)

選（えら）ぶ to choose

特 選 (alt) 选 (simp)

学 The two little worms must *choose* between two options: they either stay on the hammock with legs or take to the road.

注 通 (186) 遷 (Jōyō) 透 (Jōyō)

565 (2級)

TOGETHER, AT THE SAME TIME

キョウ

共有（きょうゆう）する to share
共同（きょうどう） combination, common
共存（きょうぞん） coexistence
共通（きょうつう） common
共産党（きょうさんとう） communist party

とも

共働（ともばたら）き both working (a couple)
共倒（ともだお）れする to fall together

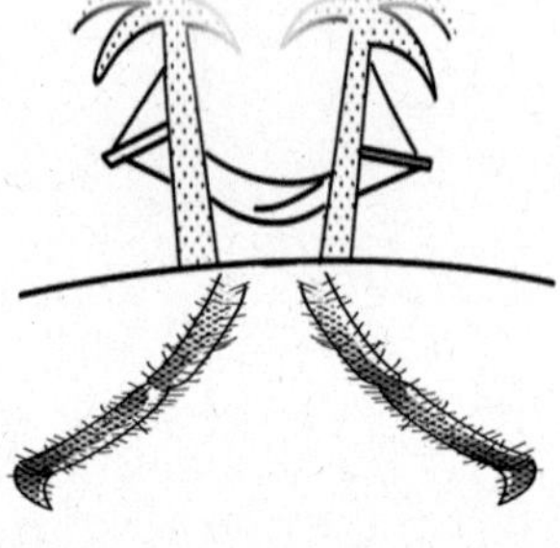

(6 strokes)

注 先 (41)
児 (574)
供 (6th)

 If you want to lie *together, at the same time*, any hammock will not do: it must be a hammock with legs.

566 (2級)

SOLDIER

ヘイ

兵士（へいし） soldier
兵隊（へいたい） troops
兵舎（へいしゃ） barracks
兵器（へいき） weapon
徴兵（ちょうへい） recruitment

ヒョウ

兵法（ひょうほう） the art of war
兵糧（ひょうろう） military provisions

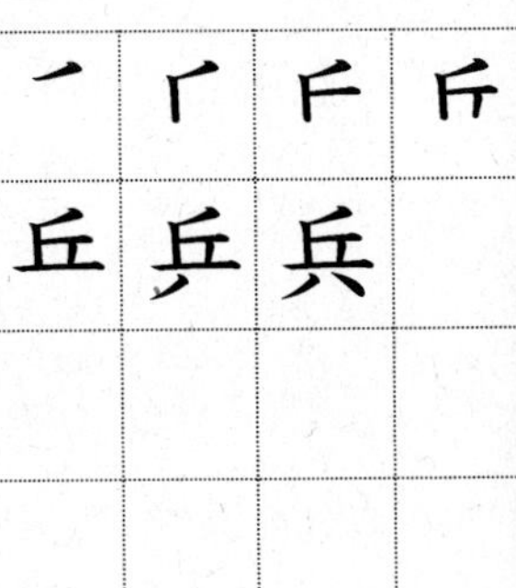

(7 strokes)

注 共 (565)
具 (413)
丘 (Jōyō)

 The secret for an impeccable uniform is that the *soldiers* iron them everyday.

567 — TO BEND, TO FOLD, OPPORTUNITY

(2級)

(7 strokes)

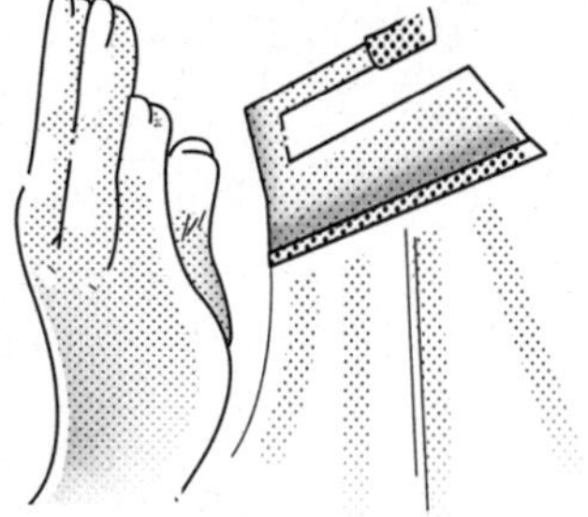

セツ

- 骨折（こっせつ） broken bone
- 曲折する（きょくせつする） to bend
- 右折する（うせつする） to turn right
- 百折不撓（ひゃくせつふとう） unbeatable, indomitable

お(る/れる/り)

- 折る（おる） to bend, to fold
- 折れ目（おれめ） (the line of) a fold
- 折り紙（おりがみ） *origami* (art of folding paper)

特

学 If you can't *bend* the spoon with your hand, try hitting it with the iron.

注 所 (438) 近 (178) 払 (Jōyō)

568 — TO RECOMMEND, TO MENTION, TO RAISE

(1級)

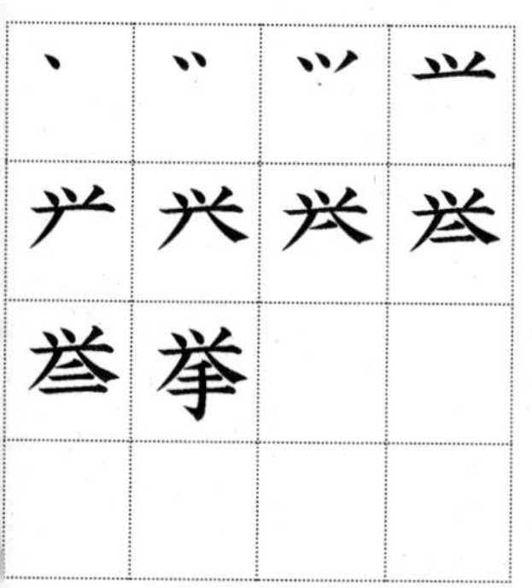

(10 strokes)

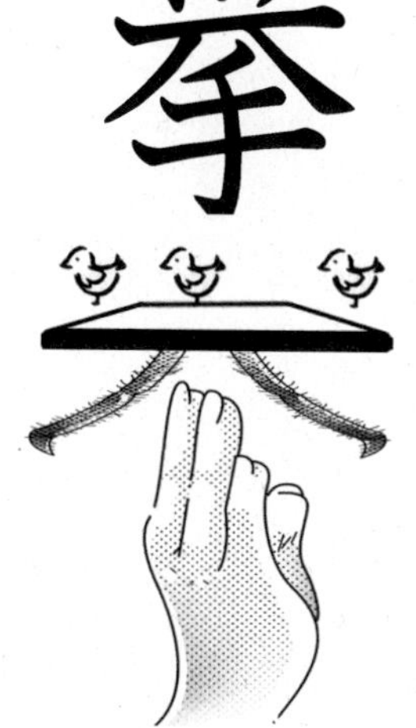

キョ

- 選挙（せんきょ） election
- 列挙する（れっきょする） to enumerate
- 挙式する（きょしきする） to celebrate a ceremony
- 快挙（かいきょ） heroic deed

あ(げる/がる)

- 挙げる（あげる） to raise, to recreuit, to celebrate (e.g., a ceremony)
- 挙がる（あがる） to be mentioned

特 擧 (ant) 舉 (alt)

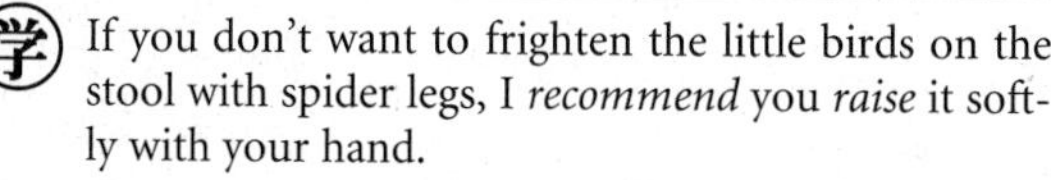

学 If you don't want to frighten the little birds on the stool with spider legs, I *recommend* you *raise* it softly with your hand.

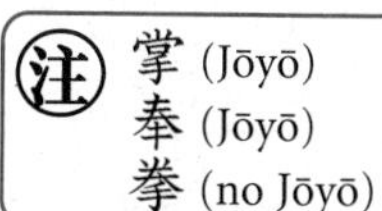

注 掌 (Jōyō) 奉 (Jōyō) 拳 (no Jōyō)

王様、この辺りで食糧や兵器と共に敵軍の兵士が大勢見つかりました。

城壁の内の輪まで達するのは初めてだ。我々を包囲するつもりだろう…せめて味方のストラビア王国と連絡できれば…

アルクツルス騎士をよんでくれ！
はい、陛下！

アルクツルスの快挙を数えればきりがない。百折不撓な騎士だ。

アルクツルス、危険な使命に選ばれた…

というわけで、ストラビア城の上を飛んだら、この手紙を落としてね。じゃ、後はまかせる。
で・でも、陛下…
了解。長距離輸送ですね。

Exercises 練習

1. Develop the stroke order of the following kanji.

初												
包												
輪												
選												

2. Choose the correct reading for each kanji or kanji combination.

a) ただいま、国連の軍隊も参加（さんか）するという連絡がありました。

We have just been informed that the forces of the United Nations will also participate.

国連: 1．くにつら 2．くにづら 3．こくえん 4．こくれん

軍隊: 1．くんたい 2．ぐんたい 3．くんだい 4．ぐんだい

連絡: 1．つらく 2．つららく 3．れんらく 4．えんらく

b) 何年ぶりの初恋の人に会った。空軍 兵士になっていた。

I have seen my first love after many years. He has become a soldier in the Air Force.

初恋: 1．しょこい 2．はじこい 3．はつこい 4．はっこい

空軍: 1．くぐん 2．くうぐん 3．くくん 4．くうくん

兵士: 1．へいし 2．へし 3．ひょうし 4．ひょし

c) 息子が周辺のちんぴら連中と付き合っている。共通点がないのに！

My son mixes with a crowd of local troublemakers. In spite of him having nothing in common with them!

周辺: 1．しゅうえん 2．しゅうへん 3．しゅうべ 4．しゅうへ

連中: 1．つらちゅう 2．れんちゅう 3．つらなか 4．れんなか

共通: 1．きょうつう 2．きょつう 3．ともつう 4．ともつ

3. Write the kanji (one or more) and the meaning of the following words.

しょきゅう ______ ______ じょうたつ ______ ______

こづつみ ______ ______ おりがみ ___り___ ______

ゆびわ ______ ______ せんきょ ______ ______

4. Correct either the reading or the writing mistakes in the following words.

己帯	ほうたい	将車	しょうぐん	骨折	こっぜつ
連る	つれる	速幸	そくたつ	供存	きょうぞん

Answers to exercises 練習解答

1. (Check them in the corresponding kanji table: #557, #559, #562, and #564)

2. a) 国連: 4 | 軍隊: 2 | 連絡: 3 / b) 初恋: 3 | 空軍: 2 | 兵士: 1 / c) 周辺: 2 | 連中: 2 | 共通: 1

3. しょきゅう: 初級, beginner's level | こづつみ: 小包, (postal) parcel | ゆびわ: 指輪, ring | じょうたつ: 上達, improvement | おりがみ: 折り紙, origami (art of folding paper) | せんきょ: 選挙, election

4. 包帯 ほうたい | 将軍 しょうぐん | 骨折 こっせつ | 連れる つれる | 速達 そくたつ | 共存 きょうぞん

Manga translation マンガ翻訳

Messenger: Your Majesty, we have discovered in the surrounding area a large number of enemy soldiers together with weapons and provisions.

King: This is the first time they've reached the inner ring of the castle wall. They probably intend to besiege us. If, at least, we could contact our allies from the kingdom of Stolavia...

King: Call Sir Arcturus!

Soldier: Yes, Your Majesty!

King (OFF): Arcturus' deeds are innumerable. He is a knight who is unbeatable.

King: Arcturus, I have chosen you for a dangerous mission.

King: ...So remember, as soon as you are flying over the palace of Stolavia, you let go of the message, OK? I leave it to you!

Knight: B-but, Your Majesty...

Soldier: Roger. Long distance delivery.

New elements 新しい部首

No new elements!

Lesson 50
第五十課

569 (2級)

PRIZE, TO PRAISE

賞

シヨウ

- 賞品 (しょうひん) prize, trophy
- 賞金 (きんしょう) (cash) prize
- 受賞する (じゅしょう) to receive a prize
- ノーベル賞 (しょう) Nobel prize
- 賞美する (しょうび) to admire
- 賞賛する (しょうさん) to praise
- 観賞する (かんしょう) to admire, to enjoy

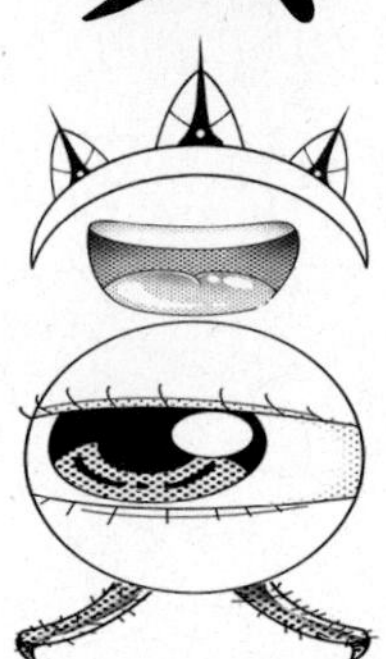

(15 strokes)

注 償 (Jōyō)
営 (5th)
覚 (471)

学 The *prize* for this year's beauty pageant is the queen's crown, and it will be awarded to the contestant with the biggest mouth: "Miss Seashell."

570 (2級)

CURRENCY, COIN, GOODS

貨

カ

- 通貨 (つうか) currency
- 硬貨 (こうか) coin
- 銀貨 (ぎんか) silver coin
- 外貨 (がいか) foreign currency
- 百貨店 (ひゃっかてん) department store
- 雑貨 (ざっか) household goods
- 貨物 (かもつ) freight
- 貨物船 (かもつせん) freighter

(11 strokes)

注 貸 (5th)
貿 (5th)
賃 (6th)

学 Look at Kim and the Indian: they are exchanging seashells, their world's *currency*.

貨 (alt)

(12 strokes)

費	費	費	費
費	費	費	費

EXPENSE

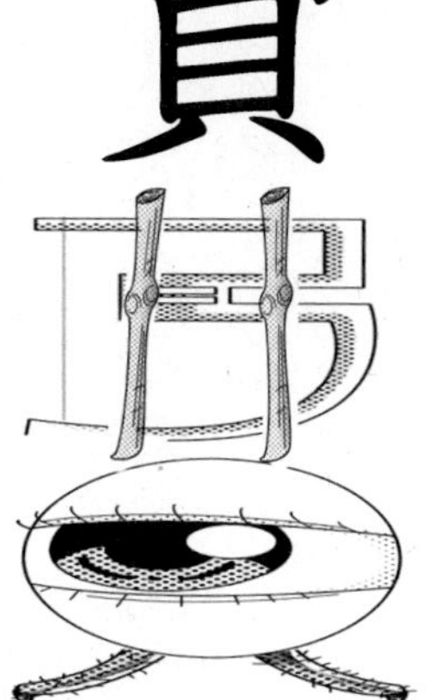

(2級)

571

ヒ

費用（ひよう） expenses, cost
出費（しゅっぴ） expenses
食費（しょくひ） food expenses
学費（がくひ） school expenses
生活費（せいかつひ） living expenses
消費（しょうひ） consumption
消費者（しょうひしゃ） consumer

つい(やす)

費やす（ついやす） to spend, to invest

学 This sure is some *expense*: using two arrows in one bow to hunt down just one seashell.

賛 (5th)
貴 (6th)
買 (111)

(12 strokes)

貯	貯	貯	貯
貯	貯	貯	貯

TO SAVE

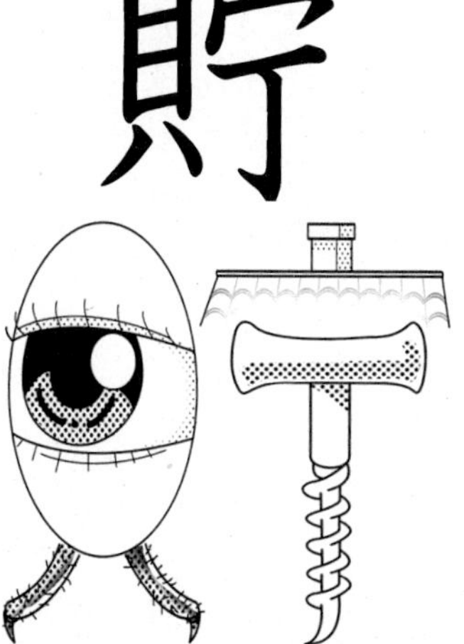

(2級)

572

チョ

貯金（ちょきん） savings
貯金箱（ちょきんばこ） piggybank
貯水池（ちょすいち） reservoir

た(める)

貯める（ためる） to save

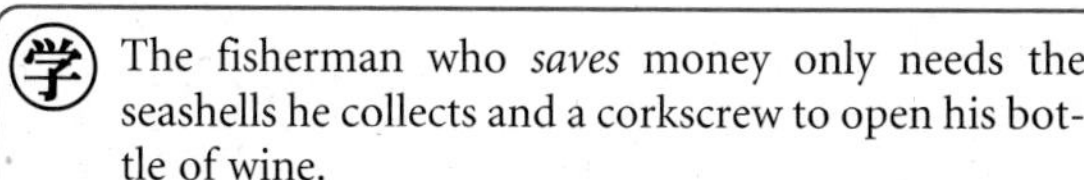

学 The fisherman who *saves* money only needs the seashells he collects and a corkscrew to open his bottle of wine.

頂 (6th)
財 (5th)
敗 (478)

573 (3級)

TO GIVE BIRTH TO, TO PRODUCE, RICHES

サン

- 出産（しゅっさん） birth, to give birth to
- 安産（あんざん） easy childbirth
- 産業（さんぎょう） industry
- 産出（さんしゅつ） production
- 財産（ざいさん） fortune, assets
- 不動産（ふどうさん） real estate
- 倒産（とうさん） bankruptcy

う(む/まれる)

- 産（う）む to produce

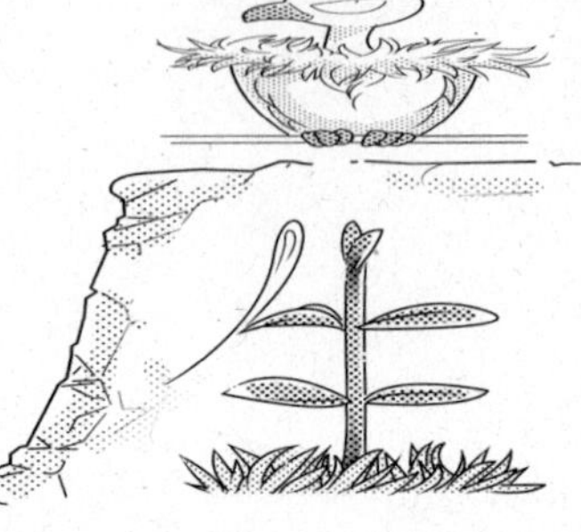

(11 strokes)

注 星 (147) 童 (331) 差 (628)

学 The vulture watches over the cliff, under which a plant *produces* the new *riches* of life.

特  産 (alt)

574 (2級)

CHILD

児

ジ

- 児童（じどう） child, infant
- 園児（えんじ） kindergarten child
- 胎児（たいじ） fetus
- 育児（いくじ）する to raise children
- 五歳児（ごさいじ） five-year-old child
- 天才児（てんさいじ） child prodigy
- 問題児（もんだいじ） problem child

ニ

- 小児科（しょうにか） pediatrics

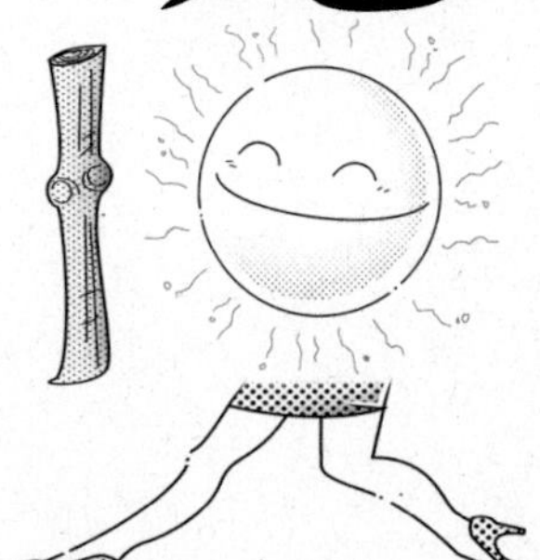

(7 strokes)

児 児 児 児 児 児 児 児

注 兄 (215) 見 (24) 免 (Jōyō)

学 The *child* plays with a stick, while his mother sunbathes her slender legs.

特  兒 (ant)

一	十	土	耂
考	老		

(6 strokes)

OLD PERSON, TO GROW OLD

老

(2級) **575**

ロウ

- 老人 (ろうじん) old person, old man
- 老後 (ろうご) old age
- 老化する (ろうかする) to grow old
- 老木 (ろうぼく) old tree
- 敬老 (けいろう) respect for the aged

お(いる)

- 老い込む (おいこむ) to grow old

ふ(ける)

- 老ける (ふける) to grow old

学 When they *grow old*, both the wise man and the Indian remain seated, because they find it hard to move.

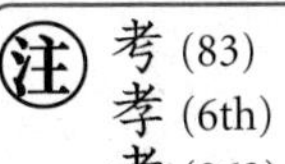
注 考 (83)
孝 (6th)
者 (262)

丨	口	口	口丨
口冂	口日	口日	口甲
唱	唱	唱	

(11 strokes)

TO SING SOFTLY, TO RECITE

唱

(1級) **576**

ショウ

- 合唱 (がっしょう) chorus
- 独唱 (どくしょう) vocal solo
- 暗唱する (あんしょうする) recite from memory
- 詠唱する (えいしょうする) to intone, to sing

とな(える)

- 唱える (となえる) to intone, to sing

Sing softly to the sun; and he will get so happy, instead of one you'll have two!

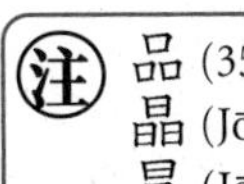
品 (354)
晶 (Jōyō)
冒 (Jōyō)

Lesson 50

577 (2級)

BLISS, HAPINESS

喜

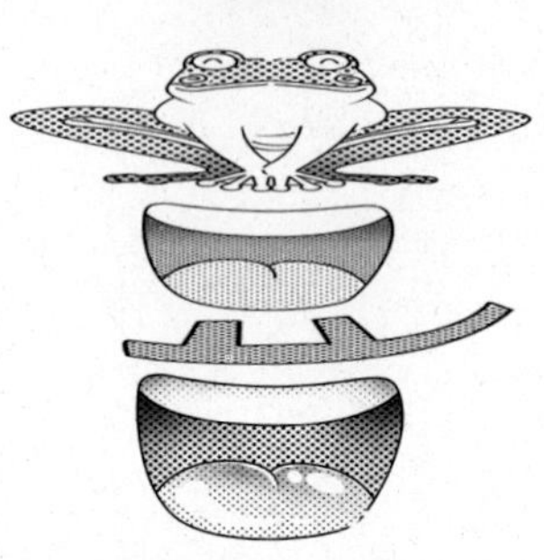

(12 strokes)

喜	喜	喜	喜
喜	喜	喜	喜

キ

- 歓喜（かんき） great happiness
- 悲喜（ひき） sadness and happiness
- 喜劇（きげき） comedy
- 喜怒哀楽（きどあいらく） emotions (delight, anger, sorrow, and pleasure)

よろこ(ぶ/ばす)

- 喜（よろこ）ぶ to be glad
- 喜（よろこ）んで with pleasure
- 喜（よろこ）ばす to delight

注 善 (6th)

学 The frog was adopted by a couple. The *happiness* caused by its arrival made their bearded mouths laugh!

特

578 (2級)

GOOD

良

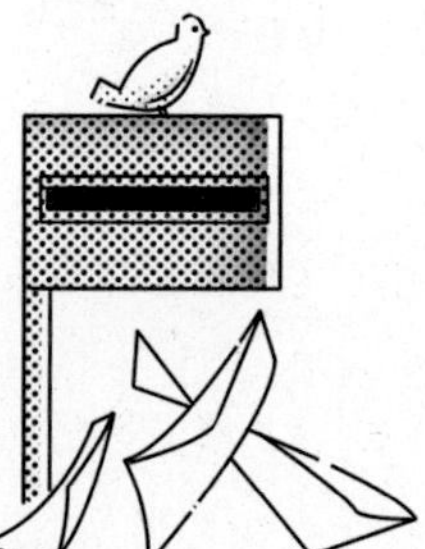

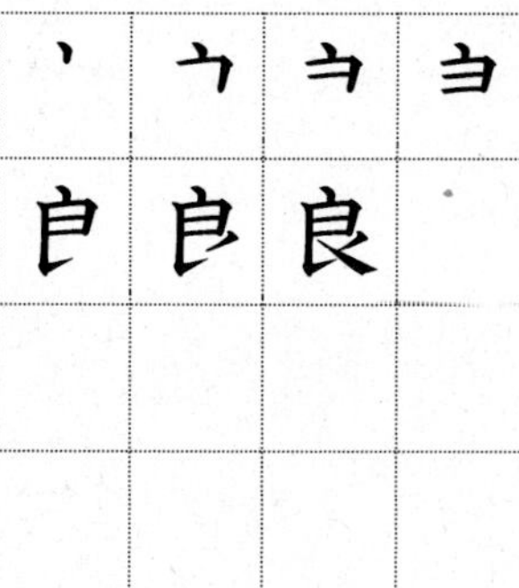

(7 strokes)

良	良	良	良
良	良	良	良

リョウ

- 良好（りょうこう） favorable, good
- 良質（りょうしつ） good quality
- 最良（さいりょう） the best, most excellent
- 不良（ふりょう） bad; scoundrel
- 良民（りょうみん） good citizen

よ(い)

- 良（よ）い good
- 良（よ）い年（とし）を Happy New Year
- 仲良（なかよ）し good friends

注 食 (130)
即 (Jōyō)
民 (514)

学 The pigeon is the messenger of *good* things.

特

579 MEAL (COOKED) RICE

(3級)

(12 strokes)

ハン

ご飯(はん) meal, rice
炊飯器(すいはんき) rice cooker
飯店(はんてん) Chinese restaurant
夕飯(ゆうはん) supper, dinner

めし

飯(めし) rice, meal
焼き飯(やきめし) fried rice
昼飯(ひるめし) lunch
飯屋(めしや) local restaurant

特 飯 (alt)

 A *meal* is what you need to get the energy that will allow you to climb that slope.

 飲 (347)
飢 (Jōyō)

580 TO NOURISH, TO EDUCATE

(1級)

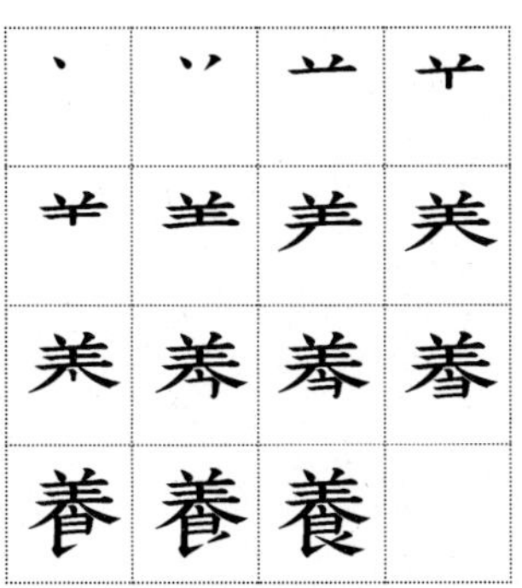

(15 strokes)

ヨウ

養子(ようし) adopted child
養成(ようせい)する to educate
教養(きょうよう)する to teach
休養(きゅうよう)する to rest
養護(ようご)する to protect and take care of
養育(よういく)する to raise
養毛剤(ようもうざい) hair-growing tonic

やしな(う)

養う(やしなう) to raise, to educate

 There is nothing as nutritious as a sheep that is well fed.

 美 (405)
着 (416)
義 (5th)

大喜びだよ！貯金、貯金して銀貨を手に入れた。お菓子をたくさん買おう！
あっ…苦しい…店が倒産したし、先週からご飯も食べてないし…
どうしよう？お菓子で費やしたいけど、この老人は栄養たっぷりの食事をとらないと、このまま…
はい、おじいちゃん。これ、あげる。
待ってください！
だまして悪かったけれど、ご覧のとおり、絶好調である。それなのに、君は大切な銀貨をくれた。
たしかに良い小児である。受賞するにふさわしい。
本当？じゃ、お菓子の山がほしい!!
それは、それは…
・・・
あ・あのぉ…呪文とか詠唱しないの？
勘違いしているよ、坊や。オレは魔法使いなんかじゃないよ。ただのごろつきさ。

Exercises 練習

1. Develop the stroke order of the following kanji.

費												
児												
喜												
養												

2. Choose the correct reading for each kanji or kanji combination.

a) ここなら、学費は(食費込みで)月３万円だって。貯金が足りるかな？

Here, the school fee (food expenses included) is 30,000 yen. I wonder if my savings will be enough.

学費:	１．がくつい	２．がっつい	３．がくひ	４．がっひ
食費:	１．しょくつい	２．しょくい	３．しょくひ	４．しょくび
貯金:	１．ちょきん	２．ちょうきん	３．ちょっきん	４．ちょぎん

b) うちは児童二人と老人二人がいるから、もう一人養子にする余裕(ゆゆう)はないですよ。

At home there are two children and two old people. I can't just adopt another one!

児童:	１．じどう	２．にどう	３．しどう	４．じいどう
老人:	１．ろうにん	２．ろうじん	３．ろにん	４．ろじん
養子:	１．ようし	２．ようこ	３．よし	４．よこ

c) 米の産出が多い日本ではご飯がよく食べられている。だから、炊飯器が必要だ。

In Japan, they produce and eat a lot of rice. That's why they need rice cookers.

産出:	１．うしゅつ	２．うで	３．さんしゅつ	４．さんで
ご飯:	１．ごめし	２．ごはん	３．ごばん	４．ごさん
炊飯器:	１．すいばんき	２．すいめしき	３．すいさんき	４．すいはんき

3. Write the kanji (one or more) and the meaning of the following words.

あんざん ______ ______ ひゃっかてん ______ ______

がっしょう ______ ______ せいかつひ ______ ______

しょうひん ______ ______ ふりょう ______ ______

4. Correct either the reading or the writing mistakes in the following words.

天才時	てんさいじ	唱る	となえる	喜こんで	よろこんで
不動山	ふどうさん	考ける	ふける	食いお年を	よいおとしを

Answers to exercises 練習解答

1. (Check them in the corresponding kanji table: #571, #574, #577, and #580)

2. a) 学費: 3 | 食費: 3 | 貯金: 1 / b) 児童: 1 | 老人: 2 | 養子: 1 / c) 産出: 3 | ご飯: 2 | 炊飯器: 4

3. あんざん: 安産, easy childbirth | がっしょう: 合唱, chorus | しょうひん: 賞品, prize, trophy | ひゃっかてん: 百貨店, department store | せいかつひ: 生活費, living expenses | ふりょう: 不良, bad, scoundrel

4. 天才児 てんさいじ | 唱える となえる | 喜んで よろこんで | 不動産 ふどうさん | 老ける ふける | 良いお年を よいおとしを

Manga translation マンガ翻訳

Child: I'm so happy! After much saving, I finally have a silver coin! I'll buy tons of candies!

Old man: Oh, I feel awful. My shop has gone bankrupt, and I have eaten nothing for a week.

Child (thinking): What shall I do? I want to spend it on candies, but if this old man doesn't eat some nutritious food, he will soon...

Child: Here, old man. It's for you.

Old man (OFF): Wait a minute!

Old man: I'm sorry I tricked you, but, as you can see, I'm perfectly well. Still, you gave me your valuable coin. You are, undoubtedly, a very good boy and you deserve a prize.

Child: Really? T-then, I want a mountain of candies!

Old man: Oh, I see...

Child: ...

Child: Ahem, aren't you going to recite a spell or something?

Old man: You are mistaken, kid. I'm not a magician, I'm just a rascal.

New elements 新しい部首

丗 buckle 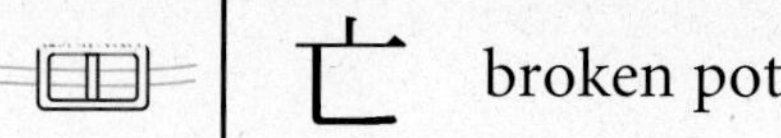 亡 broken pot 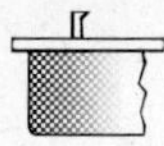

Lesson 51
第五十一課

581 (1級)

MILITARY MAN, PROFESSIONAL

シ

- 剣士 (けんし) swordsman
- 武士 (ぶし) warrior, samurai
- 騎士 (きし) knight
- 弁護士 (べんごし) lawyer
- 紳士 (しんし) gentleman
- 博士 (はくし) doctor (Ph.D), professor
- 力士 (りきし) sumo wrestler
- 同士 (どうし) fellow

一 十 士

(3 strokes)

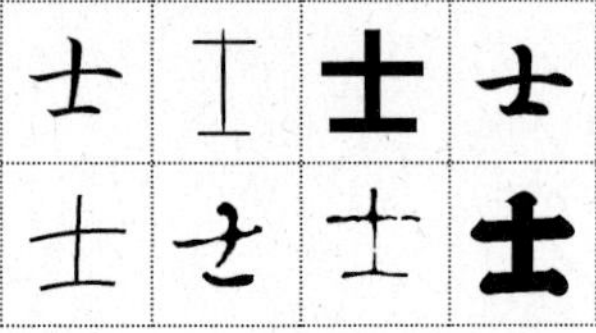

注 土 (55)
上 (2)

 Look at this *military* frog, an honorable animal.

582 (2級)

ABSENCE, LACK

ケツ

- 欠点 (けってん) defect, fault
- 欠陥 (けっかん) defect
- 欠席 (けっせき) absent
- 出欠 (しゅっけつ) to attend or to be absent
- 不可欠 (ふかけつ) indispensable
- ガス欠 (けつ) in need of gas

か(ける/かく)

- 欠ける (か) to lack
- 事欠く (ことか) to be in need of

丿 𠂊 ケ 欠

(4 strokes)

欠 欠 欠 欠
欠 欠 欠 欠

注 久 (5th)
夂 (no Jōyō)
矢 (233)

 Drunken Kim surely *lacks* tact by carrying his chair about.

 缺 (ant)

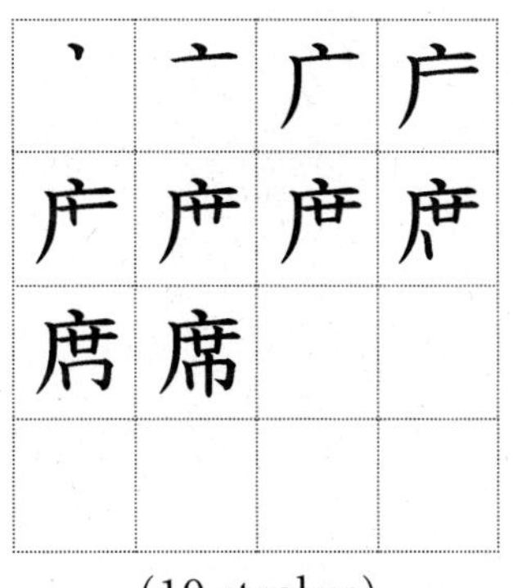

(10 strokes)

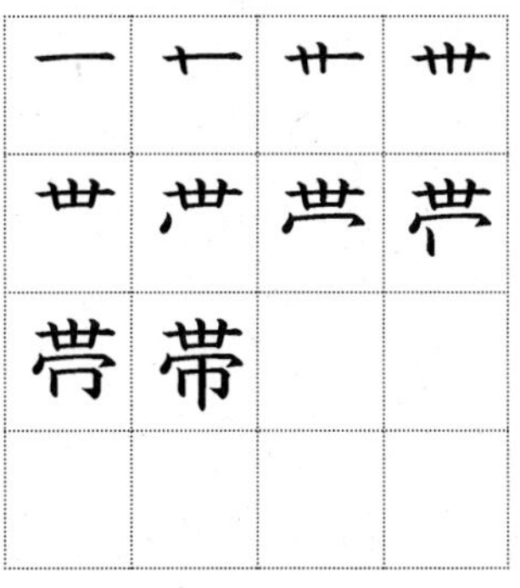

SEAT, TO ATTEND

(2級)

583

セキ

席(せき) seat
出席(しゅっせき) atender
座席(ざせき) in attendance, to be present
指定席(していせき) reserved seat
会席(かいせき) meeting place

Take a *seat* in my humble cave and taste this suckling pig, which I, with my sexy apron on, have prepared specially for you.

度 (365)
座 (6th)

BELT, TO WEAR, TO HAVE

(2級)

584

タイ

包帯(ほうたい) bandage
止血帯(しけつたい) tourniquet
声帯(せいたい) vocal cords
亜熱帯(あねったい) tropics
時間帯(じかんたい) time zone, time frame
連帯(れんたい) solidarity

おび / お(びる)

帯(おび) *obi* (belt for a kimono)
帯(お)びる to wear

(10 strokes)

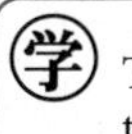

帯 (ant)

This *belt*'s buckle is too big; but there's no other way to tie a tutu on an apron.

葉 (433)
帝 (Jōyō)

585 (2級)

UNUSUAL, SCARCE, ASPIRATION

キ

希望（きぼう） hope, desire
希求（ききゅう）する to aspire to, to desire
希書（きしょ） rare book
希少（きしょう） rare, scarce

まれ

希（まれ）に rarely

(7 strokes)

注 気 (52)
布 (5th)

An *unusual* last will: a housewife asking to take to the grave chopsticks and her apron, so she can cook in the other world.

586 (2級)

TO MURDER, TO KILL

サツ

殺人（さつじん） murderer
暗殺（あんさつ） assassination
自殺（じさつ） suicide
殺菌（さっきん） sterilization
抹殺（まっさつ） massacre

ころ(す)

殺（ころ）す to kill, to murder
殺（ころ）し屋（や） hired killer
人殺（ひとごろ）し murderer / killer (of people)

(10 strokes)

注 殻 (Jōyō)
役 (246)
穀 (6th)

The actor has been *murdered* and he lies in his wooden coffin, buried by his favorite tree; his cowboy hat was left on the director's chair.

(2級) 587

LOSS, MISTAKE

失

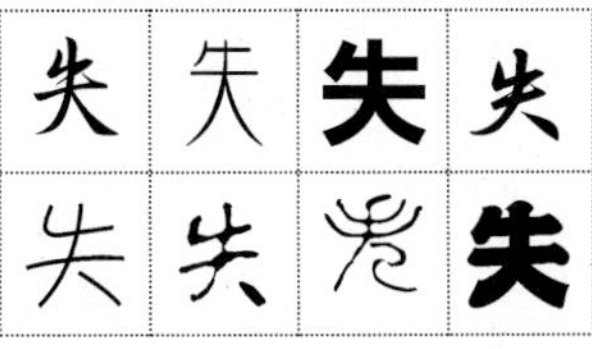

(5 strokes)

シツ

失礼(しつれい) rudeness
失神(しっしん) faint
失業(しつぎょう) unemployment
失言(しつげん) verbal slip
失敗(しっぱい) blunder, failure
消失(しょうしつ) disappearance
失望(しつぼう)する to lose hope

うしな(う)

失(うしな)う to lose
見失(みうしな)う to lose sight of

学 Be careful with the drill: you have much to *lose* if, by *mistake*, you drill too far.

 矢 (233) 天 (68) 夫 (436)

(2級) 588

WISH, HOPE

望

(11 strokes)

ボウ

希望(きぼう) hope, desire
絶望(ぜつぼう) despair
要望(ようぼう) request, demand
有望(ゆうぼう) promising
人望(じんぼう) popularity, fame
望遠鏡(ぼうえんきょう) telescope
展望台(てんぼうだい) observation platform

のぞ(む)

望(のぞ)む to hope for

 特 望 (alt)

学 Entrusting his broken pot to the moon, the king *hopes* that she will be able to repair it.

 最 (556) 聖 (6th)

589 (2級)

WORD, RESIGNATION

ジ

- 辞書（じしょ） dictionary
- 辞典（じてん） dictionary
- 世辞（せじ） compliment
- 辞令（じれい） written appointment
- 辞退（じたい） declination
- 辞表（じひょう） resignation letter

や(める)

- 辞（や）める to quit, to resign

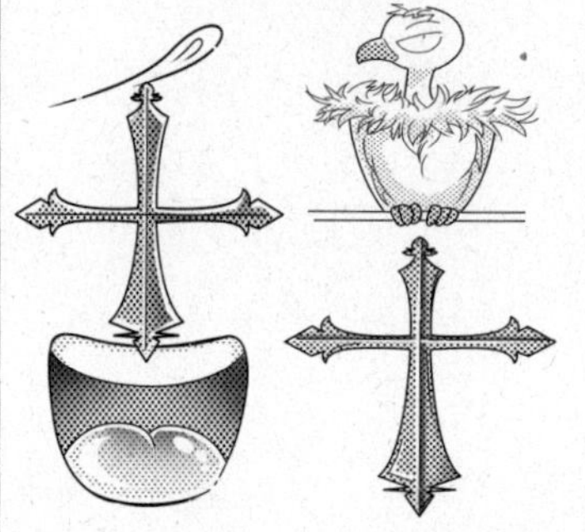

(13 strokes)

注 話 (107)
乱 (6th)
報 (5th)

学 One thousand mouths shout *words* asking the vulture to resign as the guardian of the sacred cross.

特  (ant)

590 (1級)

REFERENCE WORK, CODEX, CEREMONY

テン

- 辞典（じてん） dictionary
- 字典（じてん） kanji dictionary
- 古典（こてん） (literary) Japanese classics
- 式典（しきてん） ceremony
- 祭典（さいてん） festival
- 典型的（てんけいてき） typical, usual

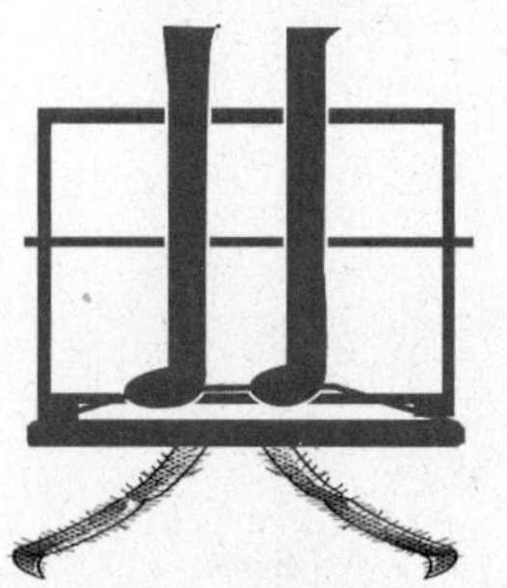

(8 strokes)

注 曲 (296)
無 (619)

 A perfectly closed pentagram is a *work of reference*, placed on a stool with legs for exhibition.

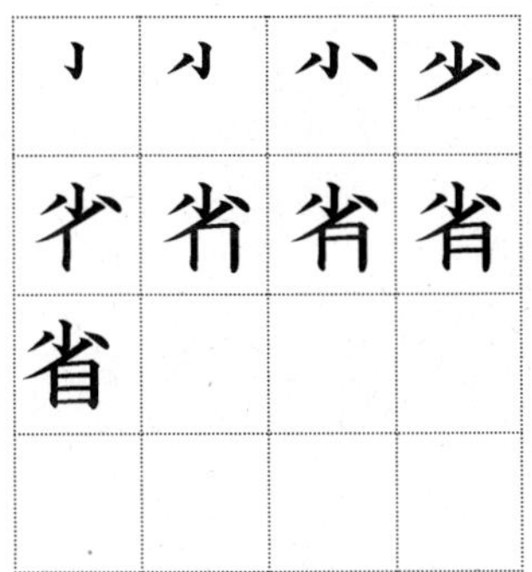

(9 strokes)

MINISTRY, REFLECTION

(2級)

591

セイ

反省(はんせい) reflection on, to think on

自省(じせい) soul-searching

ショウ

大蔵省(おおくらしょう) Ministry of Finance

省(しょう)エネ energy saving

省略(しょうりゃく) abbreviation

かえり(みる)

省(かえり)みる to reflect on

学 When it announces even a little budget cut, all eyes are on the *ministry*.

着 (416)
看 (6th)
査 (5th)

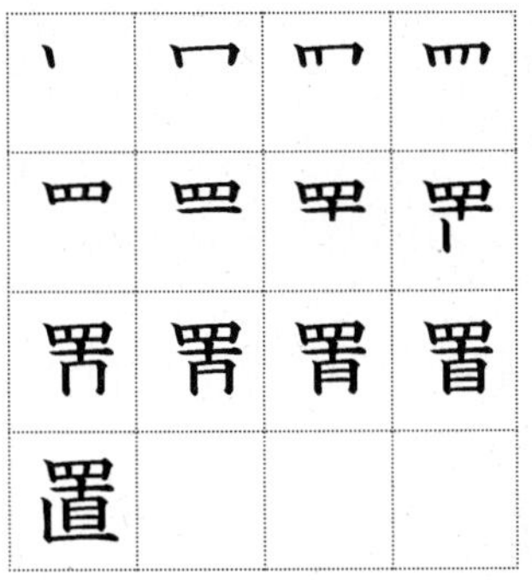

(13 strokes)

TO PLACE, TO SET UP

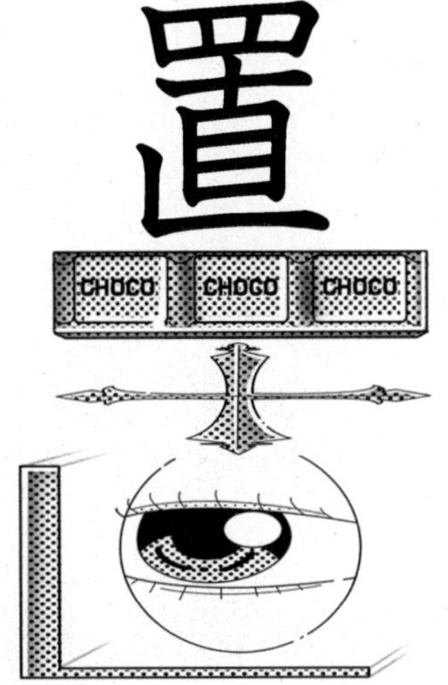

(2級)

592

チ

配置(はいち)する to arrange

装置(そうち) device

措置(そち) measures, steps

設置(せっち)する to set up, to put

放置(ほうち)する to abandon

拘置所(こうちしょ) house of detention

お(く)

置(お)く to put, place

置(お)き場(ば) warehouse

置(お)き書(が)き note

Although she knows it won't last two days, mom *places* the chocolate bar flat on the shelf.

値 (6th)
署 (6th)

マフィアの親分、逮捕

失望しないでください、親分。もう適切な措置をとり、国の一番すぐれた弁護士をやとっておきました。せいぜい、禁固六ヶ月の刑に処せられるでしょう。

なにいいい⁉
六ヶ月だって‼?
た・多分それより少ない、よく分かりません…

六ヶ月か…おやおや、しょうがないな。

前置きを省きましょう。付帯控訴しますか？
そ・そうかなぁ…ちょっと法律辞典で引かせていただきます。

おいおい、この有名な弁護士って、本当に大丈夫かい？
あのう…実は今日は病気で欠席しています。これが彼のいとこですけど…

・・・
最後の希望はあるか？
その弁護士めとバカ部下をぶっ殺すこと‼

Exercises 練習

1. Develop the stroke order of the following kanji.

帯												
希												
辞												
典												

2. Choose the correct reading for each kanji or kanji combination.

a) 「皆さんの出席は必要不可欠である」とあの弁護士は言った。
That lawyer said "everybody's attendance is necessary and indispensable."

出席: 1. でせき 2. でっせき 3. しゅせき 4. しゅっせき
不可欠: 1. ふかかく 2. ふかける 3. ふかけつ 4. ふかかつ
弁護士: 1. べんごさ 2. べんごし 3. べんごす 4. べんごそ

b) 多くの失敗を重ねると、希望を失って自殺してしまう人がいる。
There are people who, having linked several failures, lose hope and end up committing suicide.

失敗: 1. しつはい 2. しつばい 3. しっぱい 4. しっぱい
希望: 1. きのぞ 2. きぼう 3. まれのぞ 4. まれぼう
自殺: 1. しさつ 2. じさつ 3. しころす 4. じころす

c) 辞書に出てこない省略があれば、電子辞典を使って調べてみてください。
When you can't find an abbreviation in a normal dictionary, look it up in the electronic dictionary.

辞書: 1. ししょ 2. じじょ 3. しじょ 4. じしょ
省略: 1. しょりゃく 2. しょうりゃく 3. せいりゃく 4. せりゃく
辞典: 1. してん 2. じてん 3. やてん 4. しいてん

3. Write the kanji (one or more) and the meaning of the following words.

けってん ______ ______ しつぎょう ______ ______
していせき ______ ______ あんさつ ______ ______
じかんたい ______ ______ はんせい ______ ______

4. Correct either the reading or the writing mistakes in the following words.

直き場 おきば 舌める やめる 鉄う うしなう
省みる かえみりる 切希 せつぼう 人殺し ひとごろし

Answers to exercises 練習解答

1. (Check them in the corresponding kanji table: #584, #585, #589, and #590)

2. a) 出席: 4 | 不可欠: 3 | 弁護士: 2 / b) 失敗: 4 | 希望: 2 | 自殺: 2 / c) 辞書: 4 | 省略: 2 | 辞典: 2

3. けってん: 欠点, defect, fault | していせき: 指定席, reserved seat | じかんたい: 時間帯, time zone | しつぎょう: 失業, unemployment | あんさつ: 暗殺, murder | はんせい: 反省, reflection, to think

4. 置き場 おきば | 辞める やめる | 失う うしなう | 省みる かえりみる | 切望 せつぼう | 人殺し ひとごろし

Manga translation マンガ翻訳

Headline: Mafia boss arrested

Gangster: Don't despair, boss. We have taken appropriate measures, and we have hired the best lawyer in the country. You'll get six months in jail at the most.

Mafia boss: Whaaat?! Six months?!

Gangster: W-well, m-maybe less, I don't know for sure.

Boss: Six months... Oh, well, if it can't be helped.

Judge (OFF): Let's do without the preliminaries. Do you wish to lodge an additional appeal?

Lawyer: W-well, I don't know. I'll just look it up in my legal dictionary.

Boss: Hey, are you sure this famous lawyer is good?

Gangster: Ehm, frankly, he was sick today, and he couldn't come. This is his cousin.

Boss: ...

Executioner: Any last wishes?

Boss: I want to kill that damned lawyer and my good-for-nothing subordinate!!

New elements 新しい部首

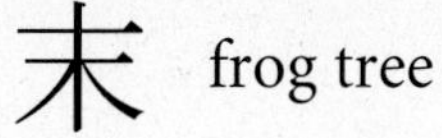

Lesson 52
第五十二課

593 (2級)

(NOT) YET

未

ミ

- 未婚 (みこん) unmarried
- 未満 (みまん) less than
- 未定 (みてい) undecided
- 未完成 (みかんせい) unfinished
- 未来 (みらい) future

いま(だ)

- 未だ (いま) as yet, still

ま(だ)

- 未だ (ま) still, not yet

(5 strokes)

 来 (135)
末 (594)

学 The tree grows taller, but it doesn't touch the sky *yet.*

594 (2級)

CULMINATION, END

末

マツ

- 週末 (しゅうまつ) weekend
- 年末 (ねんまつ) the end of the year
- 結末 (けつまつ) termination
- 始末 (しまつ) to dispose of
- 粗末 (そまつ) coarse, rough
- 端末 (たんまつ) terminal

すえ

- 末 (すえ) end, last part
- 末っ子 (すえっこ) youngest son/daughter

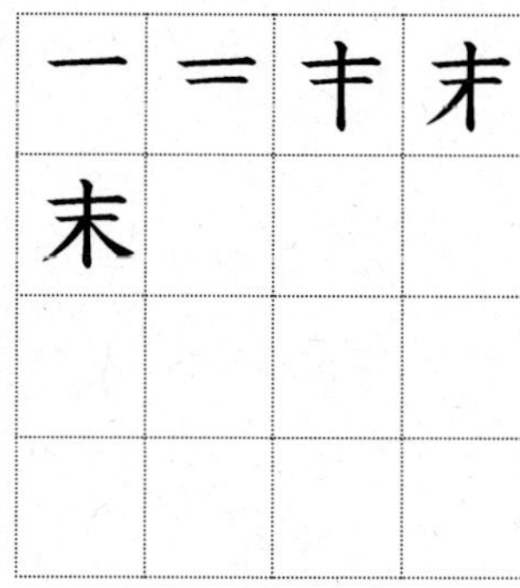

(5 strokes)

 未 (593)
来 (135)

学 This tree doesn't grow. In the *end*, it finds its *culmination* in the frog sitting high upon its branches.

595

(2級)

MONETARY NOTE/ BILL, TICKET

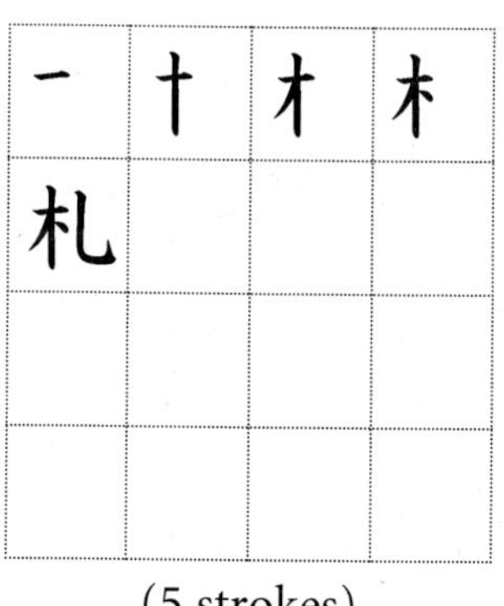

(5 strokes)

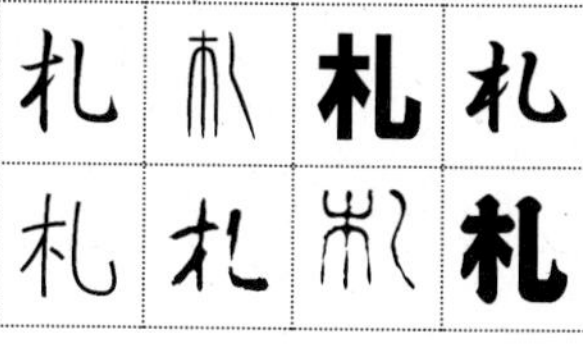

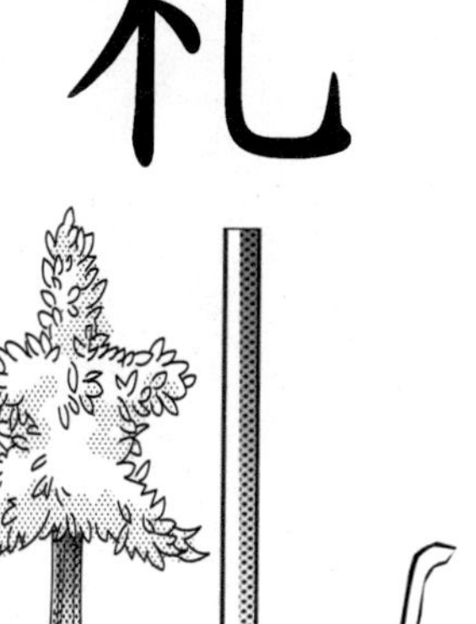

サツ

千円札(せんえんさつ) 1,000 yen bill
札束(さつばた) wad of money
改札口(かいさつぐち) ticket gate

ふだ

札(ふだ) label, sign
名札(なふだ) name tag
値札(ねふだ) price tag
切り札(きりふだ) the trump card
花札(はなふだ) *hanafuda* cards

学 To go into the forest you need a *ticket*: pay in cash to the first tree you see, then pull the hook to gain entry.

注 礼 (419) 乱 (6th) 村 (64)

596

(2級)

MATERIAL, SKILL

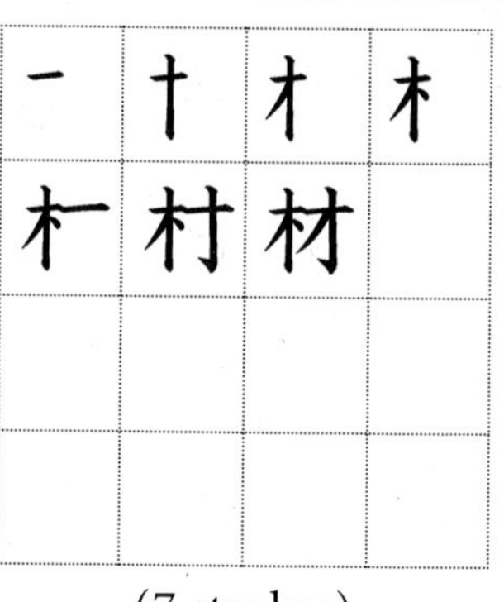

(7 strokes)

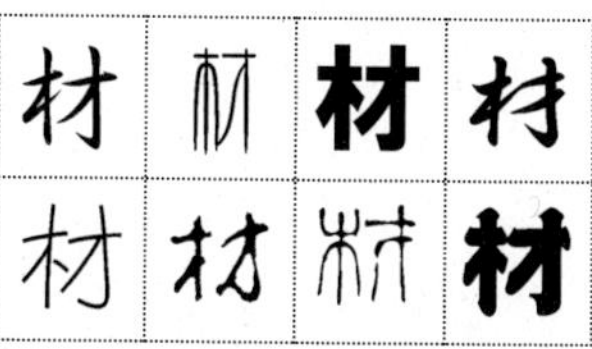

ザイ

素材(そざい) materia
木材(もくざい) wood
鉄材(てつざい) metal
材料(ざいりょう) ingredients
教材(きょうざい) teaching materials
取材(しゅざい)する to interview, to gather information
人材(じんざい) talented person

To whittle a tree down into usable *material* takes great *skill*. Only the scarecrow knows the secret.

村 (64) 枚 (6th) 析 (Jōyō)

597 (2級)

TO TIE IN A BUNDLE, TO RESTRICT

ソク
- 約束(やくそく) promise
- 結束(けっそく)する to unite, to band together
- 拘束(こうそく)する to arrest, to bind

たば / たば(ねる)
- 花束(はなたば) bouquet
- 束(たば)ねる to tie in a bundle

つか / つか(ねる)
- 束(つか)の間(ま) an instant
- 束(つか)ねる to bundle, to tie

(7 strokes)

束	束	束	束
束	束	束	束

束 (199)
京 (204)
事 (325)

The talking mouth of the wise tree is so big and speaks endlessly that it will never be *restricted* from speech by *tying it in a bundle* with other trees.

598 (1級)

PINE TREE

ショウ
- 松竹梅(しょうちくばい) decoration for celebrations
- 青松(せいしょう) green pine

まつ
- 松(まつ) Japanese pine
- 松葉(まつば) pine needle
- 松茸(まつたけ) *matsutake* mushroom

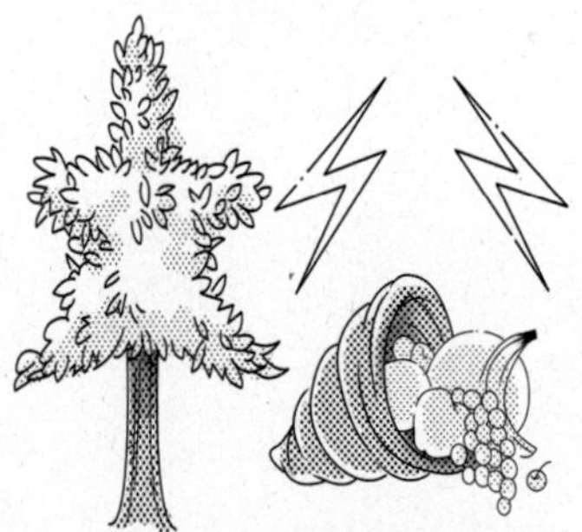

(8 strokes)

松	松	松	松
松	松	松	松

格 (5th)
枠 (Jōyō)
桜 (5th)

学 The *pine* is a tree that needs a storm to produce a cornucopia of pine nuts.

丶	丷	宀	宊
安	安	安	案
案	案		

(10 strokes)

PROPOSAL, IDEA

(2級)

599

アン

- 案(あん) proposal, idea
- 思案(しあん)する to consider
- 案内(あんない)する to guide
- 提案(ていあん) proposal
- 法案(ほうあん) a bill
- 名案(めいあん) fantastic idea
- 案外(あんがい) contrary to expectation
- 案(あん)の定(じょう) as one expected
- 案(あん)ずる to suffer, to worry

特

The man was so fed up that he *proposed* to his wife that they move to the tree house: she loved the idea!

注 策 (6th) 宴 (Jōyō) 客 (406)

一	十	丰	主
圭	青	毒	毒

(8 strokes)

毒	毒	毒	毒
毒	毒	毒	毒

POISON, EVIL

(2級)

600

ドク

- 毒(どく) poison
- 毒(どく)ガス poisonous gas
- 毒入(どくい)り poisoned
- 毒殺(どくさつ) death by poisoning
- 有毒(ゆうどく) poisonous
- 中毒(ちゅうどく) intoxication
- 消毒(しょうどく) disinfection
- 毒舌(どくぜつ) stinging tongue

A *poisonous* plant grows from the grave of this mother who had been deprived of her child; evil had taken hold of her.

毎 (218) 麦 (150) 音 (43)

601 (1級)

UME (JAPANESE PLUM TREE)

梅

バイ

梅花 (ばいか) plum blossom
梅林 (ばいりん) plum tree forest
梅雨 (ばいう) rainy season

うめ

梅 (うめ) plum
梅酒 (うめしゅ) plum liquor
梅干 (うめぼし) pickled plum

Special

梅雨 (つゆ) rainy season

(10 strokes)

注 板 (273) 植 (268) 根 (274)

学 *Ume* is the tree chosen for the garden outside the shed of this mother: with its fruit she will be able to feed her child.

楳 (alt)

602 (2級)

EXTREME, POLE

キョク

極端 (きょくたん) extreme, radical
究極 (きゅうきょく) ultimate
極東 (きょくとう) Far East
北極 (ほっきょく) North Pole

ゴク

極上 (ごくじょう) top-quality

きわ(める/まる)

極める (きわめる) to run to an extreme
極めて (きわめて) extremely

(12 strokes)

構 (5th)
械 (604)

学 This tree works *extreme* miracles like a magic lamp: next to it, ten thousand mouths can be fed with just two slices of bread placed on a chair.

603

MACHINE, AIRPLANE, OPPORTUNITY

(2級)

(16 strokes)

キ

- 機関（きかん） engine, organization
- 洗濯機（せんたっき） washing machine
- 飛行機（ひこうき） airplane
- 機長（きちょう） airplane captain
- 危機（きき） crisis, emergency
- 機会（きかい） opportunity
- 機能（きのう） function

はた

- 機織（はたおり） a weaver (of cloth)

学 A tree and two spools of thread balls is all Kim needs to invent the *machine* that will give him the *opportunity* to unmask fake Robin Hood.

 械 (604) 極 (602)

604

DEVICE

(2級)

械

(11 strokes)

カイ

- 機械（きかい） machine
- 器械（きかい） instrument, appliance

 With wood from a tree, the fake Robin Hood has created a new *device*: a gate which opens when he arrives.

 機 (603) 栽 (Jōyō) 域 (6th)

大変だ。梅の木が枯れかかっている。
年々産業化が進んでいるし、汚染が増えているから、毒殺されてしまう。

そうね。木はただの粗末な木材じゃないよ。生物だ。でも、今の人間はそれを思案しないで、札束のことしか考えない。

極端な状態だ。このまま行けば…未来はどうなるかな…

百万年後…

大変だ。ロボ松の木は壊れかかっている。
そうね。木はただの粗末な鉄材じゃないよ。機械だ。でも、今のロボットはそれを思案しないで、札束のことしか考えない。

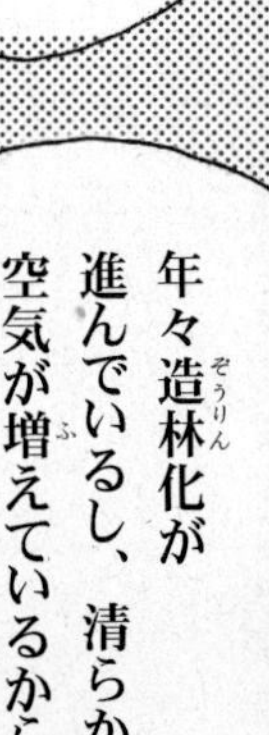
年々造林化が進んでいるし、清らかな空気が増えているから、毒殺されてしまう。

Exercises 練習

1. Develop the stroke order of the following kanji.

束												
毒												
極												
機												

2. Choose the correct reading for each kanji or kanji combination.

a) 取材の内容はまだ未定です。年末までに必ずお知らせします。

The interview contents are yet to be decided. We will inform you before the end of the year.

取材:	1．しゅうさい	2．しゅさい	3．しゅうざい	4．しゅざい
未定:	1．みてい	2．いまてい	3．まつてい	4．まってい
年末:	1．ねんすえ	2．ねんいま	3．ねんまつ	4．ねんま

b)「死ぬ前に、機会を作って、北極まで行く」と約束をした。

He promised, "Before I die, I will find the opportunity to go to the North Pole."

機会:	1．かいかい	2．かかい	3．きかい	4．ききあ
北極:	1．きたきょく	2．きたごく	3．ほっきょく	4．ほくごく
約束:	1．やくそく	2．やっそく	3．やくたば	4．やくつか

c) 毒入り梅酒で旦那(だんな)さんを毒殺したって？案外冷血な女ですね...

Did she kill her husband with poisoned plum liquor? I never expected her to be so cold blooded.

梅酒:	1．ばいしゅ	2．うめさけ	3．うめざけ	4．うめしゅ
毒殺:	1．どくさつ	2．どっさつ	3．どくざつ	4．どっざつ
案外:	1．あんぞと	2．あんそと	3．あんがい	4．あんかい

3. Write the kanji (one or more) and the meaning of the following words.

みらい	______	______	かいさつぐち	______	______
ひこうき	______	______	ざいりょう	______	______
つゆ	______	______	あんない	______	______

4. Correct either the reading or the writing mistakes in the following words.

末だ	まだ	松	ます	機危	きき
花札	はなさつ	消毒	しょうとく	極る	きわめる

Answers to exercises 練習解答

1. (Check them in the corresponding kanji table: #597, #600, #602, and #603)

2. a) 取材: 4 | 未定: 1 | 年末: 3 / b) 機会: 3 | 北極: 3 | 約束: 1
c) 梅酒: 4 | 毒殺: 1 | 案外: 3

3. みらい: 未来, future | ひこうき: 飛行機, airplane | つゆ: 梅雨, rainy season | かいさつぐち: 改札口, ticket gate | ざいりょう: 材料, ingredients | あんない: 案内, to guide

4. 未だ まだ o いまだ | 松 まつ | 危機 きき | 花札 はなふだ | 消毒 しょうどく | 極める きわめる

Manga translation マンガ翻訳

Farmer 1: That's terrible. Plum trees are withering...

Farmer 2: Industrialization is progressing and environmental pollution is increasing year after year, so they are getting poisoned.

Farmer 1: True. Trees are not just rough wood. They are living beings. But people nowadays don't think about that; they only care for wads of money.

Farmer 1: This is an extreme situation. If it continues, I don't know what will happen in the future...

Caption: A million years later...

Farmer-robot 1: That's terrible. The plum tree-robots are getting damaged...

Farmer-robot 2: Afforestation is progressing and fresh air is increasing year after year, so they are getting poisoned.

Farmer-robot 1: True. Trees are not just rough metal. They are machines. But robots nowadays don't think about that, they only care for wads of money.

New elements 新しい部首

井 well 

Lesson 53
第五十三課

605 (2級)

TYPE, MODEL

型

ケイ

模型（もけい） scale model
原型（げんけい） prototype
典型（てんけい） model, typical
型式（けいしき） model
体型（たいけい） body figure

かた/がた

型（かた） form, design, pattern; *kata* (in karate)
大型（おおがた） large size
旧型（きゅうがた） old model

(9 strokes)

注 刑 (Jōyō)
形 (189)
堅 (Jōyō)

学 Look at this torii: it has the latest *model* of braids and a base of fertile land.

特

606 (2級)

CIRCUMFERENCE, PERIPHERY

周

シュウ

周辺（しゅうへん） outskirts, environs
周囲（しゅうい） perimeter
円周（えんしゅう） circumference
半周（はんしゅう） semicircle
周期（しゅうき） period, cycle
十周年（じゅうしゅうねん） 10th anniversary

まわ(り)

周り（まわり） surroundings

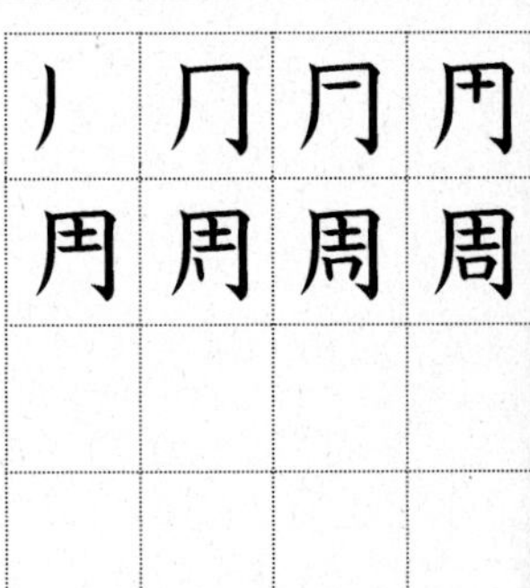

(8 strokes)

 週 (176)
同 (194)
回 (159)

 Not wanting to be discovered, the masked man always walks making detours around the *periphery*.

607 (2級)

TO SURROUND

囲

(7 strokes)

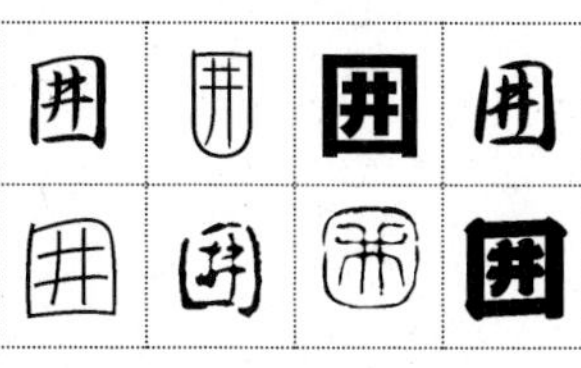

イ

- 包囲（ほうい） to be surrounded
- 範囲（はんい） range, scope
- 雰囲気（ふんいき） atmosphere, ambience
- 囲碁（いご） go (board game)

かこ(う/む)

- 囲む（かこむ） to surround, to enclose
- 取り囲む（とりかこむ） to surround
- 囲い（かこい） enclosure

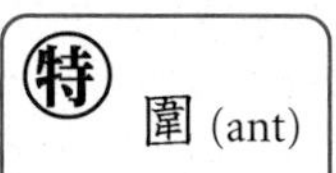

 (ant)

学 The toy car circuit *surrounds* the well. This was a bad idea: many cars have fallen inside...

- 回 (159)
- 困 (6th)
- 図 (183)

---

608 (2級)

SOLID, TO SOLIDIFY

固

(8 strokes)

コ

- 固体（こたい） solid body
- 固定（こてい） fixed, static
- 頑固（がんこ） stubborn
- 固着する（こちゃくする） to adhere fast

かた(い/める/まる)

- 固い（かたい） hard
- 固める（かためる） to harden
- 固まり（かたまり） mass, lump

学 Don't ever think of putting an old man in an enclosed place: inside, he will *solidify* like a statue!

- 国 (182)
- 団 (5th)
- 因 (5th)

609 (2級)

OFFICIAL, TO ADMINISTER

シ

- 司会者（しかいしゃ） emcee (M.C.)
- 司令官（しれいかん） commander
- 司法する（しほうする） to administer justice
- 上司（じょうし） one's superior, boss
- 寿司（すし） sushi

つかさど(る)

- 司る（つかさどる） to administer

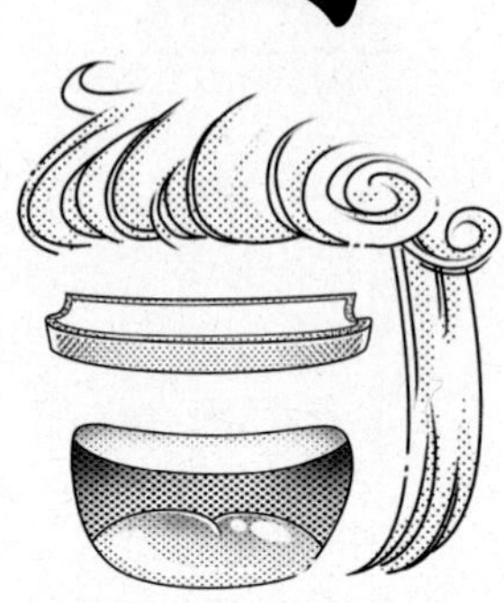

(5 strokes)

注 句 (5th)
可 (5th)

We don't have enough wigs, so I'll give you half of one, but there is one slice of bread for every mouth. To be an *official*, you must know how *to administer* resources.

---

610 (2級)

CONTAINER, INSTRUMENT

器

キ

- 容器（ようき） container, receptacle
- 器具（きぐ） tool, instrument
- 楽器（がっき） musical instrument
- 兵器（へいき） weapon
- 炊飯器（すいはんき） rice cooker
- 便器（べんき） toilet bowl
- 食器（しょっき） tableware, plates and utensils

うつわ

- 器（うつわ） container

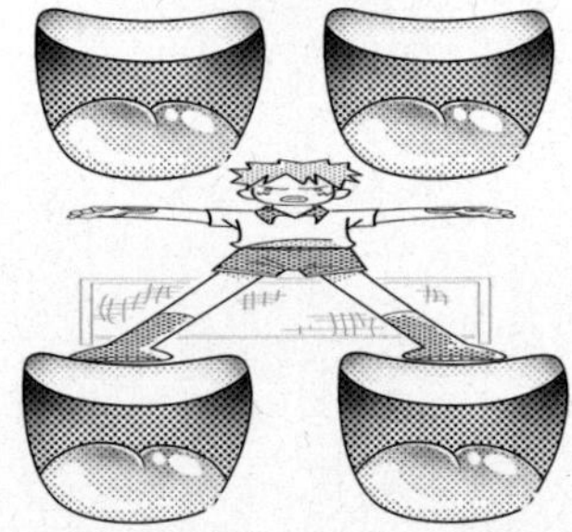

(15 strokes)

注 品 (359)

To quench the thirst of four mouths you need a big *container* full of water.

器 (alt)

611

(2級)

SALT, CHLORINE

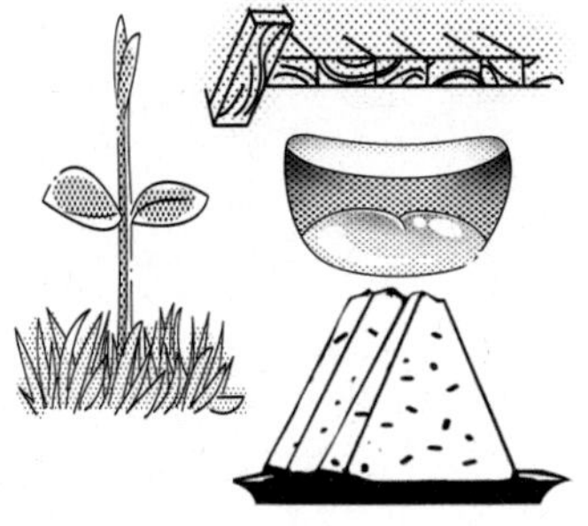

(13 strokes)

塩	塩	塩	塩
塩	塩	塩	塩

エン

- 塩分（えんぶん） salt, salinity
- 食塩（しょくえん） table salt
- 塩水（えんすい） salt water
- 塩基（えんき） (chemical) base
- 塩素（えんそ） chlorine

しお

- 塩（しお） salt
- 塩辛い（しおからい） salty
- 塩水（しおみず） salt water

特 鹽 (ant)

学 The food from the land that you eat under a shed, with your mouth, always tastes better with a pinch of *salt* on your plate.

注 増 (5th)
境 (5th)

612

(1級)

DISTRICT, STREET

街

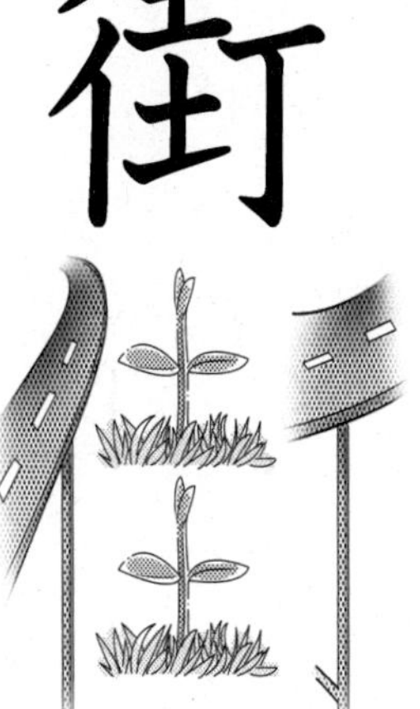

(12 strokes)

街	街	街	街
街	街	街	街

ガイ

- 市街（しがい） town
- スラム街（がい） slum district
- 街頭（がいとう） street
- 商店街（しょうてんがい） shopping area, outdoor promenade
- 繁華街（はんかがい） amusement quarter

まち

- 街（まち） district, city, town
- 街角（まちかど） street corner

 With the real estate boom, the two plots of fertile land between the highways will end up being shopping *districts.*

 術 (5th)
衝 (Jōyō)
衛 (5th)

613 (2級)

TO ACQUIRE, BENEFIT

得

トク

獲得（かくとく）する to obtain

取得（しゅとく）する to acquire

所得（しょとく） earnings

得意（とくい） good at

買い得（かいどく） bargain, good offer

え(る) / う(る)

得（え）る to get, to obtain

心得（こころえ）る to understand, to give consent

あり得（う）る possible

(11 strokes)

注 復 (5th)
徳 (5th)

学 By the highway, under a scorching sun, selling bread helps the alien to *acquire* a nice *benefit*.

614 (1級)

DIAMETER, PATH

径

ケイ

半径（はんけい） radius

直径（ちょっけい） diameter

口径（こうけい） caliber

経路（けいろ） course, route

(8 strokes)

注 経 (5th)
軽 (369)
役 (246)

学 The highway covers the *diameter* of the director's fertile patch of land, where he has decided to establish himself.

特 徑 (ant)
逕 (alt)

(10 strokes)

DISCIPLE, FOLLOWER, VAIN

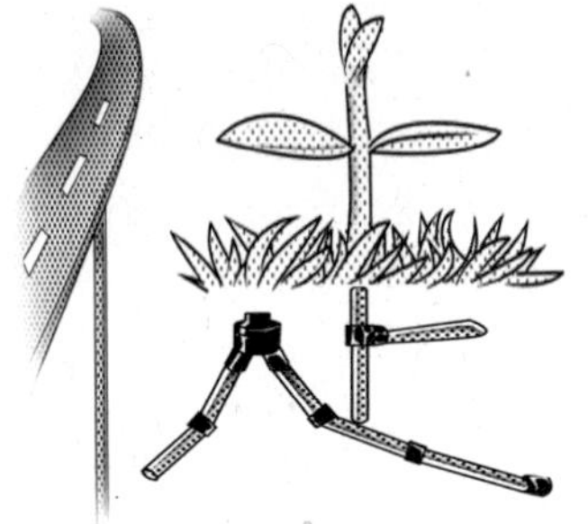

(2級) **615**

ト

- 生徒（せいと） student, pupil
- 学徒（がくと） follower, disciple
- 教徒（きょうと） religious believer
- 仏教徒（ぶっきょうと） Buddhist
- 信徒（しんと） believer
- 徒歩（とほ） to walk

学 The true *disciple* is the one who doesn't hesitate to run along the highway to the sky if the teacher says so.

注 従 (6th)
待 (248)
征 (Jōyō)

(14 strokes)

IDLENESS, CALM, BARRIER

(2級) **616**

カン

- 関係（かんけい） relationship
- 関心（かんしん） interest
- 関節（かんせつ） joint
- 関税（かんぜい） customs / duties (at the airport)
- 関東（かんとう） Kantō region
- 関西（かんさい） Kansai region

せき

- 関所（せきしょ） old border station
- 大関（おおぜき） sumo champion

特 關 (ant)

Flee from *idleness*! For it will lead you to hell's gates.

開 (426)
閉 (6th)
閣 (6th)

もう
うぅっ！
いやだ!!
どうしたんですか、先生？
インスピレーションが全然わかない！固い旧型な作品しか出てこない！
生徒よ、がっかりしたよ…
新鮮な様式を得るのが必要だ。周囲の影響を受けるために、街を歩こう。
寿司屋！寿司屋の開店！
「大口径」雑誌！武器マニアのあなたに！
輸入自動車！いまなら、関税OFF！
レストラン「マリン」！おいしい料理！塩ざけ専門！
さっすが先生！すばらしい器だわ！
まあ…ちらしのためのゴミ箱だけど…

Exercises 練習

1. Develop the stroke order of the following kanji.

囲												
固												
器												
街												

2. Choose the correct reading for each kanji or kanji combination.

a) あの頑固な生徒が先生を殴(なぐ)ってから、クラスの雰囲気が変わった。

After that stubborn pupil hit the teacher, the atmosphere in the class has changed.

頑固: 1. がんかた 2. がんこう 3. がんがた 4. がんこ

生徒: 1. せいとう 2. せいと 3. せいどう 4. せいど

雰囲気: 1. ふんかこき 2. ふんにき 3. ふんいき 4. ふにき

b) 子どもの頃から音楽に関心を持っているので、楽器を弾(ひ)くのが得意です。

He's been interested in music since he was a child, so he's good at playing instruments.

関心: 1. せきしん 2. せきごころ 3. かんしん 4. かんごころ

楽器: 1. らくき 2. らっき 3. がくき 4. がっき

得意: 1. えい 2. えるい 3. とくい 4. とい

c) あの司令官は欲しいものがあれば、兵器で取得する。

If there's anything that commander wants, he gets it with weapons.

司令官: 1. しれかん 2. しれいかん 3. つかさどかん 4. つかさどれいかん

兵器: 1. へいき 2. へきい 3. へき 4. へえき

取得: 1. しゅえ 2. しゅえる 3. しゅどく 4. しゅとく

3. Write the kanji (one or more) and the meaning of the following words.

しかいしゃ ______ ______ おおがた ______ ______

しお ______ ______ しゅうい ______ ______

しょうてんがい ______ ______ かたまり ______ ______

4. Correct either the reading or the writing mistakes in the following words.

調り まわり 心得る こころる 直経 ちょっけい

古定 こてい 原形 げんけい 間西 かんさい

Answers to exercises 練習解答

1. (Check them in the corresponding kanji table: #607, #608, #610, and #612)

2. a) 頑固: 4 | 生徒: 2 | 雰囲気: 3 / b) 関心: 3 | 楽器: 4 | 得意: 3 / c) 司令官: 2 | 兵器: 1 | 取得: 4

3. しかいしゃ: 司会者, emcee | しお: 塩, salt | しょうてんがい: 商店街, shopping area | おおがた: 大型, large size | しゅうい: 周囲, perimeter | かたまり: 固まり, mass, lump

4. 周り　まわり | 心得る　こころえる | 直径　ちょっけい | 固定　こてい | 原型　げんけい | 関西　かんさい

Manga translation マンガ翻訳

Master potter: Nooo! I've had enough!

Assistant: What's the matter, master?

Master: I have no inspiration! I can only manage works of stiff and old-fashioned forms! I'm desperate, pupil...

Master: I need to acquire a new and fresh style. I´m going for a walk in the town to get some influence from the environment.

Advertising flier man 1: Sushi! Opening of a sushi parlor!

Advertising flier man 2: "Great caliber" magazine! For weapon-freaks like you!

Advertising flier man 3: Imported cars! No custom duties if you buy now!

Advertising flier man 4: "Marine" restaurant! Delicious cuisine! Our specialty is salted salmon!

Assistant: You are a genius, master! What a wonderful vessel!

Master: Well... It's really a wastebasket for advertisement fliers, but anyway...

New elements 新しい部首

無	Trojan horse		飞	flying angel	
圥	goddess of fertility		舟	raft	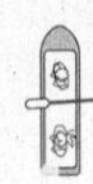

Lesson 54
第五十四課

617 (2級)

LAMP, TO LIGHT

灯

トウ

灯台（とうだい） lamp, lighthouse

灯油（とうゆ） kerosene

電灯（でんとう） electric light (fixture)

蛍光灯（けいこうとう） fluorescent lamp

ひ

灯（ひ） lamp, torch

とも(す)

灯す（ともす） to light a lamp

灯し火（ともしび） candle light, flame

丶	丷	火	火
火一	灯		

(6 strokes)

灯	灯	灯	灯
灯	灯	灯	灯

注 炊 (Jōyō) 朴 (Jōyō) 秋 (152)

学 Did you know the first *lamp* in history was made by setting fire to a corkscrew?

特  燈 (ant)

618 (2級)

TO BURN, TO ROAST

焼

ショウ

焼却（しょうきゃく） to incinerate

焼死（しょうし） burn to death

全焼（ぜんしょう） burn completely

や(く/ける)

焼く（やく） to roast, to broil

焼き物（やきもの） pottery

焼きそば（やきそば） fried noodles

焼き肉（やきにく） roast meat

目玉焼き（めだまやき） fried egg

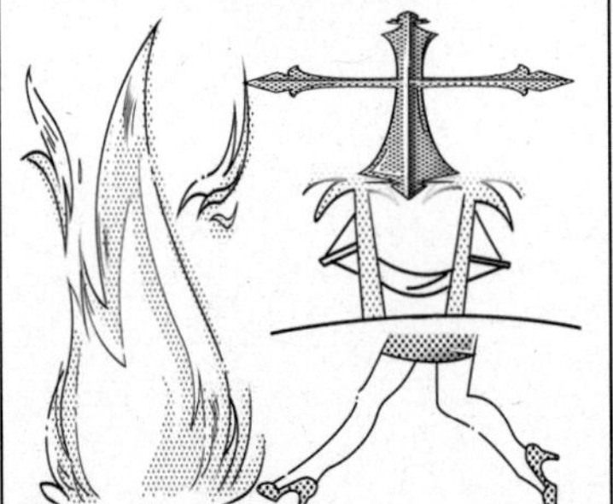

丶	丷	火	火
火一	火十	火土	火土
焼	焼	焼	焼

(12 strokes)

焼	焼	焼	焼
焼	焼	焼	焼

注 燃 (5th)  爆 (Jōyō)

学 Let your sins *burn* in fire: your little respect for the cross, your laziness, and your lust. Let them burn!

特  燒 (ant)

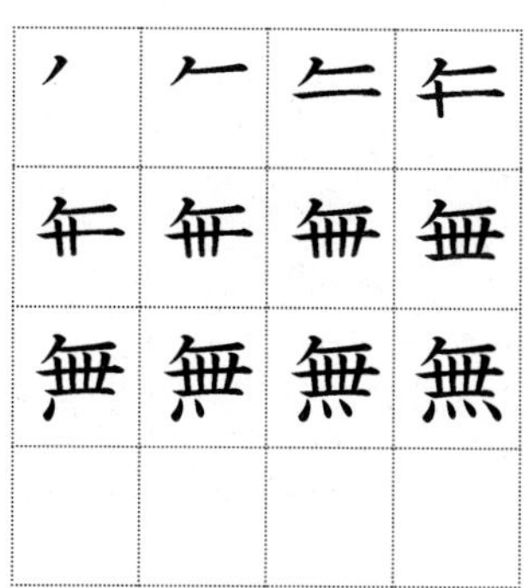

(12 strokes)

無	無	無	無
無	無	無	無

WITHOUT (UN-), NOTHING

(2級)

619

ム

無(む) nothing

無理(むり) impossible

無意味(むいみ) nonsense

ブ

無様(ぶざま) clumsy, pathetic

無礼(ぶれい) irreverence

な(い/くす/くなる)

無(な)い there isn't/arent

無(な)くなる to disappear, to die

学 The legend of the Trojan horse says that since it was made of wood and it had caught fire, it ended up being burned to ashes, leaving *nothing* behind.

焦 (Jōyō)
典 (590)
魚 (229)

照	照	照	照
照	照	照	照

(13 strokes)

TO SHINE ON, TO FEEL EMBARRASSED

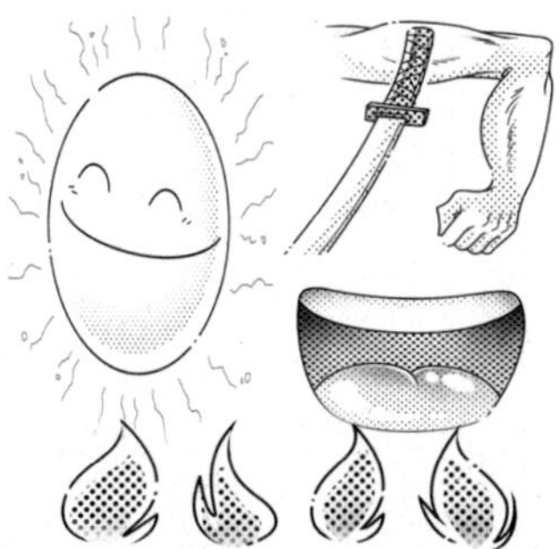

(2級)

620

ショウ

照明(しょうめい) lighting

照射(しょうしゃ) irradiation, exposure

照合(しょうごう)する to check against, to compare

対照(たいしょう) contrast

て(れる/らす)

照(て)らす to shine on

照(て)れくさい shy

照(て)れるなぁ Oh, how embarrassing...

 The sun *shines on* the scene: my sword in your mouth, and fire at your feet. Don't *feel embarrassed* of dying.

点 (223)
昭 (294)

621 (2級)

YESTERDAY, LAST (MONTH, YEAR)

昨

サク
- 昨年（さくねん） last year
- 昨夜（さくや） last night
- 昨日（さくじつ） yesterday

Special
- 昨日（きのう） yesterday

(9 strokes)

注 作 (139)

学 Remember *yesterday*, when you spent all day in the sun playing on the park slide.

特

622 (2級)

THUS, JUST AS IT IS, HOWEVER

然

ゼン
- 自然（しぜん） nature
- 全然（ぜんぜん） not at all
- 突然（とつぜん） suddenly
- 当然（とうぜん） of course
- 偶然（ぐうぜん） by chance

ネン
- 天然（てんねん） natural

しか(し/も)
- 然も（しかも） besides, moreover

(12 strokes)

注 燃 (5th)
熱 (623)

学 In the light of the reclined moon, the master relaxes and shows himself *just as he is*: a dog who likes to lounge with the fire at his feet.

特

一	十	土	圥
圥	坴	坴	坴
坴	埶	埶	埶
熱	熱	熱	

(15 strokes)

熱	熱	熱	熱
熱	热	熱	熱

HEAT, FEVER, PASSION

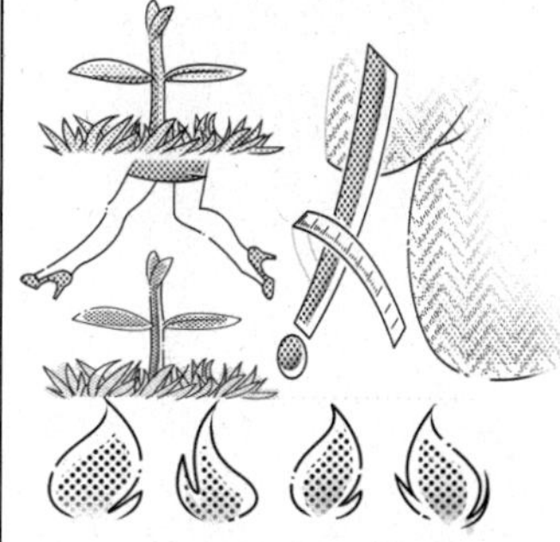

(2級)

623

ネツ

熱(ねつ) fever, passion
高熱(こうねつ) intense heat, high fever
熱帯(ねったい) tropic
熱意(ねつい) passion, zeal
熱心(ねっしん) great interest
熱血(ねっけつ) zealous
情熱(じょうねつ) passion

あつ(い)

熱(あつ)い hot, passionate

学 When the goddess of fertility finds fertile land, she becomes round, once again, because the flame of *passion* ignites inside her.

然 (622)
熟 (6th)

ノ	亻	亻	亻
亻	亻	伫	伫
倍	倍	偣	偣
億	億	億	

(15 strokes)

億	億	億	億
億	億	億	億

HUNDRED MILLION

億

(2級)

624

オク

一億(いちおく) one hundred million
十億(じゅうおく) one thousand million
百億(ひゃくおく) ten thousand million
千億(せんおく) one hundred thousand million
億万長者(おくまんちょうじゃ) billionaire

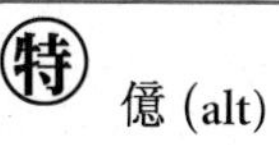

億 (alt)

Kim has won one *hundred million* yen playing the lottery, and he is incredibly happy. The sound of his heart is like a drum!

僕 (Jōyō)
憶 (Jōyō)

625 (2級)

TRILLION, PREMONITION

兆

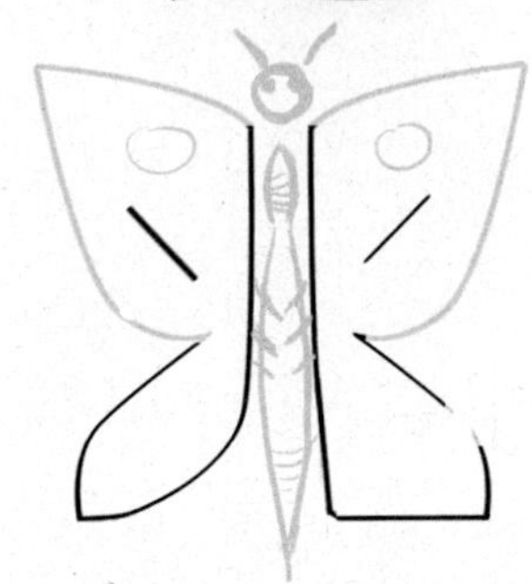

チョウ

- 一兆 (いっちょう) one trillion
- 十兆 (じゅっちょう) ten trillions
- 前兆 (ぜんちょう) omen
- 吉兆 (きっちょう) good omen
- 兆候 (ちょうこう) symptom, sign

きざ(す)

- 兆し (きざし) premonition

(6 strokes)

兆	兆	兆	兆
兆	兆	兆	兆

注 北 (197)
比 (5th)
逃 (Jōyō)

A butterfly is a good omen; however, a *trillion* is a sound *premonition* that a plague is near.

626 (2級)

TO FLY

飛

ヒ

- 飛行機 (ひこうき) airplane
- 飛行 (ひこう) flight
- 飛来する (ひらいする) to come flying
- 飛躍 (ひやく) bold leap

と(ぶ/ばす)

- 飛ぶ (とぶ) to fly
- 飛び上がる (とびあがる) to jump, to fly
- 飛び出す (とびだす) to fly out, to jump out
- 飛び魚 (とびうお) flying fish

(9 strokes)

飛	飛	飛	飛
飛	飛	飛	飛

注 戒 (Jōyō)
羽 (140)
弱 (237)

学 Can you see the *flying* angels? They are taking the torii in for repair, because the gods broke it.

627

(10 strokes)

TO NAVIGATE (BY SEA OR AIR)

(2級)

コウ

航行（こうこう） navigation, sailing
航空（こうくう） aviation
航海（こうかい） ocean navigation
潜航（せんこう）する to cruise underwater
渡航（とこう） voyage, passage
欠航（けっこう） suspension (of a flight or a ship service)
密航者（みっこうしゃ） stowaway

学 The love of *navigation* on this small raft is what unites the Mexican and the cowboy.

船 (96)
般 (Jōyō)

628

(10 strokes)

DIFFERENCE, INTERVAL

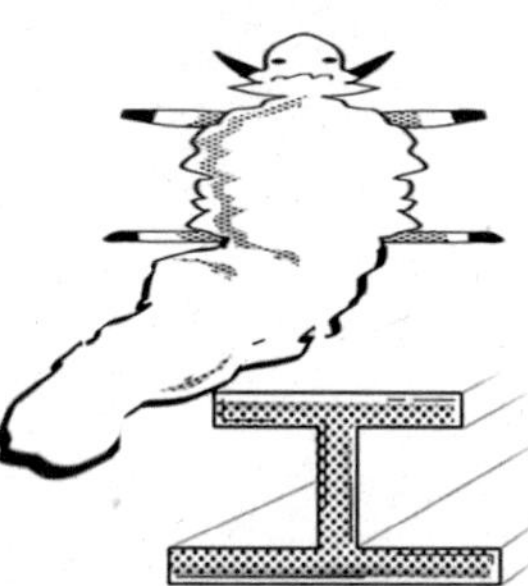

(2級)

サ

差（さ） difference
時差（じさ） time difference
時差（じさ）ぼけ jet-lag
差別（さべつ） discrimination
交差（こうさ） crossing, intersection

さ(す)

差（さ）す to give, to stick, to hold up (an umbrella), to fill
差（さ）し上（あ）げる to give (honorific)

 In a sheepskin fashion show, the *interval* between models depends on the time it takes for them to cross the iron beam from which they step up onto the catwalk.

着 (416)
美 (405)

本当におかしい…熱は高いが、病気の兆候はありません。

切れた蛍光灯が照らしつづけるかのように謎です。

最近、変わったことでもありましたか？

そうね…昨日は飛行機で海外から帰った…

そうだ！時差ボケでしょう！

いいえ、渡航といっても、ただの一時間の便だった。

でも、変わったことといえば、先週めちゃうまい焼肉を食べたぞ！

それは無関係だと思いますよ、全然…

ちなみに、お仕事は？

土地をバカ安く買ったり、めちゃ高く売ったりする。

Exercises 練習

1. Develop the stroke order of the following kanji.

焼												
無												
熱												
飛												

2. Choose the correct reading for each kanji or kanji combination.

a) 突然、照明が消えた。真っ暗になった部屋で、彼(かれ)は情熱あふれたストーリを語った…

Suddenly, the light went out. And, in the dark room, he told us his passionate story.

突然:	1．とつせん	2．とつぜん	3．とっせん	4．とつねん
照明:	1．てめい	2．ていめい	3．しょうめい	4．しょめい
情熱:	1．じょうあつ	2．じょうねつ	3．じょあつ	4．しょねつ

b) 飛行機が買いたいって？ 無理よ！あれは千億、いや、一兆(ちょう)円もするぞ！

You want an airplane? Impossible! They cost one hundred million yen. No, a trillion yen!

飛行機:	1．とこき	2．とこうき	3．ひこうき	4．ひこき
無理:	1．むり	2．ふり	3．ぶり	4．ぷり
千億:	1．せんお	2．せんおく	3．ちお	4．ちおく

c) ナナとハチは全然似ていない。つまり、対照をなしている。大差がある。

Nana and Hachi don't look alike at all. That is, there is a contrast; there's a great difference.

全然:	1．せんせん	2．せんぜん	3．ぜんせん	4．ぜんぜん
対照:	1．たいしょ	2．たいしょう	3．たいて	4．たいてら
大差:	1．だいさ	2．たいさ	3．おおさ	4．おさ

3. Write the kanji (one or more) and the meaning of the following words.

でんとう	______	______	きざし	______	______
やきそば	______	______	こうさ	______	______
ゆうべ	______	______	ねっしん	______	______

4. Correct either the reading or the writing mistakes in the following words.

昨日	さくにち	航空	くうくう	飛出す	とびだす
一意	いちおく	着別	さべつ	熱つい	あつい

Answers to exercises 練習解答

1. (Check them in the corresponding kanji table: #618, #619, #623, and #626)

2. a) 突然: 2 | 照明: 3 | 情熱: 2 / b) 飛行機: 3 | 無理: 1 | 千億: 2

c) 全然: 4 | 対照: 2 | 大差: 2

3. でんとう: 電灯, electric light | やきそば: 焼きそば, fried noodles | ゆうべ: 昨夜, last night | きざし: 兆し, premonition | こうさ: 交差, crossing | ねっしん: 熱心, great interest

4. 昨日 さくじつ / きのう | 航空 こうくう | 飛び出す とびだす | 一億 いちおく | 差別 さべつ | 熱つい あつい

Manga translation マンガ翻訳

Doctor: That's strange. You have very high fever, but no symptoms of sickness. It's a mystery, like the fluorescent lamps that keep shining even after they have gone out.

Doctor: Has anything weird happened to you lately?

Patient: Well, I returned from overseas by plane yesterday...

Doctor: Of course! It could be jet-lag!

Patient: I don't think so. Although it was a trip overseas, it was only a one-hour flight.

Patient: But, speaking of unusual things, last week I ate some delicious roast meat.

Doctor: I don't think that has anything to do with it, at all...

Doctor: By the way, what do you do?

Patient: I buy plots of land at ridiculously low prices, and I sell them at very high prices.

Doctor: Aha! You are suffering from speculation fever!

Patient: Really? Oh dear, and yet this month I've only earned two hundred million yen...

New elements 新しい部首

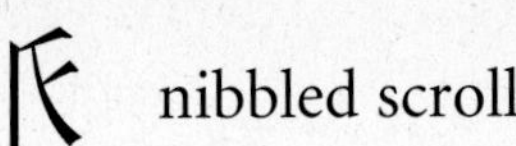

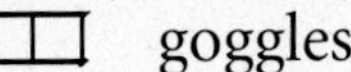

Lesson 55
第五十五課

629 (1級)

PULSE, VEIN/ARTERY

ミャク

- 脈(みゃく) pulse
- 脈拍(はくみゃく) pulse
- 動脈(どうみゃく) artery
- 静脈(じょうみゃく) vein
- 山脈(さんみゃく) mountain range
- 人脈(じんみゃく) personal connections, social network
- 文脈(ぶんみゃく) context

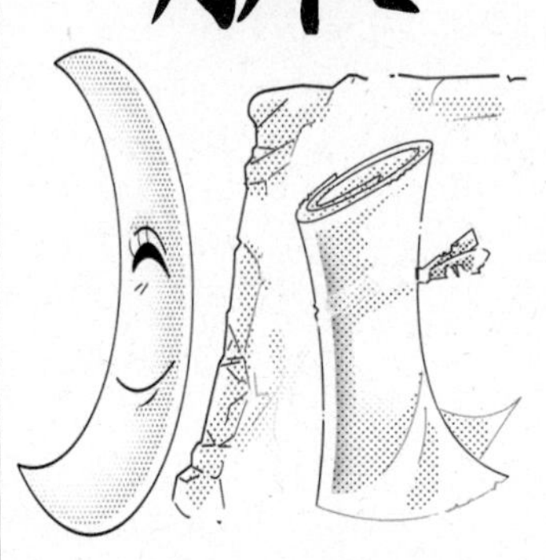

丿	月	月	月
月⺈	肵	肵	脈
脈	脈		

(10 strokes)

注 服 (288)
肌 (Jōyō)
派 (6th)

学 The moon keeps her finger on the *pulse* of history. She shines upon the cliff which keeps the first manuscript, an old nibbled scroll, which contains the *veins* of the past and *arteries* of the future.

脉 (alt)

630 (1級)

INTESTINES

チョウ

- 腸(ちょう) intestines, entrails
- 小腸(しょうちょう) small intestine
- 大腸(だいちょう) large intestine
- 盲腸(もうちょう) appendix
- 胃腸(いちょう) stomach and intestines
- 浣腸(かんちょう) enema

丿	月	月	月
月	月冂	肙	肙
腭	腭	腸	腸
腸			

(13 strokes)

注 陽 (323)
傷 (6th)
腹 (6th)

The farmer's *intestines* work at night only. Of course, this is because he works while the sun is out with his plow, so his innards have no other time to do their job!

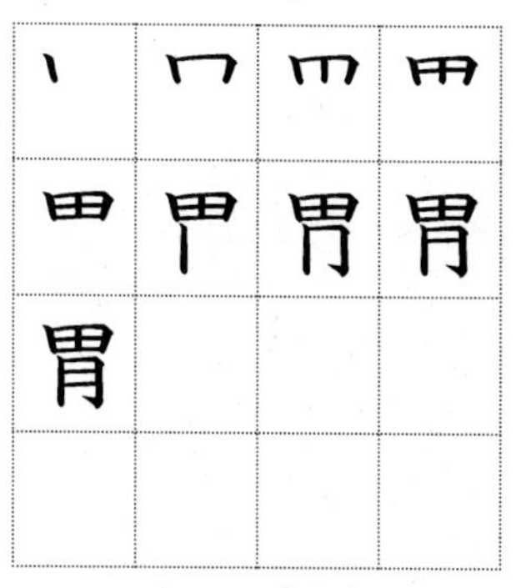

(9 strokes)

STOMACH

胃

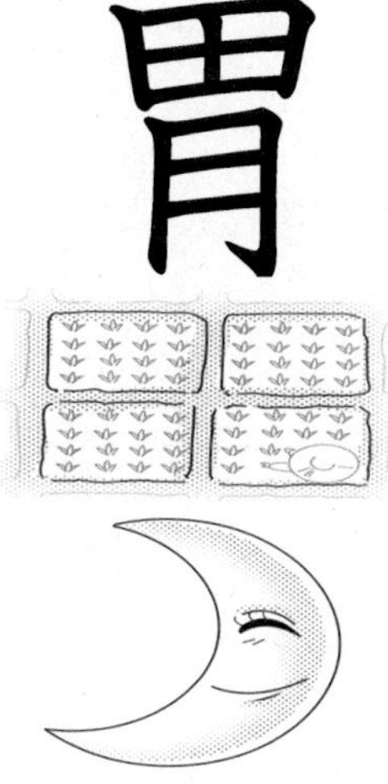

(2級)

631

イ

- 胃（い） stomach, tummy
- 胃袋（いぶくろ） stomach
- 胃炎（いえん） gastritis
- 胃潰瘍（いかいよう） stomach ulcer
- 胃癌（いがん） stomach cancer

特

 Our *stomach* depends on the rice field, which, in turn, depends on the moon's care.

 思 (221) 畑 (424) 員 (355)

(12 strokes)

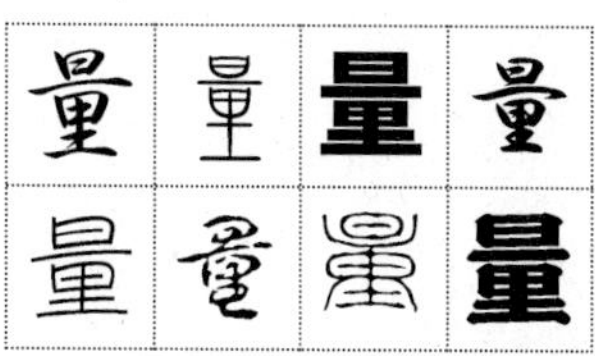

AMOUNT, TO MEASURE

量

(2級)

632

リョウ

- 量（りょう） amount
- 大量（たいりょう） large amount
- 重量（じゅうりょう） weight
- 容量（ようりょう） volume
- 量産（りょうさん） mass production
- 測量（そくりょう） to measure, to weigh
- 器量（きりょう） ability, capacity

はか(る)

- 量る（はかる） to weigh, to measure

 The sun must always be offered bread by the village; however, the villagers can never remember the right *amount* that they should give.

 童 (331) 重 (289)

633 (2級)

TO RECORD (ON, PAPER OR TAPE), TO REGISTER

録

ロク

- 記録(きろく) chronicle, record
- 録音(ろくおん)する to record voice or sound
- 録画(ろくが)する to record videotape
- 登録(とうろく)する to register, to enroll
- 目録(もくろく) catalogue
- 付録(ふろく) appendix, supplement

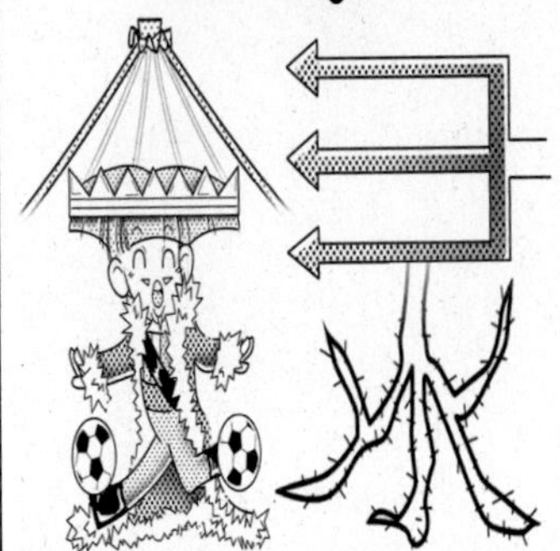

(16 strokes)

注 緑 (335)
銭 (5th)

学 Money hunted with a trident must be *registered.* That way, it takes root, and you can prove it belongs to you.

特  錄 (alt)

634 (1級)

MIRROR

鏡

キョウ

- 鏡面(きょうめん) mirror surface
- 顕微鏡(けんびきょう) microscope
- 望遠鏡(ぼうえんきょう) telescope
- 潜望鏡(せんぼうきょう) periscope

かがみ

- 鏡(かがみ) mirror
- 手鏡(てかがみ) hand mirror

Special

- 眼鏡(めがね) glasses

(19 strokes)

注 鐘 (Jōyō)
鎮 (Jōyō)
鋭 (Jōyō)

学 Just imagine the amount of money the vulture makes holding a *mirror* for the sun, who loves looking at his slender legs.

特  (alt)

635 郡 REGION, DISTRICT, COUNTY

(10 strokes)

郡	郡	郡	郡
郡	郡	郡	郡

郡

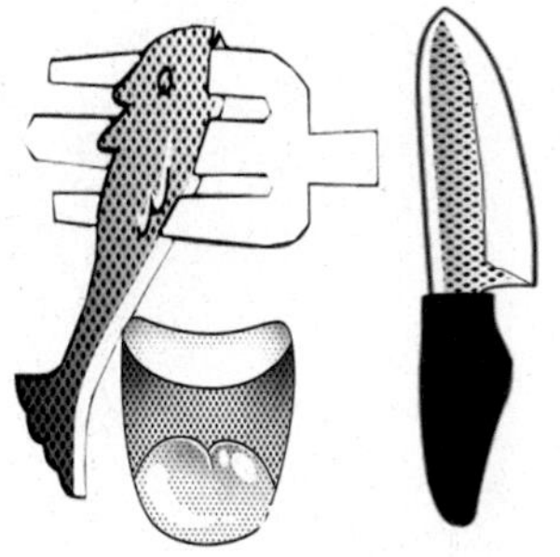

(1級)

グン

郡(ぐん) county, region

郡部(ぐんぶ) county, rural district

郡長(ぐんちょう) county headman

三島郡(みしまぐん) Mishima county (in Osaka)

 You, fisherman! Defend your *county* with a knife, if necessary!

 部 (261)
朗 (Jōyō)
邸 (Jōyō)

636 陸 LAND, SOLID GROUND

(11 strokes)

陸	陸	陸	陸
陸	陸	陸	陸

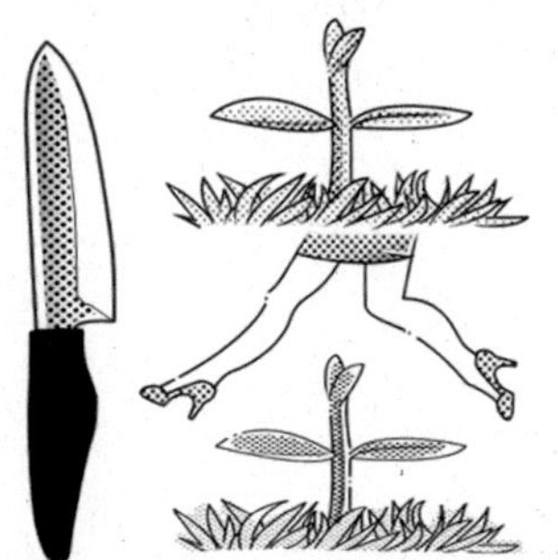

(2級)

リク

陸(りく) land, solid ground

陸地(りくち) land

上陸(じょうりく) (ship) landing

着陸(ちゃくりく) (airplane) landing

離陸(りりく) (airplane) takeoff

大陸(たいりく) continent

陸軍(りくぐん) infantry (troops)

陸上(りくじょう) athletics

 At last, the goddess of fertility has arrived on the continent. With her divine knife, the goddess will cultivate the *land* and make it fertile.

 陵 (Jōyō)
障 (6th)
勢 (5th)

637 (1級)

TROOPS, GROUP (OF PEOPLE)

タイ

- 軍隊 (ぐんたい) troops, army
- 隊長 (たいちょう) troop leader
- 隊員 (たいいん) troop member
- 艦隊 (かんたい) fleet, navy
- 自衛隊 (じえいたい) Japan Self Defense Forces
- 楽隊 (がくたい) musical band
- 捜索隊 (そうさくたい) search party
- 探検隊 (たんけんたい) exploration party
- 親衛隊 (しんえいたい) bodyguard

(12 strokes)

隊	隊	隊	隊
隊	隊	隊	隊

注 像 (5th) 墜 (Jōyō) 豚 (Jōyō)

学 Look at those funny Viking *troops*: they are armed with knives, horns, and bread. Wait a second... they are actually winged piglets!!

 隧 (alt)

638 (1級)

FLAG

旗

キ

- 国旗 (こっき) national flag
- 星条旗 (せいじょうき) Stars and Stripes banner (USA)
- 日章旗 (にっしょうき) Rising Sun flag (Japan)

はた

- 旗 (はた) flag

(14 strokes)

旗	旗	旗	旗
旗	旗	旗	旗

注 期 (287) 族 (381)

学 That person who hangs his *flag* on the door is a painter: in his shed he has an easel.

(12 strokes)

PHENOMENON, ELEPHANT

象

(2級) **639**

ショウ

- 現象 (げんしょう) phenomenon
- 気象 (きしょう) meteorology
- 対象 (たいしょう) object (of study)
- 抽象 (ちゅうしょう) abstract
- 印象 (いんしょう) impression
- 象徴 (しょうちょう) symbolization

ゾウ

- 象 (ぞう) elephant
- 象牙 (ぞうげ) ivory

学 A paranormal *phenomenon* makes the winged piglet, armed with a flash and goggles, look like an *elephant.*

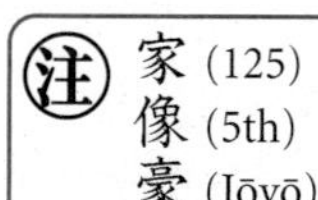

注 家 (125) 像 (5th) 豪 (Jōyō)

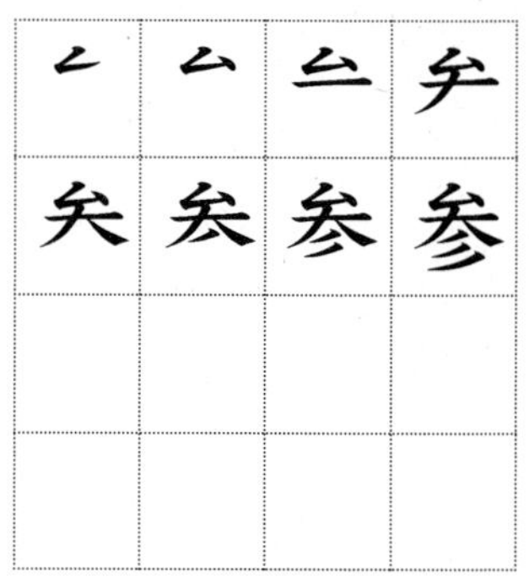

(8 strokes)

TO TAKE PART, TO GO (FORMAL), TO VISIT

参

(2級) **640**

サン

- 参加する (さんか) to take part, to participate, to join
- 参戦する (さんせん) to enter a war
- 参拝する (さんぱい) to visit a temple
- 参考する (さんこう) to consider
- 降参 (こうさん) to give up

まい(る)

- 参る (まい) to come; to go (formal)
- 墓参り (はかま) visit to a cemetery

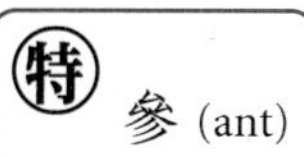

特 参 (ant)

学 *Visit* the cornucopia of the giant: everybody can *take part* in the banquet until their stomachs get three folds of fat from so much food.

注 冬 (155) 寒 (409) 珍 (Jōyō)

記録によると、先探検隊はこの山脈まで参着した。
すると、変な現象が起こって、皆が胃腸病でたおれた。
酸素不足か、住んでいた郡や陸地との気圧の違いだったろう…
ま…まさか…望遠鏡を！
あっ！そ・その旗は…
しょ・食事が大量…もう食べられない…
FAST FOOD M
いてぇ…腹がいたい…

Exercises 練習

1. Develop the stroke order of the following kanji.

脈												
録												
旗												
参												

2. Choose the correct reading for each kanji or kanji combination.

a) 敵国の軍隊が上陸した時、日本の自衛隊は覚悟(かくご)ができていた。

When the enemy troops landed, the Japanese Self Defense forces were ready.

軍隊:　1．ぐんたい　2．ぐんだい　3．ぐんだむ　4．ぐんだぬ

上陸:　1．うえりく　2．あがりく　3．あげりく　4．じょうりく

自衛隊:　1．じえいたい　2．じえいだい　3．じえいだむ　4．じえいだぬ

b) クラスに参加したかったから、登録した。でも、難(むずか)しすぎて、すぐ降参だった。

I wanted to participate in that class, so I enrolled. But it was too difficult and I soon gave up.

参加:　1．まいか　2．まか　3．さんか　4．さっか

登録:　1．とうろく　2．とうどく　3．とうぞく　4．とうもく

降参:　1．ふるまい　2．ふるさん　3．こうまい　4．こうさん

c) バックには手鏡、お守りの象と... 浣腸が入っていた。

In the bag there was a hand mirror, an elephant-shaped amulet and... an enema.

手鏡:　1．しゅきょう　2．しゅっきょう　3．てかがみ　4．てがガみ

象:　1．しょう　2．しょ　3．そう　4．ぞう

浣腸:　1．かんい　2．かんちょう　3．かに　4．かんみゃく

3. Write the kanji (one or more) and the meaning of the following words.

ぶんみゃく ______ ______　いえん ______ ______

じゅうりょう ______ ______　ぐん ______ ______

めがね ______ ______　こっき ______ ______

4. Correct either the reading or the writing mistakes in the following words.

参いる	まいる	動脈	どうみやく	大陸	たいにく
印像	いんしょう	旗	ばた	記録	きおく

Answers to exercises 練習解答

1. (Check them in the corresponding kanji table: #629, #633, #638, and #640)

2. a) 軍隊: 1 | 上陸: 4 | 自衛隊: 1 / b) 参加: 3 | 登録: 1 | 降参: 4

c) 手鏡: 3| 象: 4 | 浣腸: 2

3. ぶんみゃく: 文脈, context | じゅうりょう: 重量, weight | めがね: 眼鏡, glasses | いえん: 胃炎, gastritis | ぐん: 郡, county, region | こっき: 国旗, national flag

4. 参~~て~~る まいる | 動脈 どうみゃく | 大陸 たいりく | 印象 いんしょう | 旗 はた | 記録 きろく

Manga translation マンガ翻訳

Expedition leader: According to this register, the previous expedition made it to this mountain range.

Expedition leader: Then, a strange phenomenon took place, and they all become sick with a gastrointestinal disorder.

Expedition member: The lack of oxygen or the atmospheric pressure, which is different in the land or district they lived in, I guess...

Expedition leader: No... It can't be that... Pass me the telescope!

Expedition leader (OFF): Oh! T-that flag is...

Expedition leader: What a huge amount of food. I can't eat any more...

Expedition member: Ouch, my tummy...

Review of Grade 4

小学校四年生まとめ問題

Review of Grade 4 四年生・まとめ問題

1. Link the kanji with their corresponding *kun'yomi* and *on'yomi* readings.

1.	あたま	歩	タ
2.	ある(く)	頭	ハイ
3.	あつ(い)	様	キ
4.	よろこ(ぶ)	流	シュウ
5.	くば(る)	待	ショ
6.	さま	喜	フ
7.	なが(れる)	短	タイ
8.	なら(う)	習	タン
9.	ほか	他	ト
10.	ま(つ)	都	トウ
11.	みじか(い)	暑	ヨウ
12.	みやこ	配	リュウ

2. Write the missing kanji in the following text.

へいせい　ふつか　わたし　きょうと　つ　えき　まわ

______二十年十月______。私が______に___く日です。___から出たら、___りを見て、

あつ　さむ　きょうと　す

「これは今日から私の街だ」と思いました。夏は___すぎて、冬は___すぎる______はとても

わたし　じぶんじしん　せんたく

みにくい所だと聞いていました。それでも私はここにした。__________の______でした。

October 2nd, year 20 of the Heisei era (2008). This is the day I arrived in Kyoto. As soon as I left the station, I looked around me, and I thought that this will be my city from now on. I heard it's too hot in summer and too cold in winter, that living here is difficult. However, I've made up my mind. This has been my own decision.

へいせい　はつか　さいしょ　くろう

______二十一年三月________。来日してからもう六ヶ月ですが、______から______

けんきゅう　しゅっせき

しています。ずっと______室に閉じ込められています。授業に______するだけでなく、

しゅくだい　べんきょう　あそ

______や______もあるので、___べません。

March 20th, year 21 of the Heisei era (2009). It's now six months since I've arrived in Japan. It's been hard from the start. I spend all day shut up in the study room. It's not only attending classes, there are also homework and studying. I can't have fun.

へいせい　ついたち　も　とつぜん

______二十一年十月______。身体が___たなかった日。______目の前のものが真っ

いらい　おぼ　きゅうきゅうしゃ　びょういん　はこ

白になって、それ______何も___えていません。__________で______へ___ばれた

けんこう

のでしょう。______が大事なのに…

October 1st, year 21 of the Heisei era. The day my body can't bear it any longer. Suddenly, all becomes white before my eyes, and, from this very moment, I can't remember anything else. They probably took me to a hospital in an ambulance. And health is so important...

3. Choose the correct reading for each kanji or kanji combination.

a) 政府で働きたい。給料のいい、残業のないポストを希望しています。

I want to work for the government. I hope for a position with good wages and no overtime.

政府:	1. せいぶ	2. せぶ	3. せいふ	4. せふ
働き	1. どうき	2. はたらき	3. はらたき	4. とうき
給料:	1. きゅうりょ	2. きゅりょう	3. きゅりょ	4. きゅうりょう
残業:	1. ざんぎょう	2. ざんごう	3. のこぎょう	4. のこごう
希望:	1. まれのぞ	2. きぼう	3. まれのそ	4. きぼ

b) 海兵隊 航空団(だん)の人が飛行機に乗れないって？笑わせるな！

You're saying that somebody from the Marine air force can't fly an airplane? Don't make me laugh!

兵隊:	1. ひょうたい	2. ひょたい	3. へたい	4. へいたい
航空:	1. こうくう	2. こうく	3. こく	4. こくう
飛行機:	1. とこうき	2. ひこき	3. ひこうき	4. とこき
乗れ	1. のれ	2. どれ	3. もれ	4. これ

c) 村田(むらた)博士の説明のおかげで、オレは卒業できたと思う。

I think I graduated thanks to professor Murata's explanations.

博士:	1. はかせ	2. はかし	3. はくせ	4. はっくし
説明:	1. とめい	2. とうめい	3. せつめい	4. せめい
卒業:	1. そっぎょう	2. そつぎょう	3. そしぎょう	4. そぎょう

4. Choose the correct kanji for each reading.

a) ちゅうおう区の土地がていかしている内に、ちょきんして、マンションを買わなきゃ。

Now that prices in the Chūō district are going down, we must save money and buy an apartment.

ちゅうおう:	1. 仲央	2. 仲英	3. 中央	4. 中英
ていか:	1. 低下	2. 氏下	3. 底下	4. 紙下
ちょきん:	1. 貯金	2. 貯全	3. 停金	4. 停全

b) がくれきのため、しけんのけっかがすべてだ。頑張(がんば)って！

For your academic background, exam results are everything. Keep it up!

がくれき:	1. 学止	2. 学歴	3. 学暦	4. 学磨
しけん:	1. 試験	2. 試駅	3. 武験	4. 武駅
けっか:	1. 結早	2. 結課	3. 結巣	4. 結果

c) まごがいもかんせつも痛(いた)いおばあさんにはなたばをあげた。

The grandson brought a bouquet of flowers to his grandmother, who was suffering from stomach ache and painful joints.

まご:	1. 子	2. 孫	3. 系	4. 係
い:	1. 青	2. 胃	3. 員	4. 田
かんせつ:	1. 間節	2. 関節	3. 閑節	4. 聞節
はなたば:	1. 花束	2. 花木	3. 花東	4. 花味

Answers to exercises 練習解答

1.	あたま	頭	トウ
	ある(く)	歩	フ
	あつ(い)	暑	ショ
	よろこ(ぶ)	喜	キ
	くば(る)	配	ハイ
	さま	様	ヨウ
	なが(れる)	流	リュウ
	なら(う)	習	シュウ
	ほか	他	タ
	ま(つ)	待	タイ
	みじか(い)	短	タン
	みやこ	都	ト

1. 平成二十年十月二日。私が京都に着く日です。駅から出たら、周りを見て、「これは今日から私の街だ」と思いました。夏は暑すぎて、冬は寒すぎる京都はとても住みにくい所だと聞いています。それでも私はここにした。自分自身の選択でした。

平成二十一年三月二十日。来日してからもう六ヶ月ですが、最初から苦労しています。ずっと研究室に閉じ込められています。授業に出席するだけでなく、宿題や勉強もあるので、遊べません。

平成二十一年十月一日。身体が持たなかった日。突然目の前のものが真っ白になって、それ以来何も覚えていません。救急車で病院へ運ばれたのでしょう。健康が大事なのに...

3. a) 政府: 3 | 働き: 2 | 給料: 4 | 残業: 1| 希望: 2
b) 兵隊: 4 | 航空: 1 | 飛行機: 3 | 乗れ: 1
c) 博士: 1| 説明: 3| 卒業: 2

4. a) ちゅうおう: 3 | ていか: 1 | ちょきん: 1
b) がくれき: 2 | しけん: 1 | けっか: 4
c) まご: 2 | い: 2 | かんせつ: 2 | はなたば: 1

Indexes
索引

Kanji index 漢字索引

357 商
358 局
359 屋
360 去
361 反
362 取
363 受
364 祭
365 度
366 庭
367 庫
368 乗
369 軽
370 転
371 路
372 面
373 身
374 運
375 返
376 追
377 送
378 速
379 進
380 遊
381 族
382 放
383 整
384 旅
385 岸
386 両
387 炭
388 島
389 負
390 急
391 相
392 想
393 息
394 意
395 悲
396 悪
397 和
398 秒
399 委
400 始
401 安
402 守
403 定
404 実
405 美
406 客
407 宮
408 宿
409 寒
410 究
411 研
412 写
413 具
414 真
415 県
416 着
417 申
418 神
419 礼
420 福
421 世
422 界
423 鼻
424 畑
425 問
426 開
427 式
428 感
429 病
430 歯
431 苦
432 落
433 葉
434 薬
435 荷
436 夫
437 駅
438 所
439 列
440 州
441 付
442 府
443 氏
444 底
445 低
446 仲
447 伝
448 位
449 信
450 借
451 便
452 例
453 側
454 別
455 印
456 刷
457 副
458 利
459 種
460 積
461 働
462 功
463 加
464 努
465 勇
466 労
467 協
468 博
469 栄
470 堂
471 覚
472 観
473 停
474 候
475 健
476 建
477 康
478 敗
479 散
480 改

No.	Kanji
481	求
482	救
483	牧
484	特
485	争
486	静
487	清
488	泣
489	治
490	浴
491	法
492	満
493	漁
494	浅
495	残
496	験
497	単
498	戦
499	成
500	果
501	巣
502	課
503	訓
504	試
505	議
506	説
507	祝
508	競
509	不
510	以
511	衣
512	卒
513	臣
514	民
515	告
516	各
517	変
518	愛
519	念
520	必
521	結
522	給
523	紀
524	続
525	約
526	的
527	令
528	冷
529	倉
530	順
531	願
532	類
533	料
534	粉
535	笑
536	節
537	管
538	官
539	完
540	害
541	察
542	票
543	標
544	要
545	好
546	季
547	孫
548	央
549	英
550	芸
551	芽
552	菜
553	歴
554	史
555	景
556	最
557	初
558	辺
559	包
560	連
561	軍
562	輪
563	達
564	選
565	共
566	兵
567	折
568	挙
569	賞
570	貨
571	費
572	貯
573	産
574	児
575	老
576	唱
577	喜
578	良
579	飯
580	養
581	士
582	欠
583	席
584	帯
585	希
586	殺
587	失
588	望
589	辞
590	典
591	省
592	置
593	未
594	末
595	札
596	材
597	束
598	松
599	案
600	毒
601	梅
602	極
603	機
604	械

605 型
606 周
607 囲
608 固
609 司
610 器
611 塩
612 街
613 得
614 径
615 徒
616 関
617 灯
618 焼
619 無
620 照
621 昨
622 然
623 熱
624 億
625 兆
626 飛
627 航
628 差
629 脈
630 腸
631 胃
632 量
633 録
634 鏡
635 郡
636 陸
637 隊
638 旗
639 象
640 参

Readings index 読み方索引